The Army of the Caesars

The Army of
the Caesars

Michael Grant

M. Evans & Company, Inc.
New York

Library of Congress Cataloging-in-Publication Data

Grant, Michael, 1914–
    The army of the Caesars / Michael Grant.
        p.   cm.
    Originally published: New York : Scribner, 1974.
    Includes bibliographical references and index.
    ISBN 0-87131-705-2
    1. Rome—History, Military. 2. Rome—Army. 3. Rome—
    Politics and government—30 B.C.–476 A.D.   I. Title.
[DG89.G7   1992]
322'.5'0937—dc20   92-6179
                                                                CIP

M. Evans and Company, Inc.
216 East 49th Street
New York, New York 10017

Manufactured in the United States of America

9 8 7 6 5 4 3 2 1

Contents

Contents

Maps

Acknowledgements

The author and publishers would like to thank the following for granting permission to quote from copyright sources: Heinemann and Harvard University Press, the Loeb Classical Library, for Suetonius, vols. I and II, Ammianus Marcellinus, vol. I and Dio, vol. VIII; Macmillan for A.H.M.Jones (ed.), *A History of Rome through the Fifth Century*; New American Library for Rex Warner (trans.), *War Commentaries of Caesar*; Penguin Books for Tacitus, *The Annals of Imperial Rome* (trans. M.Grant), *The Histories* (trans. K.Wellesley); University of California Press for *Herodian of Antioch's History of the Roman Empire* (trans. E.C.Echols), reprinted by permission of the Regents of the University of California.

Preface

The Roman imperial army was the earliest of the world's standing armies in which the soldiers were regularly recruited, and cared for, and finally pensioned off, by the state. This situation did not come about all at once. But when it did, it continued for five hundred years, and exercised profoundly far-reaching effects on all subsequent history. For this was one of the greatest and most formidable armies that has ever existed. Moreover it was the conditions the Roman army created which enabled Rome to bring into effect its vast, peculiar and specific contributions to civilization, which have to such a large extent made our modern life, for better or worse, what it is. The army, therefore, which produced these far-reaching and permanent results deserves continuing investigation and analysis.

In this book I have attempted to provide a brief history of the army of the Roman emperors, with a prior discussion of the circumstances that preceded their arrival. This is a very large subject, which a great deal of archaeological and literary material has survived to illustrate. This evidence, taken all in all, suggests that the Roman army owes its lasting significance to two causes. First, it conquered the Roman empire and kept the peace in its provinces – 'the immeasurable majesty of the Roman peace', as a fleet commander, Pliny the elder, aptly described it. Second, the army played an enormous part in the policies and political decisions of successive emperors of Rome, and in the multifarious and enormous events that flowed from these policies and decisions – often thwarting and reversing their intentions in the process.

The first of these two roles of the army, comprising the military operations by which the empire was conquered and the Roman Peace which those conquests brought into being, makes a remarkable story which has often been told. The second role of the army, too, relating to the part it played in the internal affairs of the capital and the empire, cannot fail to receive some attention in any general historical account of the period. Yet it has not, as far as I know, been the subject of a special study in recent times. This, then, is the main theme of the present book. It will take note of the principal military operations, and will begin with a general description of the Roman soldier and his activities. But it will chiefly consider the impact of the Roman army, including the praetorian guard, upon the life of the empire itself, and particularly upon the behaviour and destiny of its government. Such a study can, I believe, reveal aspects of imperial rule which do not always receive sufficient emphasis, and which, moreover, have a bearing upon the management of states in later centuries, including our own; and it will also show a number of individual emperors in an unfamiliar light. We are accustomed to learn from the works of ancient historians, who were mostly staunch supporters of the senate and opponents of military influence, which rulers they consider 'good' or 'bad'. Looked at from the standpoint of the army, the good and bad rulers often turn out to be quite different. And to study the empire from this point of view is at least as legitimate as to study it from the viewpoint of the senators, since it was on the army, in the last resort, that everything depended. This is an ultimate, basic fact of which it is too easy to lose sight when one studies non-military aspects of the empire, such as the constitution which papered over the stark reality of army domination.

I want to thank Mr Michael Crawford, Professor Henri Godin, Mrs Bezi Hammelmann, Mr J.C.T.Oates and Miss Betty Radice for their help, and I owe an acknowledgement to Dr J.P.V.D.Balsdon for an adaptation from a legionary distribution table. I am also very grateful to Miss Eileen Wood, of Messrs Weidenfeld and Nicolson, for her editorship of the volume, to Miss Barbara Gough and Mrs Hilary Walford for their assistance, and Mr Derek Dooley for his preparation of the maps. And the book could never have been written without the constant help of my wife.

MICHAEL GRANT

Introduction: The Roman Soldier

It is with the massive power of the Roman army as a corporate force that this book is mainly concerned. But before this corporate institution, and its character, can be properly estimated, something must first be said about the individual soldiers who each made their small contribution towards it. The toughness, endurance and courage of the Roman soldier at his best need no special emphasis. But the authorities who controlled him also devoted intense thought to furnishing him with weapons and equipment which would enable him to exploit these qualities to the uttermost. So comments must first be made about these, and also about the various other means that were employed to develop his personal efficiency to the highest possible level.

In the late Republic and early empire a Roman legionary on the march carried two javelins – throwing spears, in place of the thrusting spears which had been Rome's national weapon in the First and Second Punic Wars against the rival power of Carthage (264–41, 218–01 BC). The change had already been brought into effect by the second century BC, when the Greek historian Polybius, a great admirer of the Romans and their army, offered a description of these javelins.

Some of these are thick, some thin. Of the thick ones, some are round, with a diameter of about three inches, while others are square, with a side about three inches in width. The light javelins, which they carry along with the heavy ones, resemble moderate-sized hunting spears. The shafts of all their javelins are about four and a half feet long [later, they attained a length of seven feet]. On each one there is fitted a barbed iron head of the same length as the shaft. They make sure that it will be attached tightly enough to be useful by pushing the iron head right into the shaft, to a point about half-way up, and they bolt it in place with thick-set rivets. The result is that before the binding could be loosened through use the iron head would break, although it is a finger and a half in thickness at the bottom where it joins the shaft. Such is the effort and foresight that they put into attaching the head.[1]

Later on, during the first century BC, when a standard type of javelin came into universal use, an impressive refinement had been added. For now the smiths tempered only two parts of the iron head: its lower end, which was hammered out to provide a socket for the shaft, and its ten-inch-long point, which was left in its original soft state. This meant that, if the enemy stopped the missile with his shield, it stuck there at an angle and he could neither go on using his shield nor throw the javelin back, because it was bent and buckled. And if the javelin missed the enemy's body and shield alike and fell to the ground, the result was the same; and once again it could not be thrown back. This missile had a fatal range of something like ninety feet. A leather thong was attached to its wooden shaft at the point of balance, so that it flew through the air like a bullet ejected from a spiral barrel, with a twisting, spinning motion, which added impetus and penetration to its flight.[2]

When he had hurled his javelins, the legionary charged in. Then, at close quarters, he used his formidable sword. It was lodged in a leather or wooden scabbard, reinforced with metal at top and bottom, out of which he drew his sword with his right hand. The scabbard was carried high up on the right side of his body. At first sight this looks an encumbering location but it kept scabbard and sword clear of his shield-bearing left arm. Moreover it prevented them from becoming entangled with his legs. The sword was a short one, only two feet long. Its short two-inch-wide blade possessed a double edge, for cutting and thrusting, but the legionary used the weapon less for these purposes than for stabbing. Its bone handle was notched with a groove, to provide a firm grip, and was topped with a round or square pommel. On the left side of the body was slung a short leaf-shaped dagger, which could be used, if the sword got lost, for hand-to-hand fighting, but at other times was generally employed as a knife.

The dagger, too, was carefully placed to prevent it from getting in the way of the shield, which was carried on the same side. This shield (*scutum*) was equipped with two leather straps, one to fit on to the legionary's forearm and the other to hang from his left shoulder on the march. In earlier times Roman shields had been light and round, but by the later days of the Republic a rectangular shield had been introduced instead. Polybius already knew of this, though in his time it had not yet come into general use, as it did subsequently. 'The width of the convex surface of the shield', he records, 'is two and a half feet, the length four feet, and the thickness at the rim three inches.' The change to these substantial means of protection made it unnecessary for the legs to be protected by greaves (shin-pieces), as in earlier days, so that they went out of use – and the mobility of the soldiers was correspondingly increased.

The shield is made [Polybius continues] of a double thickness of planks, joined together with glue derived from bulls' hides. The outer surface is wrapped first with canvas, then with calf-skin. Along the rim, at the top and bottom, the shield has an ornamental binding made of iron, which protects it from the cutting strokes of swords and from damage when it is set on the ground. It also has fitted to it an iron boss, which deflects the more destructive blows of stones, long javelins and heavy missiles in general.[3]

The interior of the boss provided the soldier with space to alter his grip on the shield, and the curve of its cylindrical surface helped to deflect blows (like the curved surface of a tower incorporated in a wall or castle). Its outer face was ornamented with a wide diversity of decorative designs, which stood for different units and services. These designs, represented conventionally but with care, can be seen on the spiral reliefs of the Column of Trajan (AD 98–117) in his Basilica at Rome,* though what these do not show is that the devices, in their original state, were variously and garishly coloured.

The main feature of the legionary's clothing was his cuirass or corselet (*lorica*), which likewise assumed a number of different forms. In the first century AD, to judge by sculptural representations, the normal wear was a leather jacket with leather shoulder-pieces. But in the next century AD, the time of Trajan, a corselet in common use possessed overlapping breast- and backplates of metal, strengthened by iron hoops, fastened at the front with studs and slots, and made flexible by hinges at the back, which allowed freedom of movement – or alternatively the fastenings, fore and aft, were leather cords. Further strips of metal served as shoulder-pieces. Sometimes a scarf was worn to prevent the metal plates from chafing the skin. There were also several

* See Chapter 8.

types of mail armour, one of which consisted of a series of interlocking rings, while another comprised metal scales sewn in overlapping rows on a leather coat.[4]

Over this corselet, round his waist, the legionary wore a wide belt studded with various ornaments and fastened with an elaborate buckle.[5] Attached to this belt, to protect the genitals, was a kind of sporran consisting of thick leather strips which swung between the wearer's legs, and were sometimes fastened in loops. This protective addition covered the lower portions of a woolen tunic or undervest which was sleeveless or left one shoulder bare. On long, hot marches, when everything else had been stripped off, this remained as the one and only garment. In cold weather a soldier kept himself warm with a thick, brown woollen cloak, and sometimes, too, he wore tight-fitting leather trousers reaching below the knee. But most important of all were his heavy boots (*caligae*), or rather sandals, which were in many ways more serviceable than modern army boots. Their soles, made of several layers of leather and heavily studded with hollow-headed nails, varied considerably in thickness; perhaps three-quarters of an inch was about the average. Strips of cloth or fur were sometimes placed inside the sandals, and they were fastened to the foot by ankle thongs.

What the legionary wore at his other extremity, his helmet, assumed various shapes, at different times and places. This head-gear was generally of bronze, fitted inside with an iron skull-cap lined with leather or cloth. A heavier type of helmet, which was worn in the Rhine and Danube armies, terminated at the top with a ring, into which a crest of red plumes was inserted for full-dress parades (on Trajan's Column, legionaries are shown going into battle wearing these crests, but it is unlikely that they normally did so). Visors for frontal protection were not worn, but a small metal peak jutted out in front, and at the back a plate extended downwards to protect the neck. There were also hinged cheek-pieces at the sides. In Britain the legionaries seem to have worn a lighter sort of helmet, with an upward-curving back.

A successful soldier was able to display spectacular decorations. These included collars or necklaces, arm-bands and round discs worn in a leather harness strung over the corselet. Awarded usually in sets of nine, these discs often bore the portrait of the emperor. Open to all ranks, too, was the glorious Civic Crown, a wreath of oak-leaves (later made of gold) awarded for saving the life of a fellow-citizen. But if the possibilities of winning decorations were impressive, the various punishments in force, too, were, by modern standards, tough.

Soldiers appear to have been laden with a large quantity of gear – alarmingly large according to some accounts. Cicero wrote of 'the toil, the great toil, of the march: the load of more than half a month's provisions, the load of any and everything that might be required, the load of the stake for entrenchments'.[6] Normally, perhaps, a legionary carried rations for three days, not the two weeks to which Cicero refers. But he took with him, in addition, a bronze food box or mess-tin, a kettle and perhaps a portable hand-mill. Since, moreover, he was not only a fighting man but an engineer and a builder of camps and roads – those greatest of all Roman military monuments[7] – he also carried a length of rope or a leather thong; a pickaxe, slung from his belt in a bronze sheath; a chain, a saw and a hook, all kept in a tool-bag; stakes for constructing entrenchments;* and a wicker basket for moving earth.[8] The tool-bag and basket were attached to a staff or forked stick, which was carried over the left shoulder. It has been estimated that the legionary, over and above his armour and weapons, was burdened with equipment weighing as much as sixty pounds. Rightly did Gibbon suggest that this weight 'would oppress the delicacy of a modern soldier'.

However each eight-man section (*contubernium*), who shared a tent between them, sometimes also shared a mule, which could be used to transport millstones (for grinding their food) and other heavy baggage. The army on the march was also accompanied by two-wheeled carts loaded with heavy weapons and siege-machinery,† and carefully packed supplies. Probably by that time such forms of transport were increasingly employed to lighten the soldier's personal burden. Slaves, too, were utilized as batmen and carriers; there is evidence that soldiers possessed slaves of their own, and bought and sold them. In due course there was legislation prescribing lenient treatment for soldiers who were absent from duty too long because they were in pursuit of absconding slaves.

Officers, of course, displayed grander uniforms than the men under their command. In particular they wore elegantly shaped cuirasses. These varied in style according to personal taste, but generally took the form of tight leather jerkins on which curved sections of bronze were fastened by stitching, in order to give an exaggerated impression of muscular development. The officers also wore pleated kilts of leather or cloth, sometimes strengthened and ornamented by metal strips arranged according to rank. Rank, too, determined the colours of

* See Appendix 3.
† For siege-machinery, see Appendix 4.

officers' cloaks, which varied between white, red and purple. Lined ankle-boots of an ornamental appearance were also worn. The centurions, the principal professional officers of the Roman army who did a lion's share of the work,* were permitted to wear lighter footwear than the soldiers, resembling sandals though still studded with nails. When they went on parade they wore shin-pieces, sometimes coated in silver.† The centurions also carried staffs of hard vine-wood, which served as symbols of their rank and as instruments for beating legionaries.

The decorations for which officers were eligible, according to rank, included an imposing variety of different types of wreath and crown – of which a plain gold crown was the commonest – a silver spear-head and (at the highest level) a miniature silver standard.[9] A very senior general might well be the holder of as many as four crowns, four spear-heads and four standards.

The cavalrymen of the legions, who were comparatively few in number, probably wore lighter corselets and helmets, and carried a circular or oval shield and a thrusting spear or heavy lance. Their horses had no saddles, and stirrups were not yet invented.

The auxiliary troops who, in the imperial epoch, became as numerous as the legionaries,‡ but unlike them were not normally Roman citizens and did not obtain citizenship until they were discharged, wore uniforms quite distinct from those seen in the legions. Moreover these styles of dress varied considerably from one auxiliary unit to another, since they originated from different parts of the empire. Fluttering capes and other distinctive features are to be seen, and the irregulars (*numeri, symmachiarii*) of the second century AD appear on Trajan's Column stripped to the waist, or in short tunics leaving one shoulder exposed. They wore long trousers, rolled up to form a waistband, and they marched and fought barefoot. Auxiliary infantrymen often carried thrusting spears and long broad swords (*spathae*), probably of German origin. It was from the auxiliary cavalry in the second century AD that there developed the iron-clad horseman of eastern type who became a vital part of the Roman army a century later.§

---

* See the end of this Introduction, p. xxxiii.

† For the uniform of centurions (and of the various grades of standard-bearer who ranked below them), see Appendix 2.

‡ For the auxiliaries, see Chapter 3.

§ For the uniforms of auxiliary cavalrymen, auxiliary infantrymen and *numeri*, see Appendix 2.

A word should also be said about the Roman soldier's diet. In general he went without breakfast, a fate which would not attract his modern counterpart, at least in northern countries. Nor perhaps would he welcome the Roman concentration on cereal as the main feature of the legionary's diet. What he ate was not barley, which was regarded as a punishment, but wheat. This was eaten in the form of porridge, or bread, which he himself ground over hot stones or embers. On campaigns the grain was baked into hard biscuits. This cereal diet was supplemented by soup, lard and vegetables. As for meat, Tacitus comments on an occasion when it proved the only food available: and then it was by no means appreciated.[10] All the same, the soldiers ate meat when they could, mostly salted and mostly pork. Graham Webster had a look for food remains on the site of a fort in Dorset, and although the number of bones was too small to provide comprehensive statistics, his conclusions were interesting:

Cattle and sheep were present, but very little pig. Bird bones included doves' and pigeons' and a fair amount of fowl. In the latter case, however, there were six cocks' spurs indicating gaming birds and five neatly severed skulls suggesting sacrificial victims. What was interesting was the Giant Wrasse (?), now held inedible on account of its large number of bones. There were also the inevitable remains of shellfish.[11]

In other words soldiers ate what they could when they could. Very often they washed their food down with vinegar, which they carried about them and mixed with water. And, true to the continuing tradition of their country, they drank wine whenever it was available; hence a large number of casks, stacked in carts, represented upon Trajan's Column.

The Roman legionaries were vociferous. This did not surprise other ancient peoples such as the Greeks, whose soldiers had always been highly articulate and critical. But it would cause raised eyebrows, to say the least, among the officers of such modern armies as have any claim to efficiency. The first ten books of Livy's *History of Rome*, written in the time of Augustus, are full of stories of soldiers shouting at their generals and questioning their wisdom. Admittedly he is dealing with mythical times and drawing upon his imagination. Yet the way in which he writes about these incidents suggests that he was reproducing an authentic type of situation. It may be that the severe discipline of the Roman army during the First and Second Punic Wars somewhat inhibited this Mediterranean flow of eloquence. But subsequently, in 168 BC, Lucius Aemilius Paullus, after he had taken over the command in Macedonia, found his soldiers so talkative and bent on interference that they seemed to be behaving 'as though they were all commanders'. In consequence he issued an order that they should concentrate on having ready hands and keen swords, and leave the rest to him.[12] Yet the tendency towards loud self-expression remained.

One of its results was that generals, too, had to be extremely articulate, and this likewise emerges strongly from Livy. Almost all ancient historians insert numerous set speeches by commanders, whether delivered before battle, on parade, in council or on a variety of other occasions. Many of these orations are at best plausible, and more probably quite fictitious. Nevertheless it becomes clearly apparent that eloquence was a far more important qualification in generals than it is now. And fortunately, being products of an educational system based on rhetoric, they were much more likely to possess some talents in this direction than their modern counterparts. The generals, as a religious duty, ensured that every soldier swore an oath (*sacramentum*) to the Roman state (and until 216 BC to their own comrades as well[13]). A gold coin depicts the ceremony.[14] Soldiers were made liable to summary execution[15] – and were feared, as Gallius records. When a levy was made and they were enrolled, the military tribune administered an oath to them in the following words:

In the army of the consuls such and such and for ten miles around it, you will not with malice aforethought steal, alone or with others, anything worth more than a *sestertius* [quarter of a *denarius**] in any one day; and excepting a spear, spear-shaft, wood, fruit, fodder, a wineskin, a purse or a torch, if you there find or carry off anything which is not your own and is worth more than one *sestertius*, you will bring it to one of the consuls, or to whomsoever either of them shall designate, or you will report within the next three days whatever you have found or carried off with malice aforethought, or you will restore it to the owner to whom you believe it belongs, acting in good conscience.[16]

Naturally, in times of civil war, mutiny or other disturbance, this sort of correctness went entirely by the board. Moreover, even in times of peace, the satirist Juvenal – writing some two generations before Gellius – took pains to point out, in a poem which he wholly devoted to this theme, that soldiers possessed a good many more privileges than the rest of the population. A large part of the poem is lost, but what

* For the Roman currency, see Appendix 5.

remains shows that it was an exhaustive demonstration of the advantages, and seemingly unfair advantages at that, which were enjoyed by the soldiery.

> Who can count up the rewards of a successful
> Army career? If you do well during your service
> The sky's the limit, there's nothing you can't hope for.
> Find me a lucky star to watch over my enlistment
> And I'd join up myself, walk in through those barrack-gates as
> A humble recruit . . .
> Let us consider first, then, the benefits common to all
> Military men. Not least is the fact that no civilian
> Would dare to give you a thrashing – and if beaten up himself
> He'll keep quiet about it, he'd never dare show any magistrate
> His knocked-out teeth, the blackened lumps and bruises
> All over his face, that surviving eye which the doctor
> Offers no hope for. And if he seeks legal redress,
> The case will come up before some hobnailed centurion
> And a benchful of brawny jurors, according to ancient
> Military law: no soldier, it's stated, may sue or be tried
> Except in camp, by court-martial. 'But still, when an officer's
> Trying a guardsman, surely the proceedings must be conducted
> With exemplary justice? So if my complaint is legitimate
> I'm sure to get satisfaction.' But the whole regiment
> Is against you, every company unites, as one man, to ensure
> That the 'redress' you get shall be something requiring a doctor,
> And worse than the first assault. So since you've a pair of shins, it's
> Stupidity past belief to provoke all those jackboots, and all
> Those thousands of hobnails . . .
> > Easier find a witness
> To perjure himself against a civilian than one who'll tell
> The truth, if the truth's against a soldier's honour or interest . . .
> > And it's in any commander's interest
> To see the bravest soldiers obtain the best recompense,
> That they all have decorations and medals to show off, that all . . .[17]

And there the half-ironical survey breaks off – which is a pity, since no other Greek or Roman social critic discusses this important subject at any length. However some light is thrown on another aspect of the same theme by papyri discovered in the sands of Egypt. In one of these a businessman lists – among normal overheads – payments and bribes 'to the soldier on his demand'.[18] Moreover this is a theme which had already made its appearance in St Luke's Gospel. Soldiers on service, it was stated in the Gospel, had come to see Jesus and had asked him how they should behave. And to them he said: 'No bullying; no blackmail; make do with your pay.'[19]

But of course to be content with one's pay, whether it was generous or otherwise, was something which not every soldier was prepared to do; and among the papyri from Egypt is a letter one of them wrote to his parents on this very subject:

My dear Mother,

I hope that this finds you well. When you get this letter I shall be much obliged if you will send me some money. I haven't got a penny left, because I have bought a donkey-cart and spent all my money on it. Do send me a riding-coat, some oil and above all my monthly allowance. When I was last home you promised not to leave me penniless, and now you treat me like a dog. Father came to see me the other day and gave me nothing. Everybody laughs at me now, and says 'his father is a soldier, his father gave him nothing'.

Valerius's mother sent him a pair of pants, a measure of oil, a box of food and some money. Do send me money and don't leave me like this. Give my love to everybody at home.

Your loving Son.[20]

There speaks the individual soldier. And it is he who has hitherto been the subject of this discussion. When the army is found continually influencing and transforming the course and direction of affairs, such are the men, multiplied by thousands, who produce these far-reaching repercussions. And yet, obviously, in these major matters of state, it is only rarely that the soldier as an individual will emerge. What will become evident, instead, is his impact *en masse*. This was both military and political. The present book will have a lot to say about his political impact. But since his role was, in the first resort, intended to be military, let us conclude with one or two pictures showing the army at those military tasks for which they were primarily designed.

First, training. For these Roman soldiers, in the intervals between vociferous protests and mutinies, were famous for their fine discipline: and this was because they were extremely well trained. Indeed, theirs was the best trained army that there had ever been. The methods adopted by the Romans are described by Vegetius.* The first stages of

---

* See Bibliography, Section B, Roman Writings. Vegetius is late, but his material is based on earlier works dating from various periods of the empire.

the training programme, which were based on the system in force at the schools for gladiators, are described by him in these terms:

The ancients (as we find in their writings) trained their recruits in this manner. They made round wickerwork shields, twice as heavy as those of service weight, and gave their recruits wooden staves instead of swords, and these again were of double weight. With these they were made to practise at the stakes both morning and afternoon. The employment of stakes is of the greatest benefit both to soldiers and to gladiators. No man has ever distinguished himself as invincible in armed combat either in the gladiatorial arena or in the Field of Mars [an area outside the original walls used for army exercises] who was not carefully trained and instructed at the stakes ... A stake was planted in the ground by each recruit, in such a manner that it projected six feet in height and could not sway. Against this stake the recruit practised with his wickerwork shield and wooden stave, just as if he were fighting a real enemy. Sometimes he aimed as against the head or the face, sometimes he threatened from the flanks, sometimes he endeavoured to strike down the knees and the legs. He gave ground, he attacked, he assaulted, and he assailed the stake with all the skill and energy required in actual fighting, just as if it were a real enemy; and in this exercise care was taken to see that the recruit did not rush forward so rashly to inflict a wound as to lay himself open to a counter-stroke from any quarter. Furthermore they learned to strike, not with the edge, but with the point. For those who strike with the edge have not only been beaten by the Romans quite easily, but they have even been laughed at.[21]

Arms-drill of this kind alternated with target-practice, running, jumping and tree-felling. Moreover three times a month, according to Vegetius, there were long route marches for recruits, on which the pace varied from the normal marching rate to a rapid trot.[22]

When the Romans crushed the rebellious Jews, in the First Jewish Revolt or First Roman War (AD 66–73), the historian Josephus, who served his compatriots for a time as a commander, was deeply impressed by the discipline of the Roman army:

This vast empire of theirs has come to them as the prize of valour, and not as a gift of fortune.

For their nation does not wait for the outbreak of war to give men their first lesson in arms. They do not sit with folded hands in peace-time only to put them in motion in the hour of need. On the contrary, as though they had been born with weapons in hand, they never have a truce from training, never wait for emergencies to arise. Moreover their peace manœuvres are no less strenuous than veritable warfare. Each soldier daily throws all his energy into his drill, as though he were in action. Hence that perfect ease with which they sustain the shock of battle. No confusion breaks their customary formation, no panic paralyses, no fatigue exhausts them. And as their opponents cannot match these qualities, victory is the invariable and certain consequence. Indeed, it would not be wrong to describe their manœuvres as bloodless combats and their combats as sanguinary manœuvres . . .

By their military exercises the Romans instil into their soldiers fortitude not only of body but also of soul. Fear, too, plays its part in their training. For they have laws which punish with death not merely desertion of the ranks, but even a slight neglect of duty. And their generals are held in even greater awe than the laws. For the high honours with which they reward the brave prevent the offenders whom they punish from regarding themselves as treated cruelly.

This perfect discipline makes the army an ornament of peace-time and in war welds the whole into a single body – so compact are their ranks, so alert their movements in wheeling to right or left, so quick their ears for orders, their eyes for signals, their hands to act upon them. Prompt as they consequently ever are in action, none are slower than they in succumbing to suffering, and never have they been known in any predicament to be beaten by numbers, by ruse, by difficulties of ground, or even by fortune – for they feel surer of victory than of fortune's power. Where counsel thus precedes active operations, where the leaders' plan of campaign is followed up by so efficient an army, no wonder that the empire has extended its boundaries on the east to the Euphrates, on the west to the ocean, on the south to the most fertile tracts of north Africa, on the north to the Danube and the Rhine.

One might say without exaggeration that, great as are their possessions, the people that won them are greater still. If I have dwelt at some length on this topic, my intention was not so much to extol the Romans as to console those whom they have vanquished – and to deter others who may be tempted to revolt.[23]

In peace-time the efficiency of the Roman army was displayed in spectacular parades. Arrian, who wrote a tactical manual in the second century AD, supplies a description of the auxiliary cavalry's ceremonial:

The horsemen enter the exercise ground fully armed, and those of high rank or superior horsemanship wear gilded helmets of iron or bronze to draw the attention of the spectators. Unlike the helmets made for active service, these do not cover the head and cheeks only but are made to fit all round the faces of the riders with apertures for the eyes . . . From the helmets hang yellow plumes, a matter of ornament as much as of utility. As the horses move forward the slightest breeze adds to the beauty of these plumes. They carry oblong shields of a lighter type than those used in action – since both agility and smart turnout are the objects of the exercise – and they improve the appearance of their shields by embellishment. Instead of breastplates the horsemen wear tight leather jerkins embroidered with scarlet, red or blue and other colours. On their legs they wear tight trousers, not loosely fitting like those of the Parthians and Armenians. The horses have frontlets carefully made to measure, and also wear side-armour.[24]

Graham Webster adds a comment on such parades:

It is difficult for us in this day and age to understand the motives behind the expense and trouble of providing this special equipment merely for the parade. But ceremony has always played a very important part in army life. In giving pride in appearance, it deepens the feeling of superiority. The flashing splendour of these arms and the elegant and skilful drill movement must have produced a deep effect on both Roman and barbarian alike. Nor must we forget the deeper religious significance. This was no mere show to impress an audience, like the Royal Tournament, but an affirmative identification of the army with the gods. Perhaps we may see this in the presence of the gilded parade masks. The swarthy barbarian faces were hidden behind this uniform, classical façade. This must have been to make them all look either like Romans or like gods. It may be significant that there was a similar practice in the classical theatre. Not all the masks are classical; some are definitely barbarian or have eastern features with flowing locks, and the suggestion has been made that the cavalry enacted the battles of the Trojan War in the annual festival celebrating the founding of Rome.[25]

Later in this study we shall read the appreciative words spoken by Hadrian to various categories of his troops on parade (Chapter 8, p. 239).

Perhaps one of the severest tests of the Roman soldier's discipline was his fortitude in erecting camps of remarkable elaboration.

For the Romans [remarked Josephus] never lay themselves open to a surprise attack. For, whatever hostile territory they may invade, they engage in no battle until they have fortified their camp. This camp is not erected at random or unevenly. They do not all work at once or in disorderly parties. If the ground is uneven, it is first levelled: a site for the camp is then measured out in the form of a square. For this purpose the army is accompanied by a multitude of workmen and of tools for building.[26]*

The Roman order of march was equally systematic. The men marched in columns of ten, and in spite of the two or three hours spent on camp construction normally covered about fifteen miles a day, or twenty-five on forced marches with light equipment. On campaigns

---

* For the Roman camp, see Appendix 3.

there was a recognized order of march, though it was variable within limits. When Julius Caesar moved his army from place to place in Gaul, it was led by an auxiliary cavalry regiment with its baggage. Then came the legions, each accompanied by its own baggage, with their rear and flanks protected by further auxiliary cavalry.[27] When Vespasian moved a legion against the Jewish rebels the formation of his column was as follows: light-armed auxiliaries to repel harassing attacks and explore ambushes; detachments of legionary infantry and cavalry; ten men from each century to erect camps; road-makers; the baggage of the commander-in-chief and his generals, accompanied by a cavalry escort; the commander-in-chief himself, with a picked infantry and cavalry guard; the major part of the small cavalry forces of the legions; mules with siege equipment including siege-towers carrying battering rams;* the commanders of the legions with their senior subordinate officers and an escort to guard them; the standard-bearers (*aquiliferi*) with their legionary Eagles, followed by trumpeters; the legions them-selves (with their baggage), each under the marching orders of a centurion; the legionary servants, with laden mules and other beasts of burden; the main body of the auxiliaries who had not marched in the vanguard; and finally a rearguard of legionary and (auxiliary) infantry, with a considerable force of cavalry.[28]

The psychology and tactics of the battlefield itself were the subject of further discussions by Vegetius. In the battle, he says, each man required a lateral space of three feet, while the distance between ranks should have been six. Thus ten thousand men could be placed in a rectangle about fifteen hundred yards by twelve yards – and it was advisable not to extend the line much beyond this. The disposition of particular units depended upon circumstances and above all, of course, upon the formation adopted by the enemy. The normal arrangement was to place the infantry in the centre and the cavalry on the wings. The function of the latter was to prevent the centre from being outflanked, and, once the battle was turned and the enemy started to retreat, the cavalry could move forward and cut them down. If your cavalry was weak it should be stiffened with lightly-armed auxiliary foot-soldiers.

Vegetius then goes on to describe the tactics known as the wedge and the saw. Legionaries commonly employed a 'wedge' formation when they moved to the attack; this enabled small groups to be thrust well into the middle of the enemy, and, when these groups expanded, the

* For siege-machinery, see Appendix 4.

enemy troops were pushed into restricted positions, making hand-to-hand fighting difficult. This is where the short legionary sword, held low and used as a thrusting weapon, became invaluable, whereas the long Celtic or German sword would have been impossible to wield. If the enemy formed a wedge, the correct opposing tactic was to form indentations in the line to accommodate the wedges and prevent penetration. The 'saw' was a detached unit which operated immediately behind the front line and engaged in lateral movements so as to block any holes which might have appeared, or to develop a thrust where a sign of enemy weakness became apparent.[29]

When battle was joined legions were often formed up into three lines, so that at any one moment nearly two-thirds of the legion remained outside the zone of slaughter and exhaustion. One behind the other, these lines of closely formed legionaries advanced against the enemy shoulder to shoulder, with their shields almost meeting in a solid wall.

The classic armies that won the Roman Republic's wars of expansion were about fifteen to twenty thousand men strong. Each of them was commanded by one or both of the annually elected consuls, who represented both the sovereign Roman people and the advisory senate which guided its actions – these forming the *senatus populusque Romanus* (SPQR) which comprised the state itself.

In Republican times such armies were made up of two parts, Roman citizens and non-citizen Italian 'allies' (*socii*), theoretically in equal numbers.[30] These allies were the forerunners of the auxiliaries of the imperial epoch. As for the citizens, the units known as legions (from *legere*, to gather together) to which they belonged dated from very ancient times. In later days the Romans liked to compare any and every legion to a wholly self-contained 'armed state', wherever it might find itself.[31] The legion was divided into thirty smaller infantry units called maniples – ten for each of the three lines of battle. Each maniple, in its turn, comprised two centuries, perhaps originally consisting of a hundred men, though in historical times the strength was eighty. Thus the mess-units of eight men, sharing a tent and a mule, were ten to each century.

However, from shortly before 100 BC, the maniple largely lost its importance to the cohort. This unit, which was tactical rather than administrative and possessed no particular officers or staff of its own, consisted of three maniples, so that there were ten cohorts in every legion, and six centuries in every cohort. (The small cavalry sections in each legion gradually vanished at this time, though, as we shall see, they were revived later on.)

In theory the army of the Republic was a citizen militia, levied and controlled by the state officials for a single season of service. But service came to be extended to much longer periods, and Polybius is already able to speak of citizens, of various ages between seventeen and forty-six, enrolling for a sixteen-year period of service, or twenty years in an emergency. Yet even in the following century, during the turbulent last days of the Republic, legions were, at least theoretically speaking, raised, if not for one given year, at least for one given war, and released when it was over. And this was what the legionaries expected.

The Organization of the Legion

Legion
|
10 cohorts
|
(3 maniples in each cohort)
|
2 centuries (of 80 men) in each maniple,
6 in each cohort
|
10 mess-units (*contubernia*) in each century

They had been recruited, traditionally, by conscription. This resulted in something of a paradox, since the levy was restricted to the possessors of a certain property qualification – a necessary method, it was held, of ensuring that all who might be called upon to defend the state would have reason to feel the desired emotions of loyalty. The soldiers were paid, and this practice, it was believed, had been introduced in about 400 BC, at the time when the need for campaigns extending over more than a single year was first beginning to be apparent. However, for a long time thereafter, since Rome's citizens, who served as soldiers, were only doing their duty, their emoluments continued to be thought of as merely covering their expenses. For this reason, it still remained customary for the cost of their food and equipment to be deducted from the sums they received; and the cost of their clothing, too, was at first deducted, though for a time during the later Republic this deduction was remitted.

The senior officers of the Republican army were the military tribunes (*tribuni militum*), elected by the Roman people, that is to say by the Assembly.* These tribunes ranked as state officials. There were six of them to each legion and they were attached, not to individual maniples or cohorts, but directly to legionary headquarters. The Italian and Roman officers who shared the command of 'allied' units were known as prefects. This was also the title of officers appointed by legionary commanders to act as camp commandants (*praefecti castrorum*), and of others who directed their building and engineering operations (*praefecti fabrum*). Officers of the latter rank had experts at their disposal, though they may sometimes have possessed a certain amount of specialist knowledge themselves. But other officers of Republican times were often strangely deficient in professional knowledge; and when one considers the enormous successes the Roman armies gained, this becomes all the more remarkable. The fact was that the more or less aristocratic Roman society from which they came disdained technical qualifications. Fortunately, however, it insisted on a versatile experience; and its young men were made to perform training exercises of a kind in the Field of Mars.[32] This, however, was not enough to prevent most Republican wars from beginning with disasters, however triumphantly they were to conclude.

Continuity was provided by the centurions, of whom there were six in each cohort. These formidable men combined the functions and prestige of a modern company commander and sergeant-major or top sergeant. The historian Livy writes of such an officer of the early second century BC, Spurius Ligustinus. By the time he was in his fifties and had undertaken twenty-two years of service, he had acted four times as the senior centurion of his legion, and had won thirty-four decorations including six Civic Crowns.[33] According to Polybius the men the Romans chose as their centurions were those who could keep cool in an emergency. Daredevils were not what was wanted. Centurions in battle

---

* Later the tribunes of only four legions were elected by the people, the rest being nominated by commanders.

were required to be cautious about moving their men forward: though under no circumstances should they retreat without an order. During the Republic they were usually promoted from the ranks, probably through one or more of what would now be called non-commissioned officer ranks.[34] When they reached the centurionate, they started by serving in the lowest of its grades. From there they were able to move upwards through the remaining grades of the same office, grades which differed considerably one from another in importance and comprised a whole hierarchy of what were virtually different ranks. However until the last days of the Republic centurions, even of the highest level, did not succeed in obtaining further promotion to the military tribunate or other official posts: it was largely the achievement of Augustus to open wider horizons to these invaluable officers.

Part I
Two Styles of Leadership

I

Army Leadership in the Failing Republic 107–31 BC

In a warlike nation such as the Roman Republic it was evident that those generals who commanded many troops and won great successes would acquire massive and, before long, excessive prestige. The tendency of Roman legionaries to get on talking terms with their commanders has already been mentioned; and after a victory they formed the habit of saluting them by a special title of honour, *Imperator*, the commander *par excellence*. The first man unmistakably to have been hailed in this way is Lucius Aemilius Paullus Macedonicus, after military operations in Lusitania (Further Spain) in 189 BC. However he may not have been the absolute first, for it was believed that his brother-in-law, Scipio Africanus the elder, whose triumph over Hannibal brought the Second Punic War to a victorious close in 201 BC, had likewise been saluted *Imperator*. Scipio Africanus the elder also made a further move towards the personality cult by leading armies which, although armies of the state, consisted largely of men who were, and felt themselves to be, his own personal followers. The younger Scipio Africanus (Aemilianus), too, the adoptive grandson of Scipio the elder and the son of Paullus, pursued the same process further in his campaigns against the Carthaginians in the Third Punic War (146 BC) and then against the Spaniards (134–3 BC). These operations resulted in the extension of Roman rule over the province of Africa (Tunisia) and over two-thirds of Spain. Nevertheless, when the wars were over, the younger Scipio, like his grandfather, scrupulously

3

refrained from attempting any perilous exploitation of the potential political power which his successes had placed in his grasp.

But exploitation of this kind came not much later – owing to a series of developments which did not aim at such a result at all. During the second century BC, in which Rome was creating its empire in the eastern Mediterranean area, the property qualification required of legionaries was twice substantially reduced. Then, in 107 BC, the great general Gaius Marius, who was fighting against Jugurtha the king of Numidia (west of the African province), found himself faced with a desperate shortage of manpower. In consequence he opened the legions to men without any property qualification whatever, thus abandoning the idea that possessions guaranteed a man's loyalty to the state. Not so many years earlier the aristocratic brothers Tiberius and Gaius Sempronius Gracchus (d. 133 and 122 BC), in the interests of efficiency and relief from oppression, had endeavoured to make the senate a more responsible body, subject to constitutional checks. They had died in street-riots, but Rome was never the same again and new and more liberal ideas were in the wind. Under Marius – an educated personage whose depiction as a humble man of the people is a rhetorical untruth – these ideas found expression in army reforms. From now on it was enough that recruits to the legions should be Roman citizens, however poor.

At the same time, for the campaign against Jugurtha, he rejected conscription in favour of voluntary enlistment. For at least a century past conscript levies had, on occasion, been supplemented by volunteers. But Marius's combination of a thoroughgoing volunteer system with the abandonment of any property requirement created a mass of soldiers who became, inevitably, more and more professional in character, and who depended on their general far more closely than had ever been the case before. It was to join his service that they had volunteered, and since many of them had no possessions it was upon him, once their military service was over, that they continued to depend for their livelihood.

Soldiers had long been able to look forward to booty, which it was customary for a general to distribute at the end of a successful campaign. But what these landless peasants wanted above all else was land. Land allotments had been made after the Second Punic War, if not after earlier wars as well. But then the senate had discontinued the practice. They felt it was too expensive and the redistribution of soil which it involved seemed to hint unpleasantly at social revolution. They

4

disapproved of Marius's partial democratization of the army, and the more pressing demands for allotments that this inevitably created met with their adamant resistance. When Marius was raising troops to fight German invaders, holding out to them the expectation of subsequent land-grants, the attempts of a popular politician, the tribune of the people Lucius Appuleius Saturninus,* to settle the veterans in Africa and then in the recently acquired province of Transalpine Gaul (Gallia Narbonensis, south France) were among the major causes of violent rioting at Rome. Saturninus lost his life (100 BC), but his territorial assignations were apparently carried out.

The other reform of Marius which, looked at with hindsight, proved to be of particular significance was the bestowal upon each legion of its own silver Eagle, the emblem of Rome. Represented with spread wings, its claws sometimes resting upon a thunderbolt, it was carried, on the march, by an Eagle-bearer (*aquilifer*), who came next to the centurions in rank. When the legion was stationary the Eagle stood in the middle of the camp, on the top of a pole fastened into a low base. Later, in imperial times, it was lodged, together with the standards of the lesser units and images of the emperor, in a special chapel, where it was attended by a daily guard of honour.† Whether that had already been the practice under the Republic we do not know. But right from the moment of Marius's institution of the Eagle it contributed greatly to a new feeling of legionary *esprit de corps*: a feeling which, owing to the growing reliance of the soldiers upon their general, was increasingly directed to him instead of to the state. And so these legionaries came to be known as 'Marius's mules'. The exact reason for this nickname was disputed,[1] but its reference to their very personal link with their remarkable general was clear enough.

From 91 to 87 BC raged the terrible war fought by the Italians against Rome, whose senate had grudged them citizenship and other privileges. The hostilities were known sometimes as the Marsian War, after the central Italian people who took a leading part, and sometimes as the Social War since these Italians had, constitutionally speaking, been the *socii* (allies) of Rome. The Romans ultimately won the war largely because they conceded Roman citizenship to all Italy (with the exception of the north, Cisalpine Gaul, which was not yet thought of

---

* Tribunes of the people were traditionally empowered to 'protect the people' by intercession, veto and punitive action.

† For the uniforms of these standard-bearers, the *aquiliferi*, *signiferi* and *imaginiferi*, see Appendix 2.

5

as Italian). This meant that henceforward the legions would be full of Italians as well as Romans – and propertyless Italians at that. By his abandonment of the property qualification, that is to say, Marius had unwittingly prepared the way for the political unity of Italy. And now the Social War and the results which flowed from it gave new significance and shape to what he had done.

Since moreover many of these Italians felt little loyalty to the Roman government and senatorial class, against which they had so recently been fighting, another step had been taken towards the diversion of the soldiers' loyalty from the state to individual generals. And the Social War had another major military consequence too. Now that the Italians were legionaries, their 'allied' contingents to the Roman army had vanished. Henceforward instead the Romans began, slowly at first, to supplement their legions by auxiliary units drawn from outside Italy altogether, that is to say from the various provinces of the empire. In particular these provincial units were used to supplement two traditional deficiencies. First, the legions were heavy-armed infantry (they had in earlier days included light-armed detachments consisting of the youngest and poorest citizens, but these were now no more). Second, the legionary cavalry was abolished as well; the small units of legionary cavalry that had existed before disappeared for the time being from the military scene. So it was for light-armed infantry and for cavalry in particular that the commanders of the first century BC started to draw upon provincial manpower, employing it not only to create new legions, but to form separate auxiliary units.

As the Social War drew to its close, a series of events of sinister military and political significance occurred. The brilliant nobleman Lucius Cornelius Sulla, who had fought successfully in the campaign, was entrusted by the senate with a potentially glorious and lucrative eastern command. It was directed against the hostile King Mithridates VI of Pontus in northern Asia Minor, flanking and threatening the enormously wealthy Roman province of Asia, which comprised the western portions of the peninsula, and had been annexed in 133 BC. But Marius, who was greatly senior to Sulla, wanted the command for himself, and a politician named Publius Sulpicius Rufus, collaborating with Marius and mobilizing a private army to protect his own person, secured the cancellation of Sulla's appointment.

Thereupon Sulla, at the head of the troops he had been commanding in the Social War, marched on Rome and took it by force, fighting back the civilian population which opposed him. This was a flagrant breach of a tenacious Roman tradition – that soldiers should not be allowed in the capital city. But it was much worse than that. For Sulla had made himself the first Roman to lead an army against Rome. He had also in all probability become the first Roman to compel his troops to take their military oath not to the state but *to their general*, in circumstances which would compel them to fight against the official representatives of the Roman state. Not that his soldiers needed much compelling. Indeed they almost forced him to march on Rome – because the eastern war was likely to bring them loot, and they did not intend to lose it. As for Marius and Sulpicius, it had apparently never occurred to them that Sulla might refuse to allow himself to be deprived of his eastern command. By refusing, he launched the Roman army into the violence that was to bring the Republic down in ruins. And Plutarch,* looking back from the tranquil times of two hundred years later, sees the novel favours he felt obliged to lavish on his soldiers as no less fatal.

The generals of this later period were men who had risen to the top by violence rather than by merit. They needed armies to fight against one another rather than against the public enemy: and so they were forced to combine the arts of the politician with the authority of the general. They spent money on making life easy for their soldiers, and then, after purchasing their labour in this way, failed to observe that they had made their whole country a thing for sale, and had put themselves in a position where they had to be the slaves of the worst sort of people in order to become the masters of the better ... It was Sulla more than anyone else who set the example. In order to corrupt and win over to himself the soldiers of other generals, he gave his own troops a good time and spent money lavishly on them. He was thus at the same time encouraging the evils both of treachery and of debauchery. All this required much money.[2]

Sulla then proceeded to the east, where he won the war against Mithridates. But his victory could not be made definitive and permanent, since he agreed to a premature peace so that he could turn back to deal with his enemies among the Romans, the heirs of Marius who, after his death, retained their hostility to Sulla unabated. Calming his discontented army with Asian loot, he brought it back to Italy, established himself as dictator (82 BC) and retained this supreme post for more than twice as long as the six months which was supposed to be the limit of its supposedly emergency tenure. In this office he used the

* See Bibliography, Section A, Greek Writings.

7

soldiers, of whom his dictatorship made him commander-in-chief, to bring into effect the brutal proscriptions, which caused many deaths. These harrowing events raised an issue which was to dominate discussions of military affairs for centuries to come. The dilemma was this: which was worse, tyranny enforced by the army, or the civil war that might sometimes be the only alternative?

Sulla abdicated from his dictatorship – an action which seemed to Julius Caesar, in later times, unduly quixotic, and therefore mistaken. Before his abdication Sulla seems to have initiated the custom of keeping armies permanently in certain provinces; though they still possessed no regular garrisons, no standard tactical weapons and no adequate non-combatant services. As for the legionaries who had been discharged, he gave them extensive Italian lands, situated strategically in areas where they could not only, as the orator Cicero noted, serve as 'bulwarks of empire',[3] but could render him political services. But most land distributions to ex-soldiers in the later Republic failed in their purpose, and Sulla's were no exception. 'Most of his veterans,' commented the historian Sallust, 'ruined by extravagant living, looked back regretfully to the plunder which past victories had brought them, and longed for civil war.'[4] Sulla's purpose was to revive the senatorial oligarchy, but the retired legionaries were too restless to encourage the return of a stable situation.

Almost at once one of the consuls for 78 BC, Marcus Aemilius Lepidus, led the armies of Transalpine and Cisalpine Gaul in open insurrection. In Spain, too, Quintus Sertorius held out, in the Marian interest, for nearly a decade. When at last the young Pompey defeated him (73–2 BC), the senate, taking an action which did not come at all easily to them, actually voted lands to the victorious soldiers – though they never implemented the vote, and in general persisted in their unwise refusal to grant the veterans the allotments they wanted. Once again, therefore, the men turned to their generals; though in this transitional period there were few who had the power to satisfy their demands for land. Indeed, some generals of the period proved failures even before the need to provide for discharged veterans ever arose. One of these was Lucius Licinius Lucullus, who carried on the war against Mithridates. For Lucullus, though gifted as a strategist and tactician, lacked the understanding of his troops' reactions which was now more than ever an essential qualification for any Roman general.

At this period Roman armies still consisted partly of conscripts. For example there were levies throughout Italy in 87 and 84–2 BC. Yet this method was not sufficient to supply the needs of the time. When, therefore, the Roman government had to fight Sertorius or Mithridates, it was obliged to raise special emergency armies, consisting, in accordance with Marius's innovation, of volunteers from every social class. Increasingly these men, volunteers and conscripts alike, became pressure groups embodying and serving political power. They did not, as in the past, regard their service as a natural, routine phase in their duty as citizens. On the contrary they served either for a livelihood, or because they had to. It has been estimated that only about one man out of six wanted to protract his service when it had come to an end. The others could not wait for their rewards – which no one but their generals was willing to try to provide.

The legion was changing in certain respects. Its size at this period is uncertain. Probably it now comprised rather less than six thousand men – perhaps between four and five. Officers were becoming more professional. Moreover the hierarchy was slightly more flexible, since the occasional centurion could now win promotion to a senior post. On the other hand, now that Rome possessed a huge empire and was chiefly preoccupied with holding it down, many officers acquired an evil reputation for their oppressive dealings with provincials. Certain governors, such as Verres in Sicily who was prosecuted by the orator Cicero (70 BC), became notorious. But military men were often just as bad. There had been complaints at least since the early second century BC.[5] And now, in Asia, for example, declared Cicero,

there is no city large enough to slake the insolent pretensions of one single military tribune. I say nothing of commanders-in-chief and their lieutenants ... The sort of commanding officer who has sold, and still sells, centurions' commissions cannot be held in the smallest esteem. Nor is it possible to ascribe noble, elevated patriotic sentiments to the kind of man who is so eager to retain his provincial command that he doles out to Roman officials the money he drew from the treasury for the conduct of the war – or who, alternatively, is so acquisitive that he has left these funds profitably invested at Rome.

Gentlemen, I hear from your disapproving murmurs that you do not fail to identify the functionaries who have acted in this way. But I name no names, and in this way anyone who resents what I have said will be visibly admitting how well the cap fits. For it is common knowledge that this grasping behaviour by generals has caused our armies to spread devastation wherever they go. Think of the tours they have made in recent years all over Italy, among lands and municipalities that are the property of Roman citizens. Then you will find it easier to imagine how such men act among foreigners. Ask yourselves which, in these years, have reached the larger total – enemy towns destroyed by your soldiers, or allied communities ruined by the rapacity those same troops have shown when they requisition winter quarters.[6]

In consequence the richer towns were prepared to pay large sums to avoid military oppression – to escape, for instance, from having Roman soldiers billeted on them for the winter.[7] And even Caesar's future assassin Brutus, a man famous for his high principles, saw nothing wrong, when he instructed his agent to collect a debt at Salamis in Cyprus, in arranging for cavalry to lay siege to the senators of the town until some of them actually perished of starvation.[8] It was not surprising that underground literature, throughout the east, prophesied that the oppressed peoples would rise and take their revenge.[9] Cicero insisted that '*it is by defending our allies* that our people has become master of the whole world'.[10] But those days were past. No doubt honest and decent officers still existed, but in a rough age too many possessed neither of these qualities.

Moreover from the time of Sulla to the time of Augustus there was almost incessant turbulence and civil strife. It was an age to which military men and politicians of later epochs looked back with horrified fascination. Ancient historians, true to their ethical preoccupations, placed the blame on moral decline. And indeed one may well detect moral degradation in the Romans' gross ill-treatment of their slave population, causing the three terrible slave-revolts in which great numbers of slaves, now employed in vast ranches in place of the small-holdings which had produced the soldiers of Rome, rose up against their masters. In the last of these risings Spartacus raised ninety thousand desperate rebels and defeated three Roman armies before he was finally cornered (71 BC). The potential menace of Italy's masses of slaves remained an anxiety that was never forgotten.

But the economic crisis had many other ramifications too. For example Italy, after the upheavals of the Social War and the depreda-tions and largely unsuccessful veteran settlements of Sulla, was full of displaced persons, roaming around in aggressive poverty. Many of them flocked into the capital. And meanwhile there was danger of another kind too. For Rome's ancient city-state constitution was proving quite inadequate to shoulder the political control and military defence of Italy, let alone a large empire.

In these hazardous circumstances the tendency for Roman armies to depend upon their generals rather than upon the state became sharper all the time. Since a general must above all enrich his men, the bond that linked them to him – if he gave them what they wanted – not only continued after their discharge from the army, but was transmitted to his and their descendants.[11] No wonder the wealthiest person in Rome, Crassus, remarked that no one deserved to be called a rich man unless he was capable of maintaining an army on his own resources. And then, as the senate stood ineffectually in the side-lines – only concerned, it sometimes seemed, to deprive the veterans of their rewards – the time came when one private army clashed with another, and the whole fabric of the empire was threatened. For the frontiers themselves were now wide open at the mercy of external powers. As Sallust makes Lepidus, the rebel of 78 BC, observe, 'our frenzy has brought it about that Roman armies are pitted against each other, our arms turned away from the enemy and against ourselves'.[12] As all efficient military action against foreign enemies was paralysed by these events, the greatest of them, Mithridates, tried to strike a bargain with one of the Roman civil war combatants, Sertorius: it was the merest good fortune for Rome that, being unusually high-minded, Sertorius declined these overtures, since he was not prepared to cede Roman territory to foreigners.[13] Yet it remained a constant nightmare fear that, tempted by Rome's civil strife, her various enemies would join forces against her. It is remarkable, in fact, how rarely they ever did so. But the idea haunted Roman strategic thinkers for centuries.

In the meantime the leaders continued to strive savagely among themselves, with military action an ever-present threat. Their aristocratic society had always been highly competitive, and it was in these years that its internal strife attracted the condemnation of the philosophical poet Lucretius. He saw those noblemen as

> men lost,
> Confused, in hectic search for the right road,
> The strife of wits, the wars for precedence,
> The everlasting struggle, night and day,
> To win towards heights of wealth and power.[14]

Yet hitherto these noblemen had at least seen themselves as embattled heroes striving against one another for the benefit of the state. Now, amid the vastly increased personal opportunities granted by the empire, the state was a shadow, and it was for their own private benefit alone that they pitted their huge followings against one another. And these followings included Italian legionaries and provincial auxiliaries alike, as well as discharged veterans distributed far and wide in Italy and elsewhere.

A portent of this new world was Pompey (Cnaeus Pompeius Magnus). Under Sulla he had already held important commands while only twenty-three – far below the statutory age for such posts. What he had done, significantly enough, was to raise an army from his own father's retainers.[15] After his successes Sulla, with reluctance, had allowed him to celebrate a Triumph (80 BC) – an improper proceeding because only senators could triumph, and Pompey had not yet held any of the offices that qualified him for senatorial rank. After further victories over Sertorius and Spartacus, Pompey induced the senate to grant him an equally premature consulship (70 BC). This was followed by a command against eastern Mediterranean pirates (67 BC), for which purpose, invested with unprecedented powers, he was granted a fleet of two hundred ships – thus enabling him to begin the revival of the Roman navy, which had received a massive build-up in the First Punic War, but had been allowed to decline during the second century BC.

After disposing of the pirates, Pompey was entrusted with a major eastern campaign, the third war against Mithridates of Pontus. This and its aftermath proved his greatest achievement. By Pompey's skilful generalship, concentrating on the speedy exploitation of meticulously prepared preponderance of force, Mithridates was duly finished off; and then, away to the south, Syria was annexed as a province of the Roman empire. Pompey won a gigantic booty not only for Rome but for himself and replaced Crassus as the richest man in Rome. While he had been away in these Asiatic lands, the rising turbulence in the capital and in Italy almost led to a revolt, in which many of the destitute and discontented were prepared to take part. But their leader Catiline, a nobleman who was keener on anarchy than on reform, was out-manœuvred by Cicero, now occupying the consulate (63 BC). By a judicious blend of military force, inflammable oratory, wide-ranging espionage and private bodyguards, which were increasingly coming into fashion, Cicero suppressed the conspiracy.

When Pompey returned to Italy the senate inevitably tried to frustrate his attempts to settle his veterans. So, to get the better of it, he joined forces with Crassus and the ambitious Julius Caesar, now forty years of age, in the autocratic First Triumvirate. Although informal and extra-constitutional, this pact virtually completed the abolition of the Republican government in favour of government by military force. The force was provided by Pompey's veterans and by Caesar's legionary

1   Italy and Sicily

army which was about to start conquering the northern three-quarters of Gaul.[16] In 56 BC the triple compact was renewed at Luca. Crassus was now to conquer Rome's eastern neighbour Parthia, the only external power of any importance which bordered upon the empire, extending eastwards from the Euphrates to the borders of India. He was destined to fail in the task, and three years later, defeated at Carrhae

13

(Haran) and faced with a near-mutiny of his own soldiers, he agreed to confer with the Parthians, and went to his death. As for Pompey, he was allotted the huge province of Spain, rich in potential dependants and valuable metals. He set a significant precedent for the future by governing this territory *in absentia*, through his personal representatives (*legati*), while himself remaining in Italy, a short distance outside Rome. But meanwhile in the capital the 50s BC witnessed ferocious and almost incessant gang violence. The absence of a garrison and the non-existence of a police force rendered the city almost ungovernable. Nevertheless, when one of the principal gang-leaders was murdered and his chief opponent exiled, Pompey succeeded in re-establishing some sort of order.

The other result of the conference at Luca was that Caesar, who had now spent two seasons in Gaul, received *carte blanche* to complete the conquest of the country, a task which he interspersed by armed reconnaissances across the Rhine and the English Channel.

Certain features of his generalship exercised a powerful influence upon the centuries to come. As a commander, 'he could play the tunes of his time on an unrivalled instrument which others had made but which he perfected'.[17] But this process almost amounted to a trans-figuration, for its by-products pervaded every field of military science. Tactical innovations appeared, camp-structure and weaponry were over-hauled, intelligence services gained greatly in efficiency, training methods were revolutionized. Here at last was something really like a professional army. And its morale, on the whole, was unprecedentedly high.

This was partly because Caesar greatly increased the soldiers' pay. For more than half a century a legionary had been paid $112\frac{1}{2}$ silver *denarii* a year, less deductions for food and arms.* Now, although an additional deduction for clothing (customary in earlier times) was revived, the number of *denarii* paid him annually was raised to 225. For all his early life, Caesar, who inherited no riches himself, had been trying to raise the big sums that the political position he aimed at seemed to demand. Now, near the outset of his Gallic campaigns, he persuaded his fellow-triumvirs to back the huge expenditure that the 100 per cent increase in the legionaries' pay necessitated: and before long, by his vast and lucrative conquests in Gaul, he would almost have been able to defray the whole amount himself, if the state had refused to pay. Moreover, at least once – for hard work in 52 BC towards the

* For the *denarius*, see Appendix 5.

end of the campaigns – he allotted supplementary bonuses (*donativa*) in lieu of booty. The sums thus distributed amounted to 50 *denarii* for every legionary, and 500 for every centurion.[18] And perhaps he had already provided other bonuses on occasions which, in his *Commentaries*, he preferred not to mention, so as not to make his soldiers sound too mercenary.

These inimitable *Commentaries*, the *Gallic War* and *Civil War*, tell the truth – but not always the whole truth, because that is beyond any man's power, and Caesar, as the Roman commander, inevitably had his own point of view. Nevertheless the *Commentaries* are much better military history than any of the ancient world's academic historians had ever been able to produce. For Caesar provides us with an incomparable picture of himself and his legionaries in action.

At the outset, for example, we see them attacking the Celtic tribe of the Helvetii, Celts who had been driven from south Germany into Switzerland and now wanted, against the wishes of Rome, to migrate across the whole of Gaul to the Atlantic coast. Not far from Bibracte (Mount Beuvray), as Caesar moved away from the Helvetian host to obtain supplies of grain, he found they were pursuing him and harassing his rearguard. Caesar tells us how he dealt with the emergency.

Seeing what was happening, I withdrew my forces to the nearest hill and sent forward the cavalry to hold up the enemy's attack. In the meantime I formed up the four veteran legions in three lines halfway up the hill. Behind them, on the summit, were posted the two legions that had recently been enlisted in Italy, and all the auxiliary troops. So the whole hillside was covered with men. Meanwhile I ordered the packs to be collected in one place which was to be entrenched by the troops in line on the higher ground. The Helvetii, with all their wagons, came after us. They deposited all their heavy baggage in one place, and then, fighting in very close order, drove back our cavalry and came on in a dense mass up to our front line.

I first of all had my own horse taken out of the way and then the horses of other officers. I wanted the danger to be the same for everyone and for no one to have any hope of escape by flight. Then I spoke a few words of encouragement to the men before joining battle.

Hurling their javelins from above, our men easily broke up the enemy's mass formation and, having achieved this, drew their swords and charged. In fighting the Gauls were seriously hampered because several of their over-lapping shields were often pierced by a single javelin; the iron head would bend and they could neither get it out nor fight properly with their left arms. Many of them, after a number of vain efforts at disentangling them-selves, preferred to drop their shields and fight with no protection for their bodies. In the end the wounds and the toil of battle were too much for them, and they began to retire to a hill about a mile away. This hill they occupied, and our men pressed on after them. However we were now attacked by the tribes of the Boii and Tulingi, who, some fifteen thousand strong, had been the rear-guard in the enemy's column of march. They now launched an attack on our exposed right flank, and swept around behind us. The Helvetii who had retired to the hill saw them go into action and themselves began to press forward again in a counter-attack.

We formed a double front. The rear line faced about to meet the new attack, while the first and second lines went on fighting against those whom they had already defeated and driven back. This fighting in two directions went on for a long time and was bitterly contested. Finally, when they could stand up to us no longer, one division of the enemy retired, as they had begun to do originally, towards the higher ground and the others fell back on the stockade sheltering their wagons and baggage train. In the whole of this battle, which had lasted from midday until the evening, not a single man was seen to turn and run.[19]

One fact which emerges clearly enough from this and many other passages of the *Commentaries* – even allowing for an element of self-praise – is that Caesar's success was largely due to his personal relations with his men. This was something which later Roman emperors, compelled by domestic preoccupations and fears to remain far away from their soldiers, had reason to ponder upon with painful envy and anxiety. The *Gallic War* of Caesar shows in a hundred ways why he enjoyed such success with his soldiers: it was basically because he treated them like human beings. The same point is brought out by the biographer Suetonius.

Caesar did not take notice of all their offences or punish them by rule, but he kept a sharp look out for deserters and mutineers, and chastized them most severely, shutting his eyes to other faults. Sometimes, too, after a great victory he relieved them of all duties and gave them full licence to revel, being in the habit of boasting that his soldiers could fight well even when reeking of perfumes. In the assembly he addressed them not as 'soldiers', but by the more flattering term 'comrades', and he kept them in fine trim, furnishing them with arms inlaid with silver and gold, both for show and to make them hold the faster to them in battle, through fear of the greatness of the loss. Such was his love for them that when he heard of the disaster to Titurius Sabinus [a general whose legion was ambushed and destroyed by the Belgic Eburones (who lived near the Moselle) in 54 BC], he let his hair and beard grow long, and would not cut them until he had taken vengeance.[20]

The need for a Roman general, if he wanted to be successful, to *communicate* with his soldiers by word of mouth is abundantly illustrated by the practice of Caesar. One of the best orators of his day, he developed military speech-making to a fine art, and allotted it the highest priority. Before a perilous battle in 57 BC against the Belgic tribe of the Nervii (in Hainault and Flanders), he records: 'I only gave the orders that were most essential, and then ran down to address the troops where I could first find them.'[21] When another campaign, against Vercingetorix of the Arverni who led the great revolt against him in 52 BC, ran into difficulties because Caesar's siege of Avaricum (Bourges) hung fire, he reasoned with his own men successfully – and the results justified his somewhat complacent tone.

I used to go and speak to the men of each legion while they were working. I would tell them that, if they found their privations unbearable, I was quite ready to raise the siege; but one and all they would beg me not to do so. They had now, they said, served under me for many years without ever disgracing themselves or ever failing to finish any task to which they had set their hands; they would count it as a disgrace if they were to abandon this siege which they had begun; and they would rather undergo any hardship than fail to avenge the Roman citizens who had been treacherously massacred by the Gauls at Cenabum [Orléans]. Messages to the same effect were given by the troops to their centurions and military tribunes with the request that they should be passed on to me.[22]

Later in the same year, Caesar was quite seriously defeated by Vercingetorix in front of the hill-fortress of Gergovia (Gergovie) because his troops had acted impetuously and disobeyed orders. When he addressed them soon afterwards, he was faced with a task that required all his oratorical skill.

I called a meeting of the soldiers and reprimanded them for the over-eagerness and lack of restraint which they had shown in having ventured to decide for themselves where they ought to go and what they ought to do, in failing to halt when the signal for retreat was given, and in disobeying the orders of their generals and their officers. I pointed out what the effects could be of having to fight in the wrong position, and reminded them that it was this very thing which I myself had been so concerned about at Avaricum [Bourges], when, after I had caught the enemy without their commander and without their cavalry, I nevertheless chose to forgo a certain victory rather than incur even slight casualties by fighting on unfavourable ground.
Much, I said, as I admired their magnificent spirit, which no obstacle had been able to check – not the fortifications of the camp, nor the height of the

17

mountain, nor the actual wall of the town – I was just as much offended by their insubordination and by their presumption in imagining that they knew more than their commander-in-chief about how to win victories and how battles would turn out. 'From my soldiers', I said, 'I expect not only courage and gallantry in action but also discipline and self-control.'

After making these points I said a few words at the end of my speech to raise the soldiers' spirits, telling them that they must not be discouraged by what had happened and must not think that their losses were due to the warlike qualities of the enemy, when in fact they were caused by fighting on unfavourable ground.[23]

As the poet Lucan later declared about Caesar:

> Urging advantage he improved all odds,
> And made the most of fortune and the gods.[24]

His fabulous speed and vigour proved too much for all his enemies in the end. Nevertheless he would never have been able to surmount crisis after crisis if he had not been able to establish this unique relationship with his men. Later on, at an awkward juncture in the civil war, an officer observed the magnetism he exerted. In a dangerous situation, this observer recorded, 'their one comfort was in the bearing of their commander himself, in his energy and his remarkable cheerfulness. For he displayed an exalted and alert spirit. The men found reassurance in this, and they all hoped that his experience and foresight would make everything plain sailing for them.'[25]

The soldiers of this period had a great belief in the magic luck of a good commander; and Sulla had played on these feelings by adopting the name 'Felix' as a personal property of his own. Julius Caesar was realistic about this factor, and indeed almost modest. He often noted sweeping reversals of fortune, and pointed out that they could be brought about by the most apparently insignificant turn of events. Chance played a large part, he knew – 'and so let us not leave it in charge of anything more than we can help'.[26] Caesar himself had no intention of doing so as far as human precautions could avail. And his own report on all that he had to do, when a great horde of the Nervii swooped down upon his army, shows what it meant to have one of the greatest generals of all time as your commander – and a general who, although nobody else was as good as himself, knew perfectly well not only how to command but – a rarer quality still – how to delegate.

They swept on down to the river, moving at such an incredible speed that to us it looked as though they were at the edge of the woods, in the river, and on top of us all in the same moment. With the same extraordinary speed they swarmed up the opposite hill towards our camp and fell upon the men who were engaged in fortifying it.

I had everything to do at once – hoist the flag (which was the signal for a call to arms), sound the trumpet for action, call the men back from their work on the entrenchments, bring in the others who had gone farther afield to get material for the rampart, form the troops up in battle order, address them, give the signal for attack. As the enemy were practically upon us, there was simply not time for doing most of these things, but in this very awkward situation we were helped by two factors. First, the training and experience of the troops themselves, who from their knowledge of previous battles were able to dispense with orders and judge on their own what should be done; and second, the order which I had issued to commanders of legions, instructing each of them to stay with his own unit while it was at work and not leave until the fortifications were finished. Thus the legionary commanders, seeing the enemy so close and advancing so fast, did what they thought best on their own initiative, without waiting for orders from me.[27]

'For heaven's sake, satisfy *somebody*,' said Edmund Burke; and Caesar satisfied his soldiers. A large section of the traditional Roman governing class did not care for him, and indeed regarded him with the deepest suspicion. But his military expertise, his unique personality and his close personal *rapport* with the whole army impressed themselves deeply upon his legionaries. Their fatherland was Caesar's camp, and their patriotism was loyalty to Caesar. But in all this he set a terribly high standard for his imperial successors, who shared his need to satisfy their soldiers – if they themselves were to survive – but lacked his opportunities and his gifts.

The increased professionalism of Caesar's army meant that he needed a better type of officer; and he took steps to make sure that he got it. His centurions of course were a tower of strength – and he delights in recording tales of their intrepid gallantry. One such set piece, melodramatic and sentimental, occurred when the Nervii rallied from their defeat and attacked the winter camp of Quintus Cicero, the orator's brother (54 BC). The legion that conducted the successful defence, according to Caesar, contained two absolutely first-class senior centurions, Titus Pullo and Lucius Vorenus.

These two never stopped arguing about which of them was the better soldier, and every year when it came to the question of promotion each one would try to outdo the other. Now, when the fighting round the rampart was at its fiercest, Pullo shouted out: 'What are you waiting for, Vorenus? Do you want a better chance of showing how you can fight? Today will settle the argument between us.' With these words he went forward beyond the fortifications and charged into the enemy at the point where their ranks were thickest. Vorenus, of course, was not going to stay behind. He knew what people would think of him if he did, and so he went straight after Pullo.

When a little way from the enemy, Pullo hurled his javelin and transfixed one of the Gauls who had run forward to meet him. The Gaul was struck down unconscious, but his comrades covered him with their shields, while from all sides weapons rained down on Pullo so that he had no chance of retiring. One javelin went right through his shield and stuck in his sword belt. This twisted his scabbard out of position so that when he tried to draw his sword he could not at first seize the hilt. While he was struggling to do so, the enemy surrounded him. But now his rival Vorenus came up and got him out of his difficulties. Thinking that Pullo had been killed by the spear, the Gauls all turned away from him and immediately set upon Vorenus, who, fighting with his sword at close quarters, killed one man and was beginning to drive the others back. But in pressing forward too eagerly, he stumbled and fell into a depression in the ground. Now it was his turn to be surrounded and the turn of Pullo to come up and rescue him.

After killing a few more of the enemy, both centurions came back together safe and sound to the shelter of the fortifications. Each of them had deserved the highest possible praise, and in this bitter rivalry of theirs, fortune had produced a situation in which each of the two enemies had been the friend and saviour of the other; so that it was quite impossible to decide which should be considered the better or the braver soldier.[28]

Moreover, Caesar's centurions were not only soldierly and heroic: they were also outstandingly loyal to him personally, and he employed them as valuable allies and political agents – and intermediaries between himself and his troops.

At the higher military and social level, comprising the military tribunes, things were at first somewhat difficult. Caesar began his Gallic campaigns by feeling considerable dissatisfaction with some of these officers, and particularly with the young men from Rome who had joined him, as he says, in order to cultivate his friendship, while remaining lamentably ignorant about military affairs. Towards the outset of the fighting they became very frightened. After Caesar had defeated the Celtic Helvetii he turned against a powerful German chieftain, Ariovistus, who was encroaching on the territory of pro-Roman Gallic tribes. When Caesar had just managed to forestall Ariovistus at the fortress of Vesontio (Besançon) (58 BC), the final engagement which witnessed the destruction of the German army was preceded by a

Roman setback, allegedly because of low morale among these officers. For, at this point,

many of these tribunes now began asking me for leave, each finding some excellent reason why it was necessary for him to go. Others had rather more self-respect and, not wanting to look as if they were cowards, stayed behind. All the same they could not control the expressions on their faces and sometimes even burst into tears. They hid themselves away in their tents, where they spent the time bewailing their fate or else commiserating with their friends about the terrible danger in which they all stood. All over the camp, people were making their wills and getting them signed.

The panic and the general conversation of these people gradually began to have a disturbing effect even on others with considerable experience in the army – soldiers, centurions and cavalry commanders. Some of these, who did not want to appear as frightened as they were, declared that they were not at all afraid of the enemy – it was rather the narrow routes and the great forests between us and Ariovistus which gave cause for anxiety, or else the question of the grain supply and the possibility of a failure in its delivery. Some actually told me that when I gave the order to strike camp and advance the soldiers would not obey orders and would be too frightened to move.[29]

At once, Caesar says, he told his officers that it was none of their business to discuss where they were being led or for what reason, or even to think about such matters at all. But he is possibly being just a little disingenuous in blaming the officers' attitude on cowardice. For their objections to his plans may well have been prompted by his political enemies in Rome, who wanted to make capital out of what they considered to be the unnecessary and unsuitable nature of Caesar's entire operations. At all events, during the years in Gaul that followed he saw to it that the military tribunes he appointed were much more suitable officer material, and knew their jobs more thoroughly – and were impeccably loyal to himself.

Most of them were not senators, but *equites* or, according to the misleading modern equivalent, 'knights'. These *equites*, the knightly or equestrian order, were the next social stratum in Rome below the senators. To be either a senator or a knight it was necessary to satisfy a property qualification. The qualification for the knights was assessed at a level somewhat below half the figure finally established for the senate. They formed a huge section of the influential Italian upper and upper-middle class. Many of them were agriculturalists and landowners, like the senators – and indeed many *equites* were young men whose fathers were members of the senate. But a considerable number of businessmen of knightly rank, especially those who, to the anger of many senators, specialized in securing lucrative tax-farming contracts, had converted their order into a political force. Moreover, in the course of this process, a long-standing argument over the membership of the official benches of judges had set the knights corporatively against the senate. Sulla had eliminated the knights from judgeships. But subsequently in the 60s BC, strengthened by the enfranchisement of Italy, enriched by the wealth of the empire and wooed by the politically ambitious Pompey, they had greatly increased their influence in national affairs; but they remained disunited, and were a ready prey for unscrupulous leaders. Caesar employed knights as his principal advisers. And he also recruited them as military tribunes of the new efficient type that he wanted, thus bestowing upon their order a permanent stake in the army.

However he did not give the knights the biggest military posts – which went, as in earlier days, to senators. But these top posts were now transformed, for it was largely to Caesar that Rome owed the creation of the highest general's rank, that of the legionary commander (*legatus legionis*), who was a member of the senate. During the immediately preceding years of the Republic, senatorial *legati* had already appeared, not as generals in command of legions, but as members of provincial governors' staffs; and Pompey, governing Spain by remote control from Italy, appointed such officials to administer the country on his behalf. But what Caesar did was to give them the command of legions or other large bodies of troops. The men he selected for these posts, though they made mistakes, were, as might have been predicted, pretty good. Perhaps, however, in one respect they constituted Caesar's weakness. For, although he knew so well how to delegate, he does not really do their contribution justice in his *Commentaries*. And they, in return, do not seem to have felt any great affection towards him. It may be that his extravagantly versatile talents, which made him aware of his own uniqueness, seemed too much for them to take (and many other senators felt the same). In consequence some of the best of these senior officers, including the very best of all, Titus Labienus, decided, in the civil war that followed soon afterwards, to fight against him.[30] And others of his principal lieutenants, Gaius Trebonius and Decimus Junius Brutus Albinus, were subsequently among the men who plotted and achieved his murder.

Pompey and Caesar were too ambitious for the Roman world to have room for them both. The civil war which broke out between them in 49 BC was even more devastating and traumatic than any of the other wars between Romans that had taken place during the previous forty years. Even towards the end of the 50s BC, when relations between Caesar and the conservative allies of Pompey were already severely strained, there had seemed some hope that the two great warlords themselves would stop short of the fatal step. As late as 53 BC it was still possible, when Caesar wanted to mobilize new troops, for Pompey to give him a hand, as Caesar was careful to record.

I sent a message to Pompey, who was now proconsul [of Spain], but for political reasons was staying near Rome while retaining his military command. I requested him to mobilize the recruits whom he had sworn in in Cisalpine Gaul (northern Italy) when he was consul for the second time in 55 BC and to send them into Transalpine Gaul to join my army. In my view it was very important, for the future as well as for the present, that the Transalpine Gauls should realize that in Italy we had such reserves of manpower that, if we did suffer any misadventure in war, we could in a very short time not only make good our losses but take the field with larger forces than before.

Pompey, acting like a patriot and like a friend, did as I asked. The new troops were quickly raised by my own staff officers, and before the end of the winter three new legions had been formed and had been brought to Transalpine Gaul. The size of these reinforcements and the speed with which they had been assembled were indications of the efficiency of Roman organization and the strength of Roman resources.[31]

Recruitment in his province of Cisalpine Gaul, so rich in human and natural resources, was of prime importance to Caesar, and he was soon to tie the region even more firmly to his own allegiance by extending Roman citizenship to its inhabitants (49 BC). This proved invaluable to his cause in the civil war that now followed. For the fairly happy relations which, according to Caesar, had still made cooperation possible as late as 53 BC drew irreparably to a close. And then finally, after endless diplomatic and propagandist manœuvrings on both sides, the fatal evening of 11 January 49 BC arrived. Under cover of night Caesar, who as long as he remained governor of Transalpine and Cisalpine Gaul was not permitted to set foot in Italy, broke the law by leading his troops across the little stream of the Rubicon which at that time was the border between Cisalpine Gaul and Italy.

Now at last the illusion of an aristocratic, senatorial Republic – a basically civilian Republic – was at an end. The soldiers on both sides had sworn to obey their generals and follow the standards of their

2   Gaul and Britain

generals' legions, and, except for turncoats and deserters, they remained faithful to this oath, regardless of the constitutional niceties: the idea of loyalty towards the state as such had disappeared from view. Anxious, therefore, to retain this personal fidelity, Caesar felt it advisable to issue bonuses of five hundred *denarii* apiece.[32] This was a very personal war, in which a soldier captured by Caesar could say: 'I wish I were a soldier of yours rather than of the commander on the other side!' Of being a soldier of Rome he made no mention. And by the same token, one of Caesar's veteran centurions, Crastinus, could address his men in these terms: 'Follow me – and give your general the service you have promised! Only this one battle remains. After it, *he will recover his position*, and we our freedom!'[33]

This was after Pompey had been ejected from Italy to the Balkans, as very soon happened. His levies of legionary recruits in Italy, and the recruiting of personal dependants by the great nobleman Lucius Domitius Ahenobarbus, had proved of little avail to his cause. But when Pompey arrived in the Balkans, he organized the most ambitious mobilization of non-citizens that had ever been known. This was an occasion when for the first time whole legions began to be formed of non-Italians. Moreover there were huge expansions of auxiliary light-armed infantry and cavalry. Both commanders-in-chief had now wholly abandoned the traditional Republican reluctance to arm provincials. Spaniards had already been extensively enrolled by both sides and now Pompey mobilized peoples such as the Dardani and Bessi as far afield as the Danube. As for Caesar, he disposed of cavalry from Gaul and Germany, and archers and slingers from the Balearic islands. Roman armies were becoming much more cosmopolitan. And these soldiers of many races felt little interest in the Roman state, which had now become a rather vague and abstract conception. All that mattered was their own commander, with whom they were indissolubly linked by bonds of mutual indispensability.

However, in addition to all these foreigners, there were thousands of Italians fighting against Italians – and it was among these that the better-trained men were to be found. In his *Civil War* Caesar makes it clear how much their training counted: the old soldiers were much better than the new. When, for example, his war fleet made for the eastern shores of the Adriatic, there was an emergency which brought this out clearly. Two ships got behind the rest and were seized by Otacilius Crassus, Pompey's commander at Lissus (Lesh in Albania).

Of these two vessels, one had on board 220 men from a legion recently recruited, and the other rather less than 200 veterans. The sequel will show what a help it is to have a resolute and determined spirit. The recruits were terrified at the number of craft coming up and were also in a bad state because of the rough sea and their seasickness. After receiving a guarantee that the enemy would do them no harm, they surrendered to Otacilius, who had them all brought before him and then, in violation of the solemn pledge that he had given, had them cruelly killed in front of his eyes. The soldiers of the veteran legion, on the other hand, who had suffered just as much as the others from the storm and the filthy bilge water, remembered their long record of valour and determined to live up to it. They spun out the first part of the night in discussing terms of a possible surrender, then made the pilot run the ship ashore, found a good position, and passed the rest of the night there. At dawn Otacilius sent out against them about four hundred horse and detachments from the town garrison. But the veterans beat off the attack and, after killing a number of the enemy, retired without loss and joined up with our main body of troops.[34]

Then, after Caesar had extricated himself from a desperately perilous situation at Dyrrhachium (Durrës), there followed the decisive battle of Pharsalus in Thessaly (48 BC). The historian Appian* brings out the full horror of the situation: a fratricidal horror which for generation after generation later Romans never forgot. On the field of battle the two armies of compatriots confronted each other with many tragic emotions.

When all was in readiness on both sides they waited for some time in profound silence, hesitating, looking steadfastly at each other, each expecting the other to begin the battle.

They were stricken with sorrow for the great host, for never before had such large Italian armies confronted the same danger together. They had pity for the valour of these men (the flower of both parties), especially because they saw Italians embattled against Italians. As the danger came nearer, the ambition that had inflamed and blinded them was extinguished, and gave place to fear. Reason purged the mad passion for glory, estimated the peril and laid bare the cause of the war, showing how two men contending with each other for supremacy were throwing into the scale their own lives and fortunes – for defeat would mean the lowest degradation – and those of so large a number of the noblest citizens.

The leaders reflected also that they, who had lately been friends and relatives by marriage and had cooperated with each other in many ways to gain rank and power, had now drawn the sword for mutual slaughter and were leading to the same impiety those serving under them, men of the same city, of the same tribe, blood relations and in some cases brothers against brothers.[35]

Then followed the battle, which Caesar describes.

Between the two armies there was just enough space left for them to advance and engage each other. Pompey, however, had told his men to wait for Caesar's onset, and not to move from their positions or allow the line

* See Bibliography, Section A, Greek Writings.

to be split up. He was said to have done this on the advice of Gaius Triarius, with the intention of breaking the force of the first impact of the enemy and stretching out their line, so that his own men, who were still in formation, could attack them while they were scattered. He also thought that the falling javelins would do less damage if the men stood still than if they were running forward while the missiles were discharged. Moreover Caesar's troops, having to run twice the distance, would be out of breath and exhausted. It appears to us that he did this without sound reason, for there is a certain eagerness of spirit and an innate keenness in everyone which is inflamed by desire for battle. Generals ought to encourage this, not repress it, nor was it for nothing that the practice began in antiquity of giving the signal on both sides and everyone's raising a war-cry. This was believed both to frighten the enemy and to stimulate one's own men.

Our men, on the signal, ran forward with javelins levelled. But when they observed that Pompey's men were not running to meet them, thanks to the practical experience and training they had had in earlier battles, they checked their charge and halted about halfway, so as not to approach worn out. Then after a short interval they renewed the charge, threw their javelins and, as ordered by Caesar, quickly drew their swords. Nor indeed did the Pompeians fail to meet the occasion. They stood up to the hail of missiles, and bore the onset of the legions. They kept their ranks, threw their javelins and then resorted to their swords. At the same time the cavalry all charged forward, as instructed, from Pompey's left wing, and the whole horde of archers rushed out. Our cavalry failed to withstand their onslaught. They were dislodged from their position and gave ground a little. Pompey's cavalry thereupon pressed on the more hotly and began to deploy in squadrons and surround our line on its exposed flank. Observing this Caesar gave the signal to the fourth line, which he had formed of single cohorts. They ran forward swiftly to the attack with their standards and charged at Pompey's cavalry with such force that none of them could hold ground. They all turned and not only gave ground but fled precipitately to the hilltops. Their withdrawal left all the archers and slingers exposed, and, unarmed and unprotected, they were killed. In the same charge the cohorts surrounded the Pompeians who were still fighting and putting up a resistance on the left wing, and attacked them in the rear.

At the same time Caesar gave the order to advance to the third line, which had done nothing and had stayed in its position up till then. As a result, when fresh and unscathed troops took the place of the weary, while others were attacking from the rear, the Pompeians could not hold out, and every one of them turned tail and fled.[36]

Pharsalus was won by Caesar because of his personal military superiority. Pompey, at the age of fifty-eight, though still a realistic strategist, clever tactician and fine organizer, lacked insight into Caesar's improvisations and was hampered by obstreperous colleagues and subordinates. But Pharsalus also went the way it did because Caesar's veterans were now so skilful that, when they saw Pompey wanted them to charge, they spontaneously and instinctively checked their advance. A century later Lucan wrote his great poem the *Pharsalia* about this civil war. That Roman generals and soldiers could thus turn against one another seemed to him a repudiation of the most solemn of all human bonds, an invitation to all hostile foreigners to conspire with one another and invade the Roman empire – what a sad contrast to all the foreign territory which could have been won for Rome, and which the Romans, by fighting among themselves, had so fruitlessly squandered.[37]

> Make Rome the foe of all the nations, but
> Spare us a civil war . . .
> O wrathful Father, in one instant smite
> Both sides, both leaders, ere they yet have earned
> Their doom. From such a crop of novel crime
> Seek they to prove which shall be lord at Rome? . . .
> When men shall read of war, this tale shall still
> Move hope and fear alike, or futile wish . . .
> Nor Fortune lingered, but decreed the doom
> Which swept the ruins of a world away.[38]

For Lucan, as he grew increasingly disenchanted with the imperial regime of Nero under which he lived, saw this battle as the end of liberty, the triumph of military rule.

Thoughtful men of the time, such as Cicero, were well aware of the intolerable dilemma. For the only alternative to civil war, he was sure, was tyranny – tyranny by Caesar, or, for that matter, tyranny by Pompey and his friends, which would scarcely be better. For even if, in his hatred for Caesar, he had to take the side of Pompey and the conservatives, he felt no faith in the results of a Pompeian victory. Though vacillating continually, Cicero advised Pompey that peace even on the most unjust terms is better than the justest of civil wars.[39] And he himself, in the end, had duly but gloomily put in his appearance at Pompey's headquarters in Greece. But the desertions and treacheries of civil war were appalling. 'Loyalists, good God!' cried Cicero about his compatriots. 'Just see how they are running to meet Caesar, and sell themselves to him!'

After Pharsalus Pompey fled to Egypt, where the government of the Ptolemies had him killed on the sea-shore. Soon afterwards Caesar arrived in the same country and fought a sharp campaign there, when besieged by the enemies of his mistress Cleopatra. Then he defeated Pompey's sons Cnaeus and Sextus and their friends at Thapsus (Ras Dimas) in north Africa and Munda in southern Spain. The war was becoming increasingly savage and atrocities multiplied. In Africa, for example, the Pompeian leader Metellus Pius Scipio had Caesar's veterans who fell into his hands separated from the recruits and taken outside the ramparts, where they were tortured to death.[40]

Both Thapsus and Munda were perilously close run. At Thapsus, Caesar's legions, when they saw a chance of victory, had forced his hand by attacking on their own account before they were fully deployed. That was the sort of thing that could happen in civil wars, when the border between discipline and chaos was elusive. At Spain near the beginning of the war (for Caesar had defeated the Pompeians there on an earlier occasion, four years before Munda), his soldiers, by his own account, 'had gone about openly saying that, because a good chance of victory was being thrown away, they would refuse to fight next time I asked them to.'[41] Such demonstrations showed that they knew very well how much Caesar, who was treated by the other side as a rebel, depended on their own goodwill.

Much worse, there were two serious mutinies. The first was in 49 BC at Placentia (Piacenza) in Italy, when Caesar's men complained that they had not been given anything to plunder, and protested that the war was being deliberately prolonged so that their promised donative need not be paid. The second mutiny took place in 47 BC at Rome, where the mutineers settled down in the Field of Mars demanding that they should either receive their rewards or be discharged. These were severe tests for Caesar. At Placentia, declares Lucan, he could feel the pinnacle, from which he gazed down on the rest of the world, sway beneath his feet. And the incident is omitted altogether from Caesar's *Commentaries*. However his prestige and persuasiveness proved equal to both occasions, as the descriptions by Suetonius, in his *Twelve Caesars*, reveal.

Caesar's soldiers did not mutiny once during the ten years of the Gallic war. In the civil wars they did so now and then, but quickly resumed their duty, not so much owing to any indulgence of their general as to his authority. For he never gave way to them when they were insubordinate, but always boldly faced them, discharging the entire ninth legion in disgrace before Placentia, though Pompey was still in the field, reinstating them unwillingly and only after many abject entreaties, and insisting on punishing the ringleaders.

Again at Rome, when the men of the tenth legion clamoured for their discharge and rewards with terrible threats and no little peril to the city, though the war in north Africa was then raging he did not hesitate to appear before them, against the advice of his friends, and to disband them. But with a single word, calling them 'citizens' instead of 'soldiers', he easily brought them round and bent them to his will. For they at once replied that they were his 'soldiers', and insisted on following him to Africa, although he refused their service. Even then he punished the most insubordinate by the loss of a third part of the booty and of the land that had been intended for them.[42]

After the Placentian mutiny the condemned ringleaders to whom Suetonius refers were reduced, at the plea of the military tribunes, to only twelve. In the wake of the Roman disorder the legions were at once ordered to prepare for the African campaign, and, later on, whenever occasion offered, the men who had led the mutiny were unobtrusively eliminated. But every future ruler of Rome carefully noted these two crises encountered by Caesar, and were deeply anxious in case they should be repeated. For, if so, would they be able to deal with such a crisis as well as he had?

It was imperative that the rewards Caesar gave his soldiers should be enough to satisfy their expectations. He had captured extensive loot in Gaul, and it was this that made the bonuses he handed out in 49 BC a practical possibility. In the same year, entering Rome on the heels of the Pompeians, he had forcibly seized the Treasury – thus, as Lucan declared with some accuracy, for the first time making Rome poorer than a Caesar.[43] In 46 BC one of his lieutenants, Aulus Hirtius, issued masses of gold coins,[44] of which a great many went to the army. At Caesar's Triumphs in 46 and 45 BC he gave every infantryman of his veteran legions six thousand *denarii* as booty. He also inaugurated an extensive scheme of land allotments for discharged ex-soldiers, comprising entire towns in Italy and a number of provinces, together with the territory that went with them. In some of these 'colonies of Roman citizens', the soldiers were settled alongside civilians. But at others Caesar settled whole units of his former troops in a single place, scarcely transformed from soldiers at all except that they were now in civilian dress. Like the colonies of Sulla before him, Caesar's were to be bulwarks of his own political support, which was guaranteed by his generous rewards to the settlers.

He was now autocrat of the entire Roman state. Constitutionally his position was expressed in a succession of dictatorships, making him commander-in-chief of the whole army. In 46 BC he was granted this office for ten years, far in excess of the tenure of Sulla. Moreover, in order to signalize his special position as the military leader who had won unprecedented triumphs, he was declared to be *Imperator* with a peculiar and novel significance. On a previous occasion, at a late stage in his conquest of Gaul, Caesar had allowed himself to be saluted by this title, like other successful generals of the Republic. But now, after his victories in the civil wars, when he was named *Imperator* once again, it appears likely that the title was expressly conferred on him by the senate as his specific personal appellation.[45] He was also granted the laurel-wreath as a permanent symbol of his ever-triumphant role.[46] It could hardly have been made clearer that the command of the armies was what had given Caesar his unique power, and what was still the cause of its prolongation.

Most Romans did not mind this very much. Indeed many of them positively applauded it. For after the convulsions of anarchy what people want above all else is order, as the poet Lucretius, a decade or two earlier, had already pointed out. For they become:

> Sick of their feuds and weary to exhaustion
> Of violence piled on violence.[47]

The only men who really objected to Caesar's dictatorial rule were a section, a sizeable section, of the ruling class. For men of this class were devoted to their traditional competition for the leading, senatorial offices of state headed by the annually elected consulships – offices which had formerly carried with them vast and lucrative power. Nowadays, however, although the consulships and other offices still existed, they were totally eclipsed by the dictator: and when the noblemen went out to the provinces to take up military commands, these commands were now, with equal completeness, overshadowed by Caesar as commander-in-chief.

In 44 BC this situation was about to assume an acute form. For Caesar was due, in March, to depart for a gigantic campaign against the only accessible external power, the Parthians. This might well have made him a new Alexander the Great, a conqueror of the east on a massive scale. But the Roman noblemen, if they were going to the war with him, saw little advantage in becoming the new Alexander's lieutenants. And it would be even worse for those of them who stayed at home. For in spite of all the consuls and praetors and the rest who would still hold their offices, and in spite of the continued existence of the senate of which they were members, the agents whom Caesar was going to leave behind at Rome, to take charge of everything on his behalf, were not these high officials and senators, but two of his own trusted personal henchmen, Gaius Oppius and Lucius Cornelius Balbus – men who held no offices of state at all but were merely knights. And to these knights the senators would now have to defer. Worst of all Caesar's dictatorship was now extended into perpetuity, so that this situation would never end – unless violent measures were taken to conclude it.

That was why Marcus Brutus, and Cassius, and Decimus Brutus Albinus, and the rest, only a few days before Caesar was due to leave and join his eastern armies, cut him down. And Cicero, despite his earlier reflection that civil war was worse than tyranny, applauded.[48] Caesar himself, a little earlier, had dismissed the armed bodyguard of Spanish soldiers that had formerly attended him. For he had often stated the view that his death would not be to anyone's advantage, since it would merely result in much worse civil wars than there had been before.[49]

As it turned out he was wrong to think that this would deter his assassins. Yet he had been entirely right to believe that the outcome would be terrible civil strife. One of his officers, the historian Sallust, detected a general politico-military principle here. If a country, he declared, is once subjected to forcible rule, any attempt at change is bound to bring further force – bloodshed, exile and all the horrors of war.[50] And his reference to exile was very relevant to what now befell Brutus and Cassius. For they had apparently not realized before that Caesar's soldiers still under arms, and his veterans who feared for their allotments, felt such devotion towards him that the lives of his assassins were not safe anywhere in Italy. When, therefore, the senate, eager to avoid further bloodshed, offered them commands in the east, they found it advisable to accept them.

During the years from 44 to 31 BC the Roman armies were continually expanded, for the purpose of ever more formidable civil wars, ever more savage acts of cruelty,[51] ever more sweeping confiscations to supply veterans with lands and gratuities; and, from time to time, they suffered an almost total collapse of military discipline and morale. Appian analyses the reasons for this prevailing mutinous insubordination.

Its cause was that the generals, for the most part, as is usually the case in civil wars, were not regularly chosen; that their armies were not drawn from the enrolment according to the custom of the fathers, nor for the benefit of their country; that they did not serve the public so much as they did the individuals who brought them together; and that they served these not by the force of law, but by reason of private promises; not against the common enemy, but against private foes – not against foreigners, but against fellow-citizens, their equals in rank.

All these things impaired military discipline, and the soldiers thought that they were not so much serving in the army as lending assistance, by their own favour and judgement, to leaders who needed them for their own personal ends. Desertion, which had formerly been unpardonable, was now actually rewarded with gifts, and whole armies resorted to it, including some illustrious men, who did not consider it desertion to change to a like cause. For all parties were alike, since neither of them could be distinguished as battling against the common enemy of the Roman people. The common pretence of the generals that they were all striving for the good of the country made desertion easy, in the thought that one could serve his country in any party. Understanding these facts, the generals tolerated such behaviour, for they knew that their authority over their armies depended on bonuses rather than on law.[52]

The leaders, loyal to Caesar's memory, who emerged after his death to confront Brutus, Cassius and the rest, were Mark Antony, who had served as his lieutenant and was popular with the soldiery, and Caesar's nineteen-year-old grandnephew who had been adopted in his will as his personal heir. We know the youth as Octavian, and later as Augustus, though from the time of his adoption he took the name of his adoptive father, Gaius Julius Caesar. The senate gave Octavian a command (43 BC) and then snubbed him. Thereupon he joined up with Antony (hitherto his rival and enemy) and Lepidus (son of the rebel of 78 BC) to establish a combination which was as autocratic as Caesar's dictatorship had ever been. This was the Second Triumvirate.

By the orders of this joint leadership, which unlike the First Triumvirate was formally constituted, Cicero and more than a hundred other senators were proscribed and executed, and so were many knights. Brutus and Cassius were defeated and slain at the battle of Philippi in Macedonia (42 BC). Then Antony and Octavian divided the greater part of the Roman world between themselves. Antony took the east (including Cleopatra, queen of nominally independent Egypt, and her wealth), and Octavian the west—foreshadowing the permanent division of the empire four centuries later. Octavian started with a disadvantage, because he lacked Antony's military reputation — and on the battlefield of Philippi he had failed to distinguish himself. But he fought back by extracting great political profit from the fact that Caesar's official deification by the state — modelled on that of the legendary founder Romulus — had transformed himself, who was Caesar's heir, into the son of a god. Moreover, he assumed not only Caesar's personal laurel-wreath[53] but also Caesar's special title of *Imperator*, but this time *before* his name, which made it an even more specific designation of commandership and victory (*c*. 38 BC).[54]

Next Octavian suppressed Pompey's surviving son Sextus. This was the culmination of a series of huge maritime operations, in which the navy, which Pompey had begun to revive three decades earlier, was built up into a number of large squadrons. They were commanded by Octavian's brilliant admiral Marcus Vipsanius Agrippa, a living advertisement of the need, during these critical emergencies, as in Caesar's campaigns, for senior officers who were not of the traditional senatorial origin, but came from a lower social class.[55] Then, immediately after the defeat of Sextus, an attempt by Lepidus to assert himself as the third member of the Triumvirate was sharply terminated by Octavian, who sent him into permanent exile in a small country town and took over his large force of legions for himself (36 BC). However many of the numerous soldiers now under his command were nervous and mutinous, worrying about the security of their land allotments: and this general anxiety impelled him to promise that there would be no Roman civil wars ever again. At the same time he quickly distracted their attention, and took the opportunity to increase their military experience by sending an army to fight against hostile tribes in Illyricum, of which the later division into upper and lower provinces, subsequently known as Dalmatia (south) and Pannonia (north), was foreshadowed by his campaigns against the two peoples who bore those names. Meanwhile Antony fought two campaigns against the Parthians and their allies, the first a costly failure (36 BC)[56] and the second more successful (34 BC), and in the course of these operations he directed Cleopatra to build him a fleet to supplement his own.

During these years mutual suspicions between the two surviving triumvirs continually mounted, and finally the inevitable clash came. Amid a violent interchange of propaganda, Octavian publicly presented their hostilities, not as a civil war against Antony – for he had promised that there would be no more civil wars – but as a crusade against the foreigner Cleopatra. Octavian was in grave difficulties, since he had insufficient funds to pay his troops and marines. Nevertheless the ensuing campaign in the Ionian Sea brought him victory, won by his admiral Agrippa's superior naval experience, a rare prize among Romans. The operations culminated in Antony losing much of his fleet, when he and Cleopatra forced their way out of Agrippa's blockade at Actium on the north-west coast of Greece (31 BC). Antony and the queen succeeded in escaping to Egypt, but Octavian was now sole ruler of the entire Roman empire.

2

The Iron Hand in the Velvet Glove
31–18 BC

When Octavian had won the battle of Actium, he had at his disposal all the Roman armies which had been contending against each other for so long – amounting to the unprecedented total of sixty or even seventy legions, representing a quarter of a million citizen soldiers. And these soldiers now constituted the greatest of his problems. For although he was master of the Roman world he remained wholly dependent on the Roman army for the maintenance of his supremacy. This situation created a serious dilemma. For if this army-backed autocracy were too openly displayed it would prove intolerable to the traditional governing class, and he would suffer the fate of Julius Caesar. With the aim, therefore, of retaining his military autocracy and yet rendering it acceptable, he devised an exceptionally ingenious system.

But that came gradually and not just yet. His first task had to be the satisfaction of the perilously large number of soldiers, many of them potentially discontented, for whom he himself was now entirely responsible. At the very outset, therefore, as the historian Dio Cassius reports,* he hastened 'before the least sign of an uprising, to discharge some and scatter most of the others'.[1] The discharges he at once planned comprised all citizen soldiers of a certain seniority. But until he could gain possession of Cleopatra's huge treasure he had extremely little, far too little, money with which to reward them. So for the time being

* See Bibliography, Section A, Greek Writings.

36

the soldiers who were due for demobilization received nothing at all, but were retained in their units, on terminal leave – and, for safety's sake, the units were dispersed. The danger of disaffection was still acute. And meanwhile the civilian population, too, in Italy and elsewhere, was overcome by a wave of anxiety. For there was a widespread fear that their lands would be taken away from them to give to the soldiers, and that no compensation would be paid. That had happened often enough during the civil wars,[2] though Octavian himself, after his defeat of Sextus Pompeius, had instituted the custom of granting more or less adequate compensation to the townships or individuals whose land was distributed to veterans. Nevertheless after Actium there remained the gravest apprehensions, and Octavian, short of funds though he was, felt it necessary to remit taxation, in the hope of alleviating those fears.

Soon after Actium Agrippa was sent back to Italy in order to supervise these arrangements. But he found the soldiers profoundly discontented, and there were fears that, to voice their grievances, they might find themselves an alternative leader.[3] Before long open mutiny broke out at the port of Brundusium, and in January 30 BC Agrippa urgently requested Octavian to sail back from Greece. He did so, still in midwinter when navigation was exceedingly hazardous. Then somehow or other he tided over the crisis by cashiering the most insubordinate units and distributing to the rest what money and land he could find. Money and land alike were forcibly obtained from supporters of Antony, so that the fears of the civil population proved partially justified. Then Octavian returned rapidly to the east, and, by seizing the person of Cleopatra, who subsequently, like Antony, committed suicide, he took the necessary steps to get hold of her riches. While he was away from Italy, however, a young man named Marcus Lepidus, son of the exiled triumvir of the same name, plotted to assassinate him as soon as he returned home, presumably relying upon the legions that had formerly belonged to his father. Octavian's representative in Italy, the Etruscan knight, statesman and literary patron Maecenas, detected the conspiracy and put Lepidus to death. Later in the same year Octavian came back home with the Egyptian state treasure, and everything became easier. Within the next few years more than a hundred thousand veterans received land, either at older foundations or new settlements, both in Italy and the provinces. And Octavian, as after his defeat of Sextus, though on a necessarily vaster scale, paid the necessary compensation. It cost him, over the years, a gigantic sum of money.

With their anxieties on this score set at rest, the Roman public felt overwhelmingly relieved that the civil wars were now truly at an end, and their gratitude to Octavian for performing such a miracle was enormous. These sentiments are echoed constantly by coins (although admittedly these were designed by himself), and inscriptions, poets and historians all tell the same story. The era of rival military leaders is closed, the writers proclaim; the drifting vessel once again has a pilot. Much is heard, also, of the familiar theme that such internal warfare had been an open invitation to Rome's external enemies.[4] But now, pronounces Horace, everything is changed.

> While the world's bound by Caesar's laws
> I need not apprehend
> War or a violent end.[5]

The civil wars, therefore, as Lucan somewhat acrobatically observed, had turned out to be a good thing after all, since it was because of them that a new order had come into being.[6] And by the same token the battle of Actium, itself a somewhat anti-climactic engagement decided by Agrippa's previous skilful manœuvrings, was built up into a major confrontation – because Octavian himself had been present.

> Leading the Italians into battle . . .
> The Star of his Father dawning over his head.[7]

For the very essence of the position of the *Imperator* was military glory. The general theme was that Actium constituted the defeat of the east by the west, the victory of Italy over foreigners. Indeed this theme had a certain measure of justification, in that Antony and Cleopatra had envisaged an imperial system in which Greeks (though not orientals) would play a much larger part than they were designed to play under the Italian hegemony of Octavian. And so the battle came to be regarded as one of the major landmarks of Roman history.

In 29 BC Octavian celebrated a great Triumph – the historic procession of a victorious Roman general to the temple of Jupiter, Juno and Minerva on the Capitoline Hill. It was a threefold Triumph, for his successes in Illyricum (and elsewhere), at Actium and in Egypt. When the ceremonies were concluded, the conqueror placed a statue of Victory in the senate-house. Yet so pressingly did the lessons of the previous decades compel his attention that he still felt not the smallest sense of security. Indeed it is an essential feature of the military and political history of the Roman empire that hardly any ruler, at any period during all these hundreds of years, ever felt secure even for a single moment. For there was always the loyalty of the army to worry about – not to speak of the loyalty of the senators who provided their senior officers.

Octavian's cautiousness, or nervousness, was well displayed by his treatment of Egypt. On his arrival there in 30 BC, in pursuit of Antony and Cleopatra, he annexed the country as a Roman province. Sixteen years earlier Julius Caesar, when he left three legions there to protect Cleopatra, had broken every tradition by entrusting this garrison to a commander who was not a member of the senate; whereas previous commanders possessing such a high degree of responsibility had invariably been senators. Evidently, however, there was no senator in the whole of Rome whom Caesar felt able to trust with a military command offering such vast and manifest temptations. For Egypt, as the historian Tacitus observed, was difficult of access, enormously wealthy in grain, full of peculiar religions and emotional excesses and unfamiliar with the normal processes of law-abiding government.[8] Now, on coming to Egypt in his adoptive father's footsteps, Octavian bore all this in mind, and, faced with the task of creating an office which was a governorship of the country at the same time as a command, once again refused to entrust it to a senator, and instead appointed a knight – the only knight in the whole empire called upon, at this period, to govern a major province and an army.[9]

Moreover this 'prefect of Alexandria and Egypt', as he was called, represented the ruler quite as much as he represented the state. Octavian, when he departed from Egypt after its annexation, felt it necessary, in order to maintain internal order, to leave a large force behind, consisting of three legions, nine cohorts of auxiliary infantry and three auxiliary cavalry regiments. However, owing to the peculiar perils inherent in the Egyptian situation, he also believed, as Suetonius points out, that there was a grave danger that these troops would some day embark on a rebellion – a rebellion moreover which, owing to Italy's dependence on Egyptian grain, might try to starve out Rome itself. And the best way to avert this, Octavian concluded, was to ensure that the troops in Egypt remained under a governor who was in a special sense his own personal subordinate. He showed clearly, once again, that such security considerations were in his mind when he went on to ordain that senators, and knights of the highest grade, were expressly forbidden to set foot in the new province without his permission.[10]

Such, then, was the somewhat perilous heritage which the first governor and garrison commander now inherited. He was Octavian's close friend Cornelius Gallus, knight and poet.

Octavian's own constitutional position now stood in need of the most urgent attention. For it was evident enough that he would be in perpetual danger from members of the senate if he continued to present himself quite openly as the *Imperator*, the commander of troops. Yet that is what he was, and had to be. Since, however, at present he could offer no real solution to this intractable problem, he decided, for the time being, to play a waiting game and continue to hold a series of annual consulships, relying on their character as the most essentially Republican of all offices, the symbol of Republican 'liberty'. This gesture, he hoped, would see him through the next few years without disaster.

In 30 BC he chose as his consular colleague Marcus Licinius Crassus, who was not only grandson of the triumvir but furnished a link with the more ancient Republican past. Then Crassus was at once sent to be governor of Macedonia (a Roman province since 146 BC), from which he led an army northwards to confront a raiding tribe, the Bastarnae, in what later became the province of Moesia. Driving the Bastarnae northwards towards the Danube, he fought a battle in which he killed the tribal chief, Deldo, with his own hands. According to a very antique tradition Roman commanders who personally killed an enemy leader were entitled to a solemn ceremony in Rome, at which they deposited the dead man's spoils (*spolia opima*) in the temple of Jupiter Feretrius on the Capitol. This had happened three times only in the whole of Roman history and legend. But Octavian found it most inconvenient that such a brilliant military honour should go to someone else. In consequence, citing a highly dubious piece of archaeological research, he ruled that Crassus was ineligible for the distinction since he was fighting under the supreme command of another man – namely himself. Crassus was permitted to celebrate a Triumph (4 July 27 BC), but not to be hailed as *Imperator* – though others since Actium had been allowed to accept this mere title of salutation, which was recognizably inferior to the supreme designation of *Imperator* borne by Octavian himself. And Crassus was not called upon to serve again.

Meanwhile on coins of 28 BC Octavian had described himself as '*Imperator* Caesar, son of a god, consul for the sixth time, asserter of the liberty of the Roman people.'[11] Then in January 27 BC he assumed the venerable, unprecedented, name of Augustus, and officially 'restored the Republic'. This did not mean that the 'free' Republic, governed by the sovereign people on the advice of the senate, had really come back into existence. Such a method of government could no longer have held the empire together – or have paid the army; and it would have meant that Augustus was no longer in a position to protect himself against his Roman foes.[12] Besides, a people heartily tired of civil war and anarchy was entirely willing to have an autocrat who kept things in order by virtue of his army command. But the Italian upper and middle classes were only content that this should be so on the condition that the official organs of the state, even if overshadowed by Augustus himself, were at least allowed and given the chance to function once more. And that is what his 'restoration of the Republic' achieved. On his initiative the senate was once again encouraged to perform many tasks (though not those that were of major political importance), and the state officials were once again appointed by popular elections (though Augustus had ways of influencing them). For the time being he himself, encouraging the use of the vague term 'leading man' (*princeps*) to define his own position, was still one of these officials, since he still continued to hold the consulship year after year.

But the real flaw in this 'restoration of the Republic', from the point of view of a Republican, was that, even after the immediate emergency of Actium was past, Augustus retained the command of by far the greater part of the army. It was true that the governors of Africa and Macedonia, who were among those retaining the traditional appellation of proconsuls (senatorial governors), commanded five or six legions between them. But all the other legions of the empire were under Augustus. These others, after the demobilization scheme had got under way, were about twenty in number, and subsequently two or three more were added. Augustus's control over these twenty-two or twenty-three legions was made constitutionally possible by his appointment as governor of all the provinces that contained them. The provinces in question, in the first instance, were Gaul (reaching up to the German frontier), northern and western Spain (Hispania Tarraconensis and Lusitania), Syria and Egypt. Augustus ruled this huge and scattered province, or, as it is more convenient to say, these provinces, through imperial governors (*legati Augusti propraetore*), each of whom controlled their territories and legions as his representatives. There were certain precedents. In particular Pompey, in the 50s BC, had governed Spain and commanded its troops *in absentia*, through *legati*. Now however the same principle was extended to a much wider variety of regions comprising a great proportion of the entire army.

For not only was Augustus convinced that a true restoration of the Republic would have been the equivalent of passing a death sentence on himself, but he equally felt it out of the question to allow other men to command forces of any substantial size at all. And even the men who, as his own personal subordinates, commanded the large bodies of troops in his own imperial provinces were very carefully and suspiciously selected. The result was that, although many members of old Republican houses were permitted to figure among the annually elected consuls in Rome,[13] we find very few of them in the field as important imperial governors. For the latter were men chosen for their own personal suitability and loyalty, with no need to have any great social position behind them. Now that so many troops were under the control of his own subordinates and nominees, Augustus had less reason to feel afraid that the senate might attempt to take too independent a line: and no consul or other functionary outside his own personal chain of command would ever be in a position to wield anything like such great influence as himself.

However, in order to leave some gilt on the pill, his public statements remained markedly reticent about his military power and powers. For example the report he left behind him at his death (the *Res Gestae Divi Augusti*) says nothing about the legal right (*imperium*) that conferred these powers upon him. In somewhat antiquarian fashion the document prefers to speak of his first officially conferred command, sixteen years earlier.[14] Moreover the stern realities were softened in another way as well. For as soon as each of the territories under his command were 'pacified', Augustus promised that he would give them back to the senate. In general he failed to do so, and though, in minor respects, he adjusted the distribution in the senate's favour from time to time, there were also adjustments in the opposite direction.[15] However he offered a conciliatory gesture by refusing to agree that his command was permanent. For the conferment of this huge province was regarded as lapsing in ten years' time, after which the grant had to be renewed. This 'comedy', as Edward Gibbon called it, was repeated at appropriate intervals throughout the reign.[16]

Soon after the constitutional settlement which created this system, something went badly wrong in Egypt. After suppressing a rebellion up the Nile, Cornelius Gallus, Augustus's governor of the country and the commander of its troops, in some way or other – we do not know how – incurred his master's deepest suspicion and disapproval, displayed in a charge of 'base ingratitude'. Gallus was recalled, and accused by a private prosecutor in the courts; whereupon the senate passed a vote of censure upon him, and he killed himself. This incident, whatever its origin, made Augustus feel he had been right to treat the Egyptian governorship and command with unequalled caution. Nevertheless, decades after the disgrace of Gallus, he felt sufficient confidence in the local situation to reduce the garrison from three legions to two: to lessen it further was impossible, since internal disorders were always likely to recur.

Augustus was away from Italy between 27 and 24 BC. For part of the time, though his health could scarcely stand the exertion, he was directing campaigns against rebels in north-western Spain. Then, in 23 BC, he fell seriously ill. The possibility of his death raised the acutest political and military problems. For he was not an 'emperor', but the holder of traditional, Republican, offices and powers: a Roman official invested, it is true, with an exceptionally extended range of competence, yet a Roman official all the same. His offices and powers and military command, therefore, like those of any other functionary, could not be passed on or inherited by anyone else. Nevertheless this was only an attitude for constitutionally-minded sophisticates, and people in general believed he would be succeeded by an heir. Since he had no son, the obvious choice was his nineteen-year-old son-in-law Marcellus, married to his only daughter Julia. Yet Augustus, when it seemed in 23 BC that he was going to die, handed his signet-ring not to Marcellus but to the great military and naval commander Agrippa: but he was out of the question as a successor, since the nobles were almost unanimous in their dislike of him, partly because they could not tolerate a 'new man'. Augustus also handed his fellow-consul of the year a statement including a list of all the legionary and auxiliary troops.

However he recovered. And the first thing that he did, when he got better, was to readjust his constitutional position once again. He resigned the consulship, no doubt calculating that, in spite of its Republican aura, it did him more harm than good with Republicans after all, since it blocked, year after year, the post that they particularly coveted. However he did not resign his province or military command, and it is generally believed that he was also now granted a power which made him superior to the governors of senatorial provinces, including the governors of Africa and Macedonia who commanded armies. This may, it is true, have been a right of which he proposed to make only sparing use, since he did not need to invoke a legal power to influence other leading Romans. Nevertheless he was now, in all respects that mattered, commander-in-chief. And although, as has been seen, his specific tenure of his province was left subject to ostensible periodical renewals, his powers as commander, in their new sense, seem to have been granted to him in perpetuity. This was a fine distinction, but it was one which effectively safeguarded his position, while partially concealing its autocratic character.

To us, however, both the ostensible restoration of the Republic in 27 BC and the subsequent adjustment in 23 BC have a strong appearance of sham. For after all the army which had shattered the Republic into fragments was still – under Augustus's command – the true master of the state. This element of fiction was admirably summed up by Gibbon.

Although Augustus considered a military force as the firmest foundation, he wisely rejected it as a very odious instrument of government. It was more agreeable to his temper, as well as to his policy, to reign under the venerable names of ancient magistracy, and artfully to collect, in his own person, all the scattered rays of civil jurisdiction . . . To resume, in a few words, the system of the imperial government, as it was instituted by Augustus, and maintained by those princes who understood their own interest and that of the people, it may be defined an absolute monarchy disguised by the forms of a commonwealth. The masters of the Roman world surrounded their throne with darkness, concealed their irresistible strength, and humbly professed themselves the accountable ministers of the senate, whose supreme decrees they dictated and obeyed.[17]

But to the Romans, with their peculiar form of legal tradition and their traumatic experiences of the previous decades, the fiction made a good deal better sense than it did to Gibbon or does to ourselves. For Rome believed itself to be still confronted, as in the recent past, with two opposite perils: civil strife and dictatorial rule. These were the twin dread opposites summed up by Horace, perhaps during these very years, in a couple of pregnant lines.

> A mob of citizens clamouring for injustice –
> An autocrat's grimace of rage.[18]

Tacitus later makes a character in his *Dialogue on Orators* remark that you cannot have it both ways: if you want peace, you must put up with a military autocrat.[19] Yet to most Romans of the years following Actium it seemed that Augustus, by an extraordinary feat of navigation, had successfully steered a way between these two horrors. And since the old Republican offices were, after all, actively functioning once again, the element of fiction did not, even among the constitutionally minded upper and middle classes, cause a very great deal of discomfort. At a later epoch Tacitus looked back at this passivity, and commented maliciously by varying the traditional phrase 'the senate and the Roman people' to 'senate, soldiery and people' or even 'soldiery, senate and common people'. But the Roman people themselves had no objection to the new order, and as for the Greeks who were the leading element in the eastern provinces, they saw the new regime quite straightforwardly as a monarchy based on autocratic military force.[20] But that was what they were used to, and it caused them no distress.

Nevertheless it was necessary for Augustus to collaborate perpetually and intimately with the senate – which alone could ensure continuity and stability of policy. There was no simple division or dichotomy between senate and army. The senate's links with the army, through many individual senators who were or had been senior officers, were close and inextricable. The senate's position, under the principate, was excellently described by Professor A.H.M.Jones.

The senate seems at first sight to have been a powerless and helpless body. A resolute emperor could easily defy it, and could cow it into submission by accepting charges of treason against its members and either trying them himself or bullying the senate into condemning them. But emperors who thus defied the senate rarely died in their beds, and prudent emperors treated it with respect and conciliated its goodwill. The reasons for the survival of the senate as a political force are not hard to discern. Its members were the social cream of Italy and the Romanized western provinces. They were moreover immensely rich. There was a substantial property qualification for membership, 250,000 *denarii*. But most entrants owned considerably larger fortunes, while the hereditary members had accumulated vast wealth by marriages with the heiresses of extinct families, or by being adopted into the old families and thus inheriting their wealth. Wealth thus accumulated in the hands of the senatorial order from generation to generation. Above all the senate still enjoyed an immense prestige not only among the upper classes but among the general public throughout the empire, and even in the army. It included among its members the army commanders, both active and retired, and the commanders of the individual legions. An emperor who quarrelled with the senate might fear that his own generals and other higher officers might be more influenced by their loyalty to the senate than by their allegiance to himself.[21]

Indeed, even if the formal votes of the senate might not matter too much, Augustus had to have the senators, who included all his senior officers, effectively on his side. To ensure this he could exercise a safe-guard, and did. Three times (28, 18 and 11 BC), he got himself granted powers to carry out a revision of the list of senators, which was reduced, in the process, from over a thousand to about six hundred.[22] On the first of these occasions, upon which he was enrolled as the senate's chairman, he and his colleague Agrippa expelled one hundred and fifty senators and persuaded fifty more to resign (without loss of their external rank). This was not quite a political purge, but it effectively removed possible sources of trouble – the sort of trouble which might easily have spread to the army. Of course the revisions caused feelings of discontent, if not sedition – and this too might have extended to the legions. In other words there was a danger that these revisions would foment precisely the feelings of disaffection which, on a longer-term view, they were designed to avert. But Augustus was able to counteract such sentiments because he also exercised the power, when engaged in this task of revision, to create new senators. Caesar too had been granted a similar power. But Augustus employed it much more cautiously than his adoptive father. Nevertheless his measures, taken all in all, proved sufficient, since with the exception of some diehards and men with grievances, the senate as a whole became cooperative enough. And, indeed, whereas the ruler needed the senators to help him govern, it was equally true that they needed his help in order to get the jobs they wanted. Moreover, they saw that his regime was, on the whole, responsive to their interests. They were also flattered by his plans to marry some of them off to his numerous female relations.

But Augustus had to think not only of the senators but of the great municipal bourgeois class, the knights and middle ranks of the Italian towns. These people were markedly sentimental and archaistic. And so it was for their sake very largely that he took so much trouble to revive the trappings of the Republic, and exerted himself to display its antique constitution and religion in ostensible working order. Once comforted with these reassurances such men were loyal, and Augustus made sure that they remained loyal by giving them many important posts – especially, as the next chapter will show, in the army.

Loyalty and especially loyalty among the officers and troops, was a constant preoccupation of Augustus. He observed feelingly that the man who does not wish to change the existing political order is a good man,[23] though such an observation was, perhaps unconsciously, ironical, since no one had introduced greater changes than himself, however carefully he contrived to conceal them. Nevertheless, uneasy lies the head that wears a crown – even if most elaborate pains have been taken to make the crown look like something else. As a later Italian monarch, Umberto, remarked, plotters are unavoidable accompaniments of the royal profession: and Augustus's position was sufficiently royal to be liable to just the same perils. Because, as it happened, he was one of the few rulers who died safely in his bed, it is too easy to forget the fears of disloyalty, whether in the army or among the senators, that dictated so many of his actions throughout his entire life. There was no need for Maecenas to remind him, as Dio supposes he did, first that he, like Caesar, would be the target of many plots, and second that it was altogether too comfortable an illusion to suppose that all the plotters would be insignificant people who could be disregarded.[24] On the contrary the principal danger came from senators and high-ranking officers: ex-Republicans, ex-Pompeians and ex-Antonians. In consequence even the ruler's closest friends had to be distrusted, since many of them came from precisely these circles. And even if that had not been their background, and even if they had been loyal supporters of Caesar's heir, they still might have been disappointed by his failure to restore the Republic in any authentic sense: and then, harbouring such disillusionments, they would very probably have started intriguing with other malcontents who looked back longingly on the old exciting days of civil war.

And indeed Augustus was duly plotted against – more often, apparently, than the image of the Pax Augusta generally associated with his reign is likely to suggest. According to Suetonius, 'he nipped in the bud at various times several outbreaks, attempts at revolution and conspiracies, which were betrayed before they became formidable'.[25] Who betrayed them? About Augustus's secret police and military intelligence we know little (pp. 91f.) for it is not until we come to later emperors that more extensive information on this subject will become available. Another question is this: when a plot was supposedly betrayed, had it really existed? This is part of a larger problem: under the imperial regime, as Tacitus emphasized, one of the casualties was the truth. Historians were either too flattering or too vituperative about their rulers, the latter process, naturally, being reserved for an emperor who was dead.

Besides, the task of these writers was a difficult one, as Dio Cassius pointed out with considerable feeling, because it was extremely hard, even for those living at the time, to know what had happened or what had not. This blanket of obscurity descended with particular effectiveness over conspiracies and military plots. Although informers and private prosecutors had long been a recognized institution – attractive to many ambitious young men who were awarded a quarter of the estate of any person they successfully prosecuted – it was appreciated by the more reasonable sort of emperor that he ought to be fairly sceptical when they announced that a conspiracy or revolt was afoot. Nevertheless Domitian, although admittedly one of the most suspicious of rulers, was justified in complaining that it was an uphill task to induce the public to believe in the reality of a plot until it had actually succeeded![26] Dio came to a similar conclusion – he felt that emperors were often unfairly blamed for punitive action which had in fact been perfectly justified.[27]

And he added that people were particularly incredulous of supposed plots, led by men lacking the support of the army, against the *Imperator* who possessed that support.[28] Yet such incredulity was not always justified, because some plotters without military connections did make the attempt all the same. But Dio was right to lay emphasis on that particular point. For that after all was the crucial question – whether the plotters had secured military backing. The main comfort for the ruler was that those of them who lacked such support – men who were merely chancing their arm and hoping for the best – stood relatively little chance of success. And Dio knew very well what he was talking about, because he himself lived at the centre of imperial events. The fact that he lived and wrote two centuries after Augustus does not invalidate, in this respect, his comments on the Augustan age, since this particular set of circumstances had not changed.

So if Augustus, as we are told, was really advised by those around him to be lenient,[29] he could not always accept such advice. Lucan, living under Nero, was one who saw very clearly that such leniency was not always possible. He knew only too well that the peril represented by the great imperial army, weighing incessantly on every ruler's mind, imposed the need not only for continual vigilance, but for ruthless, speedy measures of precaution and suppression.

Who would be good must quit a royal court;
Virtue and sovereign power do not accord.
Blush to be cruel, and you'll always fear.[30]

Augustus's suspicions of army leaders were displayed almost immediately after the constitutional reform of 23 BC. For in the very next year Marcus Primus, governor of Macedonia – one of the provinces where proconsuls still commanded their own armies – found himself on trial for having conducted an unauthorized campaign against Thracian tribesmen, outside the boundaries of his province.[31] It was an uncomfortable case, because Primus declared that his operation *had* been authorized, either by Augustus (who had been consul in the year 23 BC) or perhaps by 'Marcellus': this may refer either to Augustus's youthful son-in-law Marcellus, who died in that year, or to a certain Marcus Claudius Marcellus Aeserninus, who held the consulship in 22 BC. Primus was duly tried under the law governing treason. But it was embarrassing that, although he was duly condemned for waging private war, several votes were cast for his acquittal. It was also embarrassing that he found an eminent defender, a certain 'Licinius Murena', one of two cousins, of whom both had held important commands.[32] We do not know what happened to Primus. But shortly afterwards this same Murena, together with another man named Fannius Caepio, was tried under the treason law and condemned for plotting to assassinate Augustus. Murena, it was said, had previously displayed a loyal record.[33] But so had many of the men who afterwards murdered Caesar. And besides, Murena's family had strong Republican and Pompeian connections.

The return of peace following the civil wars had not yet banished deep, grave anxiety and disquiet. After Actium the historian Livy, for all his support of Augustus, had prefaced his great history by words of surprising gloom; and Horace was writing grimly of guilt and atonement.[34] Nor evidently did the settlement of 23 BC dispel the miasma. Moreover there were plagues and famines, which inspired a popular move to make Augustus dictator, or at least consul for evermore. As he himself records, in order that he could deal with such emergencies he rejected powers 'contrary to the traditions of our ancestors'.[35] But he may not have been altogether sorry that such offers were made, since this suggested that he was indispensable, and that his military rule must be tolerated, for fear of something worse in its place.

A little later, perhaps in about 20 BC, he strengthened his position with the army still further by accepting from the senate the right to make peace and war on behalf of the state.[36] The case of Primus had suggested the need for this measure and partial precedents could be cited to make it sound less autocratic than it seemed.[37] In any case it could be argued that the commander whose province included most of the frontier areas should possess such a right, including the control over foreign policy which it implied.

However if Augustus possessed the right of peace and war (in addition to all other powers) in the provinces, he still lacked military authority in Italy itself, including Rome. As consul, he had possessed such authority until 23 BC, but after he had resigned from the consulship in that year he no longer held a military command within the borders of the peninsula. It appears probable that this was now rectified, and that in 19 BC he was granted the explicit right to command troops in Italy.[38] Legions were still not stationed within the peninsula, but their absence was compensated by the praetorian and city cohorts (Chapter 4).

This extension of his military powers in Italy may have been connected with a tense situation that arose in the same year, when Augustus himself was absent.[39] For a pushing character named Marcus Egnatius Rufus, on being refused permission to stand for the consulship, organized rioting and bloodshed, and was executed for plotting to murder the ruler when he returned. The senate had felt obliged to vote an armed guard to the only consul in Rome at the time (which the consul refused), and Egnatius himself had sought popularity by forming a fire-brigade of his own slaves. Augustus disbanded this body and replaced it by an official Watch. But the incident raised the nightmarish possibility of a revival of private armies, so that it clearly became advisable that the *princeps* should himself be constitutionally empowered to command troops in Italy.

This enhancement of his military power seems to have been followed by new measures designed to limit the possible military independence of other commanders who might pose a potential threat to the regime. In particular, in about 18 BC, a new treason law seems to have been passed which explicitly forbade the raising of armies or declaration of war without the specific sanction of Augustus.[40] And another landmark of military jealousy was reached at about the same time. In the previous year a senatorial governor of Africa, Augustus's Spanish protégé Lucius Cornelius Balbus (a nephew of Caesar's adviser of the same name), had been allowed a Triumph for victories over African tribes.

But he proved to be the very last general outside the imperial house who was ever permitted one of these celebrations. For since plots against the ruler were still recurring[41] – partly, perhaps, because Augustus's second revision of the senate was now at hand – it seemed more prudent that no military glory whatever should be allowed to those who did not belong to the imperial family. In this way the army's loyalty was more likely to be channelled, as it should be, in one single direction only. The faithful Agrippa duly pointed the moral when, after victories of his own in northern Spain, he refrained from requesting that he himself should be allowed a Triumph.

And yet at the same time Augustus, feeling more confident now that all outside persons were to be denied even a shred of his prestige with the army, started to prefer stressing, as far as he himself was concerned, a vague, overall victoriousness rather than the actual hard fact of his military command. For not only do the official documents persistently remain evasive about the nature of that command, but his personal appellation *Imperator* begins to appear more and more rarely on the coinage, which instead for a long time, concentrates on names and titles with a civilian, democratic and religious appeal.[42]

Part II

The Army of Augustus

3

The Imperial Army in the Provinces
31 BC–AD 6

Not long after Augustus's constitutional arrangements were more or less complete, a new sort of Roman army, at which he had been working patiently ever since Actium, was beginning to take effective shape. While developing logically from the experiences of the previous half century, it also possessed features that were original and bore the stamp of its commander's astute and powerful brain.

Augustus reduced the sixty or seventy legions, with which he had been left after Actium, to twenty-five or six, a figure which was then raised, soon after the annexation of Galatia (central Asia Minor) in 25 BC, to twenty-eight. These twenty-eight legions comprised a total of rather more than 150,000 men. This was a small number of legionaries to defend and control all the vast territories controlled by Rome. As Gibbon remarked, the *total* military strength of the empire was equalled by the army of the single French king, Louis XIV – whose rule was confined to a single province of the former Roman empire. Moreover, when serious emergencies occurred, as they inevitably did from time to time, it was always likely that the number of available legions would be found unduly small. Nevertheless, Augustus's estimate concerning the size of the army he needed was based on a meticulous, knife-edge calculation. There were several reasons why he did not make it larger. In the first place, as he himself pointed out, a sufficient number of suitable volunteers was unlikely to be forthcoming. Second, the primitive agricultural economy of the empire could not readily support a more extensive establishment. Third, a bigger army would have been a perilous security risk. After all, Augustus was in a better position than anyone else to know how large an army in the empire as a whole, and how large a garrison in each individual province, he could command without offering a potential prey to Roman military rebels.

The reorganization of the army which he planned and gradually put into effect proved singularly durable. Its main lines remained relatively untouched throughout the whole of the first two centuries of the principate.[1] As to military revolts by the officers and soldiers themselves, the results of Augustus's assessment can be judged in two divergent ways. On the one hand, during those two centuries perhaps as many as 190 years were free of military rebellions. On the other hand, the remaining ten years or so were pretty full of them.[2] However, to blame Augustus for this is scarcely fair. Even the greatest ruler cannot plan for many decades ahead. Besides, if his army had been larger its rebellions would probably have been more serious. If, however, it had been smaller still, it could scarcely have protected the empire from external invasions and raids, and from internal revolts by natives in the provinces.

One of Augustus's major innovations was to supplement these legionaries by the creation of auxiliary units on a very large scale. Such auxiliary soldiery had become a familiar feature of the armies of the civil war. But Augustus expanded the whole conception by raising the total of these auxiliaries to 150,000 or more – deliberately, it would seem, the same number as his legionaries. They were organized, however, not in legions, but in infantry cohorts of about five hundred or a thousand men each, and cavalry regiments (*alae*) of about five hundred, with a few of a thousand.[3]

Unlike legionaries, the auxiliaries were not normally Roman citizens.[4] However, at some stage during the early principate it became normal for emperors to promise citizenship to these soldiers when they were demobilized – and to their sons as well (if born from a single marriage). This reward was the principal incentive to recruitment. It also gave the recruits, and their compatriots, a general feeling of satisfaction to know that the provinces, even the outer and more primitive provinces, were being offered a share in the defence of the empire. And if it sometimes suited Rome's convenience to spend auxiliary rather than Roman blood, this was only to be expected. Nevertheless, the knowledge that this was likely to happen naturally diminished the enthusiasm of the provincials, and probably contributed to the revolts of subject peoples which periodically occurred. Indeed, such revolts were often led by men who had learnt the military art in Roman auxiliary units. However, Augustus took what precautions he could against such disasters by ensuring that the officers of these units, like those of the legions, should still be Roman citizens and Italians. Exceptions were only made in favour of a very few élite auxiliary-corps units such as those of the Batavians (from coastal Holland), who continued for a time to serve under native officers.

The auxiliaries were not uniform in organization and equipment like the legionaries, but remained, for the time being, picturesquely varied. Normally they were attached to legions for operational purposes, and were deliberately devised to counteract the more obvious legionary deficiencies, such as rigid order of battle and unsuitability for uneven ground. Moreover the legions lacked archers, because the Romans preferred hand-to-hand fighting; so auxiliary archer units were important. Besides, although Augustus revived the legionary cavalry, there were still only 120 horsemen to a legion: and even if these could sometimes serve as small fighting groups, they were for the most part little more than mounted messengers or generals' escorts. But the auxiliary cavalry units, of which the advantages had been learnt during the civil wars, were much larger and more important, not only in battle but on the march, in which they furnished the column with its principal protection.

In the later years of the Republic the continual civil wars had been fomented, or indeed caused, by the existence of temporary armies to deal with successive emergencies as they arose. The retention of such a system, founded largely on conscription, would still have had several considerable advantages. It would have meant that a large number of citizens received some military training. It would have enabled at least some of the potentially dangerous unemployed to be given something to do. And above all it would have been relatively cheap, since when there was no emergency the armies could have been disbanded. So reliance upon temporary emergency forces would have been a sound arrangement – if the soldiers and their officers could have been trusted to be loyal to Augustus.

But evidently he himself decided they could not. Dio plausibly imagines Maecenas telling him that, whatever benefits this widespread conscription and military training might confer, it would still be a mistake, for those who received it 'would always be the source of seditions and civil wars'.[5] Furthermore, they would once again tend, during their brief term of service, to become more loyal to their own individual generals than to Augustus, since it would be these generals on whom they would rely for their rewards on discharge. Besides, the sort of training that could be provided for soldiers on short-term service, and the sort of temporary expeditionary forces into which they could be enrolled, would not really afford sufficient defence for the huge frontiers of the empire. Of course, defence considerations of this kind figured largely in the deliberations of rulers upon army matters. But considerations of the other kind – those relating to their personal security – were never far from their minds either. Indeed military policy was always based on *both* these factors at the same time, imperial defence and the emperor's safety. Nor is it easy to say, at any given moment, which of the two types of consideration played the larger part in a ruler's decisions.

At all events Augustus, balancing the two factors one against the other, decided that it would be unwise and impossible to rely on a series of temporary, conscript, expeditionary forces. Instead, therefore, he opted for the only practicable alternative, a permanent standing military establishment: and that is what his army, consisting of more than 150,000 legionaries and as many auxiliaries again, was designed to be.

To maintain such a standing army was extremely expensive. For one thing, although peace reigned in many areas, there were also, from place to place, periodic and often unpredictable external and internal wars. So even if his army was intended mainly as a peace-time organiza-tion, it was necessary to maintain it on something like a war-time foot-ing. It had, in fact, to be ready for war at short notice. This was why such very large expenditure was involved, and it now becomes clearer why Augustus was so eager to keep the numbers down as far as possible. And his eagerness was all the greater because, until he could devise a system, palatable to the senate, for drawing this revenue from state funds, he himself had to defray the payments to soldiers, in service and upon discharge, out of his own pocket.

Conscription, though it was still a legal possibility, he avoided as far as the legionaries were concerned (except in two emergencies near the end of his reign [Chapter 5]). In the words of a later historian, Herodian, 'he freed the Italians' – who still contributed such a large proportion of these soldiers – 'from the necessity of working and of bearing arms'.[6] He avoided conscripting them because this would have been so unpopular, and because volunteers were more likely than conscripts to reject seditious suggestions against their *Imperator*. Although, in view of the restricted size of the citizen body from which legionaries were derived, the number of potential volunteers was too small for his liking, he reckoned that there should be just enough of them to fill the limited number of legions he proposed to maintain. But when recruitment for the auxiliaries came to be considered, he felt that the dangers of conscripting these non-citizens was less acute, and so he remained prepared, when occasion demanded, to resort to such conscription as was necessary in the provincial areas from which they came.[7]

From this army, on which the empire and he himself so greatly depended, Augustus expected a high standard of morale and discipline. As usual, Suetonius has a number of relevant anecdotes.

On one occasion he dismissed the entire tenth legion in disgrace, because they were insubordinate; and others, too, who demanded their discharge in an insolent fashion, he disbanded without the rewards which would have been due for faithful service. If any cohorts gave way in battle, he decimated them, and fed the rest on barley. When centurions left their posts, he punished them with death, just as he did the rank and file. For faults of other kinds, he imposed various ignominious penalties, such as ordering them to stand all day long before the general's tent, sometimes in their tunics without their swordbelts, or again holding ten-foot poles or even a clod of earth.

After the civil wars he never called any of the troops 'comrades', either in the assembly or in an edict, but always 'soldiers'. And he would not allow them to be addressed otherwise, even by those of his sons or stepsons who held military commands, thinking the former term too flattering for the requirements of discipline, the peaceful state of the times, and his own dignity and that of his household.[8]

On grounds of security and economy alike, therefore, Augustus did not want his army to be very large. And another reason why he deemed this unnecessary was because its chief function, henceforward, was to remain on the defensive. The principle of a mainly defensive army, a principle which continued, with occasional exceptions, to be observed throughout the imperial epoch, goes back to Augustus, and to his reasoning. He designed his army, for the most part, to keep order. Its internal duty was to nip sedition in the bud. But it was also entrusted with the prevention of minor raids and unauthorized movements from outside the frontiers. And so it was to the frontiers that its most important garrison centres tended to move. As if to underline the tendency there were no legions stationed in Italy at all. This whole strategically central area was entirely lacking in any central legionary reserve that could be thrown into the breach in an emergency. When the number of the legions was fixed at its relatively small total of twenty-eight, this was the most noticeable and striking sacrifice. It was assumed, we must suppose, that border troubles would be an unusual contingency, and that, if a crisis occurred on one frontier, diplomacy could prevent potential enemies on other frontiers from taking advantage of such a situation. Among Augustus's subtle military calculations, this was a particularly hazardous one. It was partly motivated by a desire not to look too autocratic. For it was not traditional for legions to be stationed in Italy and Rome, and to have altered this tradition would have given an un-Republican impression – would have made it seem as though the free workings of the Republic were being menaced by military pressure from Augustus. But above all the existence of a legionary army in or near the capital would have presented too ready a temptation for senior officers and other senators who might wish to make an attempt at seizing the empire for themselves.

However, it was by no means all at once that Augustus assumed a purely defensive frontier posture. Indeed it was not apparent until late in his reign, when adverse circumstances had made it imperative (Chapter 5). True, when the poets of Augustus's circle talked of him conquering Britain and Parthia, he paid no attention. His only concession to upper-class chauvinism in the latter field occurred after he had made a peaceful diplomatic arrangement with the Parthians about Armenia, whereupon his coins declared, quite falsely, that the land had been captured by a military victory (ARMENIA CAPTA, ARMENIA RECEPTA; 20 BC).[9] Nevertheless, for the greater part of his reign there was heavy, expansionist fighting in many theatres, prompted by a desire for military glory and resulting in important and widely proclaimed enlargements of the empire. Already, in the years immediately following Actium, Augustus's marshals had been very active, earning six Triumphs (before this privilege was denied them) between 28 and 26 BC. But the most sensational results were to follow. They included the annexation of Raetia and Noricum (parts of Bavaria, Switzerland and Austria) in 16–15 BC; the northward extension of the provinces of Illyricum and Macedonia right up to the Danube for its entire length (16–12 BC and later),[10] so that they incorporated, respectively, the regions of Pannonia (east Austria, west Hungary and north Yugoslavia) and Moesia (east Yugoslavia and Bulgaria), which subsequently became

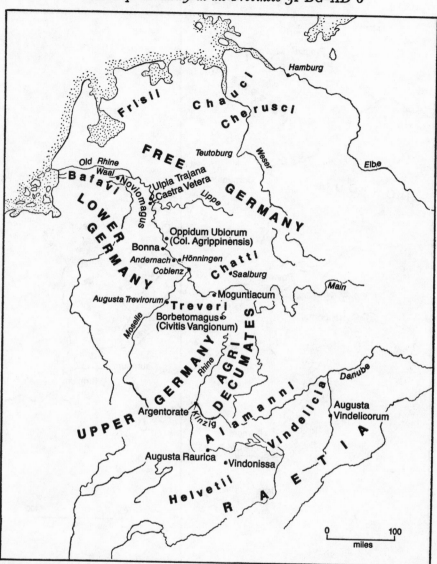

3   The Rhine Frontier

provinces on their own account; and the eastward extension of the German frontier all the way from the Rhine to the Elbe (13–9 BC).

This great outburst of activity, preparing the way for a considerable shortening of the northern border, transformed the entire configuration of Rome's imperial borders. The expansionist drive was delayed until Augustus had built up his new army into the shape he wanted it to

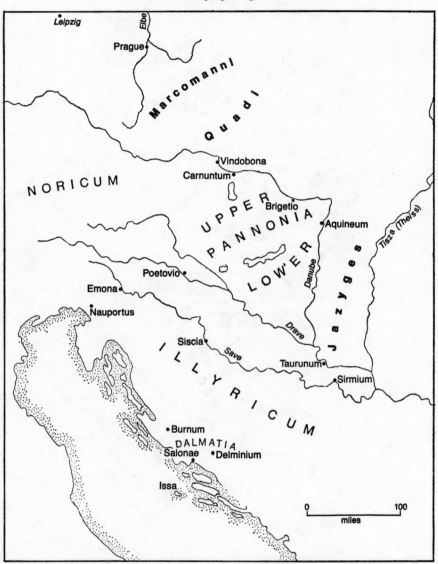

4   The Upper Danube Frontier

assume. The conquests were mainly undertaken by his stepsons,
Tiberius and Drusus senior (d. 9 BC). Augustus, however, continued to
publicize *his own* supreme victoriousness, and the Pax Augusta which it
brought,[11] and he gained a reputation as one of the greatest of Roman
warriors and generals.[12] Yet this was largely earned through the
exertions of others. He himself had never been a very successful com-

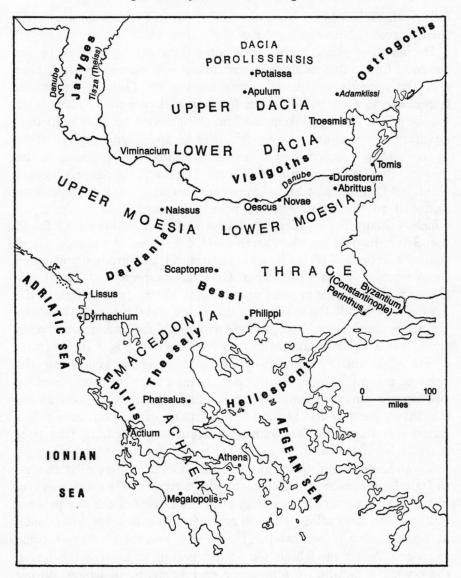

5   The Lower Danube Frontier

mander in the field, and from 23 BC onwards, for the remaining thirty-
seven years of his life, he never attempted to lead his troops in person
again. This self-denial, so profoundly at variance with the personal
leadership of Caesar, intensified his fears that others might tamper with
the army. Most later emperors, too, were similarly cut off from direct

links with their soldiers – an absence of contact which always made them nervous about the loyalty of the troops.

During these years, immediately after the great expansions, by far the most formidable military concentration was massed on the Rhine and the recently conquered areas beyond it. This concentration, formidable to enemies across the frontier, and potentially formidable (in the wrong hands) to Augustus himself, included not only numerous auxiliary units but as many as eight legions, and amounted altogether to more than 100,000 men – one-third of the total garrison of the empire. Previously much of this force had been distributed around Gaul, but Drusus senior brought up many formations to be permanently stationed on the Rhine.[13] Their principal camps, near the river, in which, initially, legionaries, auxiliaries and camp-followers all found themselves thrown together, were divided between the northern and southern sections of the west bank, territories which gradually assumed the names of lower and upper Germany respectively. The lower German garrison was centred upon Castra Vetera (near Birten in the Fürstenberg beside the junction of the Rhine and the Lippe). In upper Germany the principal base, which Drusus used for his last two expeditions, was Moguntiacum (Mainz), which stood opposite the junction of the Main and Rhine, and commanded important routes into the heart of central Europe. This upper German force was completed by two legions normally stationed in Raetia,[14] the territory comprising the Tyrol, parts of Switzerland and a section of Bavaria, in which a legion was based on Oberhausen, a suburb of Augsburg (the later Augusta Vindelicorum).

These Raetian and other upper German centres were near enough to Italy for emperors to watch them with a particularly suspicious eye. Yet at first, structurally speaking, even the largest of the camps were quite rudimentary affairs – not so much fortresses as bases, abandoned at the beginning of each campaigning season, and rebuilt when it came to an end. Across the Rhine, too, in the recently conquered territories, there were a number of temporary encampments, in which, during summer manœuvres or operations, one legion sometimes had to share its accommodation with another. But this practice caused anxiety to the ruler at Rome, who feared the temptations that might assail commanders of such massive concentrations of troops.

On the Danube legionary camps took somewhat longer to become established. Although the province of Illyricum was extended northwards through Pannonia as far as the river banks, the five legions that

6 Spain and Mauretania

it contained were at first stationed well south of the upper Danube, at Poetovio (Ptuj) on the Drave – where a great highway to the north crossed the river – and Emona (Ljubljana) on the Save, and perhaps Siscia (Sisak) on the same river.[15] These places, especially Emona, were not far from the border of Italy itself, to which they afforded protection from external enemies, as well as providing potential assistance to the

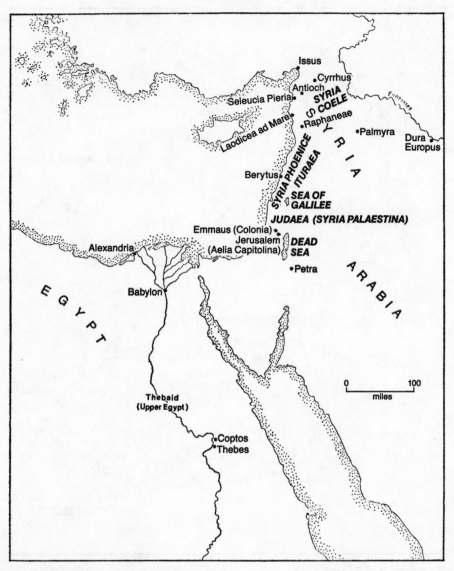

7   Syria, Judaea and Egypt

ruler if his position was threatened from within; though, as became clear later, their proximity could equally pose a threat. Further east, the portions of the Macedonian province that later became the provinces of upper (western) and lower (eastern) Moesia were overrun by Roman troops as far as the Danube. However, as in Illyricum, their legions – three in number – were still stationed, for the present, a long way south

66

of that river.[16] The Moesian legions were not suspected, at this early stage, of being able to play a dangerously subversive role in Italian affairs, since they were too far away.

In Spain, where there was heavy fighting against recalcitrant natives in 24, 22 and 19 BC, there were at first four or five Roman legions stationed in the northern territories of Callaecia (Galicia), Asturia and Cantabria.[17] At the other, eastern, extremity of the empire the legions numbered seven or eight. They were divided between Egypt and Syria. In Egypt one of its three legions was stationed at Alexandria to maintain order among the city's turbulent populations of Greeks, Jews and Egyptians, and the others were at Babylon (old Cairo) and in the Thebaid (upper Egypt),[18] where their primary task was to defend the Nile valley against Arab raids. The Syrian garrison normally consisted of four or five legions. Like their counterparts in Europe, the Syrian legions were not yet moved forward to the river frontier – the Euphrates, which divided the Roman from the Parthian empire. For frontier defence was not, at this stage, a pressing duty. That is to say it was their function not so much to stand on guard against the Parthians as to maintain internal order among the turbulent populations of Syria itself. In consequence the legions were distributed around the province.[19] However, in contrast to the Rhine and Danube legions, these Syrian formations were stationed not in relatively isolated camps but in or near large towns. In consequence their discipline suffered, and they tended not to be as effective a fighting force as the western legions, from which, before engaging in military operations, they often needed reinforcements.

In the vast Roman empire, of which the only effective cement was imperial force, the army was inevitably the most important public service. Augustus saw clearly that the relatively amateurish officers of Republican times would no longer be adequate. Julius Caesar had seen this too, and under his direction professionalism had increased. But he had died before his plans, in this or any other field, were complete, and it now remained to give the whole tendency a more logical and systematic shape.

One matter of overriding importance was to make sure that the men who commanded the legions were both efficient and loyal. In the place of the less experienced military tribunes accustomed to hold these posts under the Republic, Caesar had instituted the practice of appointing more expert officers, known as *legati*, to command his legions, as well as to take charge of other army groupings of various sizes. Following this example, Augustus regularized the rank of legionary commander (*legatus legionis*).

These commanders, who normally held their posts for between two and four years, were members of the senate. But they were young – usually, perhaps, about thirty, or sometimes not more than twenty-five. So the old idea that the armies should be commanded by whatever politician happened to be due for such a post at the time had been abandoned. For these were young men who, in their previous careers, had not yet advanced beyond the junior rank of the quaestors.

The quaestorship was a civilian post, and the legionary legate was still by no means a man who spent his whole life as a professional officer. Indeed, at intervals between military posts, he is likely to have passed through the normal stages of a non-military official career. Yet Augustus wanted his legionary commanders to be pretty good. And in spite of this apparent shortage of previous training that is what they were. For even if they spent a number of years in civilian jobs, men destined for the commands of legions were earmarked for these commands from an early age, and from that time onwards they were encouraged to take a special interest in the military career; and Augustus continued to watch them with the eye of a lynx. This was one of his safeguards; the other was their own knowledge that it was on him, and no one but him, that their future careers depended. These two factors between them made it less likely that they would have an opportunity to form any unsuitable ideas about independent action or sedition.

However once they were legionary commanders in some distant area, Augustus would not be able to watch them quite so closely any longer. True, spies could report what they were doing, and so could the imperial governor of their province, who was their immediate military superior. But on the whole, once his protégés had taken up their commands, the ruler had to rely on his own good selection, and trust them. Even so, however, he could not trust them absolutely. It is likely enough, for example, that he was advised (as Dio says) not to let consuls or praetors command armed forces during their term of office – or until a period of time had passed after its conclusion. For if this precaution was taken 'it would ensure that they will never be put in command of legions while still enjoying the prestige of their official titles – and thus be led to stir up rebellions'.[20]

An incident that arose only two years after Augustus's death showed the extraordinary sensitiveness emperors felt about this possible disloyalty of legionary commanders. A leading senator, Gaius Asinius

Gallus, proposed to Tiberius that any commander of a legion who had not yet held the praetorship should be designated as a future praetor forthwith.[21] The emperor was extremely hostile towards this suggestion, and towards the man who had put it forward. Clearly he was afraid that such commanders, having secured in advance the promotion that they were after, would in consequence feel less dependent upon himself. And that would not do at all.

The office of camp commandant (*praefectus castrorum*) also received attention from Augustus. Normally (later invariably) an ex-centurion, usually of fifty or sixty years of age, he was in charge of the organization and administration of legionary quarters, equipment and training, including the supervision of apprentice military tribunes. He was also responsible for medical services.[22] He was not a senator, but a knight. But in the absence of the legionary commander, the camp commandant could, on occasion (though not normally), be called upon to command a legion; and in a rebellion or other crisis he might have to play a key part.

As far as the unspecialized officer rank immediately below the legionary command, the military tribunate, was concerned, Augustus did a great deal to create a more regular system. Henceforward, the tribunes were by no means just the sort of amateurs whom Caesar, at the outset of his Gallic war, had found so unsatisfactory. Indeed Caesar himself had already instituted great improvements. But Augustus, as so often, placed these improvements upon a systematic basis. His military tribunes were very carefully chosen young men who were required to hold these posts for several years and were destined for further careers in the imperial service.

Within the legion definite duties were not assigned to the tribunate as a whole. But a tribune, for example, often had to be present at headquarters, in order to hear soldiers' complaints. He was also responsible for determining punishments, and for maintaining a dossier of the record and character of every soldier[23] – a useful means of checking sedition in good time. Yet he might also find himself engaged in clerical work, or checking the accounts to detect stolen stores. One way and another, then, the tribunes were given an opportunity to learn not only the art or science of war, but the details of military administration – which included a good deal of civilian-type administration as well, since, although Augustus established the nucleus of a Roman civil service (which scarcely existed before), there was still no junior civilian personnel to help administer the provinces.

Augustus divided the military tribunate into two sections. From now on the six tribunes in each legion comprised one young man embarking on an official senatorial career, the *tribunus laticlavius* (i.e. his tunic displayed the senator's broad purple stripe), and five of knightly rank, *tribuni angusticlavii* (with narrow purple stripe). Although he was only in his early twenties, it was the *tribunus laticlavius* (more often than the camp prefect) who commanded the legion when its commander was away. A senator's son himself, he could well be a family friend of the commander, and indeed may have owed him his job. Moreover Augustus himself, in all probability, was personally acquainted with his family – and may even have brought pressure on them to induce their youthful relation to undertake this military service. For even if legionaries were not conscripted, their officers virtually were.

After the young man had served as *tribunus laticlavius*, the ruler might be prepared to push him forward to a quick praetorship: if he wanted rapid promotion, this period of service as an officer was very important. True it was not an essential qualification for a senatorial career. But if a man was eager for future appointments under the emperor's own auspices, then it became not far from indispensable. And so the group of men who had served, at some stage, as *tribuni laticlavii* have been described as 'the real governing minority of the empire'. Augustus took pains to increase their numbers by appointing other men of the same rank and age to be prefects of auxiliary cavalry regiments as well. This, being a command, ranked higher than a military tribunate; and two of these youths were sometimes appointed as joint commanders of a single regiment.[24] This seems a surprising arrangement, but presumably there were experienced centurions to keep them on the right lines.

The *tribuni angusticlavii* were older than the *laticlavii*, being for the most part in their early thirties. At the headquarters of their legion they were employed as staff officers, though they might also command detachments on a campaign. Since they were and remained knights, their careers were different from those of a *laticlavius*. For the *angusticlavii* may well have served as civic officials in a town, earning selection as legionary officers on the strength of their administrative ability in municipal life. Or, alternatively, they may have been transferred to a legion after serving as prefects of an auxiliary unit, or officers of the fleet (Chapter 4).[25] For one of Augustus's greatest achievements was the creation of a wide-ranging and fruitful career for the knightly order: it was a reform which welded this great class firmly and loyally to his regime.[26] When the principate got fully under way, it became normal for a knight's career to begin with three officer posts in the army.[27] This series of posts was described as the *militia equestris*. In due course it came to be standardized as the successive tenures of three posts: prefect of an auxiliary cohort, tribune of a legion and finally prefect of an auxiliary cavalry regiment. Under Augustus most equestrian officers served in one or two of these three posts only, perhaps omitting the first. This was because, in his day, the prefects of auxiliary cohorts, if not tribal chiefs commanding their own native contingents, were often centurions. But soon the tribal units became regular auxiliary cohorts, which now came under prefects instead of centurions, and from now on the three stages of a knight's military career became almost unvarying.

As we should expect, Augustus had his methods for keeping control over such officers. They were forbidden (and indeed this applied to officers of every grade) to marry women from the provinces in which they served, so as to discourage any tendency towards separatism. There was an archaic Republican tradition that the knights were, in principle, a military order, and this was an interpretation which Augustus carefully maintained by reviving their annual parade. Nevertheless, it is a curious fact that officers of these knightly ranks, even while on active service, still remained technically civilians, so that, if found unsatisfactory, they could always be dismissed at any moment and sent back to civilian life.

However this cannot often have been necessary. For these officers, before they ever assumed their military duties, had already been very carefully screened for efficiency and loyalty alike. Suetonius happens to tell us of one way in which this was done: recommendations were sought and obtained from the authorities of the towns to which the young men belonged.[28] After their service in the army scintillating prospects were available for knights in the direct employment of the ruler, under whom they could rise to become prefect of Egypt or the praetorian guard (Chapter 4) or the grain supply. But most of these knightly officers, after their tour of military duty, returned home to their native cities where, as many inscriptions tell, they enjoyed a good deal of respect. These towns were the traditional centres of old-fashioned Roman patriotism, and it was the task of the returned officers to help convert this patriotism into loyalty to the *princeps*.

At all stages in their careers, Augustus reserved to himself the right of deciding which of these men should get on, and the results were seen in many a discreet preselection for posts. This was essentially an autocratic way of behaving. But it could also, with some plausibility, be presented as democratic. For radical politicians had, over a period of two centuries, been struggling to ensure that appointments were made on grounds of merit and not birth. And that, Augustus could say, was precisely what he was trying to do.

To us a strange feature of the system is the regular combination of military and civil posts in a single man's career. But this avoidance of a purely professional officer corps, too, could be regarded as deferential to the Republican tradition. However the real reason for the avoidance was something different: it was the fear of possible military uprisings. Professional officers spending their whole lives in the army could easily have been dangerous. They would have known altogether too much about military affairs and they might have formed far too close personal connections with their men. The creation of a military caste, therefore, had to be avoided for security reasons. On the other hand, a set of officers who were not professional enough to do their jobs or to command soldiers would have been useless. So Augustus, navigating as always a subtle, delicate course between perils and extremes, insisted that his more important helpers should hold military and civilian posts in turn.

The dilution of officers' military careers by civilian posts made it all the more necessary that they should have had some military training as boys and youths. In consequence, as in the Republic, these young men destined for the senatorial or equestrian careers were already introduced to military exercises at the age of seventeen. And even before that they may have received some form of preliminary training, perhaps for as long as three years.[29] Augustus revived the ancient annual military exercise for adolescents known as the Troy Game (*Lusus Troiae*), and built round it a cadet corps, the Juventus. Moreover similar cadet corps or clubs for young men of officer potential (*collegia iuvenum*) were instituted or revived in many or most Italian towns.

Everything possible was done to stimulate the morale of officers and stiffen their discipline. In the years 19–17 BC the coins of the capital celebrate Virtus and Honos,[30] the qualities and personifications which were particularly reverenced by military men, and Augustus revived their joint festival. Exemplary punishment was visited upon evaders of army duty. 'He sold a Roman knight and his property at public auction', declares Suetonius, 'because he had cut off the thumbs of two young sons in order to make them unfit for military service.'[31] Horace wrote praising the grand old tradition the *princeps* was so eager to renew:

Disciplined in the school of hard campaigning,
Let the young Roman study how to bear
Rigorous difficulties without complaining,
And camp with danger in the open air,
And with his horse and lance become the scourge of
Wild Parthians . . .
The glorious and the decent way of dying
Is for one's country.[32]

Propertius, on the other hand, risked imperial displeasure when he declared: 'no one of my blood is going to become a soldier'.[33] And another poet, Ovid, must have caused grave offence when he made fun of the army, continually describing the seduction of girls in the technical terms of military service.[34] It was no doubt flippancy such as this which contributed to his eventual exile to the Black Sea.

Augustus bestowed upon centurions the special attention they so amply deserved. Their different grades within the centurionate itself were maintained, and centurions' salaries, much increased by Augustus, varied enormously from about 3,750 up to 15,000 *denarii* a year.* That is to say the lowest grade of centurion received nearly seventeen times as much as an ordinary legionary, and the highest grade was paid four times as much again.

This difference corresponded with the great variety of the tasks a centurion had to perform. On the most prosaic level, as commander of an eighty-man-strong century, he had to keep track of all its arms and equipment, with two clerks to help him. It was the centurions who posted guards, conducted inspections and checked that work had been done. It was they who were responsible for the training of the rank and file, since the Roman army, for all the excellence of its training arrangements (*see* Introduction), did not possess basic camps for this purpose, and recruits had to be trained within the legions. The senior centurions, on the other hand, might even command cohorts and attend war councils, where they were called upon to state their views. At their head was the legion's chief centurion (*primus pilus*), a man aged at least fifty and probably sixty, who held office for one year and then retired with a large gratuity to enjoy a prestigious retirement. Centurions officered not only the legions but auxiliary cohorts and squadrons as well. The greatness of the Roman army still depended, perhaps depended more

---

* For Augustus's monetary system, see Appendix 5.

than ever, upon their efficiency. It was they who above all others intrepidly filled the breach and died in defence of the standards. The continuity of the army, and the perpetuity of its traditions, were in their hands.

Some centurions were commissioned direct from the legionary ranks. Others came – in mid-service or after retirement – from the praetorian guard, of which more will be said in the next chapter. Others again were brought straight in from civilian life, having been working, perhaps, in the administration of some Italian city. A centurion could be a veteran quartermaster nearing the end of his active service, a middle-aged staff officer, or a young company commander with a successful career in front of him.

This last sort of officer, though probably not unknown to Caesar, was largely the creation of Augustus. For a conspicuous feature of his system was that a man who had served as centurion could move directly upwards to the *militia equestris*, in which he would be promoted tribune of a legion or prefect of an auxiliary unit. Or alternatively he could be transferred to the civilian knightly career. Military ability, displayed during service as a centurion, had now become the most valuable of all passports to a successful future.

A man who wanted to become a centurion had to apply for his commission to the emperor,[35] whose freedman adviser known as the Minister of Notes (*a libellis*) perhaps already helped him with these matters. Tacitus deplores a civil war general who allowed his troops to elect their own centurions,[36] but in the peace-time of the imperial age too we hear of such an officer who was appointed by the vote of his legion, a certain Petronius Fortunatus.[37] Yet this was surely exceptional – and as it happens it did not, apparently, do the popular officer as much good as it might have, since, although he had only served in the army for four years before his election, he now proceeded to remain a centurion for the next forty-six years. Nor, in any case, must one suppose that his superiors had no say whatever in the appointment. For the recommendations leading to such promotions from the ranks were normally made by the legionary commander to the imperial governor of the province, and he may have taken a hand in seeing that Fortunatus's name was well regarded. The governor in his turn could either make the appointment on his own authority, or refer to Rome for a decision. When it was a question of filling a vacancy by the elevation of an obvious candidate, direct confirmation by the governor was in order. But if in the slightest doubt he would surely apply to his military superior, the supreme *Imperator*, whose personal control over commands and commissions by no means neglected or excluded the vital centurionate.

In the civil wars at the end of the Republic the centurions had been the natural leaders of the soldiers – and had sometimes taken the initiative in instigating mutinies and desertions. Julius Caesar had, on the whole, put a stop to that as far as his own army was concerned, since he had done a great deal to convert the centurions to his own purposes. Yet he, too, had been obliged to face mutinous situations. And so, in his youth, had Augustus. These experiences made him determined that such situations should never recur, and it was the centurions on whom he relied to prevent them. They were expected, now, not to foment sedition, but to repress it – to become his own firmest defenders. The good pay and prospects they were offered linked them personally with himself. Moreover he took no risks that they might become too friendly with their soldiers: for he was careful to move them about, quite frequently, from unit to unit. Indeed the danger was now that they might be so loyal to himself that the legionaries would not think of them as their spokesmen any longer. Besides, indignation was rife in the ranks because centurions often accepted bribes from soldiers who wanted leave, or hoped for exemption from heavy duty;* and some of these officers lashed around with their vine-rods too freely. In mutinies of the future, centurions who had acted in this way were the first to suffer violence themselves – at the hands of their own men.

As far as the legions stationed in the west were concerned, a proportion of their soldiers, perhaps one-fourth or one-fifth, originated from highly Romanized areas such as southern Spain, and particularly from southern Gaul which the elder Pliny described as 'Italy rather than a province'.[38] The fact that neither of these regions were included among the imperial provinces was evidently no impediment;[39] the important point was that they contained numerous Roman citizens, to whom service in the legions was still restricted. In this way the slow and gradual provincialization of the legionary army, begun under Pompey and continuing under Caesar, was still under way. But since Italy was the homeland of the majority of Roman citizens[40] it provided by far the greater proportion of the western legionaries; and in particular they came from the northern part of the country, Cisalpine Gaul. That great

---

* For Otho's removal of this abuse, see the passage quoted in Chapter 7, note 52.

reservoir of human resources had first been exploited by Caesar, who began its incorporation in the homeland in 49 BC. And now once again, on an even more extensive scale, it was called upon by Augustus to provide more than half of his Italian volunteers. Once they were in the army they became Romanized to some extent. Sometimes, however, this was quite a task. For Roman citizens though they all were, some of the soldiers from the Alpine valleys for example, despite their Roman franchise, sometimes bore names of a weirdly un-Latin appearance.[41] The feats, therefore, of cultural 'Romanization' that legionaries performed when away in the provinces, though they added up to something over the years, were necessarily somewhat limited. Nevertheless Augustus was evidently determined that the legions should remain predominantly Italian. But this was not so much in order to Romanize the empire as to make the army less sympathetic with subject peoples. For if the legionaries were Italians, there was less likelihood that they would look favourably upon revolts among the provincial populations.

The legions stationed in the eastern provinces were recruited from entirely different sources. Their officers, it is true, were still Italians. But the rank and file were easterners. For example, after the annexation of Galatia in central Asia Minor (25 BC), the royal troops of the previous client kingdom were formed into a whole legion on their own.[42] And the Galatians, being a warlike Celtic people, were also drafted extensively into other legions garrisoned in the east (as well as auxiliary units). They likewise figured prominently in the legions of Illyricum (Dalmatia–Pannonia) and Macedonia (including, for the present, Moesia). The Danube legions drew upon other regions of Asia Minor as well, though they were mainly recruited from the territories in which they were stationed. Unlike their fellow-soldiers in the west, these legionaries in the Danubian countries were by no means always volunteers; and the same applied to those in Syria and Egypt. To recruit these men, conscription was often used. But conscripts and volunteers alike, they had not, unlike the western legionaries, been Roman citizens before they joined the colours, but were given Roman citizenship on recruitment.[43]

The auxiliaries, who were not made citizens during their service, were likewise mainly conscripts. Those who came from within the Roman empire were recruited in the less Romanized provinces, and especially, to begin with, in northern and central Spain, northern and central Gaul, and Galatia. But during this initial period, comprising at least the first part of Augustus's reign, a good many auxiliaries were also provided by the dependent or semi-dependent client kingdoms which lay just beyond the frontier provinces; that is why some of these units, at first, still possessed their own native officers. But when, before long, the more important client kingdoms had been annexed and converted into Roman territory, it was normal for the officers of auxiliary units to be Italians. These contingents were often stationed away from their homes.[44] Even so some of the specialist formations, such as those of Syrian archers, still continued to obtain recruits from their distant native countries. But most of the auxiliary units now tended to replenish their numbers by recruitment in the locality in which they were serving. The emperors needed their special skills, but were not sorry to see them lose their racial *esprit de corps*, which might have encouraged disloyal and separatist thoughts.

Augustus took special care to maintain the firmest control of the gold and silver coinage which was needed to provide the troops with their pay. The superb and copious monetary system which was largely his creation served this purpose in admirable fashion, and at the same time provided an opportunity to commemorate the various aspects of his military and other policies with legends and designs inscribed on the widely circulating coins.

The basic rate of legionaries' pay, which Caesar had raised to 225 *denarii*, remained unchanged. For Augustus did not deem it either desirable or economically practicable to effect a further increase. Nor can the rate have been intolerably low, since it still stayed the same for eighty years after Augustus's death. And, although there were inevitably complaints, this total was enough, as papyri reveal, to enable some soldiers at least to save nearly one-third of what they earned,[45] and lodge it in the bank kept by their standard-bearers (p. 78). On the other hand 225 *denarii* by no means represented an outrageous or even a very large sum, when one considers that portions of it were deducted, at source, for rations, clothing, equipment and even arms and armour, not to speak of smaller deductions for feast-days and burial clubs. Auxiliary infantry received one-third of the pay of legionaries, and auxiliary cavalry two-thirds; part-mounted cohorts were later assessed at a figure between the two.

Granted that there were some careful savers, these wages might not have been enough to guarantee the soldiers' loyalty. What turned the scale, however, was the custom Augustus had inherited from the later

Republic of supplementing the soldiers' pay by special bonuses (*donativa*): 'he seduced the army with gifts', Tacitus claimed.[46] Yet his policy was by no means extravagant. It is true that after Actium the legionaries who were retained in his service received bonuses,[47] and in addition the *princeps* himself recorded that he gave 120,000 legionary veterans settled in colonies 250 *denarii** each from the spoils of war.[48] Subsequently, however, he only seems to have presented a bonus on one single occasion during the whole length of his reign. This was to celebrate the first participation of his grandson Gaius Caesar in military exercises in 8 BC,[49] and his choice of a peaceful occasion such as this, rather than a military victory, was significant, since the continued association of bonuses with victories might have meant that he came under pressure from soldiers to adopt aggressive policies at times when he might not wish to. At a later date, if not already, we learn that soldiers were obliged to place half of every bonus they received in their standard-bearer's savings bank.[50] They described these additional sources of revenue rather disparagingly as 'nail money' (*clavarium*) – enough to pay for the nails in their boots. On the other hand Augustus gained a certain reputation for generosity by letting ordinary soldiers have a good share in such decorations as he handed out, though his awards of the highest honours were sparing.[51]

Soldiers were not allowed to marry during service, and if they were already married when they joined the army their marriages had to be dissolved.[52] This was in accordance with the theory that they would often be on the move – or, perhaps, that they must not become soft, and be distracted from their jobs. This prohibition seems somewhat inconsistent with the spirit of Augustan legislation for civilians, which went to great lengths to encourage marriage and legitimate offspring. However the veto on soldiers' marriages remained theoretical rather than practical, since it was largely ignored. For in the civilian quarters which soon sprang up round their barracks the legionaries habitually kept women of local origin. Curiously enough, too, the normal forms of marriage with such partners were gone through, evidently with official connivance. Nevertheless this did not mean that the sons born to legionaries by these foreign unions gained Roman citizenship, for they could only do so if, like their fathers before them, they joined the legions. And this they frequently did – so that in effect Augustus's measure prohibiting soldiers' marriages tended to endow legionary service with a hereditary character.

* For the value of soldiers' pay, see Appendix 5.

It would have been impossible to extend the marriage prohibition to such lofty officers as the legionary commanders. Yet even they, to set an example, were not allowed to have their wives with them during the campaigning season, and could only visit them during the winter.[53]

The *sacramentum*, the oath which every soldier like every commander[54] swore on enrolment, had undergone a change of character since Republican times. During the civil wars the men had begun to swear their oaths to their generals to the neglect of their oaths to the state. And now what was sworn was still not loyalty to the state, but loyalty to the ruler – and to the state only through him as an intermediary. This oath, which was sworn once and for all but, as a reminder, was solemnly renewed at the beginning of each year, was still regarded as seriously as ever. To break it was the gravest step that could be taken. The oath-swearing scene is depicted on coins of the late first and early second century AD, on which the *Imperator*, in a toga, is shown clasping hands over an altar with an officer in military uniform, while in the background appears a soldier carrying a standard and another armed with spear and shield.[55] This oath served as a model for the oaths of allegiance that were now, since the time of the civil wars, administered to civilians as well.

This and all the other measures that were adopted to secure loyalty to Augustus proved on the whole successful. And this was in spite of the grave risk which he took, perhaps unavoidably, by ceasing for nearly four decades to take personal command of his own soldiers. After Actium the historian Livy's gloomy view of the times did not lighten when he considered the military scene. For it appeared to him, in the vast empire of his own day, that the spirit of the old soldier-citizens had gone. But he was wrong. Or even if the old type of soldier-citizen was no more, the new type was still a magnificent soldier. He was also, despite all Augustus's anxieties or because of all his precautions, by no means disposed, at least at this stage of events, to be seditious. The mutiny at Brundusium in 31–30 BC, and trouble Agrippa had with a single legion in Spain in 19 BC, were drops in the ocean during so long and eventful a reign. Besides Agrippa's mutiny was caused by an excessively tough military operation, and not by any discontent with Augustus. The soldiers, in fact, had been induced to suppress the turbulent instincts which the circumstances of the civil wars had encouraged in their predecessors. In other words the men of Augustus's legions, like the civilians who had profited from his victory and his peace, were essentially non-political. The *Imperator* called the soldiers *my* soldiers; and they were prepared to follow him loyally – if he rewarded them sufficiently well.

Rewards meant not only their pay and the occasional bonus, but above all a suitable provision for their retirement. Without that all the pay in the world would not have satisfied them.

Ex-soldiers enjoyed many privileges, and exemptions. On a papyrus of 31 BC the victor of Actium listed some of them.

> I have decided to decree that all veterans be granted exemption from tribute ... to grant to them, their parents and children, and the wives they have or shall have, exemption of all their property from taxation; and to the end that they may be Roman citizens with fullest legal right, they shall be exempt from taxation, exempt from military service and exempt from the performance of compulsory public services. Likewise, the aforementioned shall have the right to cast their votes and be enrolled in the census in any tribe they wish; and if they wish to be enrolled *in absentia*, it shall be permitted, both to the aforementioned themselves and to their parents, wives and children. Likewise, just as I desired, they may possess, use and enjoy also whatever priesthoods, offices, prerogatives, privileges and emoluments they possessed. Neither the other magistrates nor a legate nor an agent (*procurator*) nor a tribute-collector shall be in their homes for the purpose of lodging or wintering, nor shall anyone be conducted to winter quarters therein against their will.[56]

But more positive measures than these were needed to reward demobilized soldiers. For, like the veterans of previous generations, what they wanted above all was land; and the mutiny at Brundusium showed how urgently necessary its provision was. As soon as the *Imperator* had seized the Egyptian treasure, the assignation of land to the discharged legionaries was his very first priority.[57] The 'colonies' in which they were settled, like those of Sulla and Caesar, became important bastions of loyalty to the regime. Although these initial assignments took place over a period of years, Augustus, in his testamentary *Res Gestae*, reviewing the achievements of his regime, groups them together under the year 30 BC. And then he refers to a second land-settlement scheme of 14 BC; and he sums up the two occasions as follows: 'The amount which I paid for estates in Italy was about 600 million *sesterces* [150 million *denarii*], and the amount which I paid for lands in the provinces was about 260 million *sesterces* [65 million *denarii*].'[58]

These vast totals provided, throughout a period extending over more than a quarter of a century, for the settlement of about nine thousand men a year (calculated on the assumption that two out of every five men died during their service). This expenditure was defrayed, not by the state, but by Augustus himself – mainly from the gigantic resources he had acquired in Egypt. It was politically useful that he personally should pay for these settlements, as long as he could, since this reminded the soldiers that he was the source of their benefits; and he employed his own personal agents or representatives in the provinces, the procurators who ranked second to the governors, to distribute the pay.[59] Agrippa, therefore, would have been quite right to advise him (as Dio imaginatively supposes that he did) not to allow any other personage to make a contribution. For this would be perilous not only to the contributor but to Augustus, since no citizen 'would feel free to make a voluntary contribution, any more than he would readily admit that he was rich – and it is not to the advantage of the ruler that he should, for immediately such a contributor would acquire a reputation for patriotism among the masses, become conceited and incite a rebellion'.[60]

In 13 BC, after Augustus had returned from a tour of Gaul, the German frontier area and Spain, he passed two highly important new measures. First, he sought to remove the grievances that had been caused by the arbitrary durations of service which soldiers had been called upon to provide. Henceforward he declared that the term of service for legionaries should revert to sixteen years – the normal obligation of a citizen in Republican times. His object in offering this assurance, says Dio, was to prevent the soldiers 'from finding any excuse for revolt on this score'.[61] However, there was a catch. For many legionaries, after their sixteen years of service, were still to be kept with the colours (*sub vexillo*)* for four further years. These 'veteran soldiers' (*evocati*), retained in service in a special cohort under its own commander, who was known as the *curator veteranorum*, carried rods like centurions and stood next below them in rank. Theoretically at least they possessed exemption from routine duties, and were only employed actively in case of hostile attack. This was nothing new for Augustus, since during the civil wars he had recalled some of Caesar's discharged legionaries as *evocati* to serve against Antony.[62] And he could point to Republican precedents, according to which service could be extended to twenty years if an emergency so demanded. To what extent Augustus made this four-year *evocatio* into a firm obligation is not stated. Perhaps it was not obligatory for every legionary; and no doubt some of them

---

* The *vexillum* was a flaglike unit-standard, a piece of cloth attached to across-bar carried on a pole.

were quite content to stay. Nevertheless, to judge by complaints at the time of his death (Chapter 5), the additional four years became unavoidable for a good many of them – and there was widespread discontent.

The year 13 BC, in which the sixteen-year duration of service was formally announced, likewise witnessed a significant change in the form of reward that legionaries received on discharge. The allocation of land-grants was abandoned; and the demobilized soldiers were given a cash gratuity instead. Since Augustus had felt it necessary to compensate those whose lands were given to veterans, the allotment system had proved very costly. Besides land had now become increasingly hard to get. Nor, as experience had long since shown, was every old soldier a competent farmer. And another reason for the change was Augustus's desire to show himself as a good Republican. The land-grants had been a distinctive, oppressive feature of the bad, bygone period of the civil wars; so that it would be appropriate and popular to put an end to them. Henceforward, therefore, he handed out cash instead. The individual gratuity that went to each legionary totalled three thousand *denarii* (though perhaps the first beneficiaries did not receive so high a total).[63] This amounted to more than thirteen years' pay. One wonders how favourably the sum in question compared, in real value, with the land that the previous generation of Augustus's discharged soldiers had been receiving. Their land-allotments cannot have been enormously generous, because the compensation that had to be paid for them meant such a vast outlay of money. So perhaps the cash payments were not too inferior to the previous system in terms of value. 'It was not affluence,' observed P.A.Brunt, 'but the Republican veteran had possessed no entitlement at all.'

Augustus's new decision, like the regulations about length of service, was planned, as Suetonius points out, 'to keep the veterans from being tempted to rebellion after their discharge'.[64] In this the measures just about succeeded, and not much more. 'These steps', as Dio no doubt justly remarks, 'caused the soldiers neither pleasure nor anger for the time being, because they neither obtained all they desired nor yet failed to benefit altogether.'[65] This may have seemed a somewhat poor degree of gratitude in the eyes of Augustus, who, during the period 7–2 BC when the new gratuities were coming into force, claimed that they had cost him, out of his own resources, the vast sum of 100 million *denarii*. During the years that came next, between 2 BC and AD 6, there is no record of discharges. It seems that the *Imperator* foresaw a shortage of money, and began to go back on his promises about length of service. For instead of retaining the legionaries with the colours for sixteen years with the possibility of another four as *evocati*, he now resorted to the practice of making them serve twenty, plus another five (and the duration for auxiliaries was formally fixed, perhaps at this same stage, at twenty-five years). This was a calculated loyalty risk. Some soldiers were quite prepared to serve beyond their time. Others did not fancy the idea at all.[66] However Augustus no doubt estimated that his regime was by now firmly enough established to be able to ride the storm.

All these years, ever since Actium, he had continued to spend his own funds, and not the state's, on the rewarding of his discharged veterans. Admittedly there was by now a certain amount of confusion between the two sources of revenue. Nevertheless, there was sufficient distinction for Augustus, by this time, to feel unable to maintain the burden any longer. The prospect of having to continue these disbursements for the indefinite future had become intolerable. In AD 6, therefore, he put an end to the arrangement, and transferred the responsibility to the state. This he did by creating a new official, military treasury (*aerarium militare*), directed by three former praetors.

But how was this novel fund to be financed? The Roman cities of Italy, who were not accustomed to paying taxes, had a rooted objection to doing so now. And the senate, whose members would have to pay a large proportion of the bill, proved indecisive and recalcitrant. Augustus's hold on them, in his old age, was weakening, and his co-regent, Tiberius (Chapter 5), possessed many enemies in their ranks. The senators had evidently failed to learn the lesson of the late Republic, which their meanness towards the army had so signally helped to overthrow. Now however, ironically enough, when their Republic was lost to them for ever, they had to pay all the same. For Augustus, no doubt in consultation with Tiberius, decided to raise the funds for his military treasury from two new sources of national revenue, a 5 per cent tax on inheritance and a 1 per cent tax on the proceeds of sales by auction.

Augustus softened the impact, and got the military treasury under way, by making a personal contribution of 42½ million *denarii*. However, large sum though this seemed, it was only enough, at best, for fourteen thousand men, that is to say for less than two years' quota of discharged veterans. And time was clearly going to be needed before the two new taxes would bring in enough income to exercise a substantial effect on the situation. In consequence, Augustus specifically earmarked his contribution for 'soldiers who had seen twenty or more years of service'.[67] In this way the *de facto* extension from sixteen (plus four) to twenty (plus five) years of service was invested with formal authority. This was a perilous admission to make publicly, since it might have led to serious unrest. But Augustus was saved, as it happened, from any immediate repercussions by the outbreak of two successive military crises in Illyricum and Germany, which meant that demobilizations had to be postponed anyway, regardless of financial considerations (Chapter 5).

Meanwhile what he had done by establishing the military treasury was to teach the troops to look for their pensions, not to himself as an individual, but to the state. Previously he had preferred them to look to himself, however costly this might be. But now the transference was politically practicable, since he had become so manifestly the national leader that his own position as the ever-victorious *Imperator* would not suffer from this new arrangement. And he would welcome it for another reason too: because he was no longer directly the paymaster of the troops, it was also impossible for any other would-be *Imperator* to get himself thought of in this sort of capacity either: when it was recognized that all the funds came impersonally from the state, the generals would have a harder job to bribe their soldiers into seditious adventures.

4

The Protection of Rome and the Regime
31 BC–AD 14

Numerically the Roman legionary and auxiliary armies in the provinces vastly exceeded such forces as were stationed in Italy itself. But in the political and public life of the Roman commonwealth the units in the peninsula, including those in the capital itself, played parts that frequently, indeed continuously, assumed the highest importance.

These forces were varied in character, and not all were equally significant. A subordinate role, for example, was fulfilled by the fleet. This had generally been the destiny of the fleet in Roman history, but not always, since at times it had fulfilled the decisive role. One of those times had been the First Punic War (264–41 BC). Later on Pompey had shown the potentialities of the navy in his lightning campaign against the pirates of the eastern Mediterranean (66 BC). Caesar too, in his Gallic War, had built many ships on the River Loire, and had twice transported his legions across the English Channel. And then Octavian himself, the future Augustus, had used his navy, under its incomparable commander Agrippa, to win his decisive victories over Sextus Pompeius at Naulochus (36 BC) and over Antony and Cleopatra at Actium (31 BC).

He was not, therefore, likely to omit a fleet altogether from his regular military establishment. In the event of internal rebellions or external wars, its uses were obvious. And, even if there were none, the ships would be needed to police the Mediterranean. Their two main bases, those of the 'praetorian' fleets, were now to be in Italy, one on either coast. The principal naval station was at Misenum, upon the northern extremity of the Bay of Naples – a convenient point for reaching many parts of the western Mediterranean.[1] The other Italian port, on the opposite flank of Italy, was Ravenna. A location on the Adriatic Sea had been selected because trouble could still be expected from the natives of Dalmatia, the coastal portion of the province of Illyricum. These two Italian harbours, Misenum and Ravenna, were the only naval centres of strategic importance.

The other concentrations of warships were all outside Italy; and these bases were primarily intended for coastal defence and the maintenance of local order. For example there was a fleet at Forum Julii (Fréjus) on the southern coast of Gaul, from which the vessels could control the northern Mediterranean and the Rhône. Indeed this was Augustus's oldest military port, since he had already used it for his operations against Sextus Pompeius. Excavation at Forum Julii has revealed harbour-walls and many naval buildings, including the residence of the fleet-commander himself. However this Gallic base now gradually decreased in importance in favour of Misenum. There were also flotillas on the Rhine and Danube,[2] adapted to amphibious frontier operations. In the east fleets were stationed at Alexandria in Egypt and Seleucia Pieria (Süveydiye) in Syria, the latter including the Aegean in its sphere of operations.

The rank and file of the fleet consisted of two grades, the soldiers or marines (*classiarii*), and the sailors who ranked below them. These marines and sailors were mostly non-Italians, originating from various parts of the Mediterranean coasts. For example, the fleet at Misenum recruited mainly from Egypt, and the fleet at Ravenna from Dalmatia. At first Augustus enrolled in his fleet a number of slaves who had served in Sextus Pompeius's navy. But later most of the naval personnel were freedmen. They were expected to serve for twenty-six years, that is to say for a duration one year longer than auxiliaries. About the financial conditions of their service we know nothing.

The naval officers included three senior ranks: ships' captains (*trierarchi*), squadron commanders (*navarchi*) and fleet commanders or prefects, who were in charge of the bases. With the end of the civil wars the demand for great admirals had vanished. At first Augustus's prefects seem to have been army officers. But then Roman knights were usually selected for these posts,[3] and subsequently ex-slaves (freedmen) were also called upon. The handling of naval affairs at Rome was conducted by two junior officials, the *quaestores classici*. But the prefects came under the direct command of Augustus, whose military powers in 19 BC were specifically extended to Italy (Chapter 2).[4]

These military powers in the home country were very necessary to Augustus. But he needed them not so much in order to command the fleets as to protect the safety of his own person. Plotting, as we have seen, was inevitable; and plots, or alleged plots, duly materialized. For this reason Agrippa, in a speech attributed to him by Dio, takes it for granted that the *Imperator* should be carefully guarded, and Augustus's wife Livia urges that this essential precaution should never at any time be neglected.[5] When Augustus in association with Agrippa was conducting that very unpopular operation, a revision of the senate (28 BC), it was said that beneath his toga he wore mailed armour and carried a sword, that he had ten of the toughest and loyalest senators standing round his chair, and that the other senators were only allowed to approach him one by one, and even then not until they had been thoroughly searched.[6]

Obviously the warlords of the later Republic had relied heavily upon bodyguards. Sertorius, in Spain, had employed Spaniards for this purpose; and the custom of employing foreigners of more or less barbarian character as personal guards (sometimes on horseback)[7] had persisted. This was partly because of the physical strength of these men. But it was also because their imperfect acquaintance with the Latin language, and presumed lack of interest in Roman politics, meant they were less likely to be suborned into murdering the man they were supposed to protect. Caesar, who fought three campaigns in Spain, followed the example of Sertorius and enrolled a Spanish guard. Later on, however, he disbanded it. This was imprudent, according to his friends, who unsuccessfully urged him to reverse his decision. After he was dead, Octavian returned to the practice his great-uncle had abandoned, and employed a bodyguard from the Spanish town of Calagurris (Calahorra). After Actium, however, he replaced it by a guard of Germans, a race who honoured above all else the bond of personal fidelity to their selected master. Inscriptions relating to its members, known as *corporis custodes*, have survived. They were slaves and freedmen, and constituted a private body, not forming part of the Roman army.

But this German bodyguard was only supplementary to Augustus's principal guard, the praetorians, who were Roman citizens and belonged to the army. This praetorian guard had certain Republican roots. At first, it is true, the escorts with which earlier leaders had been accustomed to surround themselves, both on active service and in their civilian lives, had consisted not of army personnel, but of their own friends.[8] However one of the two Scipios, it is not clear which, was said to have employed a military guard.[9] But it seems to have been Marius who first made use of a regular military escort, when he was accompanied in Numidia by a 'bodyguard of cavalry formed of the bravest soldiers rather than of his most intimate friends' (106 BC).[10] Such guard units, whether of cavalry or infantry, came to be known as praetorian cohorts (*cohortes praetoriae*). This was because in early times Roman generals had often held the office of praetor, which was originally, before the consulship outranked it, the chief elective office of the state.

The task of the guardsmen was to intervene in order to prevent or crush mutinies, but above all to protect the person of the commander. Thus Julius Caesar, despite the impressive gesture he made by disbanding his Spanish guard, took two thousand soldiers with him when he went to dine with Cicero in his house at Cumae (Cuma) in Campania, to his host's understandable dismay.[11] And then, when he left Cicero and rode past a neighbouring dignitary's house, he ordered the whole of this guard to parade under arms on either side of him. After Caesar's death, Antony maintained a very substantial military force for his personal protection, including numerous centurions – and he accused Octavian of tampering with its loyalty. This bodyguard was said to have been six thousand strong, and the figure is not impossible when we bear in mind that later on, when for a time the two men were ostensibly reconciled, Octavian sent him a gift of two thousand picked men, splendidly equipped with full armour, to serve as praetorian guardsmen.[12] In due course Antony organized his guard into a number of cohorts. This is demonstrated by an inscription on his coinage. For when, shortly before Actium, he decided to issue a series of coins celebrating the units under his command, the praetorian cohorts are commemorated in the plural (CHORTIVM PRAETORIARVM).[13]

When Actium had been lost and won Octavian organized his own praetorian guard into no less than nine cohorts. Each contained five hundred infantrymen, divided into three maniples and six centuries of eighty men each. There was also a praetorian cavalry section of ninety men (*equites praetoriani*), consisting of three squadrons.

The victorious *Imperator* thought it best not to station more than three of the praetorian cohorts in Rome; and even for those three no permanent camp was yet established. The other six were allotted both summer and winter quarters outside the capital and around various Italian towns.[14] This was partly because he felt that the concentration of all nine cohorts in Rome would have constituted a danger rather than a protection to his life – and would have tempted other potential leaders to seduce its loyalty. Moreover, bearing in mind that the whole idea of keeping troops in the homeland was un-Republican, he was eager not to give the impression of ruling by force of arms, and so large a convergence of troops round himself might have seemed to imply this. For the praetorians, thus highly organized, already looked less like the praetorian guards of Republican generals than some guard surrounding a Greek monarch. Furthermore, in Republican times, although unofficial armed gangs had been all too painfully familiar, armed men under official military command had not normally been present at the capital at all except on the occasion of an external attack or a Triumph. Since this was now going to be changed, the change was better not made too obtrusively.

The primary duty of the praetorians was to guard the emperor, whether at Rome or elsewhere. In the city they provided him with an escort to the forum and senate, and a cohort stood on duty at the palace every day and night, changing guard between the afternoon siesta and the evening meal. While on duty in Rome the praetorians showed deference to Republican opinion by replacing their military uniforms by togas,[15] under which their weapons were ordinarily kept concealed. When they escorted the emperor to a sacrifice or a festival, they normally went unarmed. As time went on, there was a tendency to enlarge their responsibilities to the ruler considerably beyond the protection of his person. For example a praetorian cohort was normally present at performances at the theatre, where demonstrations timed to coincide with his presence often assumed a threatening aspect, and could lead to perilous riots. Moreover when there was serious fighting on the frontiers the praetorians often contributed contingents – especially when the *Imperator* himself was there, or (before long) when there was a member of his family to look after. But they were never, at this period at least, regarded in the light of a central military reserve, for nothing of the kind existed (Chapter 3).

The guardsmen were mostly recruited, Tacitus records, not very far from Rome, in the ancient central Italian regions of Latium, Etruria and Umbria.[16] Before long north Italians were added, but inscriptions and other sources suggest that only about 10 per cent of the force were provincials[17] – a considerably smaller proportion than were to be found in the legions: that is to say they were essentially an Italian force, and that is what they remained for a long time to come. 'Italy' as a meaningful term was something fairly new – a product of the first century BC in which the Social War had united the country in common Roman citizenship – and Caesar had enlarged it by adding the north Italian lands, teeming with potential recruits. When Virgil, who felt the emotive power of 'Italia' profoundly, tells how at Actium, against the eastern hordes of Antony, the westerner Octavian led *Italians* into battle,[18] some old-fashioned Romans may still have found the concept unfamiliar or even shocking. But such men belonged to the past, for Augustan thinking and writing included many a paean to the triumph won against her foreign enemies by Italy.

Indeed, as the composition of army and senate alike suggested – in both of which the proportion of non-Roman Italians showed a substantial increase – the principate could, in a sense, be described as the victory of Italy over the capital itself. But this was never openly said. What came to be emphasized instead was the identification between the two – so that there seemed nothing paradoxical about an emperor flattering the praetorians as 'the children of Italy, Rome's true warrior youth'.[19] This declaration that the guardsmen were the truest Italians, and therefore the truest Romans too, had its political dangers. Once they themselves decided to take the idea seriously, they would begin claiming that they were better able than anyone else to judge whom Italy and Rome ought to have as their ruler. However such political dangers rarely escaped the notice of Augustus: and this particular hazard provided just one more reason why he preferred to station only one-third of the praetorian cohorts inside Rome itself.

Even so, however, a bodyguard of three praetorian cohorts in the capital, amounting to over fifteen hundred men, was somewhat unwieldy viewed as a force for his personal protection. Within the ranks of the guard, as a result, there developed a special, inner corps of mounted *speculatores*.

Men of this designation were already known before Augustus's time because they had formed a regular component of the legions. Each legion normally included its own sub-unit of ten *speculatores*, acting as scouts, messengers and collectors of military intelligence. For example, a *speculator* spying for Cnaeus Pompeius junior, son of Pompey the

Great, was captured by Caesar's troops and put to death.[20] And these legionary *speculatores* still continued to exist during the empire, being especially employed for the carrying of urgent dispatches, and in addition for military police functions of various kinds. When their missions brought them to Rome, they were quartered, like other visiting or 'foreign' soldiers, in the Castra Peregrina ('foreign camp') on the Caelian Hill (*see* Chapter 8, note 69).

Meanwhile, however, a novel type of *speculatores* had also been developing. Their duties were centred upon the supreme commander himself; for example the itinerant executioners who killed the men proscribed by the triumvirs were described by this term. Antony had formed his *speculatores* into a special cohort, mentioned separately among the units honoured on his coinage (CHORTIS SPECVLATORVM).[21] In his army they were distinct from the praetorian cohorts, since the two types of soldier are commemorated under different names and on different coins. Under the emperors, however, although they proudly call themselves '*speculatores* of Caesar',[22] the central corps bearing this name belonged to the praetorian guard,[23] and, being mounted, were in effect a special reinforcement of its cavalry squadrons. These arrangements no doubt went back to Augustus himself. He is recorded to have stayed at the country house of one of his *speculatores*, and to have entertained him back.[24] These men were chosen for their impressive physique,[25] and their main task was to save the *Imperator* from assassination – that was why, as we happen to be told, one of them (not on horseback on this occasion) stood so close to his master that by mistake he nearly wounded him with his lance.[26] To preserve the ruler from assassins was likewise the task of Augustus's German bodyguard, and it might seem, therefore, that there was unnecessary duplication. But he felt safer if he had two distinct, indeed rival, groups of men devoted to this same purpose. This was partly because, in the event of an attempt on his life, if either the guardsmen or his *speculatores* happened to prove too slow, or insufficiently loyal, the other group might be able to intervene on his behalf, and ward the peril off.

This corps of mounted *speculatores* of the praetorian guard was also employed, like their legionary counterparts, for the rapid conveyance of messages and dispatches, and the provision of information, secret or otherwise, to the ruler.[27] There is also some reason to suppose that they were used for undercover activities such as espionage, arrests, the guarding of suspects and detainees, and (as under the triumvirate) the executions of condemned men. This was certainly the case in later years, and Augustus's reign saw its share of all these activities. Caesar had already done a great deal to develop military intelligence, and there is no reason to suppose that Augustus fell short of him. As regards the civilian field, although he could rely to some extent on the traditional institution of professional informers, he also had to have spies of his own, and he scarcely needed Maecenas's alleged advice that he should employ 'persons who are to keep eyes and ears open to anything which affects his supremacy'.[28] The extent to which he, like his successors, employed his praetorian *speculatores* to conduct and organize this potentially sinister necessary activity is uncertain. But it is not improbable that this was one of the functions that he required them to perform.

The praetorians were privileged above other soldiers. They always had an exceptionally good chance of catching the right eye and obtaining promotions, for example to legionary centurionates. Moreover, whereas the length of service required of legionaries was at first sixteen years and then twenty (without including their additional tenure as veterans or *evocati*), the service of praetorians was twelve years and then sixteen. And, in spite of this shorter service, they were paid considerably more than the legionaries. At first their wages were probably 375 *denarii*, while the legionaries were given 225. But then, already before the end of Augustus's reign, they were receiving as many as 750 *denarii*. Their bonuses, too, were the largest in the army. In the early part of the reign they received land settlements like other soldiers.[29] Later, when lands were replaced by cash gratuities, they were allocated 5,000 *denarii*, as against the legionaries' 3,000. In Augustus's will the differential was increased, since he left the legionaries 300 *denarii* each, but the praetorians 1,000. They were treated with this additional generosity in the will because, as the events during the next half-century were to confirm in no uncertain fashion, it was they above all others whose help would be needed to see the new ruler safely into the saddle.

All military camps and headquarters had military amphitheatres in which the soldiers could be kept amused by shows, and in the capital the praetorians were equally well looked after. At the same time, however, there were also certain disqualifications which they shared with their fellow-soldiers. For example, like the legionaries, they were not allowed to get married during their period of service. But after demobilization they were allowed, unlike all other army personnel, to contract a legally valid marriage with a foreign woman, or to legalize unions that had already been informally contracted during their service. To the existence of such informal unions, and families resulting from them, inscriptions bear witness. (They also testify to the guardsmen's possession of slaves, who were kept, like those of the legionaries, outside the camps.) The dispensation legalizing these informal partnerships meant that, after the guardsmen had been discharged, children born from such alliances became Roman citizens.[30] That accounts for the apparently anomalous fact that, unlike legionaries but like auxiliaries, they were issued diplomas when their service came to an end. This was because their unions needed formal, written sanction.

The praetorian centurions were men in whom great confidence was placed. Many of them came up through the ranks, though they could also have held centurions' posts in other branches of the metropolitan forces (*see* below, this Chapter) before becoming centurions in the guard; this became normal practice later. Once appointed to the guard centurionate, they might rise impressively through its various grades by obtaining other posts, legionary or civilian, between one grade and the next. And thereafter some of them, though not very many, were elevated to senior officer posts, or civilian equestrian offices. There were very few praetorian centurions who were not Italians.[31] They came, for the most part, from the loyal governing classes of the municipalities of Italy. These were places where, in spite of continuing reverence for ancient Roman traditions, the pretensions of the Roman senate of the day might still, even so long after the Social War was over, be regarded with something less than excessive veneration. This meant that their inhabitants' personal loyalty to the ruler, who was so plausibly claiming to restore the antique Republic, was easier to secure; and so the people of these towns became officers of the praetorian guard, upon which his safety so largely depended.

When, shortly after Actium, Augustus first established his praetorian cohorts, their highest officers were military tribunes. One of these, of senatorial rank, commanded each cohort, with other tribunes, mainly of knightly status, in support. The cohort commanders were at first under the direct command of the *Imperator* himself. The odium of stationing troops in Italy seemed less if they came directly under so august a personage, rather than under some general or another whose military power in Italy his equals would have been likely to resent.

However this arrangement soon proved impracticable. Augustus was too busy to direct the activities of the praetorians himself, and the military tribunes were not senior enough to be trusted with such large responsibilities, with obvious political implications. Accordingly, he decided to appoint prefects to take command of the guard, over the heads of the tribunes. There seems to have been no Republican precedent for this; though during Augustus's own earlier absences from Rome, when Maecenas or Agrippa had been left informally in charge of the city, it is conceivable that they were given some control over the praetorians.

The new prefects were not senators but knights. This made it less likely that they would feel a distracting loyalty to some senatorial faction. It was also in keeping with his policy of allocating some of the most important posts not only in the army (Chapter 3), but in the whole empire, to this great, influential section of non-senatorial society. Other highly conspicuous posts allotted to knights were the prefectures of Egypt (Chapter 2) and of the grain supply (*praefectura annonae*).[32] To begin with the praetorian command, though already senior to the prefecture of the grain supply, still ranked below Egypt. But over the ensuing decades it began to outshine even the Egyptian post.

The first praetorian prefects were appointed in 2 BC. They were two in number – two colleagues holding the office jointly. The initial holders of the office were Quintus Ostorius Scapula (who was later promoted to the prefecture of Egypt) and Publius Salvius Aper. This collegiate arrangement, as Dio makes Maecenas remark, had the advantage that, if one of the pair was sick, there would always be another available.[33] And the same advantage, he might have added, would apply if the loyalty of one of them was suspect.

Occasionally, in the distant future, there were to be more than two prefects at a time (Chapter 9). But, as Dio observed, this tended to lead to confusion. The initial avoidance of a sole prefect is easy to understand, since, as subsequent history would abundantly show, such an official might become so powerful that he would bring peril rather than security to his master. For this reason, throughout the whole period of more than three centuries during which the post existed, there were barely a dozen occasions on which a prefect was appointed without a colleague.

However, two of these exceptions came almost immediately, before the reign of Augustus drew to its end. For in spite of all the advantages of having joint prefects, he very quickly felt sure enough of his guard's reliability to appoint a single holder of the office – and then, after his retirement, another. The first was Valerius Ligur, and the second

Lucius Seius Strabo. The degree of eminence attained by Ligur is unknown, but Strabo, although like other praetorian prefects he only possessed knightly rank, was extremely well connected. His mother Terentia was apparently the sister-in-law of Maecenas (who had died in 8 BC), and his wife belonged to one of the very greatest families of Rome, the Cornelii Lentuli.[34]

Strabo evidently began the enhancement of the prefect's position, which was to reach its climax in the next reign when his son Sejanus had succeeded him. It was obvious enough why prefects were so important. Holding, as they did, the emperor's personal safety in their own hands, and possessing at their disposal an élite body of troops in and near the capital itself, they rapidly and inevitably came to fulfil an essential role in the inmost councils of the *Imperator*, and received his most intimate confidences. Moreover they were in a position to keep an eye on his correspondence with imperial governors and others in the provinces. For his letters to them, and their replies, were carried by the *speculatores*, who formed part of the prefect's command. The other confidential functions of the *speculatores*, such as espionage, detention and execution, were likewise subject to the prefect's direction, and added still further to his power.

The other major portion of the metropolitan garrison comprised the city cohorts (*cohortes urbanae*), which served as the police force of the capital. These cohorts were at first three in number, each containing one thousand men (later raised to fifteen hundred). Like the praetorians, they formed part of the regular army, and, like them again, they were at first billeted partly in Rome and partly in towns not far away. (There was also a single cohort at Lugdunum (Lyon), where it guarded an important mint, from which the Rhine armies were paid.)[35] The pay of these city troops by the end of Augustus's reign was probably 375 *denarii*, half the wages of the praetorians, but two-thirds as much again as those of the legionaries.

Originally the city cohorts seem to have been thought of as appendages of the praetorian cohorts, since they were to some extent numbered continuously with them. Quite soon, however, they became a wholly independent corps. This change occurred some time during Augustus's reign, but we have no idea when. It could, conceivably, have been as early as 27 BC, but a date towards the end of the reign is more likely. Perhaps Augustus, and Tiberius, who shared the administration with him during his last years, became convinced by disturbances which took place in the city during the years preceding AD 7 that such a police force was at last really unavoidable.

It was already a crying need in the later Republic. Yet senatorial opinion had then been bitterly opposed to the creation of such a force, fearing that it would merely add to the gangs that already proliferated in the city. But now the prestige of Augustus was sufficient to overcome such qualms. The praetorian cohorts were so busy guarding his own life that it was beyond their powers to police the city as well. It was to perform this necessary duty, therefore, that the city cohorts were created.[36] Theirs was the task of preventing popular demonstrations in the streets. Another of their main duties was to overawe the extensive slave population of the city, from which uprisings were still feared: and a punishment of archaic severity visited upon them in AD 61 showed how vivid such fears constantly remained. Moreover, just occasionally, as we shall see, the city cohorts were called upon to play a part in major political crises.

Each of these units was commanded by a military tribune, and in many cases these men had served previously as senior legionary centurions. The cohort commander was assisted by centurions, and both he and they could look forward to the possibility of promotion to similar posts in the praetorian guard. At the head of all the urban cohorts stood the city prefect or chief constable (*praefectus urbi*). Here the novel practice of appointing knights, which Augustus had followed in the case of the praetorian prefecture, did not seem to him so appropriate, and he therefore reserved the post for an important senator instead – a senator of the highest rank, who had served as consul. This was a conciliatory gesture to the senate, offered in the hope that they would not find the post too hopelessly un-Republican. For the same reason Augustus gave the new official an antique title, since a city prefecture had existed since very early Republican times. Its duties in the past, however, had merely been to deputize for the state officials when these attended the annual Latin Festival on the Alban Mount. The ancient custom of nominating an ex-consul for this role was revived by Julius Caesar, who appointed his cousin Lucius Caesar in 47 BC. Then two years later, when he was about to leave Italy for north Africa, Julius created a board of six *praefecti*, whose duties were not limited to the period of the Latin Festival but comprised the general administration of the city. Similarly Augustus, in *c.* 25 BC when he was about to proceed to Spain and Gaul, appointed the very distinguished and versatile Marcus Valerius Messalla Corvinus to act as city prefect, with general supervisory duties.[37] Augustus perhaps hoped that this might now become a permanent institution – and possibly that it might continue not only when he was away from the capital but when he was there. But if this was his hope, he was disappointed, because Messalla resigned after only a few days. He had no idea how to carry out his duties, he declared – and the post appeared to him to be unconstitutional (*incivilis*).[38] In other words his prefecture's somewhat tenuous links with the Republican past did not prevent him from feeling that a regular city government, with its own security forces at its disposal, displayed a somewhat sinister appearance, duplicating or clashing with the traditional administrative machinery of the state.

In spite of this setback Augustus, when he left once more for the western provinces and spent three years there (16–13 BC), again appointed a city prefect. This time he selected Titus Statilius Taurus, an eminent general with no Republican affiliations.[39] However, this still remained only a temporary arrangement: and a permanent start was not made for nearly another forty years to come.[40] Then finally, in c. AD 13 when Augustus was approaching the end of his life, the office was assumed by Lucius Calpurnius Piso, a man who, somewhat unusually at this epoch, combined highly aristocratic birth with a record of important imperial governorships and commands. After a brief initial tenure of the city prefecture – followed, we do not know why, by a short interval – he retained the office until his death nearly twenty years later.

It soon became clear that the city prefect possessed less political power than his praetorian colleague. Nevertheless he presented a more impressive façade since he was a distinguished senator and ex-consul, whereas the praetorian commander was not a member of the senate at all, but merely a knight. Furthermore, whereas the praetorian prefect apparently received his powers from the emperor,[41] the city prefects were nominally independent state officials (*magistratus*), like the consuls. As such, they, and not the *Imperator*, were the commanders-in-chief of their own cohorts.[42] They also possessed, in certain fields, their own powers of summary jurisdiction, which, as time went on, gained greatly in importance.[43] But to interpret them as agents of the senate rather than of the *princeps* would be mistaken. They were instruments of the emperor's will, just like other senior senators performing important jobs – those for example who manned the boards responsible for Rome's water supply and public works.[44] It was convenient for Augustus that his henchmen, and the chairmen and members of his key committees, should sometimes be senior senators rather than knights, so that the senate as well as his own growing personal 'civil service' should be working, and should be seen to be working, on his behalf. Upon what powers, constitutionally speaking, his orders to the city prefects and the cohorts were based, is somewhat obscure; perhaps he only gave them 'advice'. But when Messalla was appointed prefect Augustus still held the consulship: and subsequently, after the military powers of the *Imperator* had been extended to Italy in 19 BC, this may well have meant that the appointment of future city prefects was vested in himself.

Yet neither the praetorian guardsmen nor the soldiers of the city cohorts were trained to deal with one disastrous feature of the contemporary Roman scene: namely the prevalence of very serious and wide-ranging fires. In the later Republic a body of public slaves had been supposed to include fire-fighting among its duties.[45] But their resources were quite inadequate for the purpose, and in those days Rome no more possessed a fire-brigade than it disposed of a police force. When however, in 19 BC, a comparatively junior state official, Marcus Egnatius Rufus, achieved popularity by organizing a private fire-brigade consisting of his own slaves, all Augustus's customary suspicions of potential private armies were at once aroused. Egnatius himself soon came to a bad end; and meanwhile his corps had been suppressed by Augustus in favour of a body of six hundred slaves belonging to the state.

Then, after yet another particularly damaging conflagration, he effected what proved to be a permanent reorganization in this field, establishing a regular fire-brigade, seven thousand strong (AD 6).[46] These men, the Watch (*Vigiles*), were organized in seven cohorts, consisting of seven centuries each. The cohorts were commanded by military tribunes who, at the end of their tenure, were normally promoted to tribunates in the city troops. The commander of the Watch was a prefect of knightly rank, the *praefectus vigilum*, who came under the direct orders of the ruler. He was an important official, though the prefects of the praetorian guard and the grain supply ranked as his seniors.

This was the first time Augustus has assumed permanent personal control of any part of the administration of Rome. The men of the Watch were freedmen, and, by a law of AD 24, acquired citizenship after six years' service (later reduced to three). Freedmen, like slaves, were normally debarred from military service, and Tacitus's omission of the Watch from his review of the armed strength of the empire in

AD 23 confirms that they were, at least until the following year, regarded as para-military rather than as a truly military force. Nevertheless in emergencies they were sometimes transferred to the city prefect, or praetorian prefect, to strengthen the troops under his command. And in the reign of Tiberius they were to fulfil a vital role in a major crisis.

Augustus had now completed the creation of a metropolitan force which seemed adequate to deal with even the most perilous disturbances, and compares favourably with the arrangements for the preservation of law and order to be seen in many a modern city.

Part III

The Breakdown of the Augustan System

5

The Transmission of Military Power
AD 4–21

The last ten years of Augustus's life (AD 4–14), when he was ruling with his stepson Tiberius as his close associate and deputy, was an epoch of distinctive character, during which the attention of the army and the public was centred upon the delicate, gradual process of transmission of the vast Roman military power from one man to the other.

It was also an epoch from which, at first, great military triumphs were expected. For now that the new imperial army had been placed on a firm financial basis, and the home front was safely protected by effectively organized metropolitan troops, Tiberius made himself ready to launch out on fresh aggressive enterprises envisaged by Augustus's overall plan (AD 6). His target was Boiohaemum (Bohemia), which was now the home of the warlike German tribe of the Marcomanni. Under their very able monarch Maroboduus, they had migrated from southern Germany in about 9 BC, subsequently extending their control over Saxony and Silesia. Yet now that the Romans had, to all appearances, conquered northern Germany as far as the Elbe (Chapter 3), the addition of Bohemia to their conquests would mean that the imperial borders would henceforward extend roughly along a line between Hamburg, Leipzig, Prague and Vienna. When this had been attained, a great re-entrant would have been removed, and the frontier would be greatly shortened. And so a triple invasion, making use of all the armies of Germany, Raetia and Illyricum, was planned under the general direction of Tiberius.

However the entire project had to be called off. This was because of the outbreak of a huge and terrible native rebellion throughout massive areas of Dalmatia and Pannonia, the two sections of the province of Illyricum. The rebellion was due to longstanding discontentment with the humiliations of subject status. But what triggered off active resistance was Tiberius's heavy requisitioning of personnel and material for the Bohemian campaign. Moreover the rising was facilitated because Tiberius, while engaged in the subjugation of Pannonia in 12–9 BC, had neglected to ensure the permanence of his conquests by building roads throughout the interior. But above all the revolt illuminated a grave peril inherent in Augustus's new military system. For the leaders of the rebellion, and many of their men, had been trained as Roman auxiliaries. And now those auxiliaries had rebelled against the Roman government and officers who had trained them.

The suppression of the rebellion was only achieved by an exceedingly arduous series of operations, which lasted for three years and seemed to the Romans the worst military crisis they had experienced since the Second Punic War.[1] It was even being declared, amid a general feeling of panic, that an army of Pannonians could be in sight of Rome within the space of ten days. Seven or eight legions were brought to bear on the two principal theatres of operations; and they were augmented by seventy cohorts of auxiliary infantry and fourteen regiments of auxiliary cavalry. A large number of these soldiers were apathetic and threatening mutiny. Many of them were complaining that they had been kept with the colours for too long.[2] The new military treasury to provide for payments to veterans had only just got under way, and would take years to become effective (Chapter 3). And meanwhile, although there were many soldiers due for release, Augustus, in many cases, had not yet proved able to honour his undertaking to discharge them. There was no central military reserve, because he had calculated that the dangers of such a reserve would outweigh its advantages. More soldiers, therefore, were urgently needed. In utter despair[3] the *Imperator* departed from tradition by mobilizing freedmen, and slaves specially liberated for the purpose.[4] They were promised Roman citizenship and enrolled in special units of volunteers. Recourse was also had, for the first time in Augustus's reign, to the traditional but highly unpopular measure of conscription in Rome and Italy, though, out of respect for influential opinion, it was upon the section of population lacking Roman citizenship (including slaves) that the burden was made to fall.[5]

Tiberius was in command once again, and Augustus wrote to him praising his generalship in the highest terms.[6] But he included in his letter a reference to the bad morale of the army, a situation perilous not only to their fighting capacity but to himself, who might soon find their loyalty dangerously inadequate. Moreover, when the war dragged on there were reports that he was suspicious of Tiberius for delaying intentionally so that he could remain under arms, and thus be in a position to bring force to bear upon Rome. That was why (in AD 7), according to some, Augustus sent Germanicus, the twenty-two-year-old son of Tiberius's popular brother Drusus senior (d. 9 BC) to be associated in the Illyrian command. Whether this was really Augustus's motive we cannot tell. But the fact that such things were being said illustrated the hazards and anxieties experienced by a sixty-nine-year-old ruler who, on grounds of too advanced age (and too much work), was obliged, even in the most serious emergency, to delegate the command of huge forces to another man.

After the rebellion had dragged on for a full three years it was finally put down, and the whole area between the Adriatic and the Danube was reorganized. Illyricum was divided into an upper and lower province, which soon came to be known as Dalmatia and Pannonia respectively. Upper Illyricum or Dalmatia, with its capital at Salonae (Split), was now garrisoned by two legions at adjacent strategic points commanding routes into the interior, Burnum (near Kistanje), and a site at Gardun, which is perhaps the ancient Delminium. In lower Illyricum or Pannonia none of the three legions which formed the provincial garrison was yet stationed as far afield as the Danube.

Scarcely was the Illyrian rebellion over when a German rising subjected Augustus and Tiberius to an even more serious and shocking crisis. The recently conquered portion of Germany, from Rhine to Elbe, had seemed quiet enough; the latest commander of the German armies, Publius Quinctilius Varus, was entrusted with a policy of peaceful integration. But in AD 9 Varus, marching out of his summer camp near the River Weser with three legions and numerous auxiliaries, was ambushed in the Teutoburg forest or pass (perhaps somewhere near Minden)[7] by Arminius, chief of the tribe of the Cherusci. The ambush was a complete success, and Varus and his entire force were massacred. At Rome Augustus hastened to disband his German bodyguard,[8] feeling that nobody of that race could now be trusted. He was also heard crying: 'Quinctilius Varus, give me back my legions!'[9] And indeed the sudden reduction of their total from twenty-eight to twenty-five, owing

Frontier of empire
Borders of provinces
Imperial provinces and commands are indicated in capitals
Senatorial provinces in small letters

LUGDUNENSIS

BELGICA

LOW

UPPE

RA

Rhine

Da

AQUITANIA

Narbonensis

It

TARRACONENSIS

LUSITANIA

Baetica

SARDINIA

Africa

0   500
      miles

8 The Roman Empire at the Death of Augustus (AD 14)

GERMANY (Command)

GERMANY (Command)

(Region)

NORICUM

LOWER
ILLYRICUM

(PANNONIA)

UPPER ILLYRICUM
(DALMATIA)

MOESIA

Macedonia

Bithynia - Pontus

GALATIA

Asia

Achaea

SYRIA
CILICIA

Euphrates

Tigres

Cyprus

Crete

and

Cyrene

E . G . Y . P . T

Nile

to this unprecedented and wholly unforeseen catastrophe, meant not only that his impression of Germany's pacified state had proved wholly wrong, but that all his minute calculations of the total force needed to garrison the empire had gone completely astray. The unwelcome device of conscription was once again resorted to for this single occasion, as in AD 6, but this time by the drawing of lots.[10] And the hastily raised conscripts were at once sent to Germany to prevent the rebels from marching on Rome.

Yet the new recruits were not formed into new legions, so that the total number of these formations remained, for a long time, at the reduced figure of twenty-five. There were the gloomiest reports of an empire-wide shortage of manpower, and Augustus shared this deep concern. Yet he *could*, if he wished, have replaced his three lost legions – fifty years earlier there had been 200,000 Italians under arms, and to raise his own total to a similar figure, with the aid of southern Gaul and southern Spain, would surely not have been impossible. But it could only have been achieved by employing conscription on a much more far-reaching scale: and this would have damaged his personal popularity to an extent which he felt unable to risk. From a military point of view there was clearly something wrong when a local disaster, or even two successive ones, plunged the entire empire into the gravest embarrassment. But for political reasons, which had no direct bearing on the needs of military defence, the deficiency could not be made good.

In consequence Augustus abandoned his former expansionist policies altogether, and instructed his successor not to attempt their revival.[11] Maroboduus and his Marcomanni, who had escaped so narrowly in AD 6, now received a second reprieve.[12] The downfall of Varus made it necessary to evacuate the whole of northern and central Germany between the Rhine and the Elbe, with the sole exception of a coastal strip containing two tribes, the Frisii and Chauci. This evacuation turned out to be irrevocable and permanent. The fortifications of the Rhine frontier were strengthened, and the region on the Roman side of the river became a military zone, formally divided into two sections, lower and upper Germany. Each section was garrisoned by a formidably large force of four legions; and each of the two groups of legions was placed under a senior army commander. However, unlike other parts of the empire under the *Imperator*'s direct control, the two territories did not formally become imperial provinces at this stage, but remained army commands, the civilian administration of the regions being conducted by the imperial governor of the neighbouring province, Gallia Belgica.

The lower German legions had their winter quarters at Castra Vetera (Birten) and Oppidum Ubiorum (Cologne). Since two of the legions of upper Germany were stationed near by at Moguntiacum (Mainz), this meant that six of the legions of the German garrison lay in contagious proximity along a relatively short stretch of the Rhine between Castra Vetera and Moguntiacum. The two remaining upper German legions were further up the Rhine, one at Argentorate (Strasbourg) and one at Vindonissa (Windisch). Although the less defensible legionary camp at Augusta Vindelicorum (Augsburg) had been abandoned, these new locations were still too far south to serve as bases for projected invasions across the Rhine. They are indicative, rather, of a desire that two legions (separated so that they could not make corporate trouble) should be stationed not too near to Italy, but also not too far, so that the emperor could call on them if internal crises arose.

However, now that the legions available to spread round the empire were three fewer than they had been before, this massive German establishment could only be maintained by cuts elsewhere. In consequence the army in Egypt was reduced from three legions to two, and the garrison in Syria from probably five to four. It may also have been now, or partly now, that the military establishment of northern or nearer Spain (Hispania Tarraconensis) was diminished from four or five legions to three.*

Augustus had done a great deal, with success, to prevent the army from being disloyal to himself, and even the grave crises in Illyricum and Germany had only subjected its fidelity to minor strains and breaches. What he could not do, however, was to guarantee the soldiers' continued docility after his death. Indeed, what would happen when he died was, from all points of view, a major problem. He was not an 'emperor', with the implication that his role could be handed on to another. He had judiciously and ingeniously amassed in his own hands a number of traditional offices and powers, and could neither bequeath any of them singly nor bequeath his position as a whole. Even Caesar, the dictator, had only been able to adopt the future Augustus as his *personal* heir: and that was the only sort of inheritance that Augustus, too, was in a position to leave. When he was no more, therefore, it would be the easiest thing in the world for chaos to return – and the

* For the distribution of the legions in AD 20, see Appendix 1.

legions of the empire, not to speak of the praetorian guard and city troops and auxiliaries – all of which had now to be reckoned with as well – would be only too likely to become savagely warring elements in revived civil wars. This would be inevitable if an attempt was truly made to restore the Republic. And it would be equally inevitable if, without any such attempt being made, a number of rival candidates emerged to contest the succession.

Unlike many modern rulers who seem quite carefree about the deluge after their deaths, Augustus was profoundly worried about how the eventual transmission of power would come about, and he spent decade after decade trying to deal with the problem. Among other Romans feelings were divided. That he should formally nominate an heir to his uninheritable power was out of the question, since Republican opinion in the senate and elsewhere would never have tolerated such a step. Since, however, all thinking Romans dreaded the recurrence of civil war, his informal efforts to make succession arrangements that would render this less likely could expect to find a sympathetic welcome – provided that such efforts remained within the bounds of tact and tradition. And outside the ranks of those imbued with old Republican ideas there were millions who just regarded him as a Hellenistic monarch, and therefore considered it quite natural that he should train up a successor; while the army regarded a safe succession as the best, or only, guarantee that it would continue to receive its pay.

And it was on these lines, in fact, though without saying so, that Augustus proposed to act. Moreover, despite all Republican objections, he could even suggest that his intention to train up an heir was, in principle, harmonious with ancient conservative conceptions, since the Roman nobility had always regarded the hereditary succession to high office as an indispensable feature of its system. In any case, whatever niceties of constitutional thought may have been bandied around, the idea of a Julian or Augustan House gradually took shape and became accepted – especially among the legions. The idea had great value to Augustus, who used his own relatives, by blood or marriage, to conduct a lengthy succession of arduous, exhausting, military campaigns: for he felt that they were the only men he could trust with very large armies. First he made use of Agrippa in this way – but Agrippa, as a 'new man' unwelcome to the nobles, could never have become his imperial successor. Then, even before Agrippa's death (12 BC), he allotted massive commands to his own stepsons Tiberius and Drusus senior (d. 9 BC).

However, it was not they, but his own grandsons Gaius and Lucius, whom he pushed forward most pointedly,[13] making them Princes of Youth (*principes juventutis*) – honorary chiefs of the corps of the *Juventus* which supplied military training to future officers. (Their mother, Julia, did not share in their advancement, for she was exiled to an island, and one of her alleged lovers, Iullus Antonius, a son of Mark Antony, was condemned to death for harbouring designs on the throne:[14] perhaps the family of Antony still meant something to the armies.) However Lucius died in AD 2 and then Gaius in AD 4, and in the latter year Augustus, whose relations with his surviving stepson and leading general, Tiberius, had hitherto been less than satisfactory,[15] now finally indicated, obliquely but unmistakably, that he wanted him to inherit his throne. For this was surely the unspoken implication when he proceeded to adopt him as his son, so that he was known, in future, as Tiberius Caesar. However, in order that his intention should not seem too explicit, he also adopted at the same time the surviving brother of the late Gaius and Lucius, a brutish adolescent known as Agrippa Postumus. Augustus also hedged in a further fashion as well, by ordering Tiberius himself to adopt another youth, Germanicus, the scintillating nineteen-year-old son of Tiberius's brother Drusus senior who had been so greatly loved by the German legions, and had been the first to bear the name of Germanicus: he had also reputedly held Republican views. Tiberius arranged for this adoption, and even, it was said, considered making Germanicus his own adoptive son,[16] although he himself had a seventeen-year-old boy of his own, Drusus junior.

The adoption of Tiberius, although outwardly a personal and not a political event, was in truth a major turning-point. For it made it certain that the principate was going to be hereditary. That is to say, when the time came for Augustus to die, neither the army nor the senate were intended to have their say. This, then, may truly be described as a more significant landmark than AD 14, when Tiberius finally came to the throne.

Although, on adoption, he took the name of Caesar, by birth he had not been a Julius but a Claudius, one of the toughest and most perverse clans of the ancient Roman aristocracy. Other noblemen had often disliked the Claudians; and it was not only Augustus who was put off by Tiberius's grim outward behaviour. Tacitus saw Tiberius as a sinister, hypocritical tyrant, the alleged initiator of all the worst horrors of the autocracy that he himself had experienced under Domitian (AD 81–96). And he could easily find confirmatory sources for his hostile view among the future emperor's own contemporaries. It may have been in the very year of Tiberius's adoption, for example, that a certain Cnaeus Cornelius Cinna Magnus came under suspicion of plotting against Augustus's life.[17] But his real crime was the same as that of Iullus Antonius; he came of much too great a family. For this man, as his name 'Magnus' proclaimed, was the grandson of Pompey the Great himself. If a son of Mark Antony had recently felt that the advancing years of Augustus gave him a chance of winning over part of the army, then a grandson of Pompey might well harbour similar intentions (against a ruler who was now seven years older), and feel that he stood as good a chance as Tiberius. Yet Augustus, allegedly on the advice of his wife Livia, took no action against Cinna Magnus and made him consul instead. It is very possible that this conciliatory gesture was due to Livia's son Tiberius, who had Pompeian ties himself and in any case is likely to have felt that his own influence with the army was strong enough to stand minor shocks such as these.

For Tiberius was a military commander of extremely high calibre, who had endured years of splendid, gruelling service. In the eyes of many officers, soldiers and senators, this no doubt outweighed the unpopularity of his family, and his inability to make a sympathetic speech. For example one of his own officers, the historian Velleius Paterculus, who served under him for eight years in Germany and Pannonia, reminds us forcibly that Tiberius was by no means lacking in military admirers.

It was at this time that I became a soldier in the camp of Tiberius Caesar, having previously served as military tribune. For, immediately after the adoption of Tiberius, I was sent with him to Germany as prefect of auxiliary cavalry, succeeding my father in that position, and for nine continuous years as prefect of cavalry or as commander of a legion I was a spectator of his superhuman achievements, and assisted in them to the extent of my modest ability.

I do not think that mortal man will be permitted to behold again a sight like that which I enjoyed, when, throughout the most populous parts of Italy and the full extent of the provinces of Gaul, the people, as they beheld once more their old commander who by virtue of his services had long been a Caesar before he was such in name, congratulated themselves in even heartier terms than they congratulated him. Indeed words cannot express the feelings of the soldiers at their meeting, and perhaps my account will scarcely be believed – the tears which sprang to their eyes in their joy at the sight of him, their eagerness, the extraordinary delight with which they saluted him, their longing to touch his hand and their inability to restrain such cries as: 'Is it

really you that we see, commander?' 'Have we received you safely back
among us?' 'I served with you, general, in Armenia!' 'And I in Raetia!'
'I received my decoration from you in Vindelicia!' 'And I mine in Pannonia!'
'And I in Germany!'[18]

Two years after Tiberius's adoption, in AD 6 – the year of the Illyrian
crisis – taxation, famine and a serious fire produced a revolutionary
threat to public order which underlined the need of competent metropolitan troops (Chapter 4). For the masses of the population, in their
distress, 'not only openly discussed a variety of plans for a revolution,
but also posted at night an even greater variety of subversive bulletins.
Word was given out that all this had been planned and organized by a
certain Publius [Plautius] Rufus, but suspicion was directed towards
others, who were believed to be making use of his name and planning
a coup.'[19] The affair petered out. But ominous alarms and anxieties
still continued. In the next year it was felt desirable that Tiberius's
co-heir, Agrippa Postumus, whose only good quality was said to be his
massive physique, should be out of the way, and the senate condemned
him to perpetual exile. Like his mother, Julia, he was removed to an
offshore island, where he was placed under the surveillance of a military
tribune, no doubt of the praetorian guard. As Dio causes Livia to
remark, people imprisoned in places such as islands are no danger since
they cannot make contact with foreign powers,[20] or with Roman armies
in the provinces. But the possibility that such discredited and disaffected
princes and princesses might somehow obtain army support, in spite of
every precaution, was illustrated by a curious development that was now
reported. For two shady characters, Lucius Audasius, an old man who
had been in trouble for forgery, and Asinius Epicadius, a half-breed of
partly Parthian descent, were accused of an extraordinary plot. It was
said that they planned to kidnap both Agrippa Postumus and his
mother from the islands where they were confined, and then to take
them 'to the armies'.[21] Which armies the plotters had in mind (if the
story was true) we are not told. But it must be assumed that they
reckoned that these personages of Julian blood, whatever their defects,
would be more welcome to certain of the legions than Tiberius, who
belonged by birth to another family. The prestige of the house of Julius
Caesar was still pre-eminent among the troops.

Incidents of this kind deprived Agrippa Postumus of any chance of
eventual release that he may have had before. About a year after the
alleged conspiracy to rescue him, it was the turn of his sister, who was
named Julia like her mother. The husband of this Julia minor, Lucius

Aemilius Paullus, a great-nephew of the triumvir Lepidus, was charged with plotting to kill Augustus and put to death.[22] But at the same time his wife was accused of having a lover, Decimus Junius Silanus, of a family so eminent that from now onwards it was destined over a period of more than half a century to suffer almost continuous fatal casualties until it became extinct. Julia minor, like her brother and mother, was banished to an island (where she lived on, perhaps with a brief period of recall, for twenty years). For all except the destined heir himself membership of the imperial family, or even a connection with it, were disastrous, since such links might always be used to stimulate some section of the army to revolt.

In AD 13 Tiberius was granted military powers (over the provinces and armies) that were fully equal to those of Augustus himself. Their heads now appeared on either side of the gold and silver coinage.[23] The constitutional preparations for his succession – in so far as such a contradiction in terms was possible – were now complete. Then in the next year, on the nineteenth of the month that had been named after him, Augustus died.

The position after Augustus's death could not fail to be tense, but the transition went entirely smoothly, as Tiberius's adoption ten years earlier and the further steps taken subsequently had ensured. Possessing, as he already did, equal powers of command to those of Augustus,[24] once Augustus was dead he gave the watchword to the praetorian guard as its supreme commander. And in that same capacity, as Tacitus points out, he was constantly attended, from now on, by a praetorian cohort at his residence and in the forum and the senate.[25] He was careful to stress that these soldiers belonged not to himself but to the state. Nevertheless, as the historians unanimously point out, he already possessed both the outward appearance and the inward reality of power from the very moment of his predecessor's death.

He also immediately administered an oath of allegiance to the population in general – the same sort of extension of the military oath that Augustus, too, had adapted to civilians. The procedure of the oath-taking was revealing. 'The first to swear allegiance to Tiberius Caesar were the consuls of the year, Sextus Pompeius and Sextus Appuleius; then, in their presence, the praetorian prefect, Lucius Seius Strabo, and the prefect of the corn supply, Gaius Turranius; next the senate, the army and the people.'[26] The praetorian prefect, though his office was relatively new, is named immediately after the consuls –

and his precedence over both the senate and the people (like the historian's interposition of the army between them) demonstrates the shape of things to come. However one section of the army receives no specific mention in Tacitus's list. This was the corps of city cohorts. The omission of the name of their commander, the city prefect Lucius Calpurnius Piso, is strange. Perhaps the death of Augustus occurred during an interval between two successive tenures of the office by Piso; the post may even have been vacant at the time. But presumably the city cohorts were included among the metropolitan troops who swore allegiance. Nor were the legions forgotten, for at the same time *speculatores* were sent to the imperial governors and commanders in the provinces with instructions that they should administer the oath to all their legionaries and auxiliaries.[27]

The first senatorial business of the new sole reign was largely concerned with the army. For Augustus's will, when read, was not only found, as expected, to confirm the adoption of Tiberius as his personal heir,[28] but it also, during the course of a long list of bequests to the Roman people generally, specified gifts to the soldiers. The size of the sums left to officers is not recorded, but the figures for the ordinary soldiers have survived: 75 *denarii* to every legionary,[29] 125 to every member of the city cohorts and 250 to every praetorian guardsman. Not long afterwards Tiberius read out a document in which Augustus had listed the military resources of the nation, including the total strength of the army and fleet. And it was here that the late ruler had recorded his recently formed view that further imperial expansion was inadvisable.

Since Tiberius was by birth not a Julian but a Claudian, it was immediately decided that the continued existence of a Julian grandson of Augustus, namely Agrippa Postumus, presented too great a temptation to the armies, who might be persuaded to revolt in his favour. In consequence the praetorian tribune who was the young man's gaoler received orders to kill him, and these instructions were carried out by a centurion. No doubt he, too, belonged to the praetorian guard, whose officers had evidently begun their long and unsavoury career of political executions and assassinations. It has been keenly debated who was responsible for murdering Agrippa Postumus. Was it Tiberius, or Augustus who had issued the order – during his last weeks or months? Or should the blame fall on their chief adviser, Gaius Sallustius Crispus (the successor of Maecenas as *éminence grise*) – or perhaps Livia took the initiative? Be that as it may, the alleged attempt to kidnap the youth and take him to the armies must have convinced every one of them that he could not be allowed to live. And at about the same time Tiberius was said to have stopped the allowance of the elder Julia, who was Agrippa Postumus's mother. For the legions, with their attachment to the Julian house, were not likely to forget that she was Augustus's daughter, whereas Tiberius (who had at one time been married to her) contained not a drop of his blood.

Such hazards could not be allowed to endanger the new regime.[30] Indeed even without them the difficulties of starting another reign were obvious enough. It was true that in this case the vital decisions had been taken ten years earlier. Nevertheless such transitions always remained exceedingly perilous. As Gibbon observed, 'in elective monarchies, the vacancy of the throne is a moment big with danger and mischief'. And there was danger now.[31] For the situation was unprecedented, and in the absence of any traditional way of dealing with it there were noblemen quite outside the imperial house who possessed glorious ancestries and traditions of their own, and felt that the army might easily accept them as its *Imperator* quite as readily as it would welcome a Claudian. Fortunately for Tiberius there was a plurality of such potential rivals,[32] and none of them was likely to support one of the others: rather than that they would reluctantly enrol themselves among the backers of Tiberius.

Eager to dwell on the troubles of Tiberius, Tacitus, in a brilliant section of his *Annals*, gloats at disproportionate length over the embarrassing situations at the senate meetings that followed Augustus's death.[33] The dead man was duly declared a god of the Roman state like his adoptive father, Julius Caesar, before him. Next, however, the senate was compelled to take the highly un-Republican step of admitting that the new god had a successor on earth. Indeed the senators themselves, in addition to the army, had already sworn him their allegiance. They had done so, however, as individuals. As for the next step, there was general agreement – and this remained a cardinal principle for more than two and a half centuries to come – that it was now for the senate in its corporate capacity, and *not* for the much more powerful army, to perform the act investing Tiberius with that non-heritable conglomerate of powers which constituted the principate. Tiberius was the holder, as it so happened, of almost all these powers already. But since his adoptive father, until very recently, had still been alive, he, as deputy, had never yet been granted the actual supremacy – the position of emperor, as it was soon to be regarded.

During the month of September AD 14 this supremacy was decreed to him by the senate, on the motion of the consuls. Presumably their decree took the form of confirming his existing powers, without limit of time. And since the senate's decrees were technically advisory and not mandatory, the grant was made law a few weeks later by the Assembly, the organ of the sovereign though now impotent Roman people. However Augustus's special use of the title *Imperator* before his name, indicating his supreme military victoriousness, was declined by Tiberius. He modestly refrained from assuming it, now or ever – in order to minimize the invidious comparisons which, in spite of his own fine military record, so obviously presented themselves.

And indeed, throughout the period when these arrangements were being made, he had shown a certain reluctance to accept his new role. For, as he said, to occupy the principate was like holding a wolf by the ears.[34] In order to help him carry out his duties in the military sphere, he requested special powers for his nephew Germanicus[35] (now aged twenty-nine), who had already been given an army command comprising both upper and lower Germany in the previous year. On behalf of his own son Drusus junior, who was about twenty-seven, he made no similar request, since the young man was in Rome, where he was due to hold the consulate in the following year. The relative position of the two princes was left obscure. Such a duality of potential heirs occurred in a number of reigns, from the time of Augustus onwards. For all the confusion the practice caused it had certain advantages. When a ruler felt it was too dangerous to trust the large army groups to outsiders, it was helpful to have two potential commanders inside his own house instead of one. It also meant that if one of the two died or showed signs of fomenting disloyalty among the legions, another trained prince would still be available. And the inherent suggestion of the ancient Roman practice of collegiality helped to reassure the senate that the *princeps* was not going to do anything so un-Roman as to name a specific successor to the throne.

Among the legionaries this first transmission of imperial power had not gone as smoothly as seemed likely: for it turned out to have sharpened serious discontents which, for other reasons, were brewing in the frontier armies. As a result serious mutinies now broke out, in the legions of lower Illyricum (Pannonia) and lower Germany successively. The bad news from the frontiers began to arrive at Rome while the arrangements for Tiberius's accession were still being carried out. The sensational reports heightened the general tension, and emphasized that every-thing, in the last resort, depended on the loyalty of the soldiers.

Tacitus, writing over a century later, knew that the two most terrible things in the world were autocracy and civil war: and his heart was nearly torn in half by the knowledge that the second could only be prevented by the first. These are his two most solemn themes, and in his *Annals* the mutinies of AD 14 are the subject of prolonged, theatrical analysis. They are accorded this special treatment because they form an ominous forewarning of the far more serious convulsions of civil strife which were to occur just over fifty years later, within the lifetime of Tacitus himself (Chapter 7). His account of the Pannonian mutiny begins as follows:

There were no fresh motives for the Pannonian mutiny, except that the change of emperors offered hopes of rioting with impunity and collecting the profits afforded by civil war. Three legions were stationed together in a summer camp with Quintus Junius Blaesus, the imperial governor of the province, in command. When he heard of the death of Augustus and acces-sion of Tiberius he suspended normal duty for public mourning – or rejoicing. This was when insubordination and altercation began.

Before long, easy living and idleness were all the troops wanted. The idea of work and discipline became distasteful. There was a man called Percennius in the camp. Having become a private soldier after being a professional applause-leader in the theatre, he was insolent of tongue and experienced in exciting crowds to cheer actors. The legionaries, simple men, were worried – now that Augustus was dead – about their future terms of service. Percennius gradually worked on them. After dark or in the evening twilight, when the better elements had dispersed to their tents and the riff-raff collected, they talked with him.

Finally Percennius had acquired a team of helpers ready for mutiny. Then he made something like a public speech. 'Why', he asked, 'obey, like slaves, a few centurions, and fewer tribunes still? You will never be brave enough to demand better conditions if you are not prepared to petition – or threaten – an emperor who is new and still faltering. Inactivity has done quite enough harm in all these years. Old men, mutilated by wounds, are serving their thirtieth or fortieth year. And even after your official discharge your service is not finished; for you stay on with the colours as a reserve, still under canvas – the same drudgery under another name. And if you manage to survive all these hazards, even then you are dragged off to a remote country and 'settled' in some waterlogged swamp or untilled mountainside. Truly the army is a harsh, unrewarding profession. Body and soul are reckoned at five-eighths of a *denarius* a day – and with this you have to find clothes, weapons, tents and bribes for brutal centurions if you want to avoid chores.

'Heaven knows, lashes and wounds are always with us. So are hard winters and hardworking summers, grim war and unprofitable peace. There will never be improvement until service is based on a contract – pay, one *denarius* a day; duration of service, sixteen years with no subsequent recall; a gratuity to be paid in cash before leaving the camp. Praetorian guardsmen receive two *denarii* a day, and after sixteen years they go home. Yet obviously their service is no more dangerous than yours. I am not saying a word against sentry-duty in the capital. Still, here are we, on the other hand, right in the middle of tribes of savages. And you can actually see their hostile figures when you look out from our own quarters!'[36]

Tacitus may have made up Percennius's speech; for, unlike Dio Cassius describing the same events, it suits his dramatic purpose to lay stress upon these individual ringleaders. However, the Pannonian mutiny itself is an undeniable historical fact. Blaesus could do nothing against it, and had to agree to his legionaries' proposal that his own son, a military tribune, should proceed to Rome and negotiate with the new emperor. He was to demand the reduction of service from twenty years to the previous figure of sixteen (Chapter 3): and then the mutineers would send further instructions. Detachments at Nauportus (Vrhnika) looted the town, loaded their camp prefect with baggage and drove him ahead of them on long and exhausting marches, and knocked their centurions about. Then, at the main camp, another agitator, Vibulenus, cried out (according to Tacitus) that his brother had been murdered on Blaesus's orders by the gladiators whom governors kept to entertain the troops. Although Vibulenus, in fact, had no brother, the prefect of his camp and its tribunes were forcibly expelled from the lines, and their possessions were seized and plundered. Then the men turned their attention to a particularly unpopular centurion. This officer, whose name was Lucilius, 'had been given the nickname "Another-please", because every time he broke a stick over a soldier's back he used to shout loudly for another and then another'.[37] Now he was struck down and killed.

Meanwhile, Tiberius had hastened to send his own son, Drusus junior, to Pannonia to deal with the disturbance. With him were dispatched important elements of the emperor's German bodyguard, since this, following its dissolution after Varus's defeat in Germany, had now been reconstituted. Drusus was also accompanied by two praetorian cohorts, raised above their usual strength by specially picked drafts. Thus the praetorians were being called upon to escort, no longer the ruler only, but a member of what was now universally thought of as the imperial house. In command of this contingent of guardsmen was Blaesus's nephew Lucius Aelius Sejanus, who had just become joint praetorian prefect in association with his father Seius Strabo (and was later, as sole prefect, destined to elevate the office to extraordinary heights). Other leading men, too, were in the party. But 'it was Sejanus who was to be the prince's adviser, and not to let the rest of them forget what they stood to gain – or lose'.[38]

Drusus dealt with the situation effectively. With the timely aid of an eclipse of the moon, which terrified the superstitious soldiers, and with the further assistance of unceasing rain, he avoided making any immediate concessions – which, in any case, the military treasury would have found impossible to implement. Finally he felt in a strong enough position to put the chief mutineers out of the way. Vibulenus and Percennius were executed, and the other ringleaders were handed over by the soldiers themselves, or pursued outside the camp and cut down by centurions and praetorian guardsmen. Then the remaining legionaries were gradually persuaded to return to their winter quarters.

During the reorganization that followed, part of the permanent garrison of Pannonia was moved up from the south-western part of the province to Carnuntum (Petronell) on the Danube, where these troops, whose reliability was now suspect, would be nearer to their external enemies and no longer so uncomfortably close to Italy.[39] Carnuntum thus became the first legionary camp on the Danube. Farther down the river, in the eastern (lower) half of the province of Moesia which was formally created at about this time, the same process began to take place not long afterwards, when Tiberius established the first Roman fortresses on the Danube at Oescus (near Nikopol) and Novae (Svishtov). A fixed border-line on the river was now taking shape.

But meanwhile another section of the frontier on the lower Rhine was experiencing a mutiny of its own, and it was even more serious than the disturbance in Pannonia. Tacitus, that expert analyst of mass military emotion, gives a vivid picture of what happened.

At just about this time, and for the same reasons, the legions in Germany mutinied too. They were more numerous, and the outbreak was proportionately graver. Moreover they were in high hopes that Germanicus, unable to tolerate another man as emperor, would put himself at the disposal of the legionaries who would then sweep all before them. There were two armies on the Rhine bank. The army of upper Germany was under the command of Gaius Silius, the army of lower Germany under Aulus Caecina Severus.

Their overall commander was Germanicus, but he was occupied at this time in assessing the property-tax in the Gallic provinces.

Silius's legions did not regard the mutiny as their own concern and watched it with mixed feelings. But the army of lower Germany completely lost its senses. The two legions which took the initiative, the twenty-first and fifth, brought in the first and twentieth, which shared a summer camp upon the borders of the Ubii [near Cologne] and were occupied on light duties or none at all. When the death of Augustus became known the simple minds of the majority came under the influence of the masses of town-slaves who had recently been conscripted in the capital. Naturally insolent and lazy, they now argued that the moment had come for old soldiers to demand long-overdue demobilization, and for the younger men to demand an increase in pay. Everyone should insist on relief from their hardships, and retaliate against the savagery of their centurions. Here it was not just a matter of one Percennius, as in the army of Pannonia, or of soldiers nervously thinking of other and more powerful armies. This was a massive outbreak. There was a universal cry that they had won Rome's victories, her fate rested with them, and army commanders were using a surname derived from them – the name of Germanicus.[40]

In this emergency Caecina, the army commander in lower Germany, lost his nerve and did nothing. The mutinous soldiers subjected two centurions to sixty strokes of the lash, one for every centurion in the legion, and threw them out of the camp or into the Rhine, more dead than alive. Another officer of the same rank took refuge on Caecina's official dais and fell at his feet, but was dragged away by his attackers and lynched. Only one centurion, Gaius Cassius Chaerea (who later became the murderer of the emperor Caligula), fought his way through the mutineers to safety. 'Students of army psychology', remarks Tacitus, 'could see the momentous and implacable character of the revolt from the fact that its instigators were not few and far between, but there was universal, silent fury, as resolute and unanimous as if they were all acting on orders.'

Germanicus now arrived on the scene from Rome. He is one of Tacitus's principal heroes, and, although modern critics have claimed to detect in his brilliance a certain flashy superficiality, he not only enjoyed enormous popularity with his soldiers in Germany, but was revered by Romans both in his lifetime and for years and centuries after his death. The glamour that surrounded his name cannot have failed, in Tiberius's eyes, to provide a painful contrast to his own awkwardness in dealing with people – and Germanicus was not only the son of Drusus senior, so beloved by the legions, but was married to the determined, excitable Agrippina senior, who enjoyed special prestige because she was the granddaughter of Augustus. Tiberius must indeed have felt he was taking a risk when he exhibited Germanicus to the mutinous armies. For these contained strong, perhaps almost predominant, elements that wanted to reject any emperor who was not their own choice: and their choice, the historians agree, was Germanicus himself. However the young man, when he appeared among the legions, remained perfectly loyal.

But he did not deal with the mutineers as skilfully as Drusus junior had. For Germanicus only calmed them by making concessions in the emperor's name. Under no circumstances, he promised, would anyone be expected to serve for more than twenty years: soldiers who had completed this term of service were to be released immediately; and every man who had served sixteen years was to be excused from routine tasks, and strictly reserved for fighting duty. Moreover Augustus's legacies, not yet paid, were to be doubled. The men, however, knowing the condition of the military treasury, were sceptical. They did not become calm until a start had been made with putting the promised demobilizations into effect. Indeed they refused to be satisfied until the gratuities for the men to be discharged had been scraped up from Germanicus's own travelling funds.

Then Caecina took two of the legions back to winter quarters at Oppidum Ubiorum (Cologne) – where the mutiny promptly broke out all over again. This was because the soldiers whose releases had just been announced, but not yet implemented, were terrified that the promised concessions were going to be withdrawn. In the end, however, Germanicus managed to get the better of this mutineering group. In this he was much assisted by the continued loyalty of the upper German legions of Gaius Silius, which were located between himself and Rome.[41] Furthermore it was believed that Germanicus's wife, Agrippina senior, played some part in pacifying the legionaries, though her role was variously described. But meanwhile, at Castra Vetera, an even uglier situation was developing, and Germanicus got ready to transport loyal legionaries and auxiliaries down the Rhine to destroy the seditious elements. Before sending them, however, he sent notice of this impending retribution to Caecina, who read the letter privately to a number of his men he felt he could trust, including the Eagle-bearers and other standard-bearers. Then these non-commissioned officers and others, Tacitus records, sounding the men whom they thought reliable, found that the greater part of the two legions at Castra Vetera were loyal. So, in consultation with Caecina, they fixed a time at which the grossest offenders were to be struck down. At a given signal, they burst into the tents, and surprised and killed their victims. Only those in the secret knew how the massacre had begun – or where it would end.

This was unlike any other civil war. It was not a battle between opposing forces. Men in the same quarters, who had eaten together by day and rested together by night, took sides and fought each other. The shrieks, wounds and blood were unmistakable. But motives were mysterious, the outcome hard to predict. There were casualties among the loyalists too; for the culprits also had seized weapons when they realized who were being attacked. Legionary commanders, tribunes, withheld any restraining hand. Mass vengeance was indulged and glutted.

Soon afterwards Germanicus arrived in the camp. Bursting into tears, he cried: 'This is no cure – it is a catastrophe!' Then he ordered the bodies to be cremated.[42]

Such was the blood-bath that ended the ominous frontier mutinies of AD 14. Their primary cause had been Augustus's escalation of legionary service from sixteen (plus four) to twenty (plus five) years (Chapter 3)[43] – and sometimes even more. His creation of the military treasury in AD 6 would, in the end, have enabled him to rectify this grievance, but meanwhile the Dalmatian and Pannonian rebellion of AD 6–9 and the disaster to Varus in AD 9 had made any such beneficial measures impossible. It was the old soldiers who suffered. But the young soldiers too, lacking confidence in the future, joined in – including men conscripted during the emergencies, whose loyalty was below the average. Moreover, Percennius's reference to settlement in waterlogged swamps or untilled mountainsides suggests that in some cases the recently introduced system of cash payments had been abandoned in favour of a reversion to land allotments, and that these – since the former owners of the land had to be compensated – were not always generously conceived.

Nevertheless, if Augustus had remained alive, his unique prestige – despite his absence from the armies for many years – might have meant that no mutinies would have broken out at all. But his death created a situation fraught with perils, and Blaesus had compounded the danger by weakening discipline during the transitional phase. By taking advantage of this critical moment, the armies were making two significant points. First, they were giving advance notice of their decisive and disastrous future role, which was to become apparent precisely at these moments of transition between emperors, and was destined to develop from mere mutinies into major coups and rebellions, and the assassinations of emperors. And the second revelation that the army had now provided was that, although those who instigated sedition and disturbance were usually officers, this was not always or necessarily going to be the case. There had been mutinies by common soldiers in the past, even against Caesar. But now the scale had begun to be larger, and anxious Romans might foresee a time when the soldiery would get completely out of hand.

For at Rome there was the profoundest anxiety. If the mutinies had proved successful, it was said that Tiberius was ready to abdicate.[44] And perhaps he would have had little alternative. Gaius Silius, the army commander in upper Germany, privately remarked that if his own men had not remained loyal the mutineers would have pulled it off. If they had, that might have been the end of Tiberius. However it was an advantage that someone who enjoyed at least a measure of the glory of Augustus's house was on the throne, because otherwise the mutinies would have been a great deal more serious still.

Nevertheless Tiberius was strongly blamed in the capital, because he did not go to the trouble centres himself. His reasons for not doing so illustrate the dilemma facing an emperor in his relationship with his armies. If he failed to visit them, he risked losing their loyalty. If he did visit them, trouble could easily break out behind his back in Rome. There was also an additional problem: whether he went to the Pannonian or German army first, the other would be angered. Tacitus enlarges on the point, and explains that this was why Tiberius decided to send his sons instead.

Tiberius was determined not to jeopardize the nation and himself by leaving the capital. His worries were various. Germany had the stronger army, Pannonia the nearer. The former had Gaul's resources behind it, the latter threatened Italy. So which should he visit first? And what if the one placed second should take serious offence? Whereas, through his sons, he could deal with both simultaneously and keep intact his imperial dignity – which was, indeed, more awe-inspiring at a distance. Besides, it was excusable for the young Germanicus and Drusus to refer some points to their father, and resistance offered to them could be conciliated or broken by himself. If, on the other hand, the emperor himself were treated contemptuously, no expedient was left.[45]

The validity of this last argument rapidly became clear, because now that the mutinies had died down Tiberius made no move to implement the concessions Germanicus had promised in his name. Indeed in the next year he explicitly cancelled them – and henceforward inscriptions show men serving as many as thirty or forty years with the colours.

So Tiberius evidently decided that he had fared better by staying at home. For the remaining twenty-three years of his reign, therefore, he never visited his legions again – in marked contrast to his presence in their midst during so many campaigns of the past. This continued absence was hazardous, because it meant that the legionaries no longer knew him personally. However, the hazard paid off. As in the time of Augustus, who had likewise stopped leading his legions in person, they made no further trouble for the rest of his life.

After the mutinies Germanicus plunged at once into the first of three successive campaigns in which he made for the interior of 'free' Germany beyond the Rhine. These operations were, of course, under-taken on the orders of Tiberius. But they were contrary to the last instructions handed down to him by Augustus, who had specifically advised against any attempts at further imperial expansion. It was obviously desirable to make it seem that Varus was being avenged, and Germanicus duly recaptured two of his Eagles. But otherwise there was not a great deal of point in these spectacular amphibious operations. For although two victories were won against Varus's slayer – in whose tribe, the Cherusci, the Roman mutinies had dangerously encouraged the anti-Roman party – these successes led to no recovery of the lost territories. Germanicus's claim, inscribed on a trophy on the Elbe, that he had 'conquered the nations' all the way to that river from the Rhine, was untrue.[46]

The first of his expeditions, in AD 14, was little more than a rapid improvisation to take the legionaries' minds off the recent mutinies, in keeping with the military doctrine that hard work is the best way to prevent sedition.[47] The second campaign was largely designed to strengthen the pro-Roman elements across the frontier. But the massive third expedition in AD 16, was perhaps only sanctioned by Tiberius with reluctance, in order to avoid causing offence to Germanicus, so that it would not look as though the young man was being prevented from having his chance. The operations of this year are described, after a fashion, by Tacitus. Lacking the personal experience of Caesar, and writing, like other Roman historians, to display rhetorical effects rather than to impart military information, he does not usually give us a very clear idea of what happened in a battle. But his admiration of

Germanicus inspires him to present an impressive picture of the final engagement.

The Germans clamoured to fight. They were marched to a level area called Idistaviso [near Minden], which curves irregularly between the Weser and the hills; at one point an outward bend of the river gives it breadth, at another it is narrowed by projecting high ground. Behind rose the forest, with lofty branches but clear ground between the tree-trunks. The Germans occupied the plain and the outskirts of the forest. Their tribe of the Cherusci alone occupied the heights, waiting to charge down when the battle started. The Roman army moved forward in the following order: first, Gallic and German auxiliaries followed by unmounted bowmen; next, four Roman legions, and Germanicus with two cohorts of the guard and picked cavalry; then four more legions, each brought by light infantry and mounted bowmen to full strength; and the remaining auxiliary cohorts. The troops were alert and ready to deploy from columns of march into battle order.

Units of the Cherusci charged impetuously. Seeing this Germanicus ordered his best cavalry to attack their flank, while the rest of the cavalry, under Lucius Stertinius, was to ride round and attack them in the rear: and he himself would be there at the right moment. He saw a splendid omen – eight eagles flying towards and into the forest. 'Forward,' he cried, 'follow the birds of Rome, the Roman army's protecting spirits!' The infantry attacked, and the cavalry, which had been sent ahead, charged the enemy's flanks and rear. It was a strange sight. Two enemy forces were fleeing in opposite directions, those from the woods into the open, those from the open into the woods.

The Cherusci between began to be dislodged from the slopes: among them Arminius, striking, shouting, wounded, trying to keep the battle going. His full force was thrown against the bowmen, and it would have broken through if the standards of the Raetian, Vindelician and Gallic auxiliary cohorts had not barred the way. Even so, by sheer physical strength aided by the impetus of his horse, he got through. To avoid recognition he had smeared his face with his own blood. One story is that Chauci among the Roman auxiliaries recognized him and let him go. His uncle Inguiomerus was like-wise saved, by his own bravery or by treachery. The rest were massacred. Many tried to swim the Weser. They were battered by javelins, or carried away by the current, or finally overwhelmed by the mass of fugitives and collapse of the river banks. Some ignominiously tried to escape by climbing trees. As they cowered among the branches, bowmen amused themselves by shooting them down. Others were brought to the ground by felling the trees.

It was a great victory, and it cost us little. The slaughter of the enemy continued from midday until dusk. Their bodies and weapons were scattered for ten miles round.[48]

Yet even this gigantic, expensive operation led to no concrete or lasting results. After it was over Germanicus was withdrawn from the German command.

Henceforward, since it was the Rhine and not the Elbe which remained the frontier, the Rhine camps tended to become more permanent, and increasing use was made of timber to reinforce their earthen ramparts.[49] In lower Germany a barrack fortress of this kind developed at Novaesium (Neuss), which took the place of Oppidum Ubiorum (Cologne). On the whole, during the next half-century and more, the greater part of the warfare on this front, and on the Danube front as well, was destined to possess a defensive character. This was inevitable, not only because conquest beyond the rivers was virtually out of the question, but because the emperors dared neither to leave Rome themselves and command distant campaigns nor to allow other conquerors to do the job for them. Besides Tiberius did not regard it as practicable to resort to Italian conscription.[50] Yet without it, even after durations of service had become normal once again, he could not raise the large citizen forces required. And as to voluntary enlistment, he complained that it only attracted penniless vagrants.

With defensive considerations thus prevailing over the former more mobile concept of frontier policy, there gradually developed a whole elaborate network of defensive forts and supply bases, approached by a carefully designed system of communications. Yet this arrangement, as would be revealed later, bred new security perils of its own – by enhancing the local *esprit de corps* of the frontier armies until it became larger than national patriotism. Moreover the same static policy was extended to auxiliaries. These showed reluctance to be moved to provinces a long way away from their own countries; and so, to avoid trouble, they were kept more and more in the areas where they had enlisted – since the danger of discontent if they were removed apparently outweighed the danger of sedition if they remained, great though this obviously was.

Germanicus was duly awarded a Triumph, and Tiberius wrote to him as follows:

There have been enough successes, and enough misfortunes. You have won great victories. But you must also remember the terrible, crippling losses inflicted by wind and wave – through no fault of the commander. I was sent into Germany nine times by the divine Augustus, and I achieved less by force than by diplomacy.[51]

Germanicus, the letter went on, must leave his adoptive brother Drusus junior some worlds to conquer. Tacitus attributes the termination of Germanicus's German command to the emperor's jealousy. This is usually rejected, but the point is worth considering. If Germanicus had achieved great successes in Germany, then his removal from the field, certainly, would have been imperative for security reasons. For even if he himself had every intention of remaining loyal, his eight legions, flushed with victory and enthusiastic about his generalship, might well have insisted, once again, that he seek the throne for himself. As it was, however, the German campaigns had partially misfired. But once again that provided a sound reason to put a stop to the warfare – a military reason, quite apart from any considerations of jealousy.

Nevertheless, jealousy, or at least caution, could not be laid aside altogether, owing to the circumstances of Germanicus's return to Rome. While he was in Germany, two praetorian cohorts had been detached from the main corps in Italy to escort him, and serve in the campaigns – an early example of the temporary participation of these units in military operations. Now, as Germanicus, returning from the north, approached the capital, Tiberius ordered two other praetorian cohorts to go and meet him. But what happened, in fact, was a good deal more remarkable. For all seven cohorts turned out voluntarily to attend the beloved commander[52] – although he was in no sense commander of the praetorian cohorts in Italy. With the best will in the world Tiberius cannot have found this very agreeable.

After his Triumph Germanicus was given an overriding command in the eastern provinces and Drusus junior was given a similar command in Illyricum (Dalmatia and Pannonia) and probably Raetia and Noricum.[53] Tacitus delivers himself of three sneers here. He suggests that it was necessary to get Drusus away from the debauched life of the capital. He also indicates that Tiberius wanted him to win favour with the troops – as a counterpoise to the too powerful Germanicus. And finally the historian adds that Tiberius felt he would be safer if both of them were commanding armies – so that they would, so to speak, cancel one another out. However all this may be, it at least made sense that if one of the young men held a special command, the other should also. For it continued to be Tiberius's baffling, obviously impermanent, but for the time being expedient, policy that neither should be considered his heir to the exclusion of the other.

In fact Germanicus never returned from the east, but died there in AD 19. His death followed an unsavoury row with the imperial governor of Syria, Cnaeus Calpurnius Piso, who possessed less important powers than Germanicus, but had, reputedly, been told by Tiberius to keep an eye on him. When a successor came to relieve Piso, he refused to go, and waged a private war against the newcomer. Then, returning to Rome, he was prosecuted in the senate for poisoning Germanicus, and without awaiting the verdict took his own life.

Otherwise the military history of the provinces at this period consisted of two serious native revolts. One, in north Africa, was led by Tacfarinas, a Numidian who had served as a Roman auxiliary (AD 17–24). The other rising took place in Gaul (AD 21). Its leaders were tribal nobles who had inherited Roman citizenship, Julius Florus and Julius Sacrovir. The Gauls encouraged their men by declaring that the Roman army was wholly demoralized by Germanicus's death. They succeeded in seducing some auxiliary cavalry, but then the rebellion was stamped out.[54]

6

Emperors Made by the Guard
AD 21–62

There now followed a period of nearly fifty years in which the most important military development was the increased power of the praetorian guard and its prefect. This resulted, before long, in the elevation of a series of successive emperors to the throne by their agency. But first there was a prologue to this theme, in which a praetorian prefect of Tiberius became enormously powerful and narrowly missed gaining the supreme authority for himself.

This was Lucius Aelius Sejanus. While serving as joint praetorian prefect with his father Lucius Seius Strabo, he had escorted Drusus junior, with part of the guard, to Pannonia (AD 14). Less than a year later his father was transferred to the prefecture of Egypt – a transfer which at that time, officially speaking, still meant promotion. Sejanus now became sole prefect, and was in an excellent position to make full use of his political influence and social position – which was by no means as lowly as Tacitus, drawing upon hostile memoirs and his own senatorial contempt of knights, chooses to suggest.

The chief obstacle to Sejanus's ambitions was Drusus junior, because the two men did not get on; and Germanicus's death had left Drusus as heir to the throne. This was the first time a *princeps* had been given the opportunity to raise his own son to this status – and although the elevation, being foreign to the constitution, could only be implicit, it was unmistakable all the same. But in AD 23 Drusus junior died – whether Sejanus was responsible, as people said, we shall never know[1] –

and the obvious heirs now were not the dead man's own twin sons, who despite numismatic honours were far too young, at four years old, to be considered as potential successors to the throne,[2] but Germanicus's sons Nero Caesar and Drusus Caesar, aged seventeen and sixteen respectively.

The army, as always, approved of the pay guarantee represented by this continuation and continuity of the imperial house. There were members of the senate, however, who deplored such an almost overt dynastic policy as too un-Republican altogether. And Sejanus too was hostile to Nero Caesar and Drusus Caesar, as well as to their mother Agrippina senior, the restless widow of Germanicus, because he felt they would interfere with his personal aims.

For the present, as far as we know, he did nothing against Agrippina and her sons. But instead, in about AD 23, he persuaded Tiberius to take a step which enormously strengthened his own position as prefect. Earlier the nine praetorian cohorts had been distributed between Rome and neighbouring Italian towns. More recently these units had been concentrated in Rome – where they already possessed a military prison of their own.[3] They had not, however, been collected in one centre, but distributed around the city. Now they were all brought together into one barracks; and Tacitus explains the significance of this move.

The command of the praetorian guard had hitherto been of slight importance. Sejanus enhanced it by concentrating the praetorian cohorts in a single camp. Orders could reach them simultaneously, and their visible numbers and strength would increase their self-confidence and intimidate the population. His pretexts were, that scattered quarters caused unruliness; that united action would be needed in an emergency; and that a camp away from the temptations of the city would improve discipline.

When the buildings were ready, he gradually insinuated himself into the men's favour. He would talk with them addressing them by name. And it was he himself who chose their centurions and tribunes.[4]

Sejanus no doubt argued to Tiberius that the transfer of the prae-torians from their various billets into a single permanent camp would improve their discipline. It could also be claimed that their concentration in this one place would make them more effective in an emergency. As Dio put it, 'in this way the entire force could receive its orders promptly, and would inspire everybody with fear because all were together in one camp'.[5] This building covered forty acres just outside the ancient city walls, on the Viminal hill. Traces of its massive walls and gates can still be seen today, embedded in the later city wall of Aurelian. When the camp had been constructed, it appears that not

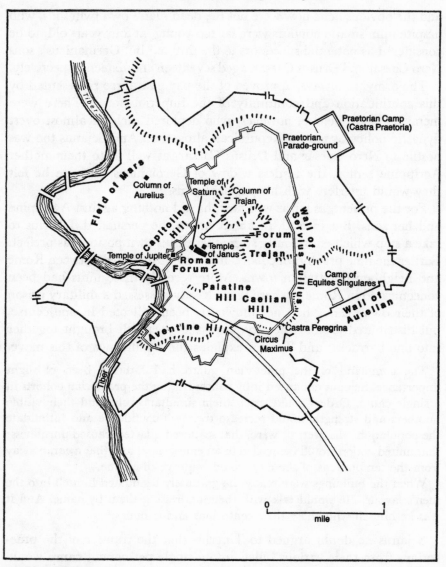

9 Plan of Rome

only all the praetorian cohorts, but the city cohorts as well, moved into this new accommodation, as well as a number of marines and sailors of the Misenum fleet who were stationed at Rome for special duties.

Clearly the main result of the change, as Tacitus points out, was to increase the importance of the praetorian prefect, Sejanus. He had already taken care to build up a party of adherents among senators and officers. His uncle Quintus Junius Blaesus, last heard of in Pannonia, was only one of a number of his followers on whom commands and honours were lavished,[6] while at the same time possible rivals to Sejanus were kept away from key posts.[7] But above all, unlike almost everyone else in the world, he had gained Tiberius's intimate confidence. The results were striking. Already in AD 20 a marriage link with the imperial house, through the betrothal of his daughter to a young prince, had been planned, though it was cut short by his prospective son-in-law's death.[8] Sejanus was also given the rank of praetor, thus becoming the first of an extremely small number of praetorian prefects to gain elevation, while still holding that office, from knightly status to the senate. As Sejanus's power precipitately increased, statues were erected to him in theatres and forums – and even at numerous legionary headquarters.[9] Indeed all the legions accorded him this honour with the single exception of those stationed in Syria,[10] where he must have failed to achieve his usual success in winning imperial governors and senior officers to his cause.

After the death of Drusus junior, when Nero Caesar and Drusus Caesar were still too young to provide Tiberius with the helpers he needed, it was not to the traditional senatorial class that he chose to turn for assistance, but to his praetorian commander. 'My Sejanus,' he called him,[11] declaring publicly in the senate and Assembly that the prefect was the 'partner of his labours'.[12] Truly Sejanus, and through him the praetorian guard which formed his power-base, had risen astonishingly high in the world. By hindsight – which is all we can achieve, since his own tame historian did not survive him[13] – he was regarded as the emperor's evil genius; Tacitus sees him as a second infamous Catiline, the sinister plotter against the Republic. But in Sejanus's greatest days the emperor, carrying his appalling burden, felt that he seemed more like a merciful reincarnation of Agrippa, the perfect helper; and he had many loyal supporters of his own who said the same.[14]

Profoundly preoccupied with problems of security, Tiberius and Sejanus had a good many influential persons sent for trial under the somewhat ambiguously expressed law of treason (*maiestas*). They were tried either by the special treason court, or by the senate, or before the emperor himself. During the whole reign it is estimated that over sixty such charges of treason were brought. This was not, perhaps, an enormous proportional increase upon the record of Augustus. But an unprecedentedly large number of these charges date from the time of

Sejanus, and are attributable to his instigation. The nagging fear, as always, was that some senator would tamper with the legions. This was a matter the praetorian prefect felt himself particularly well equipped to deal with. For once a conviction had been secured, it was convenient that he personally controlled the praetorian officers and guardsmen who could detain or execute the condemned.[15]

This is a sinister picture. Yet the suspension of the treason law, or even the failure to employ it, would have been an open invitation to conspiracy, military rebellion and assassination. For as Tiberius himself was accustomed to remark: 'Nobody willingly submits to being ruled. But men are forced to be, against their will. Subjects delight in refusing to be obedient. And, what is more, they delight in plotting against their rulers.'[16] Yet this gnawing imperial fear of revolts and plots – with an eye on the armies all the time – undoubtedly meant that Sejanus was given too free a hand. Above all he was able to rely on that recognized Republican institution, the informers. Tiberius often wearied of them, but he and his praetorian prefect made use of them all the same. When there was unpleasantness, it was convenient that they rather than he himself or Sejanus could be made to bear the blame.

In AD 25 the historian Cremutius Cordus was forced to commit suicide. This was ostensibly because he had praised the tyrannicides Brutus and Cassius, but more particularly because he had come into collision with Sejanus – who provided the prosecutors from among his own dependants.[17] And the point was brought home by an emphatic hint. For at about this time, records Dio, 'Tiberius gave the senators an exhibition of the praetorian guard at drill, as if they were unaware of the power that these troops wielded'.[18] His purpose, the historian says, was to impress the senate with his own military strength. But the inevitable result was also to remind them of the power of the prefect, which, as Josephus correctly pointed out, he directly derived from his command over the praetorian cohorts.[19]

That power reached its massive zenith when Tiberius, in AD 26, made the extraordinary decision to leave Rome and go to live on the island of Capreae (Capri). From that time onwards, although he occasionally visited the mainland, he never returned to the capital throughout all the remaining eleven years of his reign. Capreae became his permanent home, and from there he communicated with the senate by letter. This and the emperor's other correspondence was largely controlled by Sejanus, whose praetorian *speculatores*, as always, transmitted it; and he also controlled access to the presence of Tiberius himself.[20] Indeed, as Tacitus declared, it might well be said that the entire civil and military administration of the empire was now in Sejanus's hands.

From this time on the operation of the treason laws was principally directed towards removing Nero and Drusus Caesars, and their mother Agrippina. Her over-powerful position gave Sejanus both anxiety and an excuse for action. For as the widow of Germanicus she possessed great influence: and this she was said to exploit in order to provide the rallying-point for the numerous senators and officers who loathed and feared Sejanus. We are told that the imperial government now attached 'guards' and 'soldiers' to imperial personages such as herself.[21] These were, ostensibly, honorific escorts – praetorian guardsmen, perhaps *speculatores*, escorting them as they might escort the emperor. But they also sent Sejanus reports. And the reports, true or false, were passed on to the emperor – at least when they told of seditious talk.

Sejanus's campaign against Germanicus's widow and sons had been launched even before Tiberius settled at Capreae. Indeed the emperor's final withdrawal there may largely have been due to fears, deliberately heightened by Sejanus, that this family intended to kill him. Before long Nero Caesar's friends were said to be urging him to assert himself, since this was what the Roman people wanted, *and the army too*[22] – the army that had loved his father so greatly. Moreover, Sejanus's *agents provocateurs*, including no doubt praetorian guardsmen, now proceeded to suggest openly to the young man and his mother that they should take refuge with the legions in Germany.[23] For a time the presence of Tiberius's aged mother Livia, who exercised a moderating influence, prevented Sejanus from carrying out his plan. But when she died (AD 29) it was not long before Nero Caesar, Agrippina and Drusus Caesar were successively denounced, first by Sejanus and then by the emperor himself. The initial moves against Nero Caesar (for alleged homosexuality) and Agrippina (for projects of a seditious nature) significantly provoked public demonstrations, in which crowds praising them and carrying their effigies surged angrily round the senate-house itself. 'What next?' asked Sejanus. 'Before long these hordes of revolutionaries will be brandishing weapons, and hailing as generals and commanders these people whose statues they have started following like military standards!'[24] And so Nero Caesar and Agrippina were arrested and sent to islands. Within a year or two Nero Caesar was put to death or forced to kill himself. Then Drusus Caesar was cast into prison at Rome. This left, as possible heirs to the throne, the younger brother of the disgraced princes, Caligula (Gaius) aged eighteen, and one of Drusus junior's twin sons, Tiberius Gemellus, aged eleven.

In AD 31 Sejanus was consul as colleague of the absent emperor. That is to say, in effect, he was sole consul; and his other honours, too, were multiplied to extraordinary dimensions.[25] When he and his imperial colleague resigned from the consulship on 8 May he was probably granted overriding military powers, such as Tiberius had received from Augustus. Tiberius also intended to bring him into the imperial family, not this time merely through his daughter's betrothal as had been proposed eleven years earlier, but by authorizing his own engagement to the widow of Drusus junior. At this juncture, however, contrary to every possible expectation, Sejanus suffered his downfall, one of the most spectacular of all time. It was supposedly brought about, in the first place, by his proposed bride's mother Antonia, who sent her brother-in-law Tiberius a secret letter (by the hand of a servant of her own) containing fatally damaging information against Sejanus.[26] Tiberius evidently believed what he was told, and all his enormous confidence in Sejanus totally vanished – though the process of disillusionment must surely have been a little more gradual, and not so dramatically sudden as the historians maintain.[27] At all events the emperor, faced with the greatest crisis of his life, called a certain Macro (Quintus Naevius Cordus Sutorius Macro) to his aid – a man who had formerly been prefect of the Watch (Chapter 4). Tiberius told him that he was now to be the praetorian prefect in place of Sejanus, gave him orders of a highly explosive nature, and told him to go to Rome.

Macro entered the city by night, and communicated the instructions he had received to Publius Graecinius Laco, his friend and successor as commander of the Watch. Macro also took into his confidence one of the new consuls, Publius Memmius Regulus (the other was not to be trusted), and handed him a dispatch from the emperor for communication to the senate. The next morning, Macro made his way to the temple of Apollo, in which the senate was about to meet. There he sought out Sejanus, and privately told him that the message he brought from the emperor was an announcement that Sejanus was to receive the tribunician power, the supreme symbol of imperial rule. Reassured and excited by this news, Sejanus unsuspectingly went into the senate-house to attend the meeting. Macro, however, stayed outside, for he had a perilous task to perform. Confronting the praetorian guardsmen who were on duty to protect not only the senate but Sejanus himself, he disclosed to them his imperial authority, and promised them rewards if they would do what they were told. By this means he succeeded in inducing them to abandon the man who had commanded them for so long, and to return to their camp. In their place he surrounded the temple with men of the Watch, who thus for the first time were called upon to fulfil an active military and political role. They were loyal to Tiberius because, in AD 24, he had promised them that after the completion of six years' service they would become Roman citizens.

It seems strange that use was not made of the city cohorts as well. Although the absence of the emperor at Capreae had increased his reliance upon the city prefect, perhaps the holder of the post, Lucius Piso, who had been in office for nearly twenty years, was considered too old for such a crisis – his long-standing taste for drink may at last have begun to impair his effectiveness (though Seneca assures us to the contrary[28]). At all events, it was the Watch whom Macro decided to rely upon instead; leaving their own prefect Laco to direct their movements, Macro himself now proceeded rapidly to the praetorian camp, to ensure that the advantage he had precariously won with the guardsmen was pressed home.

Meanwhile the senate's deliberations started, and the consul Memmius Regulus read the emperor's letter aloud. After prolonged, verbose equivocations, the document passed on to a pathetic demand that, to ensure his endangered safety, the senate should send Tiberius a military guard, under the orders of one of the consuls, and that this should escort him to Rome. Then came a violent, amazing, denunciation of Sejanus. It took him wholly by surprise. When summoned by the consul to step forward, he rose, at the third request, only to find Laco standing beside him. Memmius did not risk a general vote – seeing that Sejanus had ensured that so many senators were his own men. Instead, he asked one senator, and one only, if the accused man should be condemned. The answer was affirmative: and thereupon Sejanus was at once taken into custody. Then, on the very same evening, although Tiberius had given no specific instructions about his fate, he was handed over to the executioner and strangled.

This bold procedure was adopted when it became clear that his praetorians were not going to do anything to help him.[29] It had been believed that his control over them was complete. Yet in the last resort they preferred their emperor to their prefect. The same choice would not always be made in the future, but on this occasion, in spite of all the disadvantages of remote control, the emperor proved the stronger of the two. Yet meanwhile Tiberius himself, waiting at Capreae, had been far from confident that his plan was going to succeed. Suetonius indicates some of the measures he had ready in case of its failure.

Distrustful and fearful of civil war, he had given orders that his grandson Drusus Caesar, whom he still kept imprisoned in Rome, should be set free, if occasion required, and empowered to take over the military command. Tiberius even got ships ready and thought of flight to some of the legions, constantly watching from a high cliff for the signals which he had ordered to be raised afar off as each step was taken, for fear the messengers should be delayed.[30]

But all was well, except for the dead man's family and friends, who were slaughtered by the new praetorian prefect Macro in a holocaust far exceeding anything that Sejanus himself had perpetrated, to the accompaniment of paeans of thanksgiving for the happy deliverance.

It was wondered in antiquity, and has often been wondered since, whether Sejanus was really guilty of a plot against Tiberius, and if so what the aims of the plot were. Clearly the emperor, in deciding to proceed against him, was not motivated by any belated regrets over the downfall of Agrippina senior and her sons, since soon after Sejanus met his end the emperor arranged that she and Drusus Caesar should be starved to death, the latter being attended, at the time, by a praetorian centurion who boasted of the brutal language he had used towards the tormented youth.[31] But Caligula (Gaius), who survived his two brothers, was old enough by now to be reckoned with, and his was the life against which Sejanus was probably suspected of plotting. He had good grounds for wanting to do away with Caligula since the young prince was unlikely, when he eventually came to the throne, to prove a sufficiently malleable master: Sejanus would have preferred the much younger Gemellus. For Caligula already enjoyed a measure of his father's popularity, not only with the populace, but among the troops. The designation by which he is known, derived from *caliga*, army boot, was an affectionate nickname they had given him because he was brought up in the German camps and even as an infant had worn military dress: there were stories that the sight of him, at the age of two, had helped to quell the mutiny of AD 14. If it was he who was the target of Sejanus's intrigues, or suspected intrigues, there was at least a measure of truth in Tiberius's own statement that he had punished Sejanus because he found him 'venting his hatred against the sons of Germanicus'.[32]

To the satirist Juvenal the downfall of this apparently all-powerful praetorian prefect seemed a classic example of that favourite rhetorical theme, the reversal of fortune.

> They're dragging Sejanus along
> By a hook, in public. Everyone cheers. 'Just look at that
> Ugly stuck-up face,' they say. 'Believe me, I never
> Cared for the fellow.' 'But what was his crime? Who brought
> The charges? Who gave evidence? How did they prove him guilty?'
> 'Nothing like that: a long and wordy letter arrived
> From Capri.' 'Fair enough: you need say no more.'
>   And what
> Of the commons? They follow fortune as always, and detest
> The victim, the failures. If a little Etruscan luck
> Had rubbed off on Sejanus, if the doddering Emperor
> Had been struck down out of the blue, this identical rabble
> Would now be proclaiming that carcase an equal successor
> To Augustus.[33]

'Such formidable servants', remarked Gibbon, 'are always necessary, but often fatal, to the throne of despotism.' Yet this first attempt by a praetorian prefect to achieve the summits of power had failed. The military were still controlled by the emperor – but only just. To him, however, and to his successors, it seemed that their most pessimistic and suspicious forecasts of the dangers which awaited them from their own commanders and soldiers were justified by the case of Sejanus. This time the perils had been avoided. But they were only avoided by a very narrow margin, and Tiberius still felt exceedingly unsafe. A senator proposed that, in future, whenever he should enter the senate, he should be accompanied by twenty of its members carrying arms. But he himself rejected this suggestion with scathing sarcasm, though magnanimously allowing the proposer to go unpunished.[34] Soon afterwards, however, he himself requested that if he came to the senate he should be permitted to bring with him a bodyguard more expert than a mere group of senators, including, that is to say, praetorian tribunes and centurions and the prefect himself. The senate passed a comprehensive resolution agreeing to his proposal, without specifying the numbers or composition of the escort, but adding that before each meeting every one of their own number should be subjected to a search. In fact, however, since Tiberius never came to Rome again, none of these measures had to be brought into effect.

His request for a personal escort of officers was intended as a gesture of confidence in the somewhat demoralized praetorian guard. The guardsmen's final reaction to the downfall of their commander Sejanus, in which they had not been called upon to play a positive part, consisted of a display of furious frustration, which impelled them to rampage around, burning and plundering. This was because they resented the implication that they had been friendly with Sejanus, and the fact that the Watch had been deemed more loyal to the emperor than themselves. In Dio's view it was perfectly true that their sympathies had been with their prefect.[35] If so, however, it was now advisable to draw a veil over this past attitude, and Tiberius, because at least they had not actively taken Sejanus's side, gave them a bonus of a thousand *denarii* each. He also added special gifts for the legions of Syria, which alone had refused to keep statues of Sejanus in their shrine.

However the emperor, although he made ample use of praetorian officers and guardsmen in the unpleasant tasks of espionage, arrest and execution which followed the alleged plot, still remained extremely nervous about their loyalty. This sensitiveness was discovered, to his cost, by a senator named Junius Gallio, when he proposed that retired guardsmen should be entitled to sit in the fourteen rows at the theatre which were habitually reserved for the knights. This proposal, though not seemingly very inflammatory, earned him an alarming letter from Tiberius.

What, wrote Tiberius, had Gallio to do with the army? They were entitled to receive their orders and rewards from the *Imperator* only. How clever of Gallio to think up something which the divine Augustus had neglected! Or was he an agent of Sejanus fomenting disaffection and rebellion – pretending to offer privileges to these politically unsophisticated soldiers, but his real aim the subversion of their loyalty?[36]

Gallio was ejected from the senate, banished and later brought back to Rome under arrest.

The prefect of the public treasury, accused of having offered Sejanus the keys of the treasury and military treasury for revolutionary purposes, committed suicide. But none of the imperial governors and commanders whom Sejanus was known to have planted throughout the empire had lifted a finger in his favour. It was true that they had not, in any case, been given any time to act. But all the same it was significant that, out of all those who were killed in the aftermath of the alleged plot, the only man of consular rank who shared Sejanus's fate was his own uncle Quintus Junius Blaesus.

However the question of the allegiance of imperial governors and senior officers was very much in people's minds. Four years after the death of Sejanus one of the prosecutors who were still assailing the dead man's friends started to threaten the powerful Cnaeus Cornelius Lentulus Gaetulicus, the army commander in upper Germany. Gaetulicus's relaxed and lenient discipline was popular with his legions, and he was well liked by the lower German army too, which happened to be under the command of his equally influential father-in-law. The prosecutor pointed out that Gaetulicus's daughter had been betrothed to one of Sejanus's sons: and it was true that the very prominent family of the Lentuli had been closely associated with Sejanus, and were gravely menaced by his fall. But Gaetulicus, according to one report, replied that he was loyal to the emperor, and that if he had made a mistake it was only the same mistake as the emperor had made himself. 'If,' he added, 'I am superseded in my command, I should regard it as a death-warning. Let us strike a bargain, Caesar: that you rule everywhere else, and that I keep my province.'[37] Whether this story was true or not the charge against him was hastily dropped, and the prosecutor found himself expelled from Rome. As for Gaetulicus, he had already been in Germany for four years, and now he remained there for another five, surviving to make trouble in the next reign.

And indeed the next reign was not at all far off; for the life of Tiberius was drawing to a close. Although some (like Sejanus) would have preferred his very young grandson Gemellus to succeed him, and although the emperor had done little or nothing to train Caligula, it was the latter, now aged twenty-five, who was unmistakably destined to succeed him upon the throne. His succession was assured because he had gained the support of the praetorian prefect Macro, who, in the emperor's old age, was even more completely in charge of the situation than Sejanus had ever been before him. When the doctor assured Macro that Tiberius would be dead in two days' time, the prefect sent out his *speculatores* to warn imperial governors and army commanders.[38] Then Tiberius died.

Caligula was at once hailed emperor by the praetorian detachment at Capreae, headed by Macro himself. He was also saluted by the fleet at the neighbouring naval base at Misenum. As soon as the news was known at Rome he was declared emperor by the senate, whose prerogative this was once again recognized to be. Later, when Caligula returned to Rome, the senate voted him, in one single enactment, the totality of the imperial powers. This was the first occasion on which such a decree had ever been passed, since when Tiberius came to the throne he had already been in possession of most of these powers, and needed only a very few more. But now, for the first time, there was a young and inexperienced emperor, who had never exercised any such powers. And so they were all granted him at once.

In spite of its outward unanimity, the senate was inwardly lukewarm about the new ruler: for most of the supporters of Germanicus's family, who would have applauded his accession, had been long since eliminated by Sejanus. The people as a whole, however, were markedly enthusiastic, and while the senate was meeting to pass its decree joyful crowds thronged round the senate-house. Moreover Caligula's succession was certain to be keenly welcomed by the troops. For not only did the army enjoy unusually good relations with the civilian population at this time,[39] so that these two sections of the Roman commonwealth might be expected to feel the same, but legionaries and praetorians alike felt special affection for the house of Germanicus. In order to please them, Caligula immediately rehabilitated his late relatives, one after another, on his coinage. The knights too, who provided the army with so many of its officers, were in favour of the new emperor, and he in turn, for the first time, explicitly associated them with the senate on his coins.[40] Oaths of allegiance were taken all over the empire by soldiers and civilians alike, not only to the new ruler but also to every member of his family, thus creating a precedent for the future.

But the new emperor and Macro felt themselves embarrassed by Tiberius's will. As everybody had surmised well in advance, it did not name Caligula as the sole heir to his personal possessions, but named a second heir also, his grandson Gemellus. There was as yet no intention of putting Gemellus to death, or at least not of putting him to death immediately. On the contrary, although there was only seven years between them, Caligula adopted him as his son, and made him Prince of the Youth, appointing his own academic and somewhat ridiculous uncle Claudius as the boy's guardian. Nevertheless Gemellus's joint personal heirship to Tiberius remained highly inconvenient to the new ruler. For it meant that the late emperor's funds would be shared between them, so that only half would remain available for all the gifts Caligula wanted to make to the army and people.[41] This was an unacceptable situation, and so, after Tiberius's will had been read to the senate by Macro, the senators were induced to declare that it was cancelled on the grounds that Tiberius had been of unsound mind. In consequence all the late emperor's property went to Caligula.

Once this had been arranged he paid out to the soldiers and people the sums that Tiberius himself had intended to leave them. These were, as far as the regular troops were concerned, the same as the bequests of Augustus, that is to say 75 *denarii* for the legionaries, 125 for the city-troops and 250 for each praetorian guardsman. Tiberius had also inserted an innovation into his will by adding bequests to the members of the Watch, who were assessed at the same rate as the legionaries.[42] This they had earned by the recent regularization of their status, and their subsequent excellent service against Sejanus. However Caligula, while carrying out these declared intentions of Tiberius to the full, also showed where he thought his best interests lay by a special gesture to the praetorians on his own account. Taking the members of the senate with him, he conducted an inspection of the entire guard, and, after watching the drilling, presented each of the guardsmen with a further 250 *denarii*, over and above the 250 bequeathed by Tiberius.

The occasion was commemorated by an issue of large brass coins displaying the emperor standing in front of the praetorian cohorts and addressing them (ADLOCVT[*io*] COH[*ortium*]).[43] Indeed, since these pieces lack the record of the senate's decree (s[*enatus*] c[*onsulto*]) which normally appeared on the brass and copper coinage, they were evidently exceptional in some way, so that it may be supposed that they probably constituted part of the actual monetary bequest itself. The coins significantly refrain from making any mention of the sums that changed hands, and this delicate omission remained a constant feature of numismatic policy throughout the entire duration of the Roman principate. It was considered respectable enough for the coinage to celebrate hand-outs to civilians in explicit detail; and in later periods it also bears many a vague reference to imperial liberality and munificence in general. But bonuses and bequests to the troops are never referred to, and it is not difficult to see why. For, in theory, all the soldiers were the loyal and obedient servants of their *Imperator*, and *that* is the aspect on which the coinage constantly dwells – particularly at times when such loyalty was not very much in evidence. In view of this propagandist stress on the fidelity of the armed forces, it was considered undesirable to call attention to the very large, increasingly large, sums which had to be disbursed in order that this loyalty should be converted from theory into practice.

Despite his initial dependence on Macro, the young emperor, who was impatient to the point of mental instability, very soon decided that he found the prefect's constant guidance boring. In consequence Macro, who seemed curiously unaware of the weakness of his position,[44] had the praetorian prefecture taken away from him, and was replaced by two joint prefects. One of them was apparently Marcus Arrecinus Clemens, who was later reputed to have done a good job.[45] The revival of the joint office meant that, individually, each of the two commanders had much less individual power than sole prefects such as Sejanus and Macro had concentrated in their own hands. However at the same time Caligula, from motives of self-protection, increased the praetorian guard itself from nine to twelve cohorts, and the city cohorts too, it would seem, from three to four.

Macro was nominated to the prefecture of Egypt, which was no longer, since the time of Sejanus, more important than the praetorian command. This proposed transfer made it possible for the current prefect of that country, Aulus Avillius Flaccus – whom Caligula hated because Avillius had prosecuted his mother – to be recalled under arrest.[46] However Macro was not allowed to set out to take his place after all; and in spring AD 38 he and his wife were forced to kill themselves. Caligula did not feel, after all, prepared to trust him with the Egyptian legions. But perhaps the real point was that Macro got on badly with the same nobles who had been the enemies of Sejanus, and Caligula may have been hoping to conciliate this large group.

Before the year was half over Gemellus too met with disaster. After Caligula had, initially, deprived him of his half-share of Tiberius's private property, his position had been further undermined when the emperor, recovering from a serious illness, had failed to name him as his own personal heir (in spite of their relationship as adoptive father and son), and had named his own passionately loved sister Drusilla instead. Now, not long afterwards, Gemellus was compelled to commit suicide. The incident throws a curious light on the professional etiquette of the military executioners, as interpreted by the emperor. For Caligula himself, who was standing by their side, instructed the praetorian tribune and centurion detailed for the purpose that they must not slay Gemellus themselves, because it was not permissible for the grandsons of emperors to be killed by outsiders.[47] In other words Caligula was insisting that even these assassins should obey the letter of their oaths of allegiance to the entire imperial house. However they were permitted to show Gemellus where he should inflict the fatal blow upon himself, and this they did. Caligula next appears to have envisaged

as his heir, not his uncle Claudius, but a distant cousin Marcus Aemilius
Lepidus, who, like himself, was a great-grandson of Augustus. And
Lepidus was now given Drusilla in marriage.

Caligula had begun to behave more autocratically than either of his
predecessors towards the senate. This might not disturb the praetorian
guardsmen and legionaries, but it could not fail to worry the senators
and senior officers who governed and commanded in the provinces. In
AD 39 Gaius Calvisius Sabinus, grandson of one of Augustus's leading
generals who won victories in Spain and at sea, had just returned from
governing lower Illyricum (Pannonia) when he was brought to trial
and forced to kill himself. He may not have been blameless of sedition,
since he had already been prosecuted on a treason charge by Tiberius
in AD 32. His wife Cornelia also found herself accused by Caligula. The
charge against her, according to Dio, was that she had made the
rounds of the sentries in the Pannonian camp, and watched the soldiers
at drill.[48] Tacitus is more detailed.

She had an unfortunate passion for inspecting the camp-site. One night
she entered it disguised as a soldier, and with no less effrontery forced herself
upon the pickets and other military activities. Finally, she had the shameless-
ness to commit adultery – in the headquarters building of all places! The
young officer involved, a certain Titus Vinius, was put under close arrest by
order of the emperor.[49]

Vinius survived to become, briefly, one of the most important advisers
of the emperor Galba thirty years later. Cornelia, on the other hand,
was obliged by Caligula to commit suicide with her husband. But the
real offence of which she had come under suspicion was treasonable
dealings with the army.

Later in the same year military treason of an unmistakable nature
was committed. This occurred in one of the huge commands of
Germany. The young emperor had already begun planning to revive
the aggressive exploits of his father Germanicus across the German
frontier, and perhaps he had intended to invade Britain as well. But in
September AD 39 he left for the north very suddenly and prematurely.
The army commander in upper Germany was still Cnaeus Cornelius
Lentulus Gaetulicus, who had been alleged, five years earlier, to have
warned Tiberius to leave him at his post, or otherwise he would revolt.
Caligula now learnt from his agents that when he himself would arrive
at Moguntiacum (Mainz) Gaetulicus proposed to have him murdered.
Probably his intention was to give the throne to Marcus Aemilius

Lepidus who, now that his wife, Caligula's sister Drusilla, had died, was believed to be enjoying a secret affair with another of the emperor's sisters, the twenty-four-year-old Agrippina junior.

Only pausing to replace the consuls of the year by two men he could trust – one of whom, it is believed, was a great general of the future, Cnaeus Domitius Corbulo – Caligula hastened north. His companions included Marcus Lepidus, Agrippina junior and his third sister Julia Livilla, none of whom it seemed advisable to leave behind. He was also escorted by part of his German bodyguard, and by praetorian cohorts: now that their number had been increased, it was possible to take some with him and yet leave a sufficient number to guard Rome in his absence. So rapidly did the party move that the praetorians, who were not accustomed to long marches, were allowed to have their standards carried by pack-animals.[50] On Caligula's arrival Gaetulicus was immediately arrested and executed. The popularity his lax discipline gave him with his troops had not been sufficient to induce them to rebel in his support. And so the first attempt to raise the great German garrisons against the central government – the prospect that each successive emperor always feared – had failed. Lepidus too was put to death, and his mistress Agrippina junior, before her expulsion to an island in banishment, was compelled by her sadistic brother to carry her lover's ashes to Rome.

The next autumn and winter were spent by Caligula in the Rhine camps and in Gaul. Certain centurions, whose conduct during the abortive revolt was judged unsatisfactory, had their discharge gratuities halved to 1,500 *denarii*. The rank and file of the legionaries, however, received a bonus of 100 *denarii* each. It may also have been at this time that two new legions were raised on the German frontier, where Bonna (Bonn) became a legionary camp.[51] Large-scale military exercises were now put into effect, to overawe the frontier tribes and restore legionary discipline. Caligula attended these manœuvres, and however unwise in other respects he may have been it was at least prudent of him to stay for a time with the legions so as to confirm their loyalty towards himself. But his enemies told ludicrous anecdotes of his military fantasies: and it is certainly true that, if he planned great German or British expeditions, they totally failed to materialize. This was largely, it would seem, because he was so conscious of senatorial unrest that he did not dare to stay too long away from Rome.

However, before concentrating once again on the affairs of the capital, he introduced two measures to strengthen his personal control over the forces of the empire. All the troops in every province were now under the command of the emperor's own subordinates, the imperial governors, except for one single legion, which was still commanded by the senatorial governor (proconsul) of Africa. Now this anomaly was removed. Senatorial governors of the province continued to be appointed, but henceforward the legion in their territory was commanded by a general (*legatus*) owing direct obedience to the ruler himself (AD 38). Moreover, in a more westerly region of north Africa, Caligula executed a client-king who had ruled Mauretania for seventeen years, and ordered that his kingdom should be converted into a province, under the control of an imperial governor or governors (AD 40). This newly annexed region (when the ensuing revolts were suppressed) provided a new and rich source of recruitment for auxiliary infantry and particularly cavalry.

When Caligula returned to Rome he celebrated an Ovation, or minor Triumph, though no victory over foreign states or tribes had been won. But he remained, with excellent reason, exceedingly nervous about his personal safety. Bearing in mind what had nearly happened in Germany, he replaced some of the officers of his German bodyguard by Thracian gladiators.[52] He was also well aware that a succession of tough actions taken by himself, culminating in the executions of Gaetulicus and Lepidus, had created a dangerous spirit of alienation among the upper class. In consequence the senate was induced to decree that, whenever he chose to be present at its meetings, he should be attended by a military guard; and that, even so, he should sit on a high platform in the senate-house, so that no one would be able to get near him.

Nevertheless at least three more plots were almost immediately launched against his life. One was in Spain. Another, led by a former consul Lucius Annius Vinicianus, was hatched among nobles who felt that Lepidus's fate sealed their own. And the third conspiracy originated inside the praetorian guard itself.[53] The first two schemes came to nothing and remained undetected, but Caligula got wind of the third and conceived a profound suspicion of the praetorians, forming a strong impression that the prefects themselves, Marcus Arrecinus Clemens and his colleague, were plotting his death. He even tackled them directly on the subject, summoning them into his presence together with a leading civilian adviser of his own, a freedman, and crying out: 'Here you are, three armed men; and I am one man and defenceless! So if you hate me and want to kill me, then go ahead and do it!'[54] After this alarming confrontation he adopted a different technique, repeatedly interviewing each of the men one by one, and trying to set them against each other.

However all these measures proved useless, because on 24 January AD 41 Caligula fell to the sword of the praetorian tribune Cassius Chaerea. Chaerea had a personal grudge against the emperor, who used to make crude fun of his sexual tastes. Two other tribunes, too, were in the plot. But it succeeded because of the cooperation of Clemens, their joint prefect. This, then, was the ominous first occasion on which senior praetorian officers murdered the emperor they were supposed to be guarding. As, in a covered passage adjoining the palace, the fatal blows were struck, the bearers of Caligula's litter tried to defend him with their poles. Then some members of his German bodyguard ran up. But, on this first occasion when they were required to perform their primary duty of protecting the emperor, they arrived too late. Nor were they able to save Caligula's wife, Caesonia, from being stabbed to death by a praetorian centurion, while her baby daughter's head was dashed against a wall.

The German bodyguard were enraged by the death of their master, which they had so conspicuously failed to prevent. They also failed to catch his murderers, but led by the Thracian ex-gladiator Sabinus, whom Caligula had made their commander, they stormed through the streets of Rome and slaughtered a number of leading senators, whether these men had anything to do with the conspiracy or not. Then the Germans charged into the theatre, in which a substantial crowd was assembled. A large-scale massacre seemed imminent, but a number of military tribunes, assisted by the powerful voice of an auctioneer who happened to be present, succeeded in calming the angry barbarians. Meanwhile some praetorian guardsmen too, who had not been privy to the plot, began rushing about Rome and looking for the murderers. But they also were somehow calmed by an eminent Gaulish senator and former consul Decimus Valerius Asiaticus, who had in fact, though the praetorians fortunately did not know it, played a prominent part in the plot.

As the German bodyguard, for all their lack of sophistication, at least dimly surmised, leading senators had participated in the murder plot. Moreover, as soon as Caligula was dead, the senate prudently moved the public funds from the treasury to a safer place on the Capitol: and there, on the very day of the murder, they proceeded to hold a meeting. But it at once became clear that they had no plan ready for the future. The consuls spoke advocating a restoration of the Republic, and the idea enjoyed some support. But it was totally unrealistic, since the army, who needed a paymaster, would never have tolerated such a move. Without a single commander-in-chief in charge, there would be military anarchy. The philosopher Seneca, who was now about forty years of age, was to show his appreciation of this when he wrote that any attempt to separate emperor from state could only mean the destruction of both.[55] Most of the other senators, too, harboured no illusions on this point. But who, then, could the new emperor be? Caligula's uncle Claudius was rejected as too preposterous a figure for serious consideration: so that for practical purposes the male imperial line was extinct.[56] Then the names began to be raised of other possible candidates to the throne, outside the imperial house: an idea which had already come to the fore before Caligula's death. Among those mentioned now, after his murder, were Lucius Annius Vinicianus, who had recently plotted an abortive rebellion against the late emperor, and Lucius Arruntius Camillus Scribonianus, the imperial governor of upper Illyricum or Dalmatia (where he will shortly be heard of again).[57]

But these discussions remained inconclusive, because it was clear enough that the attempt by any one of these men to gain the throne would have caused a bloodthirsty civil war.[58] And now the praetorian guard took matters into its own hands. For, at the prompting of their prefects, the guardsmen decided to hail a man of their own choice as emperor. He was, after all, Caligula's uncle Claudius, whom the senate had regarded as ineligible. When his nephew was killed, Claudius had run off in a panic; and Suetonius tells a dramatic tale of how his fortunes were suddenly reversed.

When the assassins of Caligula shut out the crowd under pretence that the emperor was still alive but wished to be alone, Claudius was ousted with the rest and withdrew to an apartment called the Hermaeum. A little later, in great terror at the news of the murder, he stole away to a balcony hard by and hid among the curtains which hung before the door. As he cowered there, a common soldier [of the praetorian guard], who was prowling about at random, saw his feet and, intending to ask who he was, pulled him out and recognized him; and when Claudius fell at his feet in terror, he hailed him as emperor. Then he took him to the rest of his comrades, who were as yet in a condition of uncertainty and purposeless rage. These placed him in a litter, took turns in carrying it – since his own bearers had made off – and took him to the praetorian camp in a state of despair and terror, while the throng that met him pitied him, as an innocent man who was being hurried off to execution.

Received within the rampart, he spent the night among the sentries, pleased that he had escaped death but without much hope for the future. For the consuls, with the senate and the city cohorts, had taken possession of the forum and the Capitol, resolved on maintaining the public liberty. When he too was summoned to the senate-house, by two tribunes of the people, to give his advice on the situation, he sent word that 'he was detained by force and compulsion'. But the next day, since the senate was dilatory in putting through its plans because of the tiresome bickering of those who held divergent views, while the populace, who stood about the hall, called for one ruler and expressly named Claudius, he allowed the armed assembly of the praetorians to swear allegiance to him, and promised each man 3,750 *denarii*.

And so he became the first of the Caesars who resorted to bribery to secure the fidelity of the troops.[59]

However the decision of the praetorians was unlikely to have been quite such a sudden one as all that. They did not, surely, make their first emperor entirely by default rather than by intent. For they must have been acting upon the direction of their prefects, and these had probably decided that since their own soldiers, in addition to the legionaries in the provinces, would clearly wish to have a member of the imperial house as their emperor, there was literally no alternative to Claudius. True he was accustomed to a life of learning, and suffered from a shaking head and a paralytic limp. Nevertheless he was still the brother of Germanicus and son of Drusus senior, and would inherit a large measure of their popularity.

The senate, as Suetonius pointed out, had the city cohorts at its disposal. Ten years earlier these had failed to play a part in the emperor Tiberius's coup against Sejanus. Now, however, for a brief period of time, they fulfilled a major role in public affairs, as the senate's house-hold troops. But it was a brief period indeed, for almost at once they deserted the senatorial cause and joined the praetorians. Some senators, in desperation, proposed that there should be a wholesale arming of slaves, but that too came to nothing. Then the senate dispatched representatives to extract Claudius from the praetorian camp. But he would not move. Thereupon a further senate meeting was called. Many members failed to turn up, but other suggested candidates for the throne put in an appearance – with the express intention of renouncing their claims. And now the senate capitulated to Claudius. They did so with great reluctance, because this was the first time that their right to name a new emperor had been openly ignored and contested. Such a development seemed to Gibbon to represent 'the first symptom and cause of the decline of the Roman empire'.

At all events, as on the accession of the last ruler four years earlier, the senators proceeded, with docile alacrity, to confer all the imperial powers upon Claudius *en bloc*. Like Tiberius, he was not, by birth, a member of the Julian or Augustan house but a Claudian; and unlike Tiberius, he had not even been adopted into the Julian house. Nevertheless, as a gesture to the army, he now assumed his predecessors' name of Caesar, thus setting it on its way to become a specific title denoting the imperial position. The designation 'Germanicus' he retained, since it had been part of his own name since the age of fourteen: and it was as Germanicus that he was hailed by the guardsman who hauled him out of hiding.

Yet however much Claudius needed the help of the praetorians, their officers who had assassinated Caligula could not be allowed to stay alive. For the murder of an emperor was something which, for obvious reasons, must not be encouraged or tolerated. So Chaerea was executed, and his associates likewise were removed, while the opportunity was also taken to purge other unreliable elements in the army.[60] On the other hand, as we have seen, the new emperor promised and paid each praetorian guardsman a very considerable bonus: Josephus said it was 5,000 *denarii*, not 3,750, with proportionate sums for the officers.[61] What he gave the legionaries we do not know but he gave them something. These gifts were made on his own account, because Caligula had left no will. Suetonius was justified in suggesting that this innovation set an ominous precedent for future accessions. For henceforward the troops could name the price of their support.

Claudius now began to issue two sets of gold and silver coinage, referring to the part the praetorians had played in making him emperor. One of these series of coins celebrated his admission into the praetorian camp (IMPER[*ator*] RECEPT[*us*]), and the other commemorated the oath of allegiance which the guardsmen had sworn to him (PRAETOR[*iani*] RECEPT[*i in fidem*]).[62] These issues are unique in Roman imperial numismatics and military history. No other emperor, before or after Claudius, blatantly advertised that he owed the praetorians his throne. It would have been tempting to ascribe these designs, for once, not to the directors of imperial policy, but to a momentary aberration by some mint official. But this cannot be the correct interpretation, since the same designs and inscriptions continued to appear on the coinage for a number of years. They were wholly deliberate: the emperor chose to stress and insist upon the method of his accession.

This was tough policy. Although the senate received its share of honours, Claudius knew he had not been their choice. As it happened he turned out to be a far more competent and formidable ruler than it had supposed: and, as these issues showed, he never forgot the brief but perilous interregnum when the senators had rejected him. The coins were a frank reminder to themselves, and to any other possible malcontents, that he had the praetorian prefects and their twelve cohorts behind him. Every year, on the anniversary of his accession, he gave gladiatorial games in the praetorian camp.[63] He also employed the same occasions to present the guardsmen with a further annual gift of 25 *denarii* each.[64] The coins commemorating their part in his accession may have been the actual pieces handed over at these ceremonies.

As for the legions, their enthusiasm for Caligula had somewhat waned during the course of his reign. This was the case, for example, in Germany, where his disciplinary measures against Gaetulicus and his officers inevitably caused a shock. Moreover, his failure to invade free Germany or Britain had created a poor impression. There had been indiscipline at the time; and after his death coins found in the neighbourhood of the Rhine show that his portraits were defaced. On the whole, therefore, Claudius got off to a good start with the legionaries, not only because of his family affiliations but because they were ready for a change. But their commanders and senior officers felt differently. They were senators, and could not forget how the senate had been humiliated by the circumstances of Claudius's accession.

Moreover, impulses to sedition reached them from Rome. One of the possible alternative candidates for the throne had been Lucius Annius Vinicianus. He now had an uneasy feeling that this was being remembered against him: and this impelled him to try to bring Claudius down. But he was well aware that he could not rebel alone – because he lacked that indispensable feature of any successful coup, namely military force.[65] He therefore got into touch with another of the failed candidates of AD 41, Lucius Arruntius Camillus Scribonianus, the imperial governor of Dalmatia. Scribonianus was a man who could claim descent from Pompey the Great,[66] and belonged to a family that had provided Augustus with a wife and with grandchildren earmarked for an imperial future.[67] In Dalmatia he commanded two legions, and was within easy striking distance of Rome. Like Vinicianus in the capital, Scribonianus was already planning a revolt: and the two men's plans became known to one another. Vinicianus promised the support of senators and knights, but Scribonianus evidently underestimated the supporters of Claudius, for he wrote him a menacing, insulting letter ordering him to abdicate.[68] Scribonianus also misunderstood his own troops. For when he addressed them he promised them no future emperor at all, neither himself nor Vinicianus, but the restoration of the Republic – an impracticable plan which was not what they wanted at all. Nevertheless Scribonianus persisted, and, after making his legionaries swear an oath to the senate and Roman people, ordered them to march – presumably towards Italy. Now, however, superstition was mobilized by his local opponents against him. There were religious ceremonies that must be performed before the march: the Eagles had to be adorned with wreaths and sprinkled with incense. But something, unknown, was said to be preventing this. Indeed the standards could not even be pulled up out of the ground, which was a very bad omen.[69] And so Scribonianus's soldiers failed to get started on their march on Rome. Because of these superstitious fears, and the unpopularity of their leader's Republican programme, the revolt only lasted for five days, after which the legionaries declared their loyalty to Claudius once again. Scribonianus fled to the island of Issa (Vis). There, according to one account, he was assassinated by a soldier named Volaginius, sent by the emperor. Later the man rose to a high military rank, thus showing, as Tacitus pointed out, what a successful career an army man turned murderer could now achieve.[70] Vinicianus committed suicide. The two legions that had so nearly succumbed to seduction were rewarded, for their somewhat belated remembrance of their oaths, by the conferment of the epithets Claudian, Devoted and Loyal (*Claudia Pia Fidelis*).

It had been a feeble affair; and Claudius was fortunate that it had been so badly mismanaged. But the report of these events in Dalmatia caused something like a reign of terror at Rome. A pattern relating to these matters was becoming clear. Each emperor in turn started his reign with relatively good intentions. But then, invariably, plots and military rebellions occurred, and these made him far more suspicious, severe and brutal. That a man should be popular with the army,[71] or rich or related to the imperial house, meant the end of him. Thus relatives of Scribonianus and his associates, for example, continued to be suspected, rightly or wrongly, of involvement in conspiracies at regular intervals during the half-century that lay ahead.

Claudius now began to resort to the most stringent security precautions. He made the senate pass a decree forbidding any soldier to enter the house of a senator to pay his respects.[72] He also took unprecedented steps to safeguard his own person. Everyone, of whatever age, who came into contact with him was subjected to a meticulous search. Even when he visited the sick, the beds of the patients were carefully searched for weapons. And when he went out to dinner, not only were praetorian *speculatores*, armed with lances, invariably present, but he had them wait on him at the meal, instead of his host's servants. As a result of such measures, none of the six or more conspiracies that were attempted during the remaining twelve years of his reign achieved success. These plots, and allegations of others, were said to have cost the lives of thirty-five senators and between two and three hundred knights. Such were the disastrous events set off by Scribonianus's mistaken belief that he could use the two Dalmatian legions to bring Claudius down.

However, many of these crises occurred later. Meanwhile it was the emperor's intention to remedy his lack of military glory, a shortcoming that might otherwise ultimately diminish his popularity with the army. What he proposed, therefore, was to undertake a major military aggression, in the spirit of his brother Germanicus. The enterprise he selected was the invasion of Britain, an operation which his predecessor had thought about but had then abandoned. So Aulus Plautius, the imperial governor of Pannonia, was transferred to take command of this British expedition. The army of four legions and auxiliaries which he conveyed across the Channel was not much superior in strength to the army which Julius Caesar had brought over nearly a century earlier. But it achieved much more substantial results. After winning victories (probably at the Medway and the Thames) over the forces of the Belgic kingdom which dominated south-east England, Plautius approached its royal capital of Camulodunum (Colchester). But he refrained from capturing the place until Claudius himself could appear on the scene.[73] Before long the emperor arrived, accompanied by his praetorian prefect Rufrius Crispinus and praetorian cohorts. Then, amid the cheers of his troops, he rode into Camulodunum. It had been very wise of him to come, and thus to show that he wished to command his legions in person. And the value of his own gesture was not lost on

him, since during his reign he allowed himself to be hailed *Imperator* on
no less than twenty-seven occasions. In AD 47, the centenary year of
Caesar's second visit to Britain, southern England was annexed as the
new province of Britannia, with its frontier, the Fosse Way, running
from Lindum (Lincoln) to near Isca Dumnoniorum (Exeter).

In the previous year Claudius had expanded the empire in another
direction as well. For the two client kingdoms of Thrace were annexed
and made into a new imperial province, which, like the two Mauretanias
after their pacification, increased the overall auxiliary strength of the
army.[74] On the major frontiers, however, the tendency to erect a static
defensive system became accentuated. Camps had now begun to display
stone constructions,[75] though the practice was not yet general. Nevertheless these camps were starting to assume a more permanent
appearance, and increasingly attracted traders, whose settlements
(*canabae*) outside the camps were developing into small towns. As the
legions gradually lost their mobility, and more and more of their
soldiers were recruited and served, and were then settled, in the provinces, the overall proportion of non-Italian legionaries for the first
time slightly exceeded 50 per cent.

Claudius reorganized and regularized the military career of the
knights, who now held the successive posts of prefect of an auxiliary
cohort, tribune of a legion and prefect of a cavalry squadron. That had
already been the general pattern of promotion before, but from this
time onwards it was an almost invariable practice. Such posts and the
even higher knightly offices, culminating in the prefectures of the praetorian guard and of Egypt, became such an attractive prospect that
some ambitious men preferred to renounce the senatorial career
altogether in the hope of eventually winning these prizes instead.

Meanwhile, along the frontiers, many auxiliaries were also now
stationed not far from the areas in which they had been enlisted, guarding the areas between the legionary camps. It is from the reign of
Claudius, too, that we begin to find specimens of the bronze diplomas
that were awarded to auxiliary veterans. Upon their demobilization,
after twenty-five years' service, these documents record grants of Roman
citizenship to themselves and their wives and sons. Once again Claudius
may only have been regularizing and universalizing Augustan or
Tiberian practice. But, if so, he is likely to have been very ready to do
so, since he was known to be willing enough to enlarge the citizen body.
These diplomas were preserved upon the Capitol. Under Claudius the
building selected for the purpose was the temple of Fides[76] — the

goddess or personification who stood for the loyalty of the Roman army and people.

Claudius also reorganized the fleet. Puteoli, which had hitherto been Rome's main port, and its eventual successor Ostia, where the emperor began to construct a great new harbour (Portus Augusti), received naval detachments to keep order among the seafaring populations and to prevent fires. The personnel forming these detachments was regularly moved around between these two ports and Misenum. It was also from this time that the practice of granting the marines and sailors Roman citizenship for themselves, their wives and sons after twenty-six years of service became habitual. The status of their commanders, the fleet prefects, was likewise enhanced, since the two *quaestores classici*, the young officials who had handled naval affairs at Rome, were abolished, so that the prefectures now enjoyed greater independence. Steps were also taken to integrate the posts of naval officers in a regular career, including civilian jobs from time to time. Furthermore two new fleets were created. The ships, constructed and collected at Gesoriacum (Bononia, Boulogne) for the invasion of Britain, were sent back to that port to become the British fleet (*Classis Britannica*), which subsequently had bases on the southern English coast as well. Moreover, after the annexation of Thrace, the ships at Perinthus (Ereğli), which had formerly belonged to the Thracian client kings, were taken over and formed the beginnings of a Pontic fleet.

Meanwhile, at Rome, Claudius's measures to safeguard his personal security did not prevent the outbreak of a serious crisis. Its central figure was one of the consuls designate, the rich and noble Gaius Silius, who had a grudge against the Claudian house because his father of the same name, in spite of keeping his German legions out of the mutiny in AD 14, had been forced by Tiberius, ten years later, to kill himself. Now, in AD 48, Silius became the last of a long line of lovers of Claudius's twenty-three-year-old empress Messalina – and while the emperor was at Ostia they attempted a coup, even going through a form of marriage with one another.[77] Silius calculated that the armies would not only be impressed by Messalina's descent from Augustus's sister on both sides of her family, but would also remember his own father's prestige with the German legions, which had been increased by his association, through marriage, with the house of Germanicus.[78] Perhaps Silius and Messalina intended to place Claudius's seven-year-old son Britannicus on the throne, with themselves as his guardians. In any case they seem to have won over the commander of the Watch, and the director of the imperial school of gladiators as well.

Claudius heard the news at Ostia, but was dazed by the crisis, and one of the freedmen who exercised immense power as his personal advisers, Narcissus, whose post as Minister of Letters (*ab epistulis*) gave him considerable say in strategy and defence, temporarily arranged for the command of the praetorian guard to be transferred from its joint prefects to himself.[79] He hastened Claudius to Rome and the praetorian camp, where the emperor was persuaded to deliver a brief address to the guardsmen. Meanwhile the impression spread by Claudius's return made it clear to the two chief plotters that they had thought it too easy to get the better of him. Their associates tried to disperse, but were pounced on by centurions of the guard. Silius himself was arrested, taken away to the praetorian camp, and executed. Messalina took refuge in the house of her mother. But soon a praetorian tribune and centurions arrived there, sent by Narcissus, on the ostensible orders of Claudius, to put her to death – and they were accompanied by an imperial freedman to see that they did what they were told. Then she accepted that the position was hopeless and committed suicide.

In the next year the emperor took a new wife, his fourth. She was Agrippina junior, recalled from the banishment to which she had been sentenced by Caligula. By a former marriage with a Roman aristocrat, Cnaeus Domitius Ahenobarbus (who did not belong to the imperial house, though he was a grandson of Mark Antony), Agrippina had a twelve-year-old son – four years older than Claudius's own son Britannicus, whom she intended that he should supplant as the emperor's heir. A year later she seemed well on the way to fulfilling her aim, when her boy was legally adopted by Claudius and assumed the Claudian name of Nero. Then in AD 51, at his formal introduction to public life, Nero was appointed Prince of the Youth, and allowed to head a drill (*decursio*) of the praetorian guard, sword in hand. Bonuses were distributed to the guardsmen[80] and the civil population, and the boy was permitted to appear at Circus Games wearing triumphal robes.

Britannicus, on this occasion, was still dressed as a boy. Nevertheless Agrippina was still anxious because, being the emperor's own son, he was likely to carry greater weight than Nero with the armies and in the minds of certain officers of the guard.[81] With the intention of removing these officers, she induced Claudius to replace the two joint praetorian prefects by a single commander. She explained to her husband that the guard had been split, and its efficiency diminished, by the rivalry of the present incumbents, and that unified control would mean more effective discipline. The new sole prefect, Sextus Afranius Burrus, had been selected by herself. He came from Gallia Narbonensis (southern France), and had seen service as a military tribune. He had also worked for Livia, Tiberius and Claudius in a civilian capacity.[82] As prefect, he greatly surpassed his immediate predecessors in power.[83] For example we now find him fulfilling a judicial role, under the emperor's general direction:[84] although Claudius rightly boasted of his own personal assiduity as an administrator and a judge, it may have been from this time that the praetorian prefects were called upon to bear part of the burden by presiding over civil actions, both in the first instance and on appeal.

The guard itself nowadays had some curious functions to perform. In AD 52 Claudius staged a mock naval battle on the Fucine Lake (the largest lake in central Italy, now the drained Conca del Fucino). This had been done by previous emperors as well. But Claudius outdid them all, manning the ships with nineteen thousand combatants, who presumably included numerous gladiators. Since, however, this large concourse of men might break loose and endanger public safety, their escape was prevented by the construction of a circle of rafts all round the warships. Units of praetorian infantry and cavalry were posted on these rafts behind ramparts from which they could shoot catapults and stone-throwers if the need arose.[85] The choice of cavalry seems strange, since they cannot have had their horses with them, but one must assume that they were chosen because they were expert shots.

The new praetorian prefect owed most of his power to his influence with Agrippina. Her other leading protégé was Lucius Annaeus Seneca, an eminent writer and philosopher whom she had recalled from exile, granting him a praetorship and making him tutor to Nero. In AD 53 Nero married Claudius's daughter, Octavia. Then, the following year, the emperor died; and it was generally believed that Agrippina had murdered him.[86]

She did not announce his death at once. This was because she was awaiting the propitious moment forecast by the astrologers. Like most of the imperial family she may well have believed in what they said. Besides, she deemed this precaution necessary in order to ensure the support of the praetorian cohort on duty outside the palace. For Roman soldiers, on the whole, were superstitious too. Twice, during the past forty years, their credulity had proved useful to the authorities. It had damped down a mutiny in AD 14, and it had helped to scotch a rebellion in AD 42. Now Agrippina, whatever her own beliefs, was going to make certain that it did not operate against herself. Tacitus describes what happened when the critical moment arrived.

At last, at midday on 13 October, the palace gates were suddenly thrown open. Attended by Sextus Afranius Burrus, the prefect, out came Nero to the praetorian cohort which, in accordance with regulations, was on duty. At a word from its commander, he was cheered and put in a litter. Some of the men are said to have looked round hesitantly and asked where Britannicus was. However, as no counter-suggestion was made, they accepted the choice offered them. Nero was then conducted into the guards' camp. There, after saying a few words appropriate to the occasion – and promising gifts on the generous standard set by his father – he was hailed as emperor.[87]

The transition to the new reign was smoothly managed, and in the provinces too the legions showed no hesitation in expressing their allegiance; for the army was not likely to object to the great-grandson of Augustus. But it was the praetorian prefect and guard who made Nero emperor. He was the third consecutive ruler who had to thank them for his elevation. However Nero did not, like his adoptive father and predecessor, openly publicize the dominant part they had played in his accession. Nevertheless, when he attended the senate, his speech (composed by Seneca) acknowledged not only the support of that body but the 'unanimous backing of the army'.[88] As on previous occasions the senate voted him the imperial powers *en bloc*.

But there were certain discomforts. One of them was Agrippina's interpretation of her own functions as regent – or something more than regent. Her attitude was shown by coins which actually displayed her position as more important than the young emperor's. This was a situation which, although both undesirable and constitutionally inconceivable, had to be tolerated for the present. The other current embarrassment was the continued existence of the late emperor's son Britannicus. Like others before him, Claudius, as a concession to senatorial Republicanism, had named not one single heir to his personal property but two, his son Britannicus and his stepson Nero. But since it was obvious that he had intended the latter to be his *political* heir, it was now decided that his will should not be read out.[89] For the less opportunity that was given to talk about Britannicus the better, since the support he enjoyed in the army extended to praetorian tribunes and centurions who were inconveniently conscious of their oaths of allegiance to Claudius's house.[90] Some of these supporters of Britannicus, it is true, had been eliminated, or pushed upstairs by promotion. But no doubt the feeling still remained in a number of officers' hearts. However, early in the next year, Britannicus died. His death was generally attributed to Nero, though inscriptions show that the official version, ascribing it to natural causes, was accepted in the provinces.[91]

Since Nero was still only eighteen the controllers of the empire were his former tutor Seneca, who now became his chief minister, and the praetorian prefect Burrus. They decided, as had likewise been decided on the accession of Claudius, that the new unwarlike emperor's prestige needed boosting by a major military operation. This time the theatre of war was to be the east, where Armenia, which the Romans were accustomed to claim as a protectorate, had been overrun by the Parthians. Throughout its history Rome never succeeded in its numerous attempts to win a decisive victory over Parthia. Augustus had come to a diplomatic settlement with its monarch of the day. But what Nero now needed was a military triumph; and in anticipation a coin of AD 55–6 already celebrates the Imperial Victory (VICT[*oria*] AVG[*usti*]).[92]

Nero himself, however, who liked the theatre, music, riding and dissipation, showed no interest in military activities, and did not intend to imitate his stepfather by displaying himself to the armies and camps. This refusal, as Burrus and Seneca knew, might prove a great disadvantage. Nevertheless the emperor's temperament could not be changed, and there was no other member of his family to take on the eastern command. It was therefore entrusted to a leading general, Cnaeus Domitius Corbulo, who could not claim membership of the imperial house. Nevertheless, his connections were impressive. His wife may have belonged to the great family of the Cassii, and through his mother, too, who had married six times, he could boast of a large number of important relations. Indeed, one of his half-sisters had been an empress, Caesonia, the wife of Caligula – and that emperor, during his absence in the north, had apparently left Corbulo himself in joint charge of the capital. Then, under Claudius, he had served as army commander in lower Germany, where he fought successfully against the tribe of the Chauci. He left Germany with the reputation of a formidable martinet; this was the only way in which peace-time generals could make a name, and his firm discipline was said to have proved an inspiration to his men.[93] That is not impossible, since Roman legionaries often responded even to the toughest treatment from generals who devoted themselves seriously to their welfare. However it is difficult to obtain a reliable impression of what sort of man Corbulo really was, because Tacitus selected him as one of his model heroes who could do no wrong. This the historian did for two reasons. First, as a conservative senator, he admired military men of the old strict school. Second, Corbulo collaborated obediently with an emperor whom Tacitus regarded as evil. Later, both Tacitus and Trajan, the emperor in whose reign he was writing, acted likewise, when Domitian was on the throne. Tacitus therefore reserved his highest praises for others who had struggled on in the same way – and prominent among them was Corbulo, who loyally served Nero.

In order to deal with the Parthians, Corbulo was entrusted with a special, unprecedented governorship and command, comprising two extensive provinces of central and eastern Asia Minor, Galatia and the frontier district of Cappadocia (annexed in AD 17). Nothing important, however, happened in his command until AD 58, by which time he had finished subjecting the rather slack eastern armies to a reorganization which earned paeans of admiration from Tacitus.

Corbulo found his own men's slackness a worse trouble than enemy treachery. His troops had come from Syria. Demoralized by years of peace, they took badly to service conditions. The army actually contained old soldiers who had never been on guard or march, who found ramparts and ditches strange novelties, and who owned neither helmet nor breastplate – flashy money-makers who had soldiered in towns. Corbulo discharged men who were too old or too weak, and filled their places with Galatian and Cappadocian recruits, augmented by a legion from Germany with auxiliary infantry and cavalry.

The whole army was kept under canvas through a winter so severe that ice had to be removed and the ground excavated before tents could be pitched. Frostbite caused many losses of limbs. Sentries were frozen to death. A soldier was seen carrying a bundle of firewood with hands so frozen that they fell off, fastened to their load. Meanwhile Corbulo himself, thinly dressed and bare-headed, moved among his men at work and on the march, encouraging the sick and praising efficiency – an example to all. All the same the harsh climate and service produced shirkers and deserters in considerable numbers. Corbulo's remedy was severity. In other armies first and second offences were excused: Corbulo, on the other hand, executed deserters immediately. Results showed that this was salutary and preferable to indulgence. For he had fewer deserters than lenient commanders.[94]

Conscription, too, was resorted to in the provinces in order to bring Corbulo's army up to full strength. Then finally, after exerting the patience which was his main quality as a general, he overran Armenia. However, after he had subsequently been removed from the theatre of operations, on transfer to the imperial governorship of Syria, Armenia was lost to the Parthians once again, and a Roman general suffered a disaster there. As a result Corbulo found himself invested with an even more important command than before, comprising overall control in the east. After moving into action against the Parthians for a second time, he was authorized by the emperor to come to terms with them (AD 63). According to this agreement, which proved remarkably durable, the Armenian monarch, Tiridates, was to be recognized by both of the great powers, Rome and Parthia alike.

While Corbulo was fighting, a native rebellion had broken out in Britain. The rebel monarch, Queen Boudicca ('Boadicea') of the Iceni (in East Anglia), sacked the towns of Camulodunum (Colchester), Londinium (London) and Verulamium (St Albans) before the imperial governor Gaius Suetonius Paulinus succeeded in gaining the upper hand (AD 60). His victory showed what a good general and his legionaries could do against a vastly superior force.[95]

Meanwhile, as the emperor began to assert his increasing determination to become independent of everyone likely to want to thwart him, Agrippina's influence had waned with great speed. She took this badly, and there were serious reasons to suppose that she hoped to work up military and other elements against her son, including, it was said, the city cohorts, or praetorian cohorts, or both.[96] Before Britannicus's death she had already reputedly declared that she would herself conduct him to the praetorian camp as an alternative to her son. Then, after Britannicus was dead, she began to show an unhealthy concern for the welfare of his sister Octavia, who was estranged from her husband Nero but had inherited some of her father's popularity with the army and the guard.

Agrippina also sneered at the praetorian prefect Burrus, referring in unpleasant terms to his deformity, since he had a crippled hand. Whether or not he had been wholeheartedly dependent on her before, he was nowadays her protégé no longer. And as to her relations with her son, to whom Burrus stood so close, their mutual suspicions were rising sharply and dangerously: and this may have been the time when the emperor began to surround himself with a bodyguard of knights.[97] Tacitus describes how matters came to a head.

Constantly meeting her own friends in secret, Agrippina outdid even her natural greed in grasping funds from all quarters to back her designs. She was gracious to military tribunes and centurions and attentive to such able and high-ranking noblemen as survived. She seemed to be looking round for a party of supporters – and for a leader of that party as well. Learning of these developments, Nero withdrew the praetorian detachment which she had been given as her bodyguard while her husband was still the emperor, and which she had retained when her son succeeded to the throne. He also withdrew the German guardsmen by which, as an additional compliment, this bodyguard had recently been strengthened. Furthermore, he succeeded in terminating her great receptions, by giving her a separate residence in the mansion formerly occupied by Antonia, the wife of Drusus senior. When he visited her there, an escort of praetorian centurions would accompany him, and he would hurriedly embrace her, and then leave at once.

The veneration people feel for another person's great position, if this has no force behind it, is the most precarious and transient thing in the world. Agrippina's house was immediately deserted. Her only visitors and comforters were a few women. They went to her because they loved her – or their motive may have been hatred.[98]

The change was violent – though not so sudden as the historian suggests, since the tense situation dragged on for another four years, gradually deteriorating all the time. Finally Nero, convinced that his mother would whip up the army or arm her own slaves, arranged for her to be assassinated (AD 59). Tacitus's description of the murder is replete with melodrama – not all of it entirely credible. However, his indication that Nero had the deed done by the fleet prefect at Misenum, a freedman of the name of Anicetus who had formerly been one of his teachers, seems to be correct. Anicetus enlisted the support of a naval squadron commander, Volusius Proculus. But the truth or otherwise of Tacitus's extraordinary story that they tried to kill her in a collapsible ship is beyond recall. At all events it was at her house beside the Bay of Naples that Anicetus, accompanied by a ship's captain and a centurion, finished her off. Whether Burrus and Seneca had been cognizant of the original scheme to murder Agrippina is uncertain. But before it was finally put into effect, they apparently became accomplices in the plan. However Burrus was said to have warned Nero that praetorian guardsmen could not be entrusted with the assassination, since they were devoted (or possibly he meant 'bound by oath') to the whole imperial house and to Germanicus's memory – so that they could not be expected to commit violence against his offspring. In consequence it was Anicetus, upon whom, as an ex-slave, the burden of his military oath perhaps lay more lightly, who had to perform the murder.

Nero was anxious about how the news would be received. But as Tacitus records, he was soon reassured. 'Hope began to return to him when at Burrus's suggestion the tribunes and centurions of the guard came and cringed to him, with congratulatory handclasps for his escape from the unexpected menace of his mother's evil activities.'[99] Before long, the emperor summoned up the courage to communicate with the senate:

The gist of his letter to them was that Agerinus, a confidential ex-slave of Agrippina, had been caught carrying a sword about to murder him, and that she, conscious of her guilt as instigator of the crime, had paid the penalty. He added older charges. 'She had wanted to be co-ruler – to receive oaths of allegiance from the praetorian cohorts, and to subject senate and public to the same humiliation. Disappointed of this, she had hated the whole lot of them – army, senate and people alike. She had opposed the awards of bonuses both to soldiers and civilians. She had also contrived the deaths of distinguished men.' Only with the utmost difficulty, added Nero, had he prevented her from breaking into the senate-house and delivering verdicts to foreign envoys. He also indirectly attacked Claudius's regime blaming his mother for all its scandals. Her death, he concluded, was a national blessing.[100]

The messages of congratulation that poured in from all sides showed that most people agreed with this assessment. The murder of Agrippina apparently did nothing to upset Nero's prestige among the troops. As to the navy, the only trouble was unimportant: one of the senior naval officers concerned, Volusius Proculus, later turned against the emperor, on the grounds that his services had not been rewarded by adequate promotion. Nero's relations with the praetorian guard – to whom he prudently presented a bonus after the murder – survived the incident undamaged. Indeed, later in the same year, when he indulged his personal tastes by organizing Youth Games (*Juvenalia*) of a dramatic and musical nature, a praetorian cohort was present with its tribunes and centurions, and the prefect Burrus himself put in an appearance as well.

The praetorians had a good deal of this kind of work to do for Nero. When he was younger the guardsmen (accompanied by gladiators) had attended him on his nocturnal debauches round the city. Now they reported for duty at his dramatic and musical performances. It had long been customary for a cohort to maintain order at the games. At first Nero ordered that these soldiers should be withdrawn, since he wanted to test how the public would behave. But it behaved badly, so the praetorians were ordered to police the games once again. When the emperor was performing himself, as increasingly occurred, they had particular responsibilities. For on those occasions praetorian guardsmen were seen strolling among the huge crowds and cuffing those who applauded inadequately or out of time. He also allowed them to participate in some of the shows themselves. For example at an animal hunt arranged for the people of Rome, the praetorian cavalry took on four hundred boars and three hundred lions. Enjoying this sort of limelight, the guardsmen bestowed many a compliment upon their emperor. Later the coinage recorded this close relation between the emperor and the guard, and gave it a more appropriately military tone, by displaying him galloping with the prefect at the annual praetorian manœuvres or ceremonial ride (DECVRSIO).[101] It is doubtful if, since the age of fourteen, he had ever undertaken this exertion, but the design possessed at least a measure of plausibility, because riding was one of his principal amusements.

Nero had some more adventurous tasks to entrust to the praetorians as well. For example he sent two of their officers and a party of guardsmen on a mission of geographical and political exploration in Africa. This took them across the southern frontier of the empire and right down into the central Sudan, where they were instructed to investigate the possibility of closer alliances with the local kingdoms.[102] Later the praetorians are found performing a task that they must have found less glamorous. For when Nero embarked on an abortive scheme to cut a Corinth canal, it was they who began digging it for him, though the project was abandoned after his death.

In AD 61 the praetorian commander's senatorial colleague, the city prefect, came into an unsavoury prominence that cost him his life. For this man, Lucius Pedanius Secundus – a Spanish compatriot of Seneca – succumbed to murder at the hands of one of his own slaves (who was rumoured to be his rival in a homosexual affair). According to ancient custom that meant that all the slaves residing under the same roof, who were numerous, had to be executed. This barbarous institution recalled the terrified fear of slave uprisings that was still deeply engrained in Roman hearts. Indeed the original plan to create the city cohorts, of which Pedanius himself, ironically enough, was in charge, had largely been conceived with precisely the object of keeping the slaves down. But there were a number of occasions in imperial history when the Roman populace displayed humanitarian feelings, and this proved to be one of them. For when it became known that the archaic sentence was going to be carried out, large menacing crowds collected and rioting began. After an emergency debate the senate decided against leniency, and the crowds became uglier still. Finally Nero, rebuking the population by edict, lined troops on either side of the entire route along which the condemned slaves were to be taken for execution. What troops he employed is not recorded. In other conditions the city cohorts would have been appropriate. However, owing to the embarrassing circumstance that the man whose slaves were being executed was their commander, he probably called on Burrus to provide praetorian guardsmen instead.

If so, it was one of Burrus's last services, since in the following year he died. Despite the usual stories that he was poisoned, what killed him was probably a tumour of the throat. His death was the sign for a rapidly accelerating breakdown of the entire political and military system established by Augustus.

Part IV

Revolution and Recovery

7

The Guard and the Armies Stake their Claims AD 62–70

During the seven or eight years that immediately followed, the Roman armed forces and their leaders began to get out of hand, and then plunged the empire into anarchy. The period falls into two sub-periods, of unequal length. During the first, which lasted for about six years, plots and conspiracies, centring round the praetorian guard and army, were rumoured, became a reality and proliferated, until in June AD 68 Nero finally fell. Then came the second sub-period, which lasted until the end of the following year and witnessed a series of gigantic convulsive civil wars, putting an end, in quick succession, to Galba, Otho and Vitellius, and bringing Vespasian to the throne.

After Burrus was dead, Nero reverted to the more general custom of employing two joint praetorian prefects (AD 62). One of them was Faenius Rufus, who had been prefect of the grain supply, and the other – a much more picturesque and dangerous character – was Gaius Ofonius Tigellinus. The son of a Sicilian of humble origin who left his native island under a cloud, Tigellinus had been brought up in the households of Agrippina junior and her sister Julia Livilla, and was exiled by Caligula for adultery with them both. After living, for a time, as a fisherman in Greece, he became a landowner and breeder of race-horses for the Roman Circus. There he attracted the attention of Nero, who made him prefect of the praetorian guard. Tacitus may, perhaps, give him a more deplorable character than he deserved, because the historian deplored social upstarts. And besides Tigellinus was the enemy and supplanter of Seneca, whom Tacitus admired. For Seneca, concluding that collaboration with Tigellinus was impossible, at once sought and obtained leave to retire from his post as the emperor's adviser.

Tigellinus continually tried to undermine his colleague Faenius Rufus. He found it easy to persuade the emperor, who was a timid man, that possible rivals to his own ambitions ought to be removed. The first two conspicuous victims both had fatally powerful and imperial connections, which inspired fears that they might seduce the legions (AD 62).[1] The same year also witnessed the downfall of Nero's own wife Octavia. Alarmed by popular demonstrations in her favour, prompted by her glorious lineage, Nero turned once again to the prefect of the Misenum fleet, Anicetus, who had conducted the murder of Agrippina. Now, once again, the fleet commander obliged by 'confessing' that he had been Octavia's lover, and Nero issued an edict proclaiming that she had been guilty of seditiously attempting to win over the fleet to her cause. She was sent to an island under the surveillance of praetorian centurions and guardsmen, and her death followed a few days later. Anicetus, who knew too much to be left around, was told to go and live in Sardinia.[2] Nero was now free to marry his latest mistress, Poppaea, the granddaughter of an eminent imperial governor (he had ruled Moesia for twenty-three years). The emperor had already sent away her previous lover or husband, Marcus Salvius Otho, to become the imperial governor of Lusitania (Portugal), where there was no legion for him to tamper with.[3]

Nero was now becoming increasingly preoccupied with his own dramatic and musical performances.[4] But Tigellinus continued his campaign against eminent noblemen, and this seemed to many senators and officers to present an intolerable peril to themselves. Accordingly, in AD 65, a large-scale plot was formed. It was sometimes known as the Pisonian conspiracy, after its figure-head Gaius Calpurnius Piso, a magnificent and popular nobleman who had been exiled by Caligula[5] and had, as he was only too well aware, been a target of Tigellinus's suspicions for the past three years. Piso may have had no great imperial ambitions, but if there was going to be a new emperor, as seemed possible in view of Nero's behaviour, then he would not like the successful claimant to be one of his own aristocratic rivals.[6] There were also other noblemen involved in the plot. But its mainstay was the joint praetorian prefect Faenius Rufus.[7] His motive was a justified fear of his colleague Tigellinus.

This, then, was a new sort of conspiracy, since it comprised, above all else, an attempted coup by one part of the praetorian guard against another. Faenius was supported by a group of praetorian officers, including the military tribune Subrius Flavus, who at one point intended to murder Nero with his own hand.[8] Faenius's alternative plan, however, was to begin by conducting Piso to the praetorian camp, and to take with them Claudius's surviving daughter Claudia Antonia, who would add imperial weight to the enterprise.[9] But here a complication arose. Subrius Flavus was prepared to break his military oath to Nero because, among other grievous defects, the emperor masqueraded as a dramatic and musical stage-performer. This meant that Flavus would scarcely be prepared to see the throne go to Piso, who was himself an actor and a singer, and indeed just another pleasure-loving dilettante, little better than Nero. Flavus and his fellow-officers therefore supported the proposition that the throne should go to Seneca, who, although not a military man, was at least an experienced, serious statesman. But whether Seneca himself was a party to this plan has always been doubtful.

Before long the plot was disclosed to the emperor. It was given away by Volusius Proculus, the naval squadron commander at Misenum. He had felt that Nero rewarded him inadequately for his part in the murder of Agrippina. Yet when he received a seditious overture from the plotters, it turned out that he was still sufficiently loyal, after all, to report what had happened. Subsequently the whole story came to light, and no less than forty-one persons were implicated. Out of these sixteen were executed or forced to kill themselves. They included Piso, Seneca, his nephew the poet Lucan, Claudia Antonia, Faenius Rufus and Subrius Flavus.[10] In addition four military tribunes were cashiered. To carry out the liquidations, Nero employed the co-prefect Tigellinus, and those of the praetorians who still seemed to be loyal. But he avoided calling upon soldiers with long service behind them, who might, he felt, support Piso. Instead, therefore, he preferred to use the services of new recruits as executioners.

As the full scale of the abortive rebellion began to emerge, the emperor sent troops all over the city, and doubled the size of his German bodyguard, who might be expected to be uninvolved in the plot: it is about this time that we find them organized in a regular corps (*collegium*), under their own head (*curator*) and with their own burial ground, and this regularization of their status no doubt represents a tribute to their reliability. Nero also addressed the loyalist praetorians, and gave them five hundred *denarii* each, ordering also that the grain they ate, for which they had hitherto paid the market price, should henceforward be free of charge. Moreover the leading personages who had taken the lead in stamping out the conspiracy received spectacular honours. Statues of Tigellinus were erected in the palace and the forum, the latter in triumphal guise. His new colleague in the prefecture of the guard, Faenius Rufus's successor, was the tall, grim Nymphidius Sabinus, the son of a freedwoman who was believed to have been Caligula's mistress; he had gained military experience as prefect of an auxiliary cavalry regiment in Pannonia. Nymphidius, too, had helped to crush the plot, and was awarded an honorary consulship as his reward. Among others who were recompensed for their assistance were Publius Petronius Turpilianus, the general who had pacified Britain after its revolt, and Marcus Cocceius Nerva, who thirty-one years later was to become emperor himself. Both of these men received honorary Triumphs.

It was not usual for such ill-omened subjects as conspiracies to be mentioned on the coinage. But this time an exception was made. For the coin inscription 'the Security of the Emperor' (SECVRITAS AVGVSTI) evidently refers to this event.[11] Since the plot could not be hushed up, it seemed just as well to celebrate its successful repression.

But further conspiracies, or supposed conspiracies, followed without a pause, and their possible links with the army continued to cause grave anxiety. In AD 65 Nero's wife Poppaea died, and one eminent senator, Gaius Cassius Longinus, was not permitted by Nero to attend her funeral. For his name Cassius, going back to Caesar's murderer, seemed sinister, and because of the honour he paid to this ancestor he was said to be planning a military rebellion.[12] Its figure-head was alleged to be Lucius Junius Silanus Torquatus, one of the last of many members of a great family to be struck down because of their imperial descent and connections. When these two men came under suspicion, Cassius was merely deported to Sardinia. But Silanus, sent to Barium (Bari), received a fatal visit from a praetorian centurion and a detachment of guardsmen.

Seized and told to open his veins, Silanus answered that he was ready to die but would not excuse his assassin the glorious duty. The officer, however, noting that though unarmed he was very strong and far from intimidated, ordered his men to overpower him. He did not fail to resist, hitting back as much as his bare hands allowed. Finally the centurion's sword struck him down, and he fell, wounded in front, as in battle.[13]

In the following year (AD 66) the casualties included a very eminent ultra-conservative Publius Clodius Thrasea Paetus, of Republican and philosophical tendencies. His failure to attend the senate was declared by his prosecutor to constitute insurrection and secession. 'In every province, every army, the official Gazette is read with special care – to see what Thrasea has refused to do.' The point seemed significant because his father-in-law had been an ally of Scribonianus, the leader of an abortive military rising against Claudius twenty-four years earlier. For consideration of the charges against Thrasea, the emperor summoned a meeting of the senate.

Two praetorian cohorts, under arms, occupied the temple of Venus Genetrix. The approach to the senate-house was guarded by further praetorians, in civilian dress but openly displaying their swords. Further detachments of troops were arrayed round the principal forums and lawcourts. Their menacing glares dwelt on the senators who entered the building.[14]

Thrasea was compelled to commit suicide, and at about the same time a former proconsul of Asia, Quintus Marcius Barea Soranus, succumbed to the charge of 'courting the provincials with revolutionary intentions, and encouraging the cities to rebellion'[15] – an unlikely accusation, since the Asian towns had no army of their own, and no local Roman army to subvert.

Like most of the acts of violence of Nero's government, these were events which concerned and distressed the senate more than the populace. For the Roman people on the whole were still well enough disposed to the emperor: and now he was preparing to display himself to their gaze in a highly spectacular role. This centred round a long-planned visit to the capital by Tiridates, the king of Armenia, whose claim to the throne, three years earlier – after Corbulo's final campaigns – the Romans and Parthians had surprisingly agreed upon. Tiridates arrived in Rome with an immense entourage, including three thousand Parthian cavalrymen. And then, at a great ceremony, Nero set the diadem on his head.

The centre of the forum was occupied by civilians, arranged according to rank, clad in white and carrying laurel-branches. Everywhere else were soldiers, arrayed in shining armour, their weapons and standards flashing like the lightning ... At daybreak Nero himself, wearing the robes of a commander celebrating a Triumph and accompanied by the senate and the praetorian guard, entered the forum. He ascended the platform and seated himself upon the chair of state, and then Tiridates and his suite approached between lines of troops in full armour.[16]

The emperor made the most of his great moment. He went in solemn procession up to the Capitol, where he dedicated a laurel-wreath; and he closed the temple of Janus, which signified that the wars were over. And it was now, as his coins reveal, that he allowed the public to acclaim him as *Imperator* and assumed it as his first name[17] – which no other emperor had ventured to do since Augustus. Nero himself, it could not fail to be noted, had never gone to the front at all. Nevertheless, his adoption of the title *Imperator* as a personal prefix meant that he claimed military victoriousness as his very special and peculiar attribute, and as the attribute, moreover, which made him the special heir and peer of Augustus.

While Tiridates was still in Rome Nero already knew that a revolt had broken out in the east. The scene of the rising was Judaea, an unruly province with a small garrison of non-Jewish auxiliaries from local towns. The Jews had notoriously failed to come to an understanding with the knights who served as their governors, and finally the incompetence of one of these officials had triggered off open rebellion. Nero had to appoint a general to suppress it. Since, however, plots and rumours of plots made him deeply suspicious of brilliant commanders, he played for safety and selected a fifty-seven-year-old former consul whose record was solid and unspectacular. This was Titus Flavius Vespasianus, the younger brother of Flavius Sabinus who was city prefect and had held that post for a number of years. Nero appointed Vespasian while on a prolonged dramatic and musical tour of Greece. He took with him praetorian units, and their joint prefect Tigellinus. One might have expected that his fellow-prefect, Nymphidius Sabinus, who presumably stayed behind at Rome, would have been entrusted with special responsibilities there. But all we hear is that two oriental freedmen were left in control.

They were confronted with a tense situation, because shortly before Nero's departure a further plot had been detected in Italy. In the course of the entertainments in Tiridates's honour, the Armenian king had expressed surprise because Corbulo, although in command of such a large army in the east for so many years, had never organized a military revolt against Nero. Tiridates was even heard saying to the emperor himself, 'my lord, in that man you have a good slave'. One of those on whom the remark was not wasted was Corbulo's own son-in-law Annius

Vinicianus, who had been detailed to accompany the king to Rome.[18] And the next we hear of Vinicianus is that he was accused of plotting against the life of Nero at Beneventum, in June AD 66.[19] Perhaps it was his intention to kill Nero there, while the emperor was on his way to an Adriatic port, where he would embark for his tour of Greece. Vinicianus's father and brother and other relatives had all perished in earlier rebellions or conspiracies, and he himself may have feared for his own safety. He had served with distinction under Corbulo, and could expect strong support from the eastern armies, which had become so much larger during Nero's reign. But he never got an opportunity to rally these troops, for he was arrested and, in spite of his great father-in-law, put to death. And so were a number of other governors, who had apparently been in secret contact with him.

Vinicianus's plot was apparently intended to place Corbulo on the throne. The senate and senior officers of senatorial rank would have greatly welcomed such a move. By now, too, certain legions, especially in the east, might have been willing to desert Nero, who had never visited their camps or led them in battle, in favour of the commander whose military distinction they knew so well. However that remains speculative, since in the crises about to come the legionaries in general still showed undiminished loyalty to the emperor. The praetorians would probably, at this stage, have proved a hard nut even for Corbulo to crack. Whether Corbulo knew of his son-in-law's plot is uncertain. But in any case he had possessed too many links with men destroyed in the Pisonian conspiracy for Nero to feel safe.[20] And so, at the end of the year, Corbulo found himself summoned to Greece. When he arrived there he received orders to kill himself. Before dying he uttered the Greek word *axios*.[21] This was a term employed for the acclamation of winners in the games, meaning 'you deserved it'. Corbulo was saying that his fate served him right. But did he mean 'I was a fool to have come' (that is to say 'to have come without my army, and to have spared Nero'), or 'yes, I am guilty'? We cannot tell.

Apparently Nero and his advisers were under the impression that Vinicianus's conspiracy had spread to the commanders of the German legionary garrisons. For at about the same time the army commanders in upper and lower Germany, who were two brothers, Scribonius Rufus and Scribonius Proculus, likewise received the same ominous invitation to report to the emperor in Greece; and they too were compelled to commit suicide. They were suspect because their family could claim descent from imperial personages and from Pompey, and because they were related to Scribonianus who had rebelled against Claudius in Dalmatia in AD 42. It had perhaps been imprudent of Nero to entrust the sensitive area of the two Germanies, which at this time contained seven legions, to two brothers[22] — and to leave them there for as long as eight years. This had given them an opportunity both to plan concerted action, and to form close links with their troops. And evidently Nero and his advisers believed that their plans had taken a sinister turn — that the rot had spread to the commanders of the great German armies. And they may have been right. If so the situation was perilous. Certainly that was what his representative in Rome believed, for, in about January AD 68 they urgently begged him to leave Greece and return to the capital.

He had been away for longer than any other ruler since the days of Tiberius's residence on Capreae. Yet now he entered the city, not in anxiety, but in triumph – a new sort of triumph, celebrating not military victories but his artistic successes in Greece. At the same time, however, he took thought for the army as well, for he issued coins bearing a legionary Eagle flanked by two military standards.[23] The same design had last appeared, in this form, on a famous coinage of Mark Antony, issued exactly a century previously. Augustus, too, had depicted an Eagle and standard on his coins. These two precedents formed an appropriate conjunction, for Nero was descended from Augustus and Antony alike. And far from adopting a defensive posture because of all the conspiracies, he now intended to outdo both of his ancestors in military renown by launching a large-scale eastern expedition. He had already ordered the creation of a new legion, consisting entirely of Italians of tall stature. He named the unit the 'Phalanx of Alexander the Great',[24] showing the grandiose ambitions which were revolving in his mind. Whether he himself would, in the end, have taken the field himself, it is impossible to say: but surely, at this climactic moment, he would at least have shown himself to the troops. His first aim seems to have been the occupation of the Caucasus, so as to make the Black Sea into as Roman a lake as the Mediterranean. It was in preparation for this project that steps had been taken, a few years earlier, to strengthen Roman power near the mouth of the Danube. A Pontic fleet, based on Trapezus (Trabzon) on the southern coast of the Black Sea, had also been created, incorporating the Thracian detachments, and Rome had annexed a long strip of the same sea's northern coast, at the same time establishing, for a time, direct rule over the grain-producing client kingdom of the Cimmerian Bosphorus (Crimea). Now the decisive move was at hand. And it was intended to lead to something even vaster and grander.

But the campaign never came. For shortly after the middle of March AD 68 Nero received news that one of his imperial governors, Gaius Julius Vindex, had revolted in Gaul. His province was probably the central region of the country, Gallia Lugdunensis. Vindex, himself a Gaul of royal birth who had been made a Roman senator, gained the support of a hundred thousand of his compatriots, especially from the rich central tribes. This partially compensated for the strangest feature of his revolt, a feature which, according to all accepted opinion, ought to have made it an impossibility. For he was governor of an 'unarmed' province, which meant that he had not a single legion under his command. Nor did the veteran colony Lugdunum (Lyon), which was the capital of his province, rally to his cause. But Vienna (Vienne), which lay farther down the Rhône in the neighbouring province of Gallia Narbonensis, declared its support of the enterprise.

Nero and his government at once accused Vindex of an anti-Roman, Gaulish, nationalism and separatism – an easy accusation since Gauls were traditionally regarded as revolutionaries.[25] But the main reason why Vindex rebelled was not because of Celtic nationalism at all, but owing to fear for his own life – now that the emperor had become so savage to provincial governors. The coins Vindex now issued, anonymously, at Vienna, associate their slogans of freedom and vengeance, not with Gallic independence, but explicitly with the name of Rome.[26] What Vindex stood for was liberation from Nero's tyranny; and he made the Gauls swear an oath to the senate and Roman people.[27] This had a Republican ring. Yet Vindex knew as well as anyone else that it was quite impracticable for the Republic to be restored, and that the Roman empire had to have an emperor. He did not aspire to this role himself, for he knew he lacked the authority to command widespread support. Instead, he offered the leadership to Servius Sulpicius Galba, the seventy-three-year-old governor of nearer Spain (Hispania Tarraconensis).

Like Vindex, Galba was not well off for troops: but Spain's single legion (to which its former garrison of three legions had been reduced) was under his control. Yet other factors operated in Galba's favour. There could be no successor to Nero from within his own family, for the emperor himself was its only surviving male member. Outside the imperial house, the elimination of so many other noblemen had left

Galba in an almost unique position. Supremely aristocratic and enormously wealthy, he was a man whom every ruler from Augustus onwards had esteemed, a man who already, twenty-seven years earlier,
after the death of Caligula, had been spoken of as a possible emperor.
And now, at a time when every eminent governor was the target of
Nero's suspicions, he had remained one of the very few great nobles
still allowed to occupy an imperial governorship. Understandably he
had tried to keep as quiet as he could. Yet even so he had become
alienated from Nero's personal agent (*procurator*) in the province – and
a letter from the emperor to that man, which Galba had managed to
intercept, seemed to give him real grounds for anxiety.

Such were the reasons why, after Vindex had got in touch with him,
he decided, after considerable procrastination and with substantial
reservations, to respond. Some sort of decision was forced upon him
when the imperial governor of Gaul's south-western province
(Aquitania) appealed to him for help against Vindex. Galba's chief
military adviser — perhaps the commander of his single legion — was the
ambitious Titus Vinius, last heard of twenty-nine years earlier as a
young military tribune in Pannonia committing adultery with his
commander's wife. When the appeal from Aquitania reached Galba,
Vinius reminded him that even to discuss such a message constituted
treason towards Nero: a decision one way or the other simply had to
be reached. And so, on 2 April AD 68, in a proclamation at Carthago
Nova (Cartagena), Galba pronounced himself to be the representative
(*legatus*) of the senate and Roman people. That did not mean that he
had agreed to be hailed as emperor. But, even so, his declaration was a
breach of his oath to Nero, and virtually made him the ally of Vindex.
Indeed, on an anonymous coinage of his own, which he now proceeded
to issue, he specifically celebrated the unity of the Spains and Gauls.[28]
He was joined by the thirty-three-year-old Marcus Salvius Otho, who
had been made governor of Lusitania (Portugal) when Nero annexed
his wife or mistress Poppaea. But Otho had no legion at all. So Galba
began mobilizing a second legion from the Spaniards.

For these men who had rejected Nero's authority were still extra-
ordinarily weak in military strength. In consequence Galba's fate, and
in the first instance the fate of Vindex who was nearer to the Rhine,
depended to a very great extent on the army commanders in lower and
upper Germany, who at this time commanded four and three legions
respectively. The legate of lower Germany, Fonteius Capito, could not
make up his mind what to do – he was a bad advertisement for Nero's

policy of appointing safe, insignificant governors and commanders.. Everything depended, therefore, on his upper German colleague, Lucius Verginius Rufus – who, in any case, was nearer than Capito to Vindex. Verginius was no rival to Galba in birth or wealth, but he had received exceptional honours from Nero, and he was one of the leaders of a group of north Italians who possessed great influence in governmental affairs. And now he planned to launch his army in support, not of Vindex, but of the emperor. It took him two months to move into action. But finally he marched south with all his legions and numerous auxiliaries.

Subsequently a great fog of untruths descended upon what happened next, because Verginius and his friends, later on, did not want it suggested that he had remained faithful to Nero. His own epitaph, for example, declared instead that what he had done was to put down a Gaulish nationalist menace.[29] In central Gaul, before joining battle with one another, he and Vindex conferred. What was said during this momentous conversation we do not know. It was rumoured that the two commanders agreed that their armies should not fight. But if so, one or the other of them must have been overruled by his own men. For at the end of May the clash came, and they fought a ferocious battle at Vesontio (Besançon): almost a hundred years after the civil wars had ended they were back again. Vindex was totally defeated, and fell, probably by his own hand. Although Nero had such grave shortcomings, and although the legionaries had never even seen him, the great upper German army had not deserted his cause in the crisis. Nor, in spite of his later denials, did its commander Verginius. After the battle his troops offered to hail him emperor – and this was not the last time that they did so. But he declined and returned to his province.

Galba, in despair, sent Verginius a plea for cooperation, which as far as we know elicited no acknowledgement; and then he withdrew to the interior of Spain. Nero seemed to have the situation well in hand. He started to recruit a new legion from the marines at Misenum,[30] and concentrated a force of four legions upon north Italy and Gaul. But there were ominous signs. For example in Africa a certain Clodius Macer, who was the commander of the province's only legion, struck out independently, raised another legion on his own account, and coined, ambiguously, as 'pro-praetor of Africa'.[31] He had designs on Sicily; and he threatened the grain supply of Rome.

More dangerous, however, to Nero was the petulant, unrealistic, indecisiveness of his own character. Because of this the legions, for all their loyalty to the imperial house, could hardly be expected to stay loyal for ever. Besides, owing to the emperor's heavy personal expenses, their pay was greatly in arrears, and so were the gratuities due to the veterans. Nevertheless it was not among the legions that the trouble started, but in Rome itself. Nero's German guard apparently retained its fidelity. But the decisive event was the defection of his joint praetorian prefects. From taking this step, even the news of Vesontio failed to deter them. One of the two commanders defected passively, and the other actively. Tigellinus just withdrew from the scene altogether and perhaps left the capital. His health was very poor, and it was easy for his colleague Nymphidius Sabinus to push him out of the way.[32] The initiative now rested with Nymphidius, and it was he who decided the course of events that followed next. Many senators, profoundly alienated by Nero's executions, had already been secretly in touch with Galba. And Nymphidius now sought these men out, and made common cause with them.

Nero as yet had no knowledge of all this. But the satisfaction he must have derived from the news of Vesontio was sharply diminished when he received a piece of bad news. We are not told what it was, but probably one of the generals appointed to take command in north Italy had abandoned his allegiance.[33] Indeed, this news, whatever it may have been, threw him into so great a panic that he decided he must leave Italy immediately. His destination was to be Egypt, traditionally the emperor's personal domain, where he believed, probably without justification, that the prefect Tiberius Julius Alexander was loyal. Sending trusted freedmen to Ostia to collect ships from the fleet, Nero moved to a house at the edge of the city and made preparations to depart. He also tried to persuade some of the tribunes and centurions of the praetorian guard to come away with him. But some were evasive, and others refused outright.

In the middle of the following night he found that the praetorian cohort guarding the house had melted away. The senate ordered their withdrawal, and they obeyed. For Nymphidius had made them a remarkable offer. If they would abandon their allegiance to Nero, he declared, they would be awarded the unprecedentedly large sum of 7,500 *denarii* each, more than twice what they had been given on Claudius's accession (the legionaries were to receive 1,250). In consequence they abandoned Nero, and as they did so they murdered a certain Scipulus or Spiculus, who was perhaps a gladiator, and may have been the commander of the emperor's German bodyguard. Nero fled to the northern suburbs, where one of his freedmen offered him refuge. As he passed the praetorian camp he heard the guardsmen inside cheering for Galba. 'They are after Nero!' declared a passer-by. But an ex-praetorian whom he encountered on the road saw who he was, and gave him a salute. When Nero reached the freedman's house, he was told that the senate had pronounced him a public enemy – an unprecedented experience for an emperor. He also learnt that they had sentenced him, according to ancient tradition, to be flogged to death. Thereupon, with assistance, he committed suicide.[34]

Galba was the first man to be raised to power by his legionaries. From now on, the imperial throne was a prize for which any and every army commander might compete. Very often the senate would find such men unpalatable, fellow-senators though they were. However, a personage of Galba's birth and qualifications was welcome to a great many of them – and even those who might have put forward rival claims for themselves thought it better not to try to oppose him. In about the middle of June news reached Galba in Spain that Nero was dead, and that the senate and praetorians alike had accepted him as emperor. With his newly raised legion he moved northwards into Gaul, and at Narbo (Narbonne), early in July, deputations from both the senate and the guard came to meet him. During the autumn he dealt with the freelance Clodius Macer in Africa, by getting the local imperial procurator to assassinate him.

In Rome, however, there had already been serious trouble. Although extremely rich, Galba was careful about money; and he evidently thought that the scale of Nymphidius's offer to the praetorians was outrageous. The prefect had already received a snub from the consuls when they did not add his seal to theirs on the senatorial decrees dispatched to Galba. Nevertheless Nymphidius still believed that he was going to dominate Galba and it came as a terrible shock to him to learn, before the new ruler reached the capital, that he had been deprived of the prefecture, and one of the emperor's close friends, Cornelius Laco, appointed in his place – an idle and ill-informed man, according to Tacitus.[35] Nymphidius immediately attempted a rebellion, apparently hoping to seize the throne for himself. He gave out that he was an illegitimate son of Caligula, and therefore of imperial blood. But although Galba was not yet in Rome, the revolt collapsed and Nymphidius was killed – perhaps by some of his own officers and guardsmen, though Galba claimed the credit for his own agents. The dead man, however, had not been lacking in partisans, and Galba cashiered a good many of them, replacing the officers by adherents of his own. He also took the courageous but imprudent step of refusing to pay the bonuses that Nymphidius had promised in his name, on the old-fashioned grounds: 'I choose my own soldiers; I do not buy them.'[36] This was too much even for the traditionally loyalist praetorians – and they were also greatly alarmed by rumours that they were going to be sent away, and posted to legions in the provinces.

As the new emperor finally approached the city in about October a most unfortunate incident occurred. He was met by the marines whom Nero had recently enrolled in a new legion, because they wanted to appeal to him to recognize their recently acquired legionary status. But skirmishing broke out and some of the demonstrators were killed. The surviving marines were disbanded by Galba, and he also dismissed his predecessors' German bodyguard – on the grounds that they were too friendly with a nobleman of suspect loyalty who lived near their camp. He behaved with equal lack of wisdom when he ordered the loyal legion that had accompanied him from Spain to go away from Rome – while the presumably disloyal one raised by Nero (the 'Phalanx of Alexander') was sent to Gaul, so that it passed out of his sight and control. Elevated references on his coinage to the Honour and Valour of his troops (HONOS ET VIRTVS)[37] did nothing to remedy such mistakes. Nor were his efforts at financial retrenchment at all welcome to the civilian population of Rome. And they were also resentful because he refused to hand Tigellinus over to them to be lynched.

Meanwhile a gravely critical situation was fast developing in Germany. The upper German legions had made a second attempt to make Verginius Rufus emperor – this time with the support of their fellow-soldiers on the Danube. He declined once again, but Galba recalled him to Rome and not only gave him no further employment but allowed a prosecutor to bring charges against him. Verginius was replaced in upper Germany by a lame, elderly friend of the new emperor named Hordeonius Flaccus. Meanwhile his colleague in lower Germany, Fonteius Capito, who had remained inactive during the recent events, was murdered by two of his legionary commanders – one of whom, the flamboyant Fabius Valens, will appear again on the scene very shortly. Fonteius's offence may have been that he refused to revolt on his own account. He was succeeded at the beginning of December by the fifty-four-year-old Aulus Vitellius. The grandson of a Roman knight, and son of Lucius Vitellius, who had for a time been the power behind Claudius's throne, the new commander was a product of the new aristocracy which had made its name in the imperial service.

After Nero was dead the legionaries in the German camps very soon revolted against Galba. If one legion in Spain could make an emperor, then seven in Germany could do the same, and do it better.* Nor, like the Spanish legion, would they need the help of their praetorian rivals, for they would be strong enough without them. The destruction of Vindex had given them a taste for loot; moreover Nymphidius had shown them what dizzy sums the cash bonuses awarded in struggles between different Roman leaders might attain – and they were exceedingly annoyed that his promises had not been carried out. Besides civil war attracted them in any case because its anarchic conditions would surely mean a relaxation of discipline. Although, therefore, the German armies had not started the civil wars, they soon figured prominently in them once hostilities had begun.

It was in upper Germany, the southern part of the Rhine frontier, that the new crisis started. Under the direction of Verginius Rufus the three legions in the area had duly sworn their oaths of allegiance to Galba. When, however, on 1 January AD 69, Verginius's infirm successor Hordeonius Flaccus called upon his men to renew these oaths, the two legions stationed at Moguntiacum (Mainz) refused to do so, and instead hurled the emperor's statues to the ground. Most of the senior officers did not intervene; only a few centurions tried to protect the sacred effigies, and they were arrested by their own men. In addition to the general restlessness among the German legions, those of upper Germany harboured a special grievance against Galba. This was because his accession had meant that their services against Vindex went unrewarded. The biographer Plutarch blames most of the disasters of these civil wars upon the common soldiers. Yet in fact this German rising was an isolated occasion, because, as far as the legionaries were concerned, it was the only time during this period when a seditious initiative originated from below.

Nevertheless the legionaries at Moguntiacum did not refuse to swear any oath at all. They swore, however, not to the emperor Galba, but to the senate and the Roman people. Tacitus comments on the archaic quaintness of the formula. The soldiers were not, of course, interested in the impracticable and unprofitable idea of reviving the Republic. What they wanted was another emperor, and one who, unlike Galba,

---

* For the distribution of the legions in December AD 68, see Appendix 1.

would not go back on promises made in his name. Hordeonius Flaccus could not meet the need, since he was a friend of Galba, and was in any case too frail. So when they swore allegiance to the senate and people of Rome, it was coupled with the demand that these organs of the Roman state should appoint Galba's successor. The numerous auxiliaries stationed in the area proved to be of the same mind.

They were at first looked upon with suspicion as their cohorts and cavalry regiments had been moved up and it was believed that an attack on the legions was being planned. But in due course the auxiliaries showed themselves keener plotters than their companions. Scoundrels find it easier to agree on warlike measures than on means to achieve harmony in peace-time.[38]

In lower Germany the four legions had duly sworn allegiance to Galba on 1 January. Some stones were thrown at his statues and the atmosphere was tense, but Vitellius, the newly appointed governor, had succeeded in administering the oaths. Later that evening, however, during dinner, he received news of what had been happening at Moguntiacum. And the next morning, upon the instigation of his legionary commanders, led by Valens, his troops saluted him emperor.

On the following day the army of upper Germany abandoned its ostensible allegiance to the senate and people of Rome, and did the same. The local populations and auxiliaries followed suit. How long the plans of Vitellius, or Valens, had been maturing we cannot say. But, although Vitellius had only held his command for a month, he had already taken steps to remove some of the grievances of his legionaries. Though gluttonous and capable of brutality, he was easy and relaxed, and accustomed to offering even private soldiers a hearty greeting and an embrace.[39] Because of Galba's irremediable unpopularity, Vitellius was the man for the moment. His total lack of a military record did not, on this particular occasion, provide an obstacle. For what the German legions wanted was their own nominee for the throne – and he was the only potential nominee they had got.

When the legions of upper Germany had dissociated themselves from Galba on 1 January, his imperial agent at Augusta Trevirorum (Trier) sent couriers giving him the bad news, which reached him at Rome on 8 or 9 January. Although the praetorian prefect Laco was his right-hand man, Galba had alienated so many guardsmen that he had little faith in the loyalty of the metropolitan garrison. He decided, however, that a useful way to safeguard his throne was to adopt a son, so as to give a comforting impression of continuity. The advisers to whom he announced this intention included the praetorian prefect Laco, and the city prefect Ducenius Geminus. His choice, however, was unfortunate. It fell on Lucius Calpurnius Piso Licinianus, a high-minded young man of the bluest possible blood, descended both from Pompey and from Crassus. Galba's principle that the empire should go *to merit* – for he made it quite clear he was appointing a successor to the throne as well as to his personal possessions – was in keeping with a principle dear to the liberal politicians of Republican times, and it was destined to an effective revival nearly three decades later. But it was only to prove successful on that subsequent occasion because the chosen heir (Trajan) was acceptable to the army. And what Galba ought to have thought of now was, likewise, military opinion about the suitability of his candidate. However Piso meant nothing whatever to the soldiers. Indeed the praetorians may have found him positively displeasing, since he was the brother of the Piso who, four years earlier, had plotted against Nero, whom they liked. In view of the poor reception Galba's choice was likely to have from the guardsmen, he decided to announce the adoption, not in the senate or forum, but in the praetorian camp – in the somewhat forlorn hope of ingratiating himself and his nominee. He also seized the opportunity of assuring his listeners that what had happened in upper Germany was only a passing phenomenon, and should not be regarded too seriously. Tacitus comments on the occasion (10 January).

Galba did not round off his speech by pandering to the troops or bribing them. Despite this, the military tribunes, centurions and front ranks raised a gratifying cheer by way of response. But throughout the rest reigned gloom and silence, as if they felt that active service had lost them the bounty customarily exacted even in peace-time. There is general agreement that it would have been quite possible to win them over by a mere token act of generosity on the part of the niggardly old emperor. His old-fashioned rigidity and excessive strictness spelt ruin. For we cannot rise to these standards nowadays.[40]

Then the adoption was confirmed by a somewhat preoccupied senate, and on the same day the aristocratic members of the priesthood named the Arval Brethren sacrificed to Security, Foresight and the Public Well-Being.

One leading Roman, however, found Piso's nomination a shattering disappointment. That was Marcus Salvius Otho. As imperial governor of Lusitania he had been the first important personage to rally to

Galba's cause, and in consequence he had confidently expected to be adopted as the old man's son and successor himself. On the way home from Spain he had carefully ingratiated himself with Galba's legionaries, expressing sympathetic concern about the unaccustomed hardships of the march. Subsequently he had turned his attention to the praetorians, and taken the same meticulous care to win favour in their ranks as well. Whenever Galba dined at Otho's house the host would hand out twenty-five *denarii* to each of the guardsmen in attendance upon the emperor, suggesting that this was to pay for their dinners; and to one of their number who was in financial straits he presented a large sum of money as a gift. Indeed generosity of this kind had plunged him so heavily into debt that something had urgently to be done. And now, after the adoption of Piso, he felt that the time for decisive action had arrived.

The plot, organized by one of Otho's freedmen, depended entirely on his seduction of the praetorians. Their first two members the freedman approached were an assistant centurion (*optio*) and orderly sergeant (*tesserarius*). Next, five members of the emperor's inner bodyguard, the *speculatores*, were brought into the scheme, and then five more. As we learn from Suetonius (whose father was one of Otho's military tribunes), each of these men was immediately paid 2,500 *denarii* by Otho's agent, with the promise of 12,500 more.[41] Subsequently other guardsmen were won over, but no attempt was made to gain the support of a great many, since Otho was confident that, as soon as he moved into action, a considerable number would join him. The praetorian prefect, Laco, apparently remained completely in the dark about all this. Otho's first idea, immediately after the adoption of Piso, was to get possession of the praetorian camp and then assault Galba himself as he was having dinner in his own palace. But this plan was abandoned because the praetorian cohort in attendance on Galba was the same unit that had deserted Nero on the last night of his life, and Otho felt that to require it to perform the same sort of treachery once again was too much to ask or expect.

Instead, he waited for another five days – by which time, no doubt, he knew of the unwelcome but not altogether unexpected report that Vitellius had been declared emperor in Germany. On 15 January Otho went for a walk by the temple of Saturn, right beside the forum. There it was arranged that twenty-three *speculatores* should publicly hail him emperor. Drawing their swords, they shouted out their salutation, and then immediately hurried him away in a closed sedan chair, intending to take him to their camp. As they went on their way, Galba soon learnt that some senator or other – it was only later that rumour said he was Otho – was being carried to the camp. On the emperor's instructions Piso, standing on the steps of the palace, delivered a reassuring address to the praetorian cohort which was on duty there for the day. The *speculatores* who belonged to the cohort did not stay to listen, but the rank and file seemed loyal enough, and the standard-bearers duly raised their standards aloft. Meanwhile an eminent general, Marius Celsus, was sent by Galba to contact a group of picked Danubian legionaries who were encamped in the Field of Mars, in the hope that he could bring them into the city; and two senior centurions were ordered to alert a contingent from the German army which was temporarily stationed inside the walls, not far from the forum itself. Both detachments formed part of the force Nero had been preparing for his eastern expedition.

The soldiers from Germany were in two minds because Galba had treated them quite well. But the Danubian troops drove Marius Celsus away with the point of their spears. The legion of marines, whose fellow-soldiers Galba had massacred, was likewise openly disloyal. Galba now decided to send Piso to the praetorian camp, but the idea was abandoned when a report arrived that Otho had been killed. The news was untrue: he had reached the camp safely, though in somewhat unorthodox fashion. For the strength of the praetorians who were carrying his sedan had wilted before they arrived there, and they had put him down on the way. Undeterred, however, he got out of the chair, and ran onwards towards his destination. When he stopped to do up his shoe, he found himself surrounded by guardsmen who took him within the camp walls upon their shoulders, brandishing their drawn swords.

There the rest of the guard welcomed him warmly, because the information that the German legions had appointed their own emperor inspired them with a feeling of fanatical rivalry.[42] In great enthusiasm, therefore, they ushered Otho to their platform – having first removed a gilded statue of Galba – and crowded round him with their standards. Meanwhile the military tribune who was officer of the day at the camp, and the other tribunes and centurions, were too uncertain of the outcome and nervous about their own fates to intervene either against him or for him. So the elevation of Otho by the praetorians, like the salutation of Vitellius by his legionaries, was a rare instance of political action originating from the ranks. Indeed the guardsmen, noting the equivocal attitude of their officers, would not even allow them to come anywhere near their nominee, but themselves administered oaths of allegiance to one another, and the legion of marines did the same. Otho, remembering the disastrous results of Nymphidius's unfulfilled promises, gave the praetorians a somewhat cryptic assurance that 'he would only keep for himself whatever they chose to leave him'.[43] Then he ordered the camp armoury to be thrown open to the praetorians, and seizing whatever weapons they could, they rushed out of the camp as a leaderless horde.

Meanwhile Galba, carried in a sedan chair, had left his palace for the forum, and Piso had joined him. So had the praetorian prefect Laco, but like his senior aides in the camp, he was ineffective and useless. Tacitus gravely describes the outcome.

By this time Galba was being carried hither and thither by the irregular impact of the surging multitude. Everywhere the public buildings and temples were crowded with a sea of faces. As far as the eye could see the view was one of doom. Not a cry came from the mass of the people. But their faces wore a frightened expression. Their eyes strained to catch every sound. There was neither din nor quiet, only the hush typical of great fear and great anger.

Otho, however, was informed that the mob were being armed. He ordered his men to move in at full speed and seize the danger-points. Thus it was that Roman troops made ready to murder an old, defenceless man who was their emperor, just as if he were some Parthian monarch whom they were casting down from his foreign throne. Forcing their way through the crowd, trampling the senate under foot, with weapons at the ready and horses spurred to a gallop, they burst upon the forum. Such men were not deterred by the sight of the Capitol, the sanctity of the temples that looked down upon them, nor the thought of emperors past and emperors to come. They were bent upon the commission of a crime that is inevitably avenged by the victim's successor.

On catching sight of the approaching party of armed men, a standard-bearer belonging to the praetorian cohort which formed Galba's escort – Atilius Vergilio, according to the tradition – ripped from his standard the effigy of Galba and dashed it to the ground, a clear indication that all the guardsmen supported Otho. It was also a signal for a mass exodus of the civilian populace from the forum. Swords were drawn to deal with recalcitrants. Near the Basin of Curtius the panic of his bearers caused Galba to be flung sprawling from his chair. His last words are variously recorded by the conflicting voices of hatred and admiration. Some say that he grovelled, and asked what he had done to deserve his fate, begging a few days' grace to pay the soldiers their bonuses. The majority of the historians believe that he voluntarily bared his throat to the assassins, telling them to strike and be done with it, if this was what seemed best for the country. Little did the murderers care what he said.[44]

It was the treachery of the praetorians that had caused the murder. Praetorian officers had killed Caligula; abandonment by the praetorian prefects had caused the downfall of Nero; but Galba was the first emperor to be brought down by the rank and file of the guard. Piso too was put to death, his killers being a praetorian *speculator* and a soldier of a British auxiliary cohort which Nero had brought to Rome for his eastern expedition. One centurion vainly tried to defend either Galba or Piso, it is not certain which. The assassins cut off the heads of their two victims, and took them to Otho in the praetorian camp. Then they moved on to the senate-house, to show their trophies there.

The senators were by now aware that Vitellius had set himself up as emperor in Germany; and there were Vitellians among their own ranks. Nevertheless the senate immediately voted Otho full powers. As regards credentials of birth, there was not much to choose between the two candidates for empire. For both Otho and Vitellius belonged to the new equestrian aristocracy of office. But Otho suffered from two disqualifications. First, he had the unhappy distinction of being the first emperor to have murdered his predecessor – for the murder had been committed with his connivance, or on his orders. Second, he enjoyed far too few useful links with the army – apart from the praetorian guard, upon whom he was more wholly dependent than any previous ruler. He endeavoured to win the support of the legions as well, by claiming to be Nero's legitimate successor. And his coins displayed inscriptions redolent of wishful thinking – the Security of the Roman People, the Peace of the Whole World, and Victory. But this victory which was still to come was not labelled 'the Victory of the [ruling] Augustus', like Nero's, because it was now necessary to distinguish between two claimants to the throne. So the inscription preferred instead was 'the Victory of Otho' (VICTORIA OTHONIS).[45]

He became emperor under something of a misapprehension. For according to Suetonius's father, who was a military tribune in one of his legions, Otho had not believed that his accession would really be contested by Vitellius. He himself would never have taken Galba on, he was heard to say, unless he had believed that matters would be settled peacefully. He was also known to feel a particular distaste for civil war.[46] Nevertheless it immediately became clear that he had to fight one; for the attempts of each competitor in turn to remove his rival first by negotiation, and then by assassination, proved unsuccessful.[47] The German armies had already begun issuing their own coins, first without any mention of Vitellius and then with his head and name. The main theme of this coinage was the 'loyalty' and 'concord' of the armies and provinces. Moreover, although the praetorian guard was on the other side, specific appeals were made to their loyalty and concord too.[48] When these issues began to depict Vitellius himself, they described him as GERMANICVS. The previous bearers of this historic designation had assumed it because of Drusus senior's victories over the Germans. Now it was revived for quite another reason – because its bearer had been nominated by the Roman legionaries in Germany. The reappearance of the name with this new connotation was a grim sign of the times, which displayed all too clearly the centrifugal, separatist role which the two greatest of the army garrisons were now playing.

Vitellius obtained the adherence of the legions of Raetia, Britain and Spain. But long before this process was complete, and even before he knew that Galba had been killed, his armies on the German frontier had set out for Italy and Rome. Vitellius himself was not with them, for he stayed behind to mobilize a reserve force and follow later at its head. But two separate forces immediately took to the road, one led by Fabius Valens, and the other under the former commander of an upper German legion, the charming and impressive Aulus Caecina Alienus. Caecina was already 150 miles from his base when he heard that Galba was dead. The news did not stop the Vitellians. It was against Galba that they had revolted, and now they were equally determined to overcome and dethrone Otho instead. Valens went though France, and Caecina through Switzerland. Although Valens's legions broke at one point into violent mutiny,[49] which was only calmed down with difficulty by his camp prefect, the marches of both of the two armies displayed a bold and lightning rapidity, culminating in the crossing of the Alps before the winter snows had dispersed. Then, descending into Italy, they successfully effected a junction at Cremona, just north of the River Po.

Meanwhile Otho had been somewhat slow in making his defensive preparations. He managed to prevent the praetorians from lynching Marius Celsus, whose recent efforts on behalf of Galba they resented. But otherwise he remained very much under their thumb – and they even set about choosing their own prefects for themselves. The prefecture was vacant, since Laco had met his death at the hands of a soldier acting on Otho's orders. To replace him the praetorians chose a pair of commanders, one of whom was a former prefect of the Watch, Plotius Firmus, an officer who had risen from the ranks.

Nevertheless, as Tacitus records, the guardsmen soon became dangerously disorderly and disaffected.

A mutiny occurred which almost had fatal consequences for the capital, though it arose out of a trifling incident where no danger was anticipated. Otho had ordered the seventeenth [city] cohort to move to Rome from the city of Ostia, and a praetorian tribune named Varius Crispinus was charged with the task of issuing arms to it. Anxious to carry out his orders with greater freedom from distraction while the praetorian barracks were quiet, he had the armoury opened and the cohort's transport loaded up at nightfall. The hour aroused suspicion, the motive was misconstrued, and the attempt to act quietly led to an uproar.

Seeing the arms, some drunken praetorians felt an urge to get hold of them. The troops raised a clamour and accused the tribunes and centurions of a treasonable plot to arm the household servants of the senators and murder Otho. Some of the praetorians were ignorant of the real circumstances and, befuddled with drink, undesirable elements seized the chance of loot, and the mass of men were, as usual, ready for any kind of excitement. Besides, the willingness of the better soldiers to obey orders had been neutralized by the darkness. The tribune and the strictest disciplinarians amongst the centurions offered resistance, but were struck down. The men helped themselves to the arms, drew their swords and rode off to Rome and the palace.[50]

According to Suetonius, however, this issue of arms to other units caused the praetorians to turn against the senate itself, whom they suspected of displaying less than wholehearted enthusiasm for Otho's cause. As a result a massacre of senators was only very narrowly averted.

For suddenly all the soldiers, without any particular leader, had hastened to the imperial palace, clamouring for the death of the senators. After putting to flight some of the military tribunes who attempted to stop them, and killing others, just as they were all blood-stained, they burst right into the emperor's dining-room, demanding to know where he was; and they could not be quieted until they had seen him.[51]

A few of the ringleaders were executed for this outrage, but Otho felt it best to be generous to the other praetorians, and presented them with a bonus of 1,250 *denarii* each. The military tribunes and centurions of the guard felt they had had enough, since the constant mutinies in these civil wars were casting a heavy strain on officers; and so they asked leave to be discharged. But finally the situation returned to something like calm.

In any case, the praetorians were not Otho's only cause for anxiety, or even his principal one. For what took precedence over everything else was his need to win backing for his cause among the officers and legionaries in the provinces. Men from the legions in Pannonia, Dalmatia and Moesia supported him, and were on their way to help him. But they might not arrive in time, and urgent overtures had to be made to the other major garrisons as well. With the need for their good-will in mind, Otho brought Verginius Rufus out of retirement and gave him a second consulship, in the hope that his great reputation with the German army would undermine the leadership of Vitellius. He also reappointed Flavius Sabinus to the city prefecture in the hope of ingratiating himself with Sabinus's brother Vespasian, who was success-fully commanding a large army against the rebels of Judaea. And finally news was given of an impending reform which, as Tacitus indicates, was designed to benefit legionaries throughout the empire.

There was a demand for the remission of the payments traditionally made to centurions to secure exemption from duty. This was a kind of annual tax payable by the other ranks. As much as a quarter of a maniple's strength would be scattered high and low on leave or loitering in the actual barracks, so long as they squared the centurion in command. The extent of these exactions and the methods employed to meet them attracted nobody's attention. Highway robbery, theft or taking on jobs as servants were the means by which they had to pay for their time off. Besides this, the richer a soldier was, the more he was subjected to fatigues and ill-treatment until he agreed to purchase exemption. Finally, when his money had given out and he had got into an idle and unhealthy state, he would return to his unit, reduced from affluence to poverty and from vigour to sloth. This process was repeated interminably; and the same destitution and indiscipline ruined man after man, driving them herd-like down the slope that leads to mutiny, dissension and, in the last resort, civil war.

However Otho had no wish to alienate his centurions by bribing their men. So he promised that the annual leave should be paid for by the imperial exchequer. There is no doubt that this was a beneficial reform, and in the course of time the practice hardened into a recognized part of the military system under the good emperors who succeeded.[52]

And so gradually the confrontation between Otho and Vitellius began. Otho delayed for two fatal months. His delay was not due to any excessive hopes that the German legionaries would desist from fighting against him now that Galba was dead. But the troops he himself was able to mobilize on the spot, apart from a single legion and some auxiliary cavalry and infantry, were metropolitan units, which had rarely, for the most part, seen action before, and whatever courage they might display had no taste for strict discipline or arduous physical effort. To supplement them, Otho even had to mobilize two thousand gladiators, an unattractive phenomenon that recurred from time to time during these civil wars. The Danubian armies had sent ahead a large vanguard to join him, but the rapid advances both of Valens and of Caecina meant that he could not wait for these reinforcements to arrive. He was already too late to close the Alpine passes; and if he had postponed moving for even a short time longer, the Vitellians would have been at the gates of Rome itself. Otho also made the serious mistake of dividing his command,[53] presumably because there was no experienced general whom he could trust as commander-in-chief.

After sending his main forces ahead, he finally left Rome himself. The troops that accompanied him included a personal bodyguard of brawny praetorian *speculatores*, the remaining praetorian units, a formation of praetorian veterans and a large number of marines. Otho had gained a reputation for soft living, but now he belied it. As Tacitus observed, 'he certainly did not travel in luxurious comfort. He wore an iron cuirass, and marched on foot before the standards, ill-shaven and unkempt.' That is high praise from this historian who on the whole did not think much of Otho. And Vitellius, though at least, unlike his rival, he had never murdered an emperor, seemed to him an even less appealing character. The civil wars of the late Republic, which had ended almost exactly a hundred years previously, were nowadays on everyone's lips. But at least they had been fought for men who were worthwhile. On this occasion, however, the victory of either despicable claimant would be a national disaster.

It is probable that Tacitus exaggerates the two men's inadequacies. But he does so for a reason which is central to his interpretation of Roman military and political history. He hates civil war more than anything else in the whole world, and one of the most serious things he hates about it is that it throws up these very inferior characters as leaders.

And their followers were just as bad. This was not even the sort of civil war in which principles or ideals were supposedly at stake. This was merely a war in which one army, one individual, wanted to get the better of the other. The historian had heard it said that the rank and file, on both sides, seriously considered putting an end to the hostilities, and coming to terms. But this, he fears, was to overestimate their ethical standards.

I find it stated by certain writers that in their dread of war or contempt for both emperors – whose wickedness and degradation became in fact daily more notorious – the two armies wondered whether they should not conclude an armistice under which they could either negotiate on their own or leave the choice of an emperor to the senate. According to these authorities, this was why the Othonian leaders suggested waiting for a while: Suetonius Paulinus, it is alleged, was particularly keen on this because he was the senior officer of consul's rank and had made a name for himself by service in the British campaigns.

For myself, I am quite prepared to grant that in their heart of hearts a few men may have prayed for peace in preference to strife and for a good and honest ruler instead of two worthless and infamous scoundrels. Yet in an age and society so degenerate, I do not believe that the prudent Paulinus expected the ordinary soldier to exercise such self-control as to lay his arms down from an attachment to peace after disturbing the peace from love of war. Nor do I think that armies so different in tongue and habit were capable of a union of this kind, or that generals and senior officers whose consciences were in most cases burdened with the recollection of a life of pleasure, bankruptcy and crime would have tolerated as emperor any other than a disreputable character from whom they could demand payment for the services they had rendered.

From time immemorial man has had an instinctive love of power. With the growth of our empire, this instinct has become a dominant and uncontrollable force ... Roman legions did not shrink from civil war at Pharsalus or Philippi, and there is even less likelihood that the armies of Otho and Vitellius would have made peace of their own free will. Now, as in the past, it was the same divine wrath, the same human infatuation, and the same background of evil deeds that drove them to conflict. That each round of the conflict was decided by a knock-out blow was merely the consequence of the feebleness of the contestants.[54]

The knock-out blow came not far from Cremona, in an engagement which is sometimes described as the First Battle of Bedriacum. Vitellius had not arrived from Germany, so that his troops were led into battle by Caecina and Valens. Otho too was absent from the front, since he remained at his headquarters south of the Po at Brixellum (Brescello). Moreover his Danubian legions had not yet arrived. Nevertheless, although numerically inferior to the enemy, he felt obliged to insist that the decisive confrontation should take place immediately – before his troops could melt away. Civil war battles were always confusing actions, since the two sides wore identical uniforms and carried identical weapons. But finally Vitellius's Batavian auxiliaries took their enemies in the flank, and the defeat of the Othonians was complete. Otho himself, when the news reached him, was urged by his supporters to fight on; and the appeal was reinforced by representatives of the Moesian army, who had now arrived on the scene with the news that an advance body of their comrades had already got as far as Aquileia.

But Otho rejected all this advice and on 16 April AD 69 he committed suicide. His leaderless troops at first were unwilling to accept Vitellius, and, for the third time, Verginius Rufus was invited to become emperor. And now we encounter a phenomenon which later became frequent. For the soldiers not only requested Verginius to assume the imperial power, but threatened his life if he insulted them by refusing. Nevertheless, he did refuse, once again, and as they broke into his residence, he escaped rapidly through the back door.

At Rome, three days after Otho's death, the city prefect Flavius Sabinus made all the soldiers in the city swear the oath of allegiance to Vitellius. The senate, too, with fulsome congratulations, declared him emperor. When this news was sent to him in Gaul, he named this date, rather than the day in January when he had first been proclaimed by the soldiers, as the day of his accession, thus tactfully conceding the right of the senate, rather than the army, to award the throne. Then he moved on towards the south. Stopping at Lugdunum (Lyon), he presented his six-year-old son to the legions as his eventual successor, thus declaring that he proposed to found Rome's second dynasty. The boy was called Germanicus like his father, and on coins that Vitellius now struck his head and his sister's both appeared.[55]

As he continued on his march, Vitellius had the disagreeable idea of showing his troops the battlefield of Bedriacum. Tacitus, appalled by the behaviour of men and armies when the restraints of peace and order are removed, sees the full horror of the event.

It was a dreadful and revolting sight. Less than forty days had elapsed since the engagement, and mutilated corpses, severed limbs and the decaying carcasses of men and horses lay everywhere. The ground was bloodstained and the flattened trees and crops bore witness to the frightful devastation. Not less callous was the spectacle presented by the high road, which the Cremonese had strewn with laurel and roses, building altars and sacrificing victims after the fashion of an oriental monarchy. These trappings afforded pleasure for the moment, but were soon to prove their undoing. Valens and Caecina were in attendance, pointing out the various localities connected with the battle: this was the starting-point for the legions' forward thrust; from that point the cavalry had fallen upon the foe; and in a third place the auxiliary forces had surrounded their victims.

Even the prefects and tribunes contributed their quota, each magnifying his own performance in a hotchpotch of lies, truth and exaggeration. The ordinary soldiers, too, turned off the high road with shouts of glee, retracing the extent of the fighting and gazing admiringly at the heaps of equipment and corpses littering the plain. There were indeed some few observers who were deeply affected by the diverse influences exerted by an inscrutable destiny. They were moved to tears and pity. But not Vitellius. His gaze was unaverted, and he felt no horror at the multitude of fellow-Romans lying there unburied. Blatantly exulting, and little knowing how near the day of judgement was, he proceeded to offer a sacrifice to the gods of the place.[56]

To Tacitus, this sums up perfectly the precipitous downfall of all morality brought about by civil war. So do the remaining incidents of Vitellius's march on Rome.

While Vespasian and his leaders were thus employed in the various provinces, Vitellius was moving ponderously towards Rome. Day by day more despicable and lazy, he made a point of stopping at every pleasant town and country seat. In his train followed sixty thousand armed men, dissolute and undisciplined. Even larger was the number of soldiers' servants, and the camp-followers were remarkable even among slaves for their over-bearing manners. So numerous was the escort of officers and courtiers that this alone would have presented problems of discipline, even if that had been strictly enforced . . . There were many dreadful incidents of bloody quarrels among the troops, for the legionaries and auxiliaries did not see eye to eye after an original outburst at Ticinum (Pavia). When it came to attacking civilians, however, they agreed well enough. But the loss of life was severest at a point seven miles from Rome. Here Vitellius was one day engaged in issuing haversack rations as if he was fattening up a lot of gladiators, and the lower classes had poured out from the capital and were milling about everywhere in the camp. Taking advantage of the fact that the vigilance of the troops was relaxed, some crude practical jokers managed to cut off their belts without the victims' knowledge, and then kept asking them where their equipment was. The soldiers were not used to being jeered at and took the joke badly, attacking the unarmed populace with their swords. Among other casualties, the father of one of the soldiers was killed in the company of his son. Then his identity was realized, and the news of his death halted the onslaught on the hapless civilians.

However there were anxious moments inside Rome, as the troops rapidly pressed forward at every point.

They made chiefly for the forum, being eager to see the spot where Galba had fallen. No less grim was the spectacle they themselves presented, thanks to the shaggy hides of wild beasts and the long deadly weapons which they wore. Not being used to crowds, they did not bother about avoiding collisions, and sometimes fell over because the road was slippery or someone had jostled them. When this happened, the answer was abuse, developing in its turn into fisticuffs and sword play. The officers, too, added to the general confusion by dashing about here, there and everywhere with armed escorts.

Vitellius himself, once the Milvian bridge was reached, mounted a fine charger, armed and wearing the full panoply of a general. In this guise he drove the senate and the people before him like a herd of cattle. However his entourage deterred him from entering Rome as if it were a conquered city; so he exchanged his uniform for a borrowed toga, and marched at the head of his troops in good order. The front of the column displayed four legionary Eagles surrounded by standards belonging to four other legions. After them came the standards of twelve cavalry regiments and the serried ranks of the infantry, followed by the cavalry. Then followed thirty-four auxiliary cohorts grouped according to nationality and type of equipment. In front of the Eagles went the camp prefects, military tribunes and senior centurions in white uniforms, while the rest of the centurions marched with their respective centuries in full dress uniform with medals worn. The other ranks, too, were resplendent in their various decorations. It was a noble sight, and an army worthy of an emperor – though not when that emperor was Vitellius.[57]

Vitellius arrived at Rome in July AD 69. By this time the praetorian guard, which had fought against him, was already the theme of instructions which he sent ahead to Valens. Care was taken to keep these cohorts out of contact with each other; and now, with the exception of 120 soldiers whose participation in Galba's murder had to be punished,[58] every praetorian was to be granted honourable discharge – presumably with the usual gratuity of five thousand *denarii*. Instead of these men, Vitellius ordered Valens to recruit an entirely new and much larger praetorian guard, comprising not twelve but sixteen cohorts, each of which consisted no longer of five hundred but of a thousand men. They were to be drawn, for the most part, from the Vitellian legions and auxiliaries that had come from Germany. When Vitellius himself finally arrived in the capital, he took a personal hand in putting these arrangements into effect. Moreover, in order to gain as much goodwill as possible, he adopted a permissive line about the recruitment of these and other troops.

His indulgence towards his generals was as nothing compared with the licence accorded to the rank and file. Every man was allowed to pick his own arm of the service. The most worthless characters were taken on the strength of the garrison of Rome if that was their preference. On the other hand really deserving soldiers were permitted to stay with the legions or auxiliary cavalry, if they so desired. There was no dearth of such volunteers among those who were sick and blamed the extremes of the Italian climate. Nevertheless, the legions and cavalry lost the pick of their men, and the prestige of service at Rome suffered a severe shock, for a procedure whereby twenty thousand men were taken from every part of the army was not selection, but chaos.[59]

The joint commanders of the new guard were a former prefect of an auxiliary cohort and a former centurion. One supported Caecina and the other Valens; this meant a serious division, because these lieutenants of Vitellius were not getting on with one another at all well. Caecina had called Valens a disreputable money-grubber, and Valens described Caecina as a pompous ass.

At this point, however, the focus of attention moves sharply to the eastern provinces. The prestige of their legions had been greatly increased by Corbulo, and, since the Jewish revolt was not yet over, almost half the total Roman army was concentrated in the east. Somewhat surprisingly these legions had taken the oath to Galba, Otho and Vitellius in turn, though in each case with a lack of enthusiasm. During the summer, however, the imperial governors and senior officers in the area began to fear that the fate of Corbulo, under whom so many of them had served, was also, according to Vitellius's intentions, to be theirs. The legionaries, too, were frightened that Vitellius would transfer them to Germany, an idea which their strong ties with the east made them extremely unwilling to contemplate.[60]

Vespasian, a cautious general, had now spent over two years wearing the Jewish rebels down. When he heard of Otho's downfall, his plan to finish them off by capturing Jerusalem was temporarily shelved. Vespasian and the imperial governor to Syria, Gaius Licinius Mucianus (one of the former officers of Corbulo), had previously been on bad terms. For until recently, Judaea had been under a minor governor of knightly rank, owing ultimate obedience to the Syrian governor, and Mucianus had resented its elevation into a senior, independent military command under Vespasian. After the death of Nero, however, the two men resumed friendly relations, and, in collusion with the prefect of Egypt Tiberius Julius Alexander, began to intrigue against Vitellius. Mucianus, like Verginius Rufus, rejected any claim upon the throne for himself – partly because he lacked a son and heir. Alexander, too, entertained no such ambitions, being a knight (and a man of Jewish origin). Instead, the plotters all agreed that the man who should be elevated to the imperial throne in Vitellius's place was Vespasian. Fortunately he had two sons, Titus (already a distinguished general in Judaea) and Domitian. It was also a help that his brother Flavius Sabinus was still city prefect at Rome – since Vitellius, perhaps as a life insurance, had kept him on. Meanwhile, throughout the east, there was judicious dissemination of an oracle declaring that Vespasian was the man from Judaea destined to rule the world. And in the western provinces, too, important agents were at work on his behalf.

An important factor was the attitude of the legions from the Danube. They had not arrived in Italy in time to fight for Otho. But Vitellius had then caused anger among their ranks by seizing a number of their centurions and putting them to death. Moreover they felt a special detestation of Vitellius's coarse and bullying legionaries from Germany. And the Moesian army was all the more anxious to appoint an emperor who would protect them, because they had reason to feel a bad conscience.

Two thousand soldiers of the three legions that made up the army in Moesia had been sent to help Otho. When word came to them after they had begun their march that he had been defeated and had taken his own life, they none the less kept on as far as Aquileia, because they did not believe the report. There, taking advantage of the lawless state of the times, they indulged in every kind of pillage. Then, fearing that if they went back they would have to give an account and suffer punishment, they took it into their heads to select and appoint an emperor, saying that they were just as good as the Spanish army which had appointed Galba, or the praetorian guard which had elected Otho, or the German army which had chosen Vitellius.

Accordingly the names of all the governors of consular rank who were serving anywhere were taken up, and since objection was made to the rest for one reason or another, while some members of the third legion, which had been transferred from Syria to Moesia just before the death of Nero, highly commended Vespasian, they unanimously agreed that he should be the man, and forthwith inscribed his name on all their standards.

At the time, however, the movement was checked and the soldiers recalled to their allegiance for a season.[61]

There were close ties between the Danubian and eastern legions, owing to the transfers to which Tacitus referred, and others in the reverse direction that had earlier been necessitated by the operations of Corbulo. Furthermore, the eastern commanders were dependent upon the attitude of the Danubian legions of Moesia, Pannonia and Dalmatia, since if they themselves proposed to invade Italy, the support of these troops would be essential. In consequence the declaration they had made in favour of Vespasian, however tentative at this stage, influenced Alexander, the prefect of Egypt, to move on to the decisive step. This he took on 1 July, when he ordered his legions to swear an oath of allegiance to Vespasian. Coins were at once issued ascribing the new claimant all the imperial titles, including, for the first time, two imperial first names in inseparable association, *Imperator* and *Caesar*.[62] It was this day, the first of July, that Vespasian ever afterwards regarded as the date of his accession, though his recognition by the senate did not follow until many months later: so that he was less deferential to the senatorial and Republican tradition than Vitellius, who had treated the day on which the senate voted him his powers as his accession date. The empire had entered a new phase of more accentuated militarism, in which salutation by legions was enough to constitute accession to the throne.

On 3 July, Vespasian's own legions in Judaea likewise hailed him as emperor, and before the middle of the month Mucianus and his Syrian army had done the same. It was now necessary to plan how best to concentrate all these distant and widely distributed forces upon Italy and Rome. The strategy that Vespasian adopted was characteristically patient. Mucianus, with twenty thousand men, was to set out for the west. But he was not to move too fast, because meanwhile Vespasian, by cutting Rome off from the vital grain supply of Alexandria, had some confidence that he could force Vitellius to surrender without a fight[63] – perhaps with the help of his brother Sabinus, the city prefect of Vitellius.

The Danubian armies now brought their plan to support Vespasian out into the open thus assuming for the first time the historic emperor-making role which was to become such a feature of third-century history. They hated Vitellius – and supported Vespasian because they had no candidate of their own. For the imperial governors of Moesia and Pannonia (and of Dalmatia for that matter, though his legion hung back for the present) were all nonentities – and, besides, the Pannonian governor was a relation of Vitellius. However in August the initiative was seized by Marcus Antonius Primus, the commander of one of the legions in Pannonia. Primus was a typical, successful product of war and civil war, a Gaul of dubious honesty, tremendous drive and forceful eloquence – the sort of military phenomenon, Tacitus believed, which proved a disaster to the state. This was the officer whom the soldiers both of Pannonia and Moesia now appointed as the general to lead them into Italy, without reference either to Vespasian or to the senate. 'So great', comments Dio, 'was the legionaries' anger at Vitellius and their eagerness for plunder! For they were doing this for no other purpose than to pillage Italy. And their intention was fulfilled.'[64]

In contrast to Mucianus, who was still far behind in the east,[65] Primus, allegedly still without orders, made a dramatic dash for Italy across the Julian Alps. On the other side Valens was ill and played no further useful part, and Vitellius's cause received a further severe blow when Caecina, now consul, conspired with the prefect of the Ravenna fleet to betray him:[66] a classic instance of the treacheries which disfigured these civil wars. Calling a meeting of senior centurions and a few ordinary soldiers,[67] Caecina urged the desirability of deserting to Vespasian, whom he evidently regarded as likely to win the war. However, his troops refused to agree and placed him under arrest. Then they joined the rest of the Vitellian army, which was seeking to hold the line of the Po at Cremona.

Before long, in October, followed the Second Battle of Bedriacum. Since, however, Vitellius himself was still at Rome, his forces went into the subsequent battle virtually leaderless, and therefore demoralized. Nevertheless, it was a desperately fought engagement, and long after darkness had fallen no decision had yet been reached. The final breakthrough was described by Tacitus.

Neither side had the advantage until, in the middle of the night, the moon rose, displaying and deceiving the combatants. But the light favoured the army of Primus, being behind them; on their side the shadows of horses and men were exaggerated, and the enemy spears fell short, though those who were hurling them imagined they were on target. But the Vitellians were brilliantly illuminated by the light shining full in their faces, and therefore without realizing it provided an easy mark for an enemy aiming from what were virtually concealed positions.[68]

So finally the Vitellians broke and fled in total defeat. It had been a short and sharp campaign: and Italy could not have endured anything else. Tacitus links the battle with a pathetic scene, the inadvertent killing of a father by his son – the sort of tragedy which must have been frequent during these struggles of Roman against Roman. And the soldiers on both sides, the historian commented, after cursing this cruellest of all wars, had gone on killing all the same, and robbing even their own kinsmen.

Tacitus reports another and vaster kind of atrocity as well, the sack of Cremona by Primus's victorious troops. This picture, too, was designed to illustrate a special horror of civil war, the distress that falls on harmless civilians. To Tacitus, a Roman, the obliteration of Cremona, a community of Roman citizens and Italians, was far worse than the destruction of a foreign city. The city had surrendered: yet it was ravaged and looted continuously for four days. Reflecting on the catastrophe, the historian ascribes such terrible events, not just to a desire for looting, but to hallucination, frenzy – and motives which defy analysis.

Then Primus pressed on through Italy. As he went on his way he supplied evidence of the revolutionary indiscipline into which civil war plunged the army. For when the time came to replace the centurions who had been killed, he gave the legionaries the right to make the appointments themselves; and they chose their future superiors by a show of hands.

Vitellius, for all the bad character given him by Tacitus, was by no means unpopular at Rome. It was true that the praetorians he had superseded possessed good reason to hate him. Nevertheless, at first he had many supporters. But after the Second Battle of Bedriacum his doom was a foregone conclusion – as he himself realized only too well. Vespasian's brother Flavius Sabinus, the city prefect, who was well known as a man with a great gift for talking, nearly succeeded in persuading him to abdicate – a thing no Roman emperor had ever done before.[69] But this political initiative, like an earlier intervention by the city cohorts in AD 41 (Chapter 6), proved short-lived. For soldiers who were stationed in Rome and still supported Vitellius joined up with the civilian population and forced him to abandon the negotiations, and Sabinus, set upon by a leaderless gang of German auxiliaries, had to barricade himself, his men and his young nephew Domitian, the second son of Vespasian, in the citadel upon the Capitoline hill.

When the Germans assailed their makeshift defences the temple of

Capitoline Jupiter itself, supreme symbol of the Roman state, was burnt to the ground. To Tacitus, this saddest of all events in military history epitomized better than anything else the nightmarish, fatal character of such wars between Romans.

It is a matter of controversy whether it was the attacking force that set fire to the houses or whether – and this is the more common version – it was the besieged who did so in an attempt to dislodge their enemies, who were forcing their way up and had made some progress. From the houses the fire spread to the porticoes adjoining the temple. Then the ancient wooden eagles in the pediment caught alight and fed the flames. Thus the Capitoline temple, its doors locked, was burned to the ground undefended and unplundered.

This was the most lamentable and appalling disaster in the whole history of the Roman commonwealth. Though no foreign enemy threatened, though we enjoyed the favour of heaven as far as our failings permitted, the sanctuary of Jupiter Best and Greatest solemnly founded by our fathers as a symbol of our imperial destiny – a temple which neither Porsenna on the capitulation of the city nor the Gauls on its capture had been able to desecrate – was now, thanks to the infatuation of our leaders, suffering utter destruction. It had already been burnt down in a previous civil war, but by an individual and mysterious act of arson. But on this occasion it was besieged, and in the broad light of day set on fire. One might well ask, for what military reasons? What advantage could compensate Rome for this heavy sacrifice?

So long as we fought in the defence of our country and not against it, the Capitoline temple stood foursquare.[70]

As the fire raged the pro-Vitellian auxiliaries burst into the citadel, and Sabinus was killed. Domitian, in disguise, made a narrow escape.

Meanwhile Primus and his army were approaching Rome.[71] Very soon they forced their way into the city, and a new degradation became apparent. For the population were seen to be standing around and just watching the carnage – with the eyes of dispassionate spectators. In the civil wars of the late Republic, the people, either spontaneously or under persuasion, had at least felt there was a cause for them to support, and had taken vigorous sides. Now they felt excluded, neutral, indifferent: this was just a meaningless war of one army against another, which had nothing to do with them.

Close by the fighting stood the people of Rome, like the audience at a show, cheering and clapping this side or that in turns as if this were a mock battle in the arena. Whenever one side gave way, men would hide in shops or take refuge in some great house. They were then dragged out and killed at the instance of the mob, who gained most of the loot, for the soldiers were bent on bloodshed and massacre, and the booty fell to the crowd.

The whole city presented a frightful caricature of its normal self: fighting and casualties at one point, baths and restaurants at another, here the spilling of blood and the litter of dead bodies, close by prostitutes and their like – all the vice associated with a life of idleness and pleasure, all the dreadful deeds typical of a pitiless sack. These were so intimately linked that an observer would have thought Rome in the grip of a simultaneous orgy of violence and dissipation. There had indeed been times in the past when armies had fought inside the city, twice when Sulla gained control, and once under Cinna. No less cruelty had been displayed then, but now there was a brutish indifference, and not even a momentary interruption in the pursuit of pleasure. As if this were one more entertainment in the festive season, they gloated over horrors and profited by them, careless which side won and glorying in the calamities of the state.[72]

Even before Primus arrived, the praetorian camp came under immediate attack, its attackers including the guardsmen whom Vitellius had cashiered. The guard which he had formed to replace them defended the camp to the end; yet finally its gates were broken down. Vitellius himself had been making further attempts to sue for peace. But they proved useless, and on 20 December, towards the end of this year of hideous events, he died one of the nastiest deaths of almost any Roman emperor. It is described by Suetonius.

As word was brought that the enemy were drawing near, Vitellius had been hurried into a sedan with only two companions, a baker and a cook, and secretly went to his father's house on the Aventine, intending to flee from there to Campania. Presently, on a slight and dubious rumour that peace had been granted, he allowed himself to be taken back to the palace. Finding everything abandoned there, and that even those who were with him were making off, he put on a girdle filled with gold pieces and took refuge in the lodge of the door-keeper, tying a dog before the door and putting a couch and a mattress against it.

The foremost of the army had now forced their way in, and since no one opposed them, were ransacking everything in the usual way. They dragged Vitellius from his hiding-place and when they asked him his name (for they did not know him) and if he knew where Vitellius was, he attempted to escape them by a lie. Being soon recognized, he did not cease to beg that he be confined for a time, even in the prison, alleging that he had something to say of importance to the safety of Vespasian. But they bound his arms behind his back, put a noose about his neck, and dragged him with rent garments and half-naked to the forum.

All along the Sacred Way he was greeted with mockery and abuse, his head held back by the hair, as is common with criminals, and even the point of a sword placed under his chin, so that he could not look down but must let his face be seen. Some pelted him with dung and ordure, others called him incendiary and glutton, and some of the mob even taunted him with his bodily defects. He was in fact abnormally tall, with a face usually flushed from hard drinking, a huge belly, and one thigh crippled from being struck once upon a time by a four-horse chariot, when he was in attendance on Caligula as he was driving. At last on the Stairs of Wailing he was tortured for a long time and then despatched and dragged off with a hook to the Tiber.[73]

Such were the horrors that could take place when one Roman army was fighting against another.

The next day Primus's soldiers entered Rome, and rushed plundering and massacring through the streets. A new praetorian prefect, Arrius Varus, was appointed, presumably on the instructions of Vespasian. But Primus himself remained in control for the present, as the new emperor's representative. The senate obediently voted Vespasian the imperial powers and they were duly incorporated into a law,[74] though he still continued to date his accession from 1 July. Then, only a few days later, Mucianus and his eastern army arrived in the city. He sent Primus's troops back to their homes, and Primus himself, though he received the insignia of a consul, gradually fell into the background. A mutiny at Rome compelled Mucianus to delay demobilization for a time, but gradually things became quieter. Meanwhile Vespasian himself, leaving his elder son Titus behind to take Jerusalem, prepared to make his way to Italy. When he arrived in the capital in about October AD 70, Mucianus, though remaining one of his principal advisers, henceforward tactfully effaced himself.

As Primus's army had advanced so rapidly into Italy during the previous summer, he was greatly afraid that Vitellius would receive reinforcements from his original German base; and he had therefore written to Julius Civilis, chief of the German tribe of the Batavians (on the 'Island', between the Old Rhine and the Waal). Although their impressive contingent of auxiliaries in the Roman army had greatly helped to win the First Battle of Bedriacum for Vitellius, since then they had been aggrieved because the Vitellians had called on them for a further draft. So Primus now requested Civilis to threaten trouble for the troops whom Vitellius had left behind in lower Germany, in order that they should be kept too fully occupied to send him any help. A similar message was sent from Moguntiacum by the upper German commander Hordeonius Flaccus, who was prepared to join Vespasian's cause. But it was a perilous thing for Romans to invite a powerful foreign tribe, rich in auxiliary soldiery, to attack other Romans in the middle of a civil war. And to Tacitus this was another classic evil of civil strife, that Rome's defences against external nations were perilously eroded. For not only these peoples on the Rhine, but also the Sarmatians and Dacians beyond the Danube, were all tempted to make serious trouble. And Parthia, too, seeing the departure of so many legions from the east, sought its opportunity to intervene.

When Civilis received these messages, he rallied behind himself eight Batavian cohorts, which boasted a fine fighting record. He also collected tribesmen from across the Rhine; and it was another ominous development that German auxiliaries should unite with the tribes of free Germany against a Roman army. Moreover the perils of such a course were particularly grave because Civilis had a grudge, not so much against the Vitellians in particular, but against the Romans in general, because he had been angered, before this particular civil war ever arose, by being falsely charged with treason to the Roman cause. In consequence he acted far more violently than Primus or Hordeonius had ever intended, and delivered a violent assault on the Vitellian camp at Castra Vetera in lower Germany. This was not only depleted of troops, but was inadequately fortified, since it had never expected to be attacked.

To relieve the beleaguered camp, Hordeonius, from upper Germany, sent two legions under one of their commanders, Dillius Vocula. For the time being Castra Vetera was saved. However, Hordeonius's sympathies for Vespasian, though shared by many of his officers, did not meet with the general approval of the rank and file. Most of the auxiliaries, it is true, had no particular objection to changing sides, since they felt little political attachment to either the one leader or the other.[75] But when Hordeonius tried to induce his own legionaries in upper Germany to take the oath of allegiance to Vespasian, it needed all the pressure the tribunes could exert to make them comply, and even then many of the soldiers managed to avoid pronouncing the new emperor's name. Finally, at Novaesium (Neuss), to which Vocula after performing his relief operation had retired, the legionaries happened to discover that Vitellius had sent the money for a bonus to be distributed to them. It had never been paid: and now they demanded it. Hordeonius duly handed it over – but in the name of Vespasian. This angered his soldiers so much that they dragged him out of bed and murdered him.

It was at this stage that the legions on the Rhine learnt of the Second Battle of Bedriacum, ending in Vitellius's fatal reverse. The victorious supporters of Vespasian no doubt hoped that they could now dismiss Civilis with thanks for his services, whereupon he would revert to his former inactivity. However that was not his plan at all. He had an army under his control, and, observing the condition of the Roman legionary garrisons, noted that the infusion of local levies to fill their numerous gaps, far from replenishing their strength, had weakened and undermined them. When he had attacked Castra Vetera, it was still possible to maintain the somewhat threadbare pretence that he was taking this action to help Vespasian. But now he dropped this pretext altogether, and openly revolted from Rome.

The trouble really became serious when Civilis's appeals to the Gallic tribes, which he had been launching for some time without much result, now began to elicit an active response. The subjection of the Gauls to Rome had furnished them with a good many grievances, which Roman civil war leaders had short-sightedly exploited. And now, at the beginning of AD 70, they broke into open rebellion. Tacitus explains the psychological background.

The Gauls screwed up their courage, imagining that our armies were in the same predicament everywhere . . . But it was above all the burning of the Capitol that had driven men to the belief that the empire's days were numbered. They reflected that Rome had been captured by the Gauls in the past, but as the house of Jupiter remained inviolate, the empire had survived. Now, however, fate had ordained this fire as a sign of the gods' anger and of the passing of world dominion to the nations north of the Alps. Such at any rate was the message proclaimed by the idle superstition of Druidism.[76]

The leaders of the rebel Gauls included two chieftains of the Treviri, the tribe whose capital was at Augusta Trevirorum (Trier). These men, Julius Classicus and Julius Tutor, were Roman citizens like Civilis, and had held important Roman auxiliary commands.[77] Here was the hazardous reverse side of Augustus's creation of Rome's great auxiliary army, and of Claudius's expansion of Roman citizenship among leading Gauls. It is uncertain to what degree Civilis had harboured nationalistic intentions from the start. But now his Gaulish allies, as their issues of coinage made amply clear, planned an independent Gallic empire, an Imperium Galliarum, under their own rule.

The threat to the lower German garrisons was now grimly intensi-fied. At Novaesium, Vocula was murdered by a legionary deserter. Classicus, who had sent the assassin, promoted him to be a senior cen-turion in the forces of the new Gallic Empire. Then he proceeded to arrest the two legionary commanders, while their soldiers just looked passively on. For a terrible and scandalous thing had happened. So low, in these times of strife, had the morale of the legionaries fallen that they gave in to the rebels without a fight. 'It was a deed of shame,' declares Tacitus, 'quite without parallel. A Roman army was to swear allegiance to the foreigner, sealing the monstrous bargain with a pledge to murder or imprison its commanders.'[78] Then these soldiers of Rome actually swore allegiance to the Gallic Empire. The garrison of Castra Vetera, too, surrendered to the rebels. Civilis, as 'Asserter of Freedom', records the name and number of the disgraced legion on his coins.[79] But as the troops that had capitulated marched out, the German soldiers of Civilis fell upon them and massacred the lot. During these upheavals, all the winter quarters of legions and auxiliaries in Germany north of Moguntiacum were destroyed.

Nevertheless the support which the leaders of the revolt obtained from the Gaulish tribes fell below their expectations. In consequence when Mucianus concentrated nine legions in upper and lower Germany, under Petilius Cerialis and Annius Gallus respectively, it was only a question of time before the insurrection was suppressed. At an early stage, Cerialis regained control of the legionaries who had joined the rebels: yet he treated them with surprising indulgence, merely incor-porating them in his own army, and ordering his men not to taunt them. Faced with these large Roman forces, the Gallic Empire soon fell apart. Then Civilis was cornered on his own island. Of his fate, and the fate of the Gaulish leaders, no record has survived. But in general Cerialis apparently considered lenient treatment the best policy since the services of the Batavians and Gauls as auxiliaries would still be required in the future.

In the same year the rebellion in Judaea was brought near its con-clusion. For in August, after a terrible siege, Titus captured Jerusalem. Outlying fortresses continued to hold out – notably Masada on the Dead Sea. But the Romans officially pronounced that the war was over, and in June AD 71 Vespasian and Titus celebrated a joint Triumph. After so many terrible months and years, a new era of internal peace had at last begun.

8

Emperor and Army United
AD 69–180

The accession of Vespasian inaugurated an entire century in which, by way of sharp contrast with the immediate past, the emperors and the whole of their armies were for the most part at harmony with one another.

There were some bad moments, including not only military revolts but a brief period when it seemed that a ruler was powerless against the praetorian guard (AD 96–7). But in general the armies of the empire, under the leadership of their rulers, were able to concentrate on what were intended to be their main duties, the defence or expansion of the frontiers, and the maintenance of the imperial peace. This was the only epoch which witnessed a more or less successful equilibrium between the military and other forces which constituted the Roman principate.

Vespasian was a new kind of emperor. This was not because he was an Italian from outside Rome, since he was not the first man of such origins to achieve power in the civil wars that were just past.[1] But he came from a lower social class than any of his predecessors. Not only was he many steps down the social ladder from the Julio-Claudians, but he was also a good step or two down from men whose families had become knights and then nobles by imperial office, such as Otho and Vitellius.[2] That is to say Vespasian's accession threw the throne open to a far wider range of future candidates. In the years to come, armies could elevate whom they wished, without bothering about antique snobberies. The new emperor himself was as well aware of these implications as anyone else. Indeed he had already shown, conservatives might feel, a somewhat brutal kind of realism when he deliberately chose to date his reign, not from his recognition by the senate, but from his earlier salutation by the army.

It soon became clear that, by widening the range of imperial selection, the legions had secured an emperor of rare merit. That might surprise those who knew him as a somewhat humdrum, pawky individual, and a general of painstaking caution. But after the terrible year AD 69 these patient, prosaic qualities – traditionally the qualities that had made the Roman nation – were just what the empire and army needed. Although the successful are not always the best, Vespasian was a better man than Galba or Otho or Vitellius. It is true that he and his son Titus punished the defeated Jewish rebels with great brutality. But his regime, for the most part, was beneficial. He also avoided the mistakes which had caused his predecessors to fall as soon as they had risen. He himself, therefore, survived for ten years – and died a natural death, unlike, it would seem, his six immediate predecessors. And then, when he died, his powers were transmitted peacefully according to his wishes.

While avoiding Galba's provocative meanness, Vespasian nevertheless showed no particular munificence to his victorious troops. He was not very prompt in paying discharged soldiers their gratuities, and he only gave those in service the modest bonus of twenty-five *denarii* each, which was what Mucianus had promised them.[3] This relative lack of generosity might have caused Vespasian's downfall and death. But it did not, since, like Augustus, he was an expert at fine and exact calculations of what could be achieved and what could not.

His old-fashioned austerity was also extended to higher ranks, as one junior officer was said to have found to his cost. For when, the story went, he came to express gratitude for his commission, Vespasian's nose detected that the young man was reeking of scent. 'I would have preferred you to smell of garlic', remarked the emperor, and revoked his appointment.[4] He was also keen that legionary commanders should be men capable of real responsibility. In consequence he raised their minimum age, insisting that when they were appointed they should never be less than thirty-one years of age, and preferably thirty-four.

Vespasian likewise did not feel it necessary to show any greater liberality to the marines and sailors of the fleet. It was customary for fleet detachments to serve successive tours of duty at Puteoli, Ostia and Rome. 'But when these men asked', reports Suetonius, 'that an allowance be made them under the head of "shoe money", not content with sending them away without a reply, he ordered that in future they should make the march barefoot; and they have done so ever since.'[5] Nevertheless Vespasian's recent experiences had imbued him with the conviction that the navy should be granted a more impressive role. For one thing, he himself had derived great benefit from the desertion of the Vitellian fleets at critical moments. During the Jewish rebellion, too, he had made effective use of ships both in the eastern Mediterranean and on the Sea of Galilee, and he subsequently issued a number of coins with the unique inscription VICTORIA NAVALIS.[6] Furthermore, his initial plan of campaign against Vitellius had been based on maritime considerations, since what he had first intended to do was to starve his Roman enemies out by preventing the Alexandrian grain ships from getting through to them.

These experiences relating to the sea were now translated into practical measures. Vespasian raised the status of the most important fleet prefecture, at Misenum, so that it became one of the most important posts in a knight's career; and, unlike, as far as we know, any other emperor, he planted the cosmopolitan marines and sailors from the Misenum and Ravenna fleets in settlements of their own when they retired. These were located at Paestum (south-western Italy) and in Pannonia respectively.

Vespasian abolished four disgraced German legions, including those which had deserted in the rebellion of Civilis and the Gauls. However he also raised several additional legions, one of which, like a similar unit formed by Nero, consisted of former marines. The new emperor regrouped the armies of the empire so as to ensure that legions which had supported Vitellius should not occupy key positions. For example no such legions were included in the two garrisons closest to Rome, those of Pannonia and upper Germany. Moreover, Vespasian began to break up the large Rhine and Danube camps, which had been so large that they constituted a political peril; and in any case they were poorly adapted for the legions' principal task, which was defence along the frontier periphery. Instead, single legions were separated and spaced out in barracks of their own. This meant that the trend towards continuous defensive lines along the frontiers became still more strongly marked. The principal winter camps were now normally constructed of stone. Moreover the troop units themselves, which the civil wars had

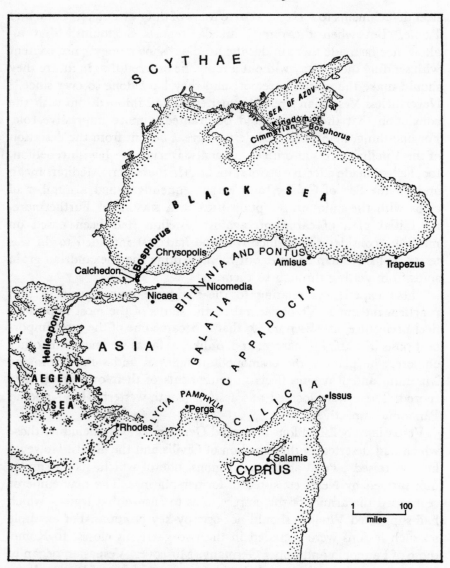

10   Asia Minor and the Black Sea

moved hither and thither in many directions, now reverted to a more static condition than ever before. A good deal of hostile capital had been made out of Vitellius's alleged unpopular intention to move legions from the countries with which they had formed ties:[7] so Vespasian could scarcely move them very often now.

It had been the legions in Syria which Vitellius's transfer plans had principally worried, thus illustrating their limitations as a fighting force, and Vespasian now thought it best to terminate their role as the only legionary garrison on the Asian continent. Instead there were now to be three such legionary centres. After the suppression of the Jewish revolt by himself and Titus, one legion continued to be posted in Judaea (under a governor of senatorial status),[8] and two were retained in Cappadocia (central Asia Minor) which had been Corbulo's first command in the area and was now united with its westerly neighbour Galatia under an imperial governor of consular rank. In Egypt, which had been Vespasian's own base of operations, two legions were retained as hitherto.

After the revolt of Civilis's Batavians and his Gaulish allies, the policy of employing numerous auxiliaries near their homes was reversed. The tendency to mix various races in a single auxiliary unit became accentuated, with the deliberate intention that locally recruited men should never form a majority. The result was that these units tended to lose their individual racial character, so that henceforward the auxiliaries display an ever increasing uniformity of arms, equipment and uniforms. Indeed auxiliary units, over the next fifty years, increasingly approximate to legions.

The termination of Civilis's rebellion at the Rhine mouth was followed by an extension of Roman territory much further up the river. For steps were now taken to shorten the more southerly stretches of the frontier, and thus to simplify its communications. This was done by annexing to the upper German command part of the area known as the Agri Decumates, which formed a re-entrant between the upper Rhine and upper Danube: so that the border-line now ran from the Black Forest to the River Kinzig (AD 74). However the German legions remained on the west bank, nearly a hundred miles in the rear.[9] In Britain anti-Roman elements had taken advantage of the civil wars to convert the kingdom of the Brigantes (Yorkshire) from a friendly buffer-state into a hostile tribe, and Cerialis, sent to Britain soon after he had brought the Rhine rebellion to an end, shattered their power and pushed the frontier upwards into northern England. The three legions of the province were now stationed at Eburacum (York) (from Lindum [Lincoln]), Deva (Chester) and Isca Silurum (Caerleon) (from Glevum [Gloucester]).

But this fighting was exceptional, since most of the enormous empire now enjoyed profound peace. The younger Pliny, writing a few years later, complained that triumphal statues were decreed to 'many who have never faced a battle, never seen a camp, never even heard the sound of a trumpet except at the theatre'.[10]

From the very outset Vespasian frankly announced that he proposed to found a dynasty, as Galba and Vitellius had tried but failed to do, by adoption and filial inheritance respectively. The new emperor's coins show how Titus was invested with all the powers that made him not only the emperor to be, but the immediate sharer of the emperor's power, like Tiberius in the last years of Augustus.[11] But whereas, in those early years of the Roman principate, Augustus had not been able to say, with constitutional explicitness, that Tiberius was going to succeed to the throne, Titus is unprecedentedly described on the coinage as DES[*ignatus*] IMP[*erator*],[12] which means, quite unambiguously, that he was intended in due course to become emperor: and that is what Vespasian persistently and openly declared was going to happen, with Titus's brother Domitian as his eventual successor.[13] For the emperor, seeing the havoc that rival candidates for military backing had wrought throughout the civil wars, appreciated clearly the advantages of having a family, and arranging that his offspring should subsequently come to the throne in their turn.[14]

Titus was a mature and experienced general, and an exceedingly reliable deputy emperor. This being the case, Vespasian now proceeded to take the logical but entirely unprecedented step of appointing him his praetorian prefect. The guard he took command of was an altogether new unit. Vitellius had disbanded Otho's praetorians, replacing them by his own, very much larger formation. Vespasian felt obliged to get rid of Vitellius's guardsmen; but he allowed some of them to join his own new guard. This was diminished in size from the sixteen one-thousand-strong cohorts of Vitellius to nine cohorts of five hundred men each – thus reverting to the strength of Augustus's original force (even if not completely to its Italian preponderance).[15] Yet, in spite of this apparently somewhat hazardous reduction of the guard's numbers, the prefecture was now regarded not as less important, but as more so. Even before the appointment of Titus to the prefecture, Mucianus, while temporarily in charge at Rome, had already recognized the new status of the post by nominating as second prefect of the reign not a knight as normally hitherto, but a senator and a relative by marriage of the emperor's house. For the man he had chosen was Marcus Arrecinus Clemens, who was the husband of Titus's sister. Clemens was also a close friend of the eighteen-year-old Domitian, who, after his brief appearance in the limelight during the siege of the Capitol, was believed to be jealous of Titus. And Clemens was also likely to be popular with the guardsmen, because his father had held the same post before him.

Nevertheless Vespasian almost immediately replaced him by Titus. This brought the guard under direct imperial control – and it is possible that the city cohorts were brought under the same command.[16] Although Titus was famous for his charm, Suetonius reports that he interpreted the intelligence duties of his praetorian prefecture with a severity that could be described as harshness.

In this office he conducted himself in a somewhat arrogant and tyrannical fashion. For whenever he himself regarded anyone with suspicion, he would secretly send praetorians to the various theatres and camps, to demand their punishment as if by consent of all who were present. And then he would put them out of the way without delay.[17]

Later Titus gained an enviable reputation as a scourge of informers. But that may have been because he could dispense with them, owing to the excellent espionage service at his disposal.

The praetorians and their officers presumably regarded his appointment to be their chief as a compliment, since their new commander was so manifestly the heir to the throne. And the legionaries, too, can have found nothing to protest against in Vespasian's clearly stated plans for the succession. The imperial house had changed, but dynastic continuity, which guaranteed that they would be paid and rewarded, still appealed to them as much as ever.

However senators of a conservative persuasion still objected to the open assumption that the principate could be handed down by heredity, like a personal estate. Vespasian, who had terminated a series of civil wars like Augustus before him, deliberately echoed Augustan propaganda upon his coinage. But Augustus had won the senators over by adhering meticulously to the outer forms of their defunct Republic; and now Vespasian clearly felt he could afford to be less careful

It was true that after a century of imperial rule most members of the senate were not as insistent on the non-hereditability of the principate as their ancestors. Some, however, still were. They had no doubt approved of Galba's choice of the 'best man' as his heir (though they would have liked it even better if they had chosen him themselves). By the same token, they had surely deplored Vitellius's nomination of his own young son. And now they were not pleased to see Titus so obviously earmarked for the throne. One such senator was Helvidius Priscus, who had married into a family of constitutional sticklers[18] and got into such trouble with Vespasian that in AD 75 he was executed apparently because he objected to the emperor's dynastic policy. As the philosopher Epictetus remarked, Helvidius's one-man protest was useless;[19] a rebellion had to have an army behind it.

Plots or alleged plots, with military implications, continued to occur under a good emperor almost as often as under a reputedly bad one. Finally, in AD 79, when Vespasian's health began to show signs of failing, his government detected a conspiracy which may well have been both authentic and serious. Among its leaders was Titus Clodius Eprius Marcellus, who had twice held the consulship – an honour to which only the most important personages could aspire – and was one of Vespasian's most intimate counsellors. Eprius Marcellus was by no means a conservative, philosophical, quasi-Republican like the late Helvidius Priscus. On the contrary he had engaged in fierce disputes both with him and with his father-in-law Thrasea, of whom he had been one of the prosecutors. Nevertheless he shared Helvidius's view that Titus ought not to be accepted as the next emperor. Perhaps he did not like the heir apparent's tough behaviour as praetorian prefect. And he may even have believed that, since Vespasian's undistinguished origins had not prevented him from becoming emperor, then his own humble background need not disqualify himself, either, from a chance of succeeding to the throne.

Nor, apparently, did Eprius make Helvidius's mistake of trying to take revolutionary action without army support. For he associated an eminent military man in his schemes. This was the almost legendary Aulus Caecina Alienus. After commanding one of the two German armies which Vitellius launched against Italy in AD 69, Caecina had then deserted to Vespasian. At that time this had earned him illwill among his former legionaries. But now, ten years later, it was suggested that he still possessed influence with the army. Indeed he was declared 'to have already got many of the soldiers in readiness for a rising'.[20] This presumably refers to some section of the metropolitan troops. Titus, as praetorian prefect, claimed to have seized the text of a speech which Caecina proposed to address to them, written in his own hand.[21] A rebellion, the authorities claimed, was due to break out that very same night, but Titus forestalled it by inviting Caecina to dinner and arranging for him to be stabbed to death in the palace. Eprius Marcellus was condemned to death by the senate, and committed suicide.

Soon afterwards Vespasian died, and Titus came peacefully to the throne. Although he was the tenth Roman emperor, it was the very first time that a son had succeeded his father. The only shadow over the occasion was the jealousy felt by his young but grimmer and more formidable brother, the twenty-eight-year-old Domitian – who could not forget his moment of importance in AD 69. When Vespasian died, Domitian was heard saying that Titus, who happened to be an expert imitator of handwriting, had tampered with his will. The real document, Domitian alleged, had declared that the two brothers should be partners in the imperial power (a formula which was not, in fact, put into practice until more than three-quarters of a century later). On his accession Titus gave the troops a bonus. We do not know how much it was, but rumour had it that Domitian toyed with the idea of doubling the sum, to win the army over to himself. However Titus, who had no son of his own, assured his brother that he would be his partner and successor – although, in fact, he gave him no share of his military powers.

After a reign of only two years, Titus died at his native town of Reate (Rieti), at the age of only forty-two. Domitian, who may or may not have been responsible for his death, rode straight from his brother's death-bed to Rome. There, on the very same day, he was acclaimed emperor at the praetorian camp. On the next day the senate voted him all the imperial powers. Though he had gone to the praetorians first, Domitian acted more constitutionally than his father, because he dated his accession from the day of senatorial recognition. Seeking for support within his family, he planned to award a consulship for the very next year to his relative Titus Flavius Sabinus, grandson of the city prefect of the same name. It was perhaps envisaged that Sabinus, who was the husband of Titus's daughter Flavia Julia, might eventually become heir.[22] About two years later, however, Sabinus succumbed to a charge of conspiracy, and Domitian's likely heir was now Sabinus's brother Flavius Clemens, and subsequently Clemens's infant sons.

Domitian was married to Domitia Longina, the daughter of the great general Corbulo, and in keeping with this alliance his principal aim was to be a successful military emperor. In particular he hoped to strengthen and push forward the empire's northern defences. In AD 83 he completed his father's endeavours to conquer the Agri Decumates, the lands between the upper Rhine and the upper Danube. When the tribe of the Chatti, who throughout this period were Rome's most powerful enemies in western Germany, had decided to take advantage of the change of emperors and make trouble, Domitian suppressed them and pushed the frontier forward to a line between the Main and the Neckar.[23] Subsequently, after the troubles of Domitian's later years, it became fashionable to belittle this achievement, but it was an authentic one all the same. Moreover, it enabled him to assume the title of Germanicus – not in the ominous sense in which Vitellius had used it, as nominee of the German legions, but with the old meaning of conqueror of the Germans. Henceforward he wore the robes of triumphant general, *Triumphator*, and even when he was attending a meeting of the senate he still kept them on.

Shortly after this German campaign he raised the pay of the army. From now on legionaries received 300 *denarii* instead of 225, and praetorians 1,000 instead of 750. The salaries of centurions, which seem hitherto to have extended between 3,750 and 15,000 *denarii*, now ranged from about 5,000 to 20,000. The emperor celebrated the pay rise by a coin of AD 84 bearing an inscription which had not appeared before: 'The Money of the Emperor' (MONETA AVGVSTI)[24] – a slogan which left it in no doubt who the armies' paymaster was. The pay increase subjected the exchequer to a heavy charge, which was to cause embarrassment to Domitian's successor. But the obvious accusation that he was pampering the soldiers, though it persisted among his critics, may have been misplaced. For one thing the currency had been showing inflationary signs, so that a *denarius* was not worth as much as it had been. Besides, the full twenty-five-year period of service, which Augustus had gradually forced his legionaries to accept without any corresponding increases of pay, was now invariable – and demanded larger remuneration.

Nevertheless Domitian's reform was significant, because it showed a characteristically objective and realistic appreciation of the army's central role in imperial policy. Domitian was popular with the soldiers, not only because he raised their wages and recognized their importance,[25] but above all because he spent so much time with them, more than any reigning ruler since the triumvirs in the previous century. Although a man whom senators regarded as oppressively harsh, he did not insist on excessive discipline in the army: and this, although his enemies later said otherwise,[26] was probably sensible enough, when it is taken into account that his prime consideration was to preserve his own life and regime. Very relevantly he issued coins showing the soldiers taking their military oath.[27]

Meanwhile the expansion in Britain begun under Vespasian was still proceeding. From AD 78 to *c.* 85 the imperial governor was Cnaeus Julius Agricola. By the end of the reign of Titus, there had been advances in Wales and Scotland, where the Tay had been reached; and the frontier-line was consolidated between the Forth and the Clyde. In three further campaigns under Domitian, Agricola turned into south-western Scotland, built and briefly occupied a legionary fortress at Inchtuthil on the Tay, and finally marched north almost as far as Inverness,[28] though without annexing any territory beyond the Forth–Clyde line. Then he was recalled, and the garrison was reduced from four legions to three, which comprised, with the inclusion of available auxiliary units, a total strength of about fifty thousand men. Agricola's son-in-law Tacitus, in a laudatory work devoted to his memory, exaggerated his achievements, and blamed Domitian for recalling him. But the emperor had rightly decided that the conquest of the whole island was impracticable. Although one would not realize it from Tacitus, he was on good terms with his generals, and the historian's returning father-in-law was granted appropriate honours. Then, however, Agricola, whose somewhat specialized experience did not make it easy to find him a job elsewhere, obediently accepted retirement, as he had obediently accepted orders all along. And so, like Germanicus and Corbulo before him, he became a typical Tacitean hero – the able general who was no political extremist but did his best to carry on, even under an emperor for whom he felt no sympathy.

Domitian's next target was Dacia. This kingdom lay beyond the lower Danube, comprising the plateau of Transylvania and extending towards the east. During the first century BC the Dacians had become an important power. Julius Caesar was only prevented from marching against them by his death, and then their chieftains were keenly sought after to strengthen the rival alliances of Octavian and Antony. Thereafter little had been heard of them until now, when their power and hostility became more formidable than it had ever been before, under a monarch named Decebalus. In AD 85 Decebalus crossed the Danube, and defeated and killed the imperial governor of Moesia. To facilitate retaliatory operations, Domitian now divided Moesia into an upper (western) and a lower (eastern) province.[29] Then, summoning re-inforcements, he himself marched to the theatre of war, establishing his headquarters in a Moesian city.

He was accompanied on his march by units of the praetorian guard. So that their employment for this purpose would not leave the metropolitan garrison short, Domitian added a further cohort to the guard, thus bringing the total to ten[30] (from which there was no further change until their disbandment in AD 312). The praetorian expeditionary contingent to the Danube was led by its prefect Cornelius Fuscus, who was also placed in command of the whole legionary force. This was an understandable arrangement when the emperor himself was at the seat of war, and was the sort of move which led to prefects becoming regarded as the emperor's military deputies. Fuscus had gained a reputation as an officer in the civil wars, when he assisted in the invasion of Italy by legions supporting Vespasian. But now, as he was penetrating into Dacia, he suffered a shattering defeat, and lost his life (AD 86 or 87).[31] This was the first but not the last time that a praetorian prefect fell in action. For the satirist Juvenal, it was a conspicuous moral example of how the mighty are fallen:

> Fuscus, who dreamed of battle lolling in marble halls,
> his guts a predestined feast for Rumania's vultures.[32]

In a disastrous retreat, the late prefect's army sustained heavy losses. However a year or two later Roman military superiority decisively asserted itself, and at a point facing the Iron Gates the Dacian army was crushed.[33]

Nevertheless the subsequent knock-out blow never materialized. This was because serious trouble was brewing along the middle reaches of the Danube, farther to the west. For at that point, beyond the frontiers of Pannonia, the German tribes of the Marcomanni and the Quadi, and the Sarmatian Jazyges, were showing unmistakable signs of hostility.[34] They had failed to help the Romans against Dacia; but their openly anti-Roman moves, which now followed, could with advantage to themselves have been timed earlier, when the Dacians were still undefeated. Nevertheless, because of the threat that these nations now posed, the Roman legions and praetorians were not launched against the Dacian capital after all. Domitian handed out bonuses to his fighting troops, and accepted his fifteenth, sixteenth and seventeenth salutations as *Imperator*. And then he made his way back to Rome.

During his absence a plot against his life had allegedly been detected. Now, however, there was an even graver development, for military rebellion broke out in upper Germany. At the outset of AD 89 its army commander, Lucius Antonius Saturninus, raised the standard of revolt. He was not a nobleman or a member of the traditional establishment, but owed his senatorial status to a recent promotion by Vespasian. Yet this recent enrolment as a senator perhaps made him a particularly fervent one, and impelled him to act. For it was already becoming clear that Domitian was less interested than any emperor before him in maintaining even a fictional partnership with the senators, other than those who served and admired him as officers of the army. Indeed, he rarely summoned the senate at all, except to impart information and issue orders. Saturninus may also have felt himself to be in personal danger. For he was said to be a sexual pervert, and Domitian, a notoriously vigorous womanizer himself, adopted a puritanical attitude towards sexual irregularity of all kinds, whether with women or men.

Saturninus launched his revolt by an unusual method. For he seized the savings banks of the two legions at Moguntiacum (Mainz) and thus made it difficult for the legionaries to avoid hailing him as emperor: which they consequently did. The garrison of Britain may also have been in the plot.[35] It was a very grave emergency indeed. Like the tribes beyond the Pannonian frontier, the rebel general must have regretted not having struck before Decebalus's Dacian army had been destroyed. Nevertheless very many of Domitian's soldiers were still tied up watching the situation in Dacia. In the east, too, hostilities were being threatened by the Parthians, in support of a pretender to the Roman throne who was claiming to be the ever-popular Nero, like two others before him.[36]

However Domitian acted against Saturninus with lightning promptitude. After receiving news of the insurrection by rapid couriers, he at once ordered to the danger spot the single legion which was now stationed in Spain, and, under its commander the future emperor Trajan, it left for Germany. Then, only eleven days after the usurper had first claimed the throne, Domitian himself, also, was already on the way to the Rhine.

The two more southerly legions of Saturninus's upper German command, stationed at Argentorate (Strasbourg) and Vindonissa (Windisch), did not join the uprising. This was perhaps why, after his salutation as emperor at Moguntiacum, Saturninus decided not to march southwards against Rome – the move it was always feared that legions in upper Germany would make. Instead he proceeded to the north in the hope of enlisting the support of the lower German army. This he failed to secure, for its commander, Lappius Maximus Norbanus, remained loyal to Domitian – and led his legions against Saturninus. Somewhere near Koblenz or Andernach, the two armies clashed. Saturninus had taken care to enlist the help of German tribesmen, the Chatti, from the other side of the Rhine. The river was frozen over, and the Chatti had intended to cross its icy surface. But when the day of the battle came the ice was thawing, and they never got across. Even so, however, Maximus was not expected to win. But he did. It was a decisive victory, and Saturninus lost his life.[37]

When Domitian arrived shortly afterwards, the disloyal officers received no mercy. The emperor was also eager to secure the files of the rebel headquarters, in order to find out what other army leaders were involved. But it now appeared that Maximus had destroyed these documents, in the hope of preventing a holocaust. It was an act of extraordinary courage, only possible because the winner of so important a victory could hardly be grudged survival and honour. Maximus's legions and auxiliary units, and the Rhine fleet, were honoured with the titles Loyal, True and Domitianic (*Pia Fidelis Domitiana*). The rising had shown what a wise policy it had been to break up camps, so that two legions were not located together:[38] and it may well have been at this time that the large troop concentration at Moguntiacum was broken up in the same way. It was also probably now that upper and lower Germany were formally converted from army commands into Roman imperial provinces and governorships, though their financial administration still remained linked with Belgic Gaul.[39] Moreover, warned by Saturninus's rebellion, Domitian ordered that the sums depositable at legionary headquarters should henceforward never exceed a certain amount.

The whole crisis had lasted a remarkably short time. Only twenty-four days after it had started, priests in Rome, the Arval Brethren, were celebrating 'the National Rejoicing' (*laetitia publica*) because of the victorious suppression of the rebels.[40] And the head of their leader Saturninus was placed on show in the forum.

Then Domitian moved on to Pannonia to lead four legions against the German and Sarmatian tribesmen. But at first they inflicted a reverse upon his army. At this point he decided that the threat from this quarter was so serious that there could be no further reckoning with the Dacians farther to the east, and that he would therefore accept king Decebalus's offer of peace. Then he was free to give the Pannonian crisis his full attention. The exact course of events remains obscure, but it seems that early in AD 92 the Jazyges crossed the Danube, and succeeded in destroying one of the Roman legions, together with the auxiliary cohorts and regiments that were supporting it. Subsequently, the situation was rectified by successful military action. But the success was not complete enough to make Domitian feel justified in celebrating a Triumph.

Before abandoning the campaign, however, he replaced the lost legion by transferring one of the upper German legions to Pannonia. He was not sorry to weaken the garrison of upper Germany, because once it became smaller there was less likelihood that the recent revolt of Saturninus would be repeated. The shift of military emphasis to Pannonia also meant that the Roman frontier had been strengthened at the point where such reinforcement seemed most likely to be needed in the future. This proved an accurate prediction, because the Danubian region was about to overtake the Rhine areas as Rome's principal battlefield against external peoples. Domitian's difficulties in the Danube zone were a dress rehearsal for even more serious emergencies nearly a hundred years later. Meanwhile there were now legionary camps on the Danube not only at Carnuntum (Petronell) but also at Vindobona (Vienna), Aquincum (Budapest) and Brigetio (Ó-Szóny).

In spite of the damaging blows that had been received as well as delivered, Domitian remained popular with the army. But he was not disposed to take any risks about this. As efficient as he was suspicious, he seems to have increased the measures of control which would ensure that his officers did not stray from the paths of strict loyalty. For one thing he apparently instituted a new kind of army personnel bureau, in which the records relating to every centurion in the army were retained and scrutinized with special care. A similar function, in all probability, had to some extent been performed by a department under the emperor's Minister of Notes (*a libellis*), but now a more thorough-going system was introduced under the Latin Secretary in the palace (*ab epistulis Latinis*). The first holder of this appointment, as far as we know, was Cnaeus Octavius Titinius Capito, working under Domitian and his two successors.[41] As a literary patron, the younger Pliny describes Capito as a haven of refuge and protection for authors.[42] But he must also have had a different side to his character, since he presided over this bureau which kept a check on centurions; and it was with his help that Domitian was enabled to exercise personal control of all their appointments, promotions and transfers.

This intensification of precautions seemed to the emperor particularly essential, since his dependence on the army was total. For, as the reign drew on, his alienation from the senate became so complete that he viewed its members with unremitting suspicion. This whole process of estrangement rapidly gained impetus after the abortive revolt of Saturninus, which had given Domitian a shock from which he never recovered. All the unpleasantnesses of treason trials were brought back, with a severity hitherto unknown. Moreover scaremongers, informers and other sinister agents received additional encouragement from the emperor's desire to lay his hands on the funds and properties of rich noblemen, in order to defray his expensive campaigns and the pay increases he had awarded to the army.

The plots or alleged plots that were now detected came thick and fast, and senatorial casualties multiplied. The emperor's childlessness increased his fears that someone would try to supplant him. In AD 95 one of the victims was his own cousin Clemens; and Clemens's young sons, who had been Domitian's intended heirs, vanished from view. Senators like Tacitus and Pliny, who obediently carried on during this perilous period, claimed after Domitian's death, as they rounded violently upon his memory, that many of the plots had been fictitious. But this remains uncertain. As Domitian himself remarked, emperors are unfortunate people because no one believes stories of plots against them until they have succeeded – and their victims have lost their lives.[43]

In this atmosphere his own assassination could not be far distant. He himself brought it nearer when, in the same year as the removal of Clemens, he prosecuted his joint praetorian prefects (we do not know their names) while they were actually in office.[44] When they were out of the way, he would have done well to replace them by a strong supporter of his own – for example Casperius Aelianus, who had already occupied the office within recent years. But the pair of prefects whom Domitian appointed instead, Petronius Secundus (who had recently been prefect of Egypt) and a certain Norbanus, noted what had happened to their predecessors, and in consequence felt highly insecure. Indeed, they almost at once formed the impression that complaints had already been lodged against them with Domitian, or were about to be.[45]

So they decided to save themselves by having the emperor killed. There is reason to suppose that the conspiracy had wide ramifications in the provinces and the legions, including those of Germany, and that the people in the know were not as discreet as they might have been. At Rome the plotters included Domitian's court chamberlain and one of his state secretaries – and his own wife Domitia Longina. Earlier on Domitian had divorced her for a time, but had subsequently reinstated her as his empress. During the initial period of their marriage she had become the first wife of a Roman emperor to have imperial coinage issued in her name during her lifetime. But the failure to revive the coinage after her reinstatement suggests that her influence was never completely restored. In consequence, being the daughter of Corbulo, she no doubt became a rallying point for those who revered his memory and hated tyrants. A freedman of Clemens's exiled widow was enlisted to do the fatal deed, and on 16 September AD 96, Domitian was struck down. His guards rushed up, and slew the assassin. But they were not in time to save their master, who was already dead.

An unprecedented development now occurred. Although the murder of Domitian was largely the work of the praetorian prefects, the new emperor, Marcus Cocceius Nerva, was the choice not of the praetorians, nor of any other section of the army, but of the senate. He declares as much on his coinage, which honours PROVIDENTIA SENATVS[46] – the Foresight the senate had shown. Nerva, who was nearly sixty-six years of age, was a respected Italian nobleman and lawyer, like his father and grandfather before him. He possessed distant imperial marriage connections, and had been a friend of Nero, who admired his poetry and rewarded him for his part in stamping out a conspiracy. Nevertheless, he also gained high favour with Vespasian, who chose him as his fellow consul (AD 71), and twenty years later Nerva had again become consul as the colleague of another emperor, Domitian.

Since he was declared emperor on the very day of Domitian's death, it seems likely that he was involved in the assassination plot; and the praetorian prefects, who had organized it, must have concurred in his choice by the senate. However the prefects, in killing Domitian, had acted without the knowledge or approval of the rank and file of the praetorian guard. For these soldiers had admired and loved him, and his murder caused them great shock, and made them dangerously restive.[47] But somehow or other, for the moment, they were calmed. This only proved possible, as Suetonius points out, because their agitation was leaderless.[48] And they were encouraged to remain inactive by the presentation of an accession bonus, recorded by an issue of coinage which displayed the new emperor addressing them in person (ADLOCVT[*io*] AVG[*usti*]).[49]

More remarkable than this initial passivity of the praetorians was the quietude of the legions in the provinces. They, too, had held a high opinion of Domitian, and Nerva was a civilian figure who had apparently never held an important governorship or military command. Nevertheless, the legionaries were persuaded to swear allegiance to him. But probably they only did so with noticeable reluctance. For it was ominous that, at the same time, he issued coins inscribed 'The Harmony of the Armies' (CONCORDIA EXERCITVVM).[50] Accompanying this inscription was the familiar device of clasped hands, holding a legionary Eagle.[51] It seems tactless of Nerva to have revived, just now, this slogan of wishful thinking, which had not appeared on the coinage since the bad old days of civil war in AD 68–70 (Chapter 7). For that terrible time of the four warring emperors, after the fall of the first dynasty, had come back to everyone's minds after the fall of the second. And it was the easiest thing in the world to see Nerva as a second Galba,[52] another ageing stop-gap who would shortly be swept away.

Before long there was an incipient mutiny at a Danube camp.[53] Then, in the second year of the new reign, there were persistent and alarming rumours about the disloyal attitude of the imperial governor of Syria, whose name cannot now be identified.[54] There were also, apparently, riots and signs of sedition in other garrisons as well.[55] In the harmony between emperor and armies, that had existed ever since the accession of Vespasian, a first breach had appeared. It was also reported that an eminent nobleman at Rome was conspiring against Nerva. This was Gaius Calpurnius Crassus Frugi Licinianus, a descendant of the triumvir Crassus, and a relative both of the Piso who had plotted against Nero and of the Piso Licinianus whom Galba had adopted as his heir. The suspect was exiled to Tarentum (Taranto).[56]

But much worse trouble followed shortly afterwards. The leading part played in Domitian's murder by the praetorian prefects Secundus and Norbanus had lost them the confidence of their own guardsmen. Because of this Nerva, immediately after his accession, had felt it advisable to remove them from office,[57] and appoint instead, with or without a colleague, Casperius Aelianus, who had held the same office during the later years of Domitian. This attempt at appeasement, however, proved disastrous, because it immediately became clear that Aelianus's sympathy with the late emperor remained undiminished. For the praetorians now rose in revolt, with himself as their leader, and demanded that Secundus should be handed over to them, together with Domitian's chamberlain, to answer for his murder.[58] Nerva barred the guardsmen's way in person, and declared that before they could take their victims they must cut his own throat first. But he was brushed aside, and the two men were seized and put to death. Then Nerva was actually forced to thank the praetorians, in public, for this execution of his friends and supporters. His humiliation loses nothing in the telling by Pliny the younger, who had himself served Domitian well but in retrospect detested his memory and was horrified by this treatment of his successor: 'The great blot on our age, the deadly wound inflicted on our realm, was the time when an emperor and father of the human race was besieged in his palace, arrested and confined ... A ruler was forced to put men to death against his will.'[59]

The reverence due to Nerva, declares Pliny, had vanished into thin air: authority was in the gravest possible peril: the whole empire was tottering to its fall, and crashing down upon the head of its emperor. And indeed those dread days of AD 68–70 truly seemed to be returning once again. It is with this crisis of Nerva's reign ever in their minds that Tacitus, Pliny and Plutarch, looking back from the tranquillity of a later regime, expressed their terrified abhorrence of civil war – and that Tacitus wrote about the year of the Four Emperors with such deep anguish in his heart.

Moreover it was to a measure of Galba's, taken during the convulsions of those times, that Nerva now had recourse once again, in order to deal with his desperate situation. Like Galba, Nerva had no son. And, like him, he now adopted, as his son and heir, a man from outside his family. His own kinsmen with eminent connections were passed over, and he chose the most suitable man he could find. But Nerva's idea of suitability was very different from Galba's. For whereas that emperor's choice had fallen on Piso Licinianus, a young nobleman whose ideals were not accompanied by any military experience, Nerva selected the most distinguished and popular general of the day, Marcus Ulpius Trajanus – and by remarkable good fortune he was as popular with the senate as with the army. Indeed he no doubt possessed a strong personal following at Rome, and, although Pliny is eager to deny a court intrigue,[60] these supporters may have brought pressure upon Nerva to reach this fateful decision.

Trajan was not an aristocrat, and had not even been born on Italian soil. For although his father belonged to a family that had originated in Italy, they had long been settled in southern Spain – and his mother was a Spaniard. A large part of the imperial soldiery came from outside the Italian borders, and now, for the first time, their emperor-to-be was of similar origin. While a legionary commander in his native country during the reign of Domitian, Trajan had been dispatched to suppress the revolt of Saturninus in upper Germany. Now, after the gift of a consulship by Domitian in AD 91, it was upper Germany to which he had returned, as one of the first imperial governors of the formally constituted province. His position in that key post no doubt weighed considerably with Nerva. Romans had not yet become used to the idea that military power was shifting from the Rhine to the Danube.[61] And, besides, the two upper German legions were in the best position of any units in the empire to risk a march on Rome. This possibility had two aspects. Trajan was well placed to help Nerva if the situation in the capital continued to get out of control. On the other hand, he would also have been excellently situated to intervene on his own behalf, if Nerva's choice of a successor had fallen on any other senator or general but himself.

Unlike Galba, Nerva announced the adoption with full publicity and legality, and word was sent to Trajan on the Rhine frontier that he had been granted the name of Caesar. His status, henceforward, could be compared with that of Titus during his father Vespasian's lifetime.[62] But in reality it was greater still, since, although Pliny missed no opportunity to exaggerate Trajan's glory, he was nevertheless right to conclude that his adoption virtually meant, in practice, that the elderly Nerva had abdicated.[63] For example, the appointments to major commands that now followed went not to Nerva's friends, but to Trajan's.

Then in January AD 98 Nerva died – a natural death. The succession of Trajan, still absent in upper Germany, followed with automatic precision. For whereas Galba's adoption of Piso had accelerated the outbreak of internal war, because Piso was a civilian, Nerva's selection of Trajan, who was a military commander, had successfully averted civil strife, and had brought peace back to the empire. But the idea behind both actions was the same – elevation on grounds of personal merit. Since Trajan, unlike Piso, was no nobleman, Pliny could plausibly affirm that he was chosen from *all* the people.[64] And since he was not a Roman, and his Italian family had been settled in Spain, it was even possible, stretching a point, to declare that he was a foreigner – the first who had ever occupied the throne.[65]

This formula of the adoption of the 'best man' proved successful and durable, since the four next emperors too, whose reigns extended over more than eighty years, were all peacefully appointed by the same means. Although the army had always preferred the continuity of dynastic succession to the senate's theory that the principate should be open to the most suitable senator, they made no move to protest against any of the accessions concerned. From this point of view it might at first seem as though this procedure represented a defeat of the army by the senate. But this was not really the case, since it was, in fact, not the senate, but the successive ruling emperors, who decided who the 'best man' was. And in deciding they took care not to adopt anyone unsatisfactory to the army.

Besides, the dynastic transfers of power which had been habitually preferred by the soldiers were not abandoned *as a principle*. They only failed to materialize, throughout all this period which lay ahead, because one emperor after another happened to be childless, or else his children had predeceased him. Even at the outset of the epoch, when Trajan was the man who was adopted, Pliny urges the gods to grant him sons and grandsons, and suggests that he, when his turn comes, should only adopt a son – as he had been adopted himself – if such heirs of his blood were lacking.[66] And as soon as a male heir became available to an emperor (Marcus Aurelius), he gave him the succession, as we shall see.

Meanwhile the practice introduced by the adoption of Trajan provided considerable satisfaction both to the army and the senate. But the real significance of his adoption lay deeper. It meant that the senate's legal right to nominate emperors, long since eroded, had now been openly shattered. Nerva's elevation to the throne had been a unique phenomenon, because to all intents and purposes, he had been a senatorial appointment – the first there had ever been. And look what had happened! The senate's nominee had been publicly humiliated by the soldiers, and in order to avert their wrath Nerva had been compelled to appoint a general as his successor.

So now, even more than ever before, the imperial regime was a military monarchy, dependent upon the troops. All other considerations were secondary. Twice in a later year (AD 238) the senate was again allowed the opportunity to appoint emperors, as was its right. And on both occasions, following within a few weeks of one another, their attempts dismally failed (Chapter 10). For the senators, except for those of them who were serving as senior officers, were not and never had been among the real masters. The army was the master – and the best an emperor could achieve was to share and guide its exploitation of the mastery.

Trajan, upon his accession, may have taken important steps for the protection of his regime and his person. For one thing it could well have been in his time that there were substantial developments in the military secret service and police. Hitherto the *speculatores*, and particularly those of the praetorian guard, had fulfilled this role to some extent, since it evolved naturally from their duties as imperial couriers. And now, in a somewhat comparable manner, a larger corps, known as *frumentarii*, likewise began to develop intelligence duties.[67] Each legion had long possessed a certain number of couriers bearing this designation, under a *centurio frumentarius*. The messages they carried were originally in connection with the imperial grain supply. But as the army supply service became more elaborate, a central unit of *frumentarii* was created and employed in the military administration. Charged with the conveyance of military dispatches,[68] these ubiquitous messengers gradually accumulated more far-reaching gendarmerie duties. They were employed, for example, to occupy observation check-points (*stationes*) in the road network which was essential to the defence of the empire and to the personal security of its ruler. And so, before long, they became known and feared as imperial spies.

It is to be supposed that the offices of imperial governors in the provinces each contained their quota of *frumentarii*. But the headquarters of these specialists were at Rome, where they were among the occupants of a camp on the Caelian Hill. Indeed, in this Castra Peregrina, first established in the mid-first century AD to house legionary detachments or individuals visiting Rome, these *frumentarii* soon became the predominant element, under centurions specially seconded from the legions. The camp also became, in consequence, a place of detention for persons awaiting trial, and its commandant the *princeps peregrinorum*,[69] who was probably in most cases a senior centurion, must have inspired a good deal of fear. There is record, too, of professional torturers and executioners (*quaestionarii*), who may have been attached to the same camp.[70] No doubt it also housed its quota of professional spies and *agents provocateurs*. The philosopher Epictetus is on record as describing the sort of thing that happened.

This is how imprudent men are trapped by soldiers at Rome. A soldier in civilian dress comes and sits by you, and begins by abusing Caesar, whereupon you, regarding the fact that he began the abuse as a sort of guarantee of trustworthiness, say all that you yourself feel. The next moment, however, you are being bound and led away.[71]

Epictetus uttered those words in *c.* AD 108, during the reign of the emperor Trajan. However, although the development of these phenomena was characteristic of this phase of the empire, it cannot be attributed with any certainty to his reign. Indeed a large part of his subsequent fame was due to his reputation for clemency. However that would not necessarily make him averse to these undercover activities, since military monarchies, however clement their direction at any one time, are inevitably compelled to protect themselves by tough and shady methods.

In any case, it does seem to have been Trajan who, at the outset of his reign, took steps to increase his personal security measures. Earlier emperors had employed both a German bodyguard and a mounted guard of praetorian *speculatores*, who performed a variety of protective duties. But the German guard had been disbanded by Galba; and Trajan evidently did not rely on the *speculatores* either, as completely as his predecessors had. For in addition he created a new mounted bodyguard altogether, known as the *equites singulares*.[72] Five hundred strong, later rising to a thousand, they were carefully picked men, mainly recruited from Germans and Pannonians who had already been serving in auxiliary cavalry regiments. These *equites singulares* had their own camp near the house of the Plautii Laterani, in the area where the basilica of San Giovanni in Laterano was later built. They stood in the same sort of relation to the praetorians as auxiliaries stood to legionaries; and they were under the command of two praetorian tribunes, so that their ultimate controller was the praetorian prefect. The creation of the corps was Trajan's way of showing honour to the auxiliaries of the empire, and of demonstrating that he trusted them with the preservation of his own person. It was also a form of reinsurance, in the event of doubts about the loyalty of praetorian guardsmen.

For Trajan had no intention that security anxieties of such a kind should distract him from his main military purposes, which were spectacular. Backed by an army which was now at its best, he intended to make use of its capacities to the uttermost, since it was his ambition to effect conquests that would outdo his hero Julius Caesar himself. 'As long', remarked Gibbon, 'as mankind shall continue to bestow more liberal applause on their destroyers than on their benefactors, the thirst of military glory will ever be the vice of the most exalted characters.'

In the first place Trajan was dissatisfied about Domitian's arrangement with King Decebalus of Dacia. In consequence he moved into warlike action against the Dacians, and in two wars (AD 101–2, 105–6) overran the country and annexed it as a new province.[73] By these campaigns he achieved the last major conquest in the history of ancient Rome, and the shift of the military balance from Rhine to Danube, which had become perceptible in recent years, was even more clearly apparent.[74] There was extensive booty, including a lot of gold. But Trajan needed it all and much more still. For he had even more massive schemes in mind.

His army in action is shown on that astonishing series of reliefs spiralling upwards on his Column at Rome, which still towers intact above the ruins of the surrounding forum of Trajan.[75]

The details of military dress [remarks D.E.Strong] and of the life and work of the army are treated with precise accuracy, and are clearly based upon full and detailed sketches made during the campaigns ... The approach of the narrative is poetic rather than prosaic ... The flow of the narrative is highlighted by the constant reappearance of the emperor in well-defined and traditional set-piece compositions.[76]

The great army displayed in these vivid reliefs was perhaps 400,000 strong. This figure, in addition to the praetorian guard and city cohorts, included some 180,000 legionaries, in thirty legions* (larger in size than in earlier days, since the first cohort of each was doubled in size†). The auxiliaries were now more than 200,000 in number; and there were perhaps about 11,000 irregulars or semi-regulars. These troops, known as *numeri* ('units') or *symmachiarii* ('allies'), comprised national companies, each about 300 strong, which could not be fitted easily into the regular army pattern. They were commanded by Roman officers, and usually served at some distance from the areas in which they had been recruited. In a sense this was a new development. But it was also, in substance, a revival and repetition of Augustus's original idea of forming auxiliary units of much the same kind. For the Augustan concept of a heterogeneous collection of auxiliary troops, preserving their varied national and racial origins in their equipment and methods of warfare, had become eroded, so that a new start was necessary. Nowadays the arms and equipment of auxiliaries were more uniform; and indeed transfers of soldiers from auxiliary units to legions had become quite common. The new irregulars represented a fresh attempt to make use of the special skills and qualities of soldiers from different countries.

* For the distribution of the legions in AD 112, see Appendix 1.
† See Appendices, note 21.

In order to fulfil his huge military requirements, Trajan compulsorily enlisted provincials as legionaries on an unusually heavy scale.[77] Complaints are recorded, and it was conceded that drafted men could offer proxies.[78] The proportion of Italians among the legionaries had now fallen from its early first-century figure of well over half to a mere 20 per cent. In frontier districts such as Pannonia the drafting of local recruits into the legions was particularly significant, because they were excellent

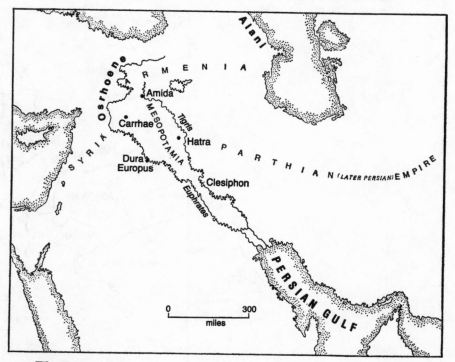

11   The East

fighting stock destined to play a large part in the future history of the empire.

In the east Trajan rounded off the frontier by annexing the client-kingdom of the Nabataean Arabs, whose capital was at Petra (now in Jordan). The country was converted into a new border province of Arabia (AD 105–6). But his real purpose, in this region, was to end the long confrontation with Parthia, not by diplomacy like Augustus and Nero, but by the utter destruction of its empire and regime. In AD 114 he annexed Armenia and upper (Northern) Mesopotamia, and in the following year captured the Parthian capital Ctesiphon and marched

Frontier of the empire
Borders of provinces
Imperial provinces are indicated in capitals
Senatorial provinces in small letters

BRITANNIA

LOWER

UPPER

AGRI

BELGICA

Rhine

Danub

RAETIA

LUGDUNENSIS

AQUITANIA

Narbonensis

TARRACONENSIS

LUSITANIA

Baetica

SARDINIA

MAURETANIA
TINGITANA

MAURETANIA
CAESARIENSIS

Africa

0   500
miles

12 The Roman Empire at the Death of Trajan (AD 117)

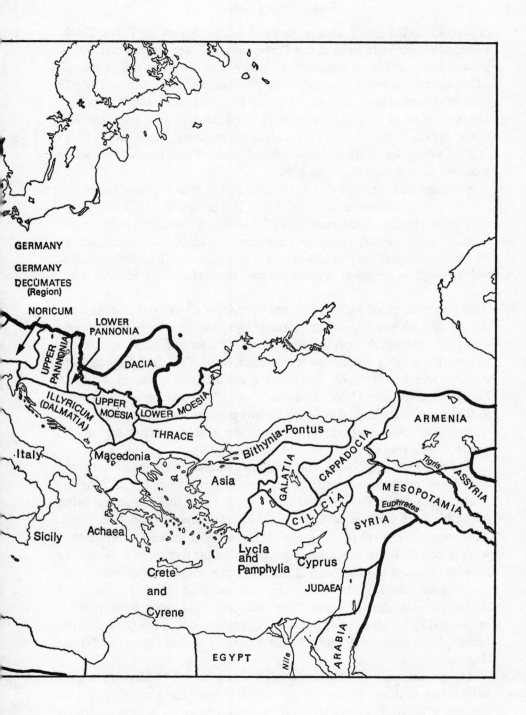

onwards into the south until he came to the estuary of the River Tigris. But in the next year Jews of the Dispersion, all over the eastern world, broke into savage insurrections. Moreover, in AD 116 southern Mesopotamia rose in revolt against the Roman occupation. Trajan's lines of communications were threatened and attacked at many points. He succeeded in setting up a puppet Parthian monarch in the palace at Ctesiphon,[79] but it was a very temporary measure. Then, in his sixty-fourth year, he turned homewards, and when he had reached south-eastern Asia Minor, he died.

His huge-scale eastern warfare had included many alleged triumphs, but they were almost entirely illusory. The campaigns had imposed a very severe strain on the resources of the empire, and had disastrously failed to produce any compensating results. The Roman army, for all its wonderful qualities and its harmonious relations with its *Imperator*, was not adapted to the great aggressions and expansions he had longed for.

This was recognized by his successor Hadrian (AD 117–38), who immediately abandoned the Parthian territories that had been precariously occupied during the previous years. This brought him serious unpopularity among conservative Romans, who also doubted, perhaps rightly, whether Trajan's supposed death-bed adoption of Hadrian had been authentic.[80] Yet Hadrian's accession was welcome enough to the army, since he had held important posts as staff-officer, legionary commander and imperial governor for the greater part of his predecessor's reign.

Hadrian's prestige with the soldiers enabled him to surmount a dangerous crisis in AD 118, before he had returned home. For his praetorian prefect Publius Acilius Attianus (who had helped to bring about his accession) felt obliged to put four leading ex-consuls to death. They were accused of plotting against Hadrian's life: and, whether they were guilty of this or not, their disapproval of his territorial evacuations may be assumed to have been intense. But the senate was so deeply and irrevocably shocked by these executions that Hadrian removed Attianus, with due honours, from his post. The new joint prefects appointed in his place were Septicius Clarus, who was the patron of the biographer Suetonius,[81] and a leading general named Quintus Marcius Turbo.

The greater part of Hadrian's reign was peaceful.[82] More than ever before the military system of the empire was based on armies permanently located on and behind its frontiers, upon which imposing defence works were built. Most impressive of all these constructions was Hadrian's Wall in Britain, extending from the River Tyne to the Solway Firth (AD 122–6). 'Old men', says Parnesius in Rudyard Kipling's *Puck of Pook's Hill*, 'who have followed the Eagles since boyhood say nothing in the empire is more wonderful than first sight of the wall.' In the static situation accentuated by such fortifications, the civil settlements beside the fortress-camps increased in size, and enjoyed a vigorous economic boom.[83] (Veteran colonies, on the other hand, ceased to be founded, because the prevalent practice of stationing legionaries and auxiliaries near their places of origin meant that special settlements on discharge were now unnecessary.)

The legionary force itself sometimes tended to be located well in the rear of the frontier defences, and came to be increasingly thought of as a strategic reserve. This was not, however, a reserve of which the legions themselves were normally available for transfer *en bloc* from one region to another. But it was not intended that the army should be wholly sedentary all the same. For although this tendency seemed to be increasing, at the same time the contrary practice developed of sending from province to province, whenever the need arose, not whole legions, since these were so hard to prise out of their camps, but smaller detachments (*vexillationes*) which were taken from a number of different legions and returned to them once their special emergency tasks had been completed. With an eye, once again, on mobility, Hadrian expanded Trajan's irregular or semi-irregular *numeri*, and made them into permanent official units of the Roman army. This differentiation between mobile and static types of troops heralded the future division of the army into two parts, a manœuvrable field force and a stationary frontier force (Chapter 10).

As befitted a provincial – for he was of Romano–Spanish origin like his predecessor – Hadrian devoted many years to making journeys round the empire, in the course of which he covered more ground than any previous emperor. His travels were prompted by a novel concept of the provinces. He regarded them no longer as conquered territories but as units of a commonwealth, each possessing its own specific character and dignity. But another and vital reason why he travelled so far and so long was in order to devote his personal supervision to all questions of military organization and defence. For these were questions which he saw to be of paramount and overriding importance. And so, although wars were few, no emperor was ever closer to his soldiers than Hadrian. He was keenly insistent on discipline, to the unique extent of commemorating this virtue (DISCIPLINA AVG[*usti*]) on his coinage.[84] And yet his constant presence with the armies, sharing their tasks and knowing all about their private affairs, their lives, their quarters and their habits, ensured him great popularity with the soldiery. He issued an unparalleled set of coins, commemorating each of his ten principal armies by name.[85] Each army, on these issues, is endowed with a special character of its own. To his successors, however, this positive en-

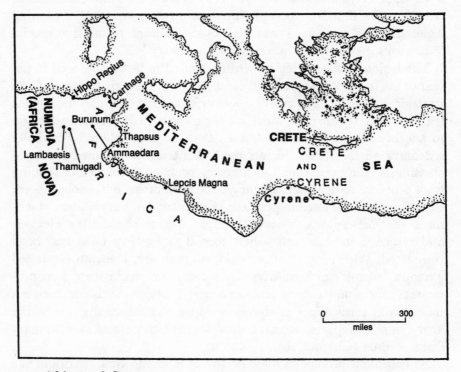

13 Africa and Cyrene

couragement of the armies' individual, separatist tendencies must have seemed a perilous innovation, since none of them produced such a series of coinages ever again.

A battered column of AD 128 at the Roman fortress-town of Lambaesis in Numidia (now Lambèse in north-eastern Algeria) displays excerpts from five addresses delivered by Hadrian to different units stationed in the place,[86] on the occasion of an imperial inspection and manœuvres conducted in the full heat of the July sun.

To the Third Legion (Augusta)

My representative [*legatus*] who is your commander has spoken for you and told me on your behalf all the allowances I ought to make for you – that a cohort is away, that every year postings are made in rotation to work in the office of the senatorial governor, that three years ago you gave a cohort and four men from each century to reinforce your sister third legion, that many various guard duties strain your strength, that you have twice within my memory not only changed your camp but built a new one. For these reasons I would have excused you if the legion had long ago abandoned manœuvres. But you have not abandoned them . . . Your senior officers and centurions were active and vigorous as they always were.

To the Legionary Cavalry

Military manœuvres have in a way their own rules, and if anything is added or subtracted, the manœuvre becomes less or more difficult. The more difficulty is added, the more elegance is subtracted. You have performed the most difficult of operations, throwing javelins while wearing breastplates . . .

To the Second (Spanish) Auxiliary Cohort

You have completed in one day works of fortification which others had distributed over several days. You have built a durable wall, such as is usually made for permanent barracks, in not much longer time than one is built of turf, which being cut in uniform blocks is easily transported and handled and is erected without trouble, since it is naturally soft and even. You used large heavy irregular blocks of stone, which no one can carry or raise or set in such a way that no irregularity appears between them. You have driven a trench straight through hard rough gravel, and have scraped it smooth. When your work was passed you entered the camp and rapidly fed and armed yourselves and followed up the cavalry which had been sent out, and greeted its return with a loud cheer . . .

I praised my distinguished colleague, the legion commander Quintus Fabius Catullinus, for putting you on to this manœuvre, which presented the appearance of a real battle, so that I can praise you, too, unreservedly. Your commander Cornelianus performed his duty satisfactorily. 'I do not approve of head-on charges' is the verdict of [name missing]. The trooper should ride across from cover and pursue with caution; if he cannot see where he is going and cannot hold in his horse when he wants, he is bound to run into hidden pot-holes.

To the First (Pannonian) Auxiliary Cavalry Regiment

You have done everything in order. You have filled the parade ground with your charges, you have thrown the javelin in a stylish manner, though using short and not easily manageable weapons; a great number of you have also thrown lances. You have jumped with speed and agility the other day. If there had been any fault, I would have noted it, and if there had been any outstanding performance, I would call attention to it. You were uniformly good throughout the whole manœuvre. Quintus Fabius Catullinus, my distinguished army commander, showed equal care on his part in the work of which he is in charge. Your commander appears to look after you carefully. You will receive a bonus, and you will perform a farewell parade on the parade ground of the Commagenians.

To the Cavalry of the Sixth Part-Mounted Auxiliary Cohort (of Commagene in north-west Syria)

It is difficult for the cavalry of a part-mounted cohort to give satisfaction in any case, more difficult for them not to cause dissatisfaction after the manœuvre of a cavalry regiment. The area of the parade ground is different and so is the number of javelin-throwers; the quality of the horses and your arms correspond with your lower pay. But you have avoided contempt by your keenness in doing what had to be done with vigour. To this you have added throwing stones with slings and combat with missiles. You have on all occasions jumped with alacrity. The special care of my distinguished legate Catullinus is apparent in your quality under his command.[87]

Meanwhile the peace-time tasks of a civilian nature, which Roman soldiers undertook as part of their duties, were becoming more and more numerous and extensive. They had long been builders and engineers; their great monument is the Roman road system, built (for the army by the army) with superb technical skill (*see* Introduction, note 7). Now, in the second century AD, we also find them – for example in lower Moesia – guarding horses, requisitioning clothes, escorting the grain supply and watching cattle.[88] From Egypt a non-commissioned officer (*principalis*) writes home to his mother congratulating himself because his rank exempts him from having to quarry stones.[89] It was also about this time that increased recognition was accorded to the existence of such multifarious non-operational tasks by the classification of a whole range of *immunes*, soldiers who were exempted from routine duties not by rank but because they had special duties of their own. There had already been a system of exemptions at earlier times, notably in the armies of Augustus and Domitian, in which veterans recalled to the colours (*evocati*), and other soldiers who had seen long service, were excused from heavy duties. But the full definition of *immunes*, as it appears in the *Digest*, seems to go back in its main lines to Hadrian.

Certain soldiers are granted by their conditions of service some exemption from the heavier fatigues. These are men such as surveyors, the medical sergeant, medical orderlies and dressers, ditchers, farriers, the architects, pilots, shipwrights, artillerymen, glassfitters, smiths, arrowsmiths, coppersmiths, helmet-makers, wagon-makers, plumbers, blacksmiths, stonecutters, lime-burners, woodcutters and charcoal-burners. In the same category there are usually included butchers, huntsmen, keepers of sacrificial animals, the workshop sergeant, sick-bay attendants (?), clerks who can give instruction, granary clerks, clerks responsible for monies left on deposit, clerks responsible for monies left without heirs, orderly-room staffs, grooms, horse-trainers (?), armoury sergeants, the herald and the trumpeter. These are all classed as *immunes*.[90]

Hadrian's care for the soldiers, then, was meticulous and their regard for him proved correspondingly great. But in the senate he never inspired confidence, since they were quite unable to forget that he had failed, immediately after his accession, to prevent his praetorian prefect Attianus from executing four of their most senior members.

Eighteen years later, in AD 136 when he was seventy years of age, he adopted a certain Lucius Ceionius Commodus as his son and successor, gave him his own name Aelius, and made him Caesar and imperial governor of both Pannonias. On the occasion of his adoption, huge bonuses were distributed to the metropolitan forces: 5,000 *denarii* to praetorians, 2,500 to city troops; apparently only 225 to legionaries. Soon afterwards, however, suspicion of disaffection fell upon Hadrian's ninety-year-old brother-in-law, Lucius Julius Ursus Servianus, a former imperial governor of upper Germany and upper Pannonia. For Servianus was believed to want the throne for the husband of his own granddaughter.[91] And so both men were driven to their deaths.

But in AD 138 Aelius Caesar too died, and Hadrian expressed regret that the bonuses handed out at his adoption had been wasted. In his place the emperor next adopted Antoninus Pius, a man of Romano–Gallic origin who, although he had held no important military command, was deeply respected by the army as well as everyone else. In his turn, Antoninus was ordered by Hadrian to adopt two boys on his own account: his Romano–Spanish wife's nephew, the austere and brilliant young Marcus Aurelius, and Aelius Caesar's son Lucius Verus. In this way the succession was guaranteed not for one reign ahead but for two.

When Hadrian died soon afterwards the empire passed peacefully to Antoninus Pius. His only difficulty was in persuading the senate to deify Hadrian, as the army must have insisted that they should. In the end, after they had heard many arguments and even threats, the senators reluctantly concurred. But the customary coinages commemorating the deified ruler were not issued. In and beyond the provinces the long reign of Antoninus that followed (AD 138–61) did not witness the unbroken peace with which it has often been credited; for fighting against frontier peoples was fairly frequent. But these hostilities remained local and peripheral. Perhaps the most important military events were in Britain, where Quintus Lollius Urbicus pushed the frontier up to the Forth–Clyde isthmus, which he spanned by constructing the Antonine wall.[92]

Antoninus felt in a strong enough position to reduce the privileges of the fleet and auxiliaries, whose children, born in service, henceforward no longer received Roman citizenship as they had before. Instead they would only obtain this by joining the legions — so that the new restriction was intended as an encouragement to legionary recruiting. In Rome there was a development rich in future significance when Antoninus appointed a series of praetorian prefects who were eminent lawyers. One of them, Marcus Gavius Maximus, held office for twenty years;[93] and he was a man as high-minded as his emperor.

Part V

The Army of the Later Empire

9
Growing Crisis and Army Domination
AD 180–235

On the death of Antoninus Pius the long period of unity between the emperors and their armies did not immediately come to an end. For, in spite of a serious military insurrection, the same harmony was for the most part maintained under Marcus Aurelius (AD 161–80). But in his reign two developments occurred which, with hindsight, proved to have permanently shattered the equilibrium. One of these happenings was a breakthrough, on an unprecedented scale, by the tribes bordering the Danube frontier, which necessitated an eventual reconsideration of the army's entire role. The other fateful occurrence was Aurelius's deliberate abandonment of his forerunners' practice of adopting a successor from outside his own family.

When Antoninus died, Hadrian's directions, twenty-three years earlier, that he should hand the throne over to the two princes he then adopted were scrupulously carried out; and the control of the empire and its armies was assumed jointly by Marcus Aurelius and Lucius Verus, who became betrothed to his colleague's daughter Lucilla. Though Tiberius, Titus and Trajan had already been invested with great authority while their predecessors were still alive, this was the first time that two emperors with absolutely equal powers (except for the chief priesthood) had ruled the empire together and operated as joint commanders-in-chief. The innovation foreshadowed a time when such formal collegiate arrangements would become normal, involving first the temporary division of the Roman army into two halves, and later the permanent partition of the entire empire and all its forces (Chapter 10).

On their accession the two new emperors went to the praetorian camp, where Verus addressed the guardsmen on behalf of them both. A bonus of five thousand *denarii* was promised, with more to the officers,[1] and the legionaries were no doubt rewarded, though on a less splendid scale. The sums were pitched high because important foreign wars were imminent. For when Parthia launched one of its periodical coups in Armenia, defeating and killing the imperial governor of Cappadocia, Verus went east to conduct a series of large-scale campaigns. He himself was something of a light-weight, but after the recovery of Armenia his able Syrian general Avidius Cassius made northern Mesopotamia a Roman protectorate (165–6). However ultimately inconclusive, the eastern fighting had at least created a peace which lasted for nearly three decades.

But now a critical emergency developed on the Pannonian frontier. The Marcomanni of Bohemia, a large and relatively advanced German people, were pushed southwards by convulsive population movements extending far back into northern Europe. In about AD 166, after a long period of restlessness, they took advantage of Rome's preoccupation with the east to surge across the Danube; while to their east, in the Danube–Tisza re-entrant, the Sarmatian Jazyges likewise burst into Pannonia. This was a collusive threat of unprecedented severity. But the Roman army, strung out behind its fortifications without a central reserve, was ill-equipped to meet the storm. As the war began to gather strength, Verus died (169) and his widow (Lucilla) was instead married by her father Aurelius to a Syrian, Tiberius Claudius Pompeianus, who had been engaged in stemming the tribal invasions as governor of lower Pannonia.

With difficulty two new legions were recruited to meet the Pannonian crisis. The chronology of the campaigns that followed is obscure, but they included two serious disasters which, according to one interpretation, both took place in the single year AD 170. Pouring across the upper and middle Danube at many points, the German tribes penetrated deep into the empire and even crossed the Alps into Italy, where they burnt the town of Opitergium (Oderzo), and Aquileia had a narrow escape.[2] And then, while this emergency was still causing the gravest disquiet, an invasion of a tribe of uncertain origin, the Costoboci, across the lower Danube overran the Balkans to within only a few miles of Athens. During the long series of painful campaigns necessitated by these disasters more than one praetorian prefect lost his life; and the empire was reduced to almost desperate financial straits.

The emperor had two main ideas for dealing with the situation. One was to admit Germans into the empire as settlers. Augustus and Nero had done the same, and later it was to become common practice. Aurelius's other proposed solution was to push forward and shorten the imperial frontier, creating two new provinces of Marcomannia and Sarmatia. Augustus had tried to do this and had failed. And Aurelius failed too. For just as it began to seem possible that his plans would bear fruit, Avidius Cassius, who now possessed wide powers in his native east, rose in revolt.[3] It may be that Aurelius's wife, Faustina the younger, was involved. She was linked to the army by a signal honour, since just as the emperor was Father of the Country, so she too had been designed Mother of the Camp (MATER CASTRORUM).[4] But her husband's health appeared to be failing, and, in case he died, Faustina may have feared for the treatment she and their fourteen-year-old son Commodus would receive at the hands of Aurelius's son-in-law Pompeianus. For it was said that she had written secretly to Avidius Cassius offering him marriage in the event of the emperor's death. Meanwhile it seems that he had received mistaken news that this had actually occurred. For he now arranged, or permitted himself, to be saluted emperor,[5] and with only two exceptions (Cappadocia and Bithynia) every one of the eastern provinces swore allegiance to his name. Aurelius hastily made peace with his northern enemies, content with only a minor territorial adjustment, the cession of a small strip of land on the other side of the Danube. Then he returned to Rome. This proved enough to demolish the uprising of Avidius, who was murdered by a centurion.

Aurelius visited the east, and then returned for a further reckoning with the Marcomanni and Sarmatians. But in AD 180 death cut him short, his purpose unachieved. It was a bitter irony that this most intellectual of emperors, the author of the introspective *Meditations*, had been compelled to spend almost the whole of his reign with his armies on active service. No previous emperor had ever filled the coinage with such abundant and varied allusions to his martial exploits. But the harsh spirit of these wars is sharply reflected in the reliefs of the Column of Marcus Aurelius at Rome. This monument, completed after his death to celebrate his German victories, resembles its Trajanic forerunner in that its pictures narrate a story of war which winds spirally upwards in successive scenes. Yet the Column of Aurelius has entered a new and more sensitive world. For its sculptors, by no means content with Trajan's extrovert sort of record, instead tell a tale of humanity and pathos. Now that the wars of Rome have become a much more serious matter, they not only appear as an exciting, triumphant enterprise, but scenes of tragic and harrowing carnage are also presented and dwelt upon. There is a much deeper and more sympathetic feeling for suffering and death, and especially for the grim fates of the barbarian enemy, who are no longer just untutored recipients of Rome's discipline, as they were on Trajan's monument, but anguished human beings. This is a world of fear and horror. It is also full of the supernatural, given haunting shape in the half-personalized Miracle of Rain, which was believed, on one historic occasion, to have saved the imperial troops from disaster.[6]

And now the eighty-two years of adoptive emperors reached an end. For during the previous decade and more Marcus Aurelius had gradually brought forward his own son Commodus, who became joint Augustus in AD 177, at the age of sixteen, and peacefully succeeded his father three years later. Since Commodus's addiction to emotional religions and gladiatorial sports made him an exceptionally eccentric ruler, his father has been greatly blamed for this reversion to the hereditary doctrine. However, unlike his predecessors, Aurelius was faced by the absence of any generally acceptable candidate – his own son-in-law Pompeianus was the most prominent personage available, but his accession to the throne would only have provoked rival candidatures and civil wars. And this at least was avoided, since the transition to Commodus was managed smoothly.

However, like Hadrian after the death of Trajan, Commodus completely abandoned his father's plans of conquest. For he judged that the dimensions neither of the imperial army nor of imperial finance were sufficient to carry an aggressive policy through. And he was probably right. Such an emancipation from the traditional policy of expansionism, which had proved so costly and ineffective, shows that at this stage at least his judgement had not become entirely warped.

So Commodus came to an agreement with the Marcomanni, and it was a much more satisfactory settlement than conservative historians were prepared to admit.[7] Then, returning to Rome, he crushed an alleged conspiracy in which Pompeianus's wife, his own sister Lucilla, was said to have been associated with the praetorian prefect he had inherited from his father – Tarrutenius Paternus, an eminent military jurist (AD 182): their aim had supposedly been to elevate a relative of the imperial house to the throne. Next, Paternus's colleague and then successor as prefect, Tigidius Perennis, became the dominant figure in the empire. First, he had Commodus's powerful court chamberlain murdered by one of the *frumentarii* who were now in demand as professional assassins. Then he arranged for the key commands in the two provinces of Pannonia to be conferred upon his own sons.[8] But in AD 185 father and sons alike succumbed. The story – or one version of it – is recounted by Dio Cassius, who was already a young public servant at the time, and saw Perennis as a much better man than the avaricious tyrant presented by other writings, notably the *Historia Augusta.**

Perennis [indicated Dio] met his end as the result of a mutiny of the soldiers. For since Commodus had given himself up to chariot-racing and licentiousness and performed scarcely any of the duties pertaining to his office, Perennis was compelled to manage not only military affairs, but everything else as well, and to stand, virtually, at the head of the state. The soldiers, accordingly, whenever any matter did not turn out to their satisfaction, laid the blame upon Perennis, and it was with him that they became angry.

The soldiers in Britain chose Priscus, a legionary commander, emperor; but he declined, saying: 'I am no more an emperor than you are soldiers!' The senior officers in Britain, accordingly, having been rebuked for their insubordination, now chose out of their number fifteen hundred javelin-men and sent them into Italy. These men had already drawn near to Rome without encountering any resistance, when Commodus met them and asked: 'What is the meaning of this, soldiers? What is your purpose in coming?' And when they answered, 'We are here because Perennis is plotting against you and plans to make his son emperor,' Commodus believed them . . . and accordingly delivered up the prefect to the very soldiers whose commander he was and had not the courage to scorn fifteen hundred men, though he possessed many times that number of praetorians. So Perennis was maltreated and struck down by those men, and his wife, his sister and two sons were also killed.

Thus Perennis was slain: though he deserved a far different fate, both on his own account and in the interests of the entire Roman empire – except in so far as his ambition for office had made him chiefly responsible for the ruin of his colleague Paternus. For privately he never strove in the least for either fame or wealth, but lived a most incorruptible and temperate life. And as for Commodus and his imperial office, he guarded them in complete security.[9]

* See Bibliography, Section B, Latin Writings.

Dio indicates that Commodus was prompted to abandon Perennis by one of the imperial freedmen, Marcus Aurelius Cleander, who hated the prefect. But if so Cleander did not obtain his reward immediately, since there followed a year or two in which the praetorian commanders, once again appointed in pairs so as to make rebellions of the guard less likely,[10] succeeded each other with lightning rapidity. One such prefect held office for only six hours – a state of affairs scarcely likely to contribute to the emperor's security. But then Commodus attempted an innovation, associating one of his couples of prefects with Cleander as their colleague and, in effect, their superior and chairman, endowed with the unique title of Minister of Protection, or, literally, of the Dagger (*a pugione*).[11] Raised to this unprecedented position, Cleander speedily rose to greater power than any prefect had ever held before. Finally, however, he succumbed to a plot organized by the prefect of the grain supply. Deliberately creating a famine in the city, this man incited the crowd and city cohorts – or it may have been the *equites singulares* – to seize Cleander and put him to death (AD 190). Commodus did nothing to save him. Indeed it may even have been he who ordered the deed to be done.[12]

As the emperor's interest in public affairs continued to wane, rebellions and suspicions of rebellion abounded. In this period the soldiers were increasingly to be seen fulfilling a sinister role as military secret police and oppressors throughout the provinces. According to one complaint, for example, perpetuated in an inscription from Asia Minor:

These men appear in the villages, doing no good but squeezing the village by unbearable requisitions of goods and by fines, so that, exhausted by the immense expenditure for these visitors and for the multitude of military police, it has been forced to give up even its public bath and has been deprived of the necessary means of subsistence.[13]

Equally hard pressed, the tenants of an imperial estate near Burunum (Soukh-el-Khmis) in north-western Tunisia petitioned the emperor against the lessee, Allius Maximus, who sent soldiers to intimidate them and beat them up:

ordering some of us to be arrested and maltreated, others to be imprisoned, and some, even Roman citizens, to be flogged and cudgelled, our only offence being that in respect of so heavy a charge, in proportion to our modest means, and to so manifest a wrong, we had written a rather bold letter to implore your Majesty's aid . . .

This compelled our miserable selves again to supplicate your divine providence . . .[14]

In reply Commodus, in a single sentence, merely directed his agents (procurators) to end the abuses.

Meanwhile at Rome, as always when there were plots and rumours of plots and an emperor who was not fully in control, the situation became more and more nerve-racking for leading citizens; whose lives were perpetually at hazard. Finally in AD 191 a new praetorian prefect Aemilius Laetus – the first African, as far as we know, to hold this post – decided that Commodus must be removed, and began to make his dispositions accordingly. The emperor's mistress and court chamberlain were of the same mind. Since, however, the attitude of the army to the summary extermination of the dynasty might well be unfavourable, careful preliminary arrangements had to be made in the provinces. First, Laetus arranged for two able African compatriots to be appointed to important imperial governorships, Clodius Albinus in Britain, and Septimius Severus in upper Pannonia, which now ranked second in the hierarchy of provinces. Next the prefect secured the appointment of another protégé, Pescennius Niger, as imperial governor of Syria, which stood at the head of all the provincial appointments. The city prefect Pertinax, a former general in Raetia and imperial governor of Britain was also in Laetus's confidence: and it was he, according to the plan now formed, who was to be elevated to the throne. Then, finally, on the last day of AD 192, Laetus arranged for a professional athlete to be introduced into the palace, and Commodus was murdered.

Laetus and the praetorian guard at once saluted Pertinax as emperor. The new ruler was handicapped, however, by the need to pay the praetorians not only his own accession bonus but also another bonus as well, which had been recently promised by his predecessor. Moreover, the efforts of Pertinax to raise and hand over these funds seemed to the guardsmen inadequate.[15] They also resented his stern discipline. The whole situation was a curiously precise echo of that never to be forgotten year AD 69, when the strict Galba had failed to establish himself after the luxurious Nero.[16] And from now on the analogy developed further, during the long period of chaos and civil war that was to follow.

Laetus soon decided that the proclamation of a martinet such as Pertinax had been a disastrous mistake. He therefore attempted to raise one of the consuls of the year to the throne instead; but this proved abortive. Next, Laetus incited his own praetorians to invade the palace. There Pertinax, deserted by everyone except his chamberlain, was struck down by a spear hurled by a German soldier, probably one of his own personal guard, the *equites singulares*.

The praetorians now found that there were two rivals for the succession, Flavius Sulpicianus, the father-in-law of the late Pertinax and his city prefect, and a rich senator named Didius Julianus. The praetorians decided to sell the throne to whichever of these men offered them the higher sum for it: and so a mock auction was held. Dio Cassius understandably deplored the sordid scene.

There ensued a most disgraceful business and one unworthy of Rome. For, just as if it had been in some market or auction-room, both the city and its entire empire were auctioned off. The sellers were the ones who had slain their emperor, and the would-be buyers were Sulpicianus and Julianus, who vied to outbid each other, one from inside the camp and the other from outside. They gradually raised their bids up to five thousand *denarii* per soldier. Some of the soldiers would carry word to Julianus, 'Sulpicianus offers so much; how much more do you make it?' And to Sulpicianus in turn, 'Julianus promises so much; how much do you raise him?'
Sulpicianus would have won the day, being inside and being prefect of the city and also the first to name the figure five thousand, had not Julianus raised his own bid no longer by a small amount but by one thousand two hundred and fifty *denarii* at one time, both shouting it in a loud voice and also indicating the amount with his fingers. So the soldiers, captivated by this excessive bid and at the same time fearing that Sulpicianus might avenge Pertinax (an idea that Julianus put into their heads), received Julianus inside the camp and declared him emperor.[17]

Perhaps these figures were not really so excessive: the rate Sulpicianus had offered had recent precedent, and Didius Julianus's supplement took account of the inflation of the *denarius*, which had become steeper owing to the warfare of Marcus Aurelius's reign.[18]* But the selling of the throne to the highest bidder was indeed a sign of the times, because it showed the military character of the power behind the throne in naked and unconcealed form. The story is taken up by a third-century historian from Syria, Herodian.

After he had performed the usual imperial sacrifices in the camp, Julianus was led out under the protection of a contingent of the guard larger than

* For the attempts by emperors to economize by issuing debased and light-weight coinage, see Appendix 5.

normal. Because he had purchased the empire shamefully, disgracefully and fraudulently, using force and opposing the wishes of the people, the new emperor rightly feared that the people would be hostile towards him. Therefore, under full arms and armour, his praetorian escort formed a phalanx, so that, if necessary, they could fight. They placed their chosen emperor in the centre of the formation, holding their spears and shields over their heads to protect the procession from any shower of stones hurled down from the houses. In this fashion they succeeded in conducting Julianus to the palace, as none of the people dared· oppose them. No one, however, shouted the congratulations usually heard when emperors were accompanied by a formal escort. On the contrary the people stood at a distance, shouting curses and reviling Julianus bitterly for using his wealth to purchase the empire.

It was on this occasion that the character of the praetorians was corrupted for the first time. They acquired their insatiable and disgraceful lust for money and their contempt for the sanctity of the emperor. The fact that there was no one to take action against these men who had savagely murdered their emperor, and the fact that there was no one to prevent the shameful auction and sale of the Roman empire, were the original causes of the praetorians' disgraceful and mutinous revolt at this time, and also of later revolts. Their lust for gold and their contempt for their emperors increased, as did assassinations also.[19]

And now the sinister events of AD 69 repeated themselves again. For just as in that year the provincial armies had been incensed by the praetorians' elevation of Otho, so now they refused to accept the guard's candidate Didius Julianus. In an attempt to ingratiate himself with the legions, he abandoned the praetorian prefect Laetus, and had him executed. But even this proved of no avail. Within a few weeks the imperial governor of upper Pannonia, Septimius Severus, was proclaimed emperor by his legions at Carnuntum, and his colleague in Syria, Pescennius Niger, was likewise saluted by his own legions there. Since the Danube was nearer than Syria to Rome, the praetorians, who realized the inadequacy of Julianus's military preparations, proved susceptible to messages from Severus. When he ordered them to arrest the murderers of Pertinax they did so: whereupon the senate proceeded to sentence Julianus to death. He had reigned only sixty-six days. Severus was hailed emperor, and within eight weeks of his proclamation he was already in Rome. Julianus's praetorian prefect Tullius Crispinus had gone out to meet his advance-guard, but had been killed. Otherwise resistance was negligible.

When Severus reached the capital he dismissed the entire praetorian guard. Once more this was an echo of AD 69, since Vitellius had done the same. But the circumstances of Severus's action were particularly dramatic, as Herodian indicates.

Severus used a trick to seize and hold prisoner the praetorian guard, the murderers of Pertinax. He quietly sent private letters to the guard's tribunes and centurions, promising them rich rewards if they would persuade the praetorian soldiers in Rome to submit and obey the new emperor's orders. He also sent an open letter to the praetorian camp, directing the soldiers to leave their weapons behind in the camp and come out unarmed, as was the custom when they escorted the emperor to sacrifices or to the celebration of a festival. He further ordered them to swear the oath of allegiance in his name and to present themselves, with good expectations of continuing to serve the imperial bodyguard.

Trusting these orders and persuaded by their tribunes, the praetorians left their arms behind and appeared from the camp in holiday uniform, carrying branches of laurel. Arriving at Severus's camp, they sent word that they were at the assembly ground where the emperor had ordered them to muster for a welcoming address. The praetorians moved towards the emperor as he was mounting the platform. Then, at a given signal, while cheering him in unison, they were all seized.

For prior orders had been issued to Severus's soldiers to surround the praetorians, now their enemy, at the moment when they were standing with their eyes fixed in expectant attention upon the emperor. They were not, however, to wound or strike any member of the guard. Severus ordered his troops to hold the praetorians in a tight ring of steel, believing that they would not resist, since they were only a few unarmed men, fearful of wounds, confronted by an armed host. When he had them netted like fish in his circle of weapons, like prisoners of war, the enraged emperor shouted in a loud voice.

'You see by what has happened that we are superior to you in intelligence, in size of army and in number of supporters. Surely you were easily trapped, captured without a struggle. It is in my power to do with you what I wish when I wish!'[20]

In place of the dismissed guard, Severus constituted a new one. It was twice the size of the last, each cohort being doubled in size from five hundred to a thousand men. The soldiers of any and every legion were eligible for transfer to the new formation, and a large proportion of those selected came from the Danubian units which the new emperor had brought with him to Rome. The legionaries were so pleased with the possibility of this promotion to a better paid job that Severus felt able to give them a much smaller initial bonus than they had originally requested. However, Dio wrote about this reconstitution of the guard in the gloomiest possible terms.

There were many things Severus did that were not to our liking. He was blamed for making the city turbulent through the presence of so many troops and for burdening the state by his excessive expenditures of money, and most of all, for placing his hope of safety in the strength of his army rather than in the good will of his associates in the government.

But some found fault with him particularly because he abolished the practice of selecting the bodyguard exclusively from Italy, Spain, Macedonia and Noricum – a plan that furnished men of more respectable appearance and of simpler habits – and ordered that any vacancies should be filled from all the legions alike. Now he did this with the idea that he should thus have guards with a better knowledge of the soldier's duties, and should also be offering a kind of prize for those who proved brave in war. But, as a matter of fact, it became only too apparent that he had, in the process, ruined the youth of Italy, who turned to brigandage and gladiatorial fighting in place of their former service in the army, and had filled the city with a throng of motley soldiers most savage in appearance, most terrifying in speech, and most boorish in conversation.[21]

But Dio, who was now a leading member of the senate and was due to become praetor in the following year, is here exhibiting conservative prejudices. And above all he is setting his face against the fact that the future salvation of the empire, and of its emperors, lay with the men of the frontier provinces, whose barbarity he, as a Roman senator and official of Greek origin, is at such pains to exaggerate. Moreover Severus also trebled the numbers of the city cohorts and doubled the Watch (who were now regarded as part of the regular army): this was not only a safeguard, in case the new guard proved unreliable, but a sop to the Italians who, even if excluded from the praetorian cohorts, were still called upon to provide the majority of these other metropolitan units. After every branch of the metropolitan troops had thus been increased, the garrison of the capital was going to be much more numerous than before.

Severus was now free to turn his attention towards the removal of his eastern rival, Pescennius Niger. But first he took a precaution in the west. The imperial governor of Britain, Clodius Albinus – latest of a series of governors of dubious loyalty in that province – was a powerful personage who enjoyed considerable influence in the senate. Severus suffered from no lack of heirs inside his own family, since he and his Syrian wife Julia Domna had two sons, of whom the elder,

Caracalla, was aged five, while the other, Geta, was still an infant. Nevertheless he felt it essential, in order to avoid trouble when he was away, to elevate Clodius Albinus to the rank of Caesar: that is to say, to adopt him as successor to the throne, for that is what such an elevation, at this period, surely meant. Then Severus set out for the east, and overwhelmed Pescennius Niger at the battle of Issus, near the junction between Asia Minor and Syria. Fleeing towards the Euphrates, Niger was overtaken and put to death, and Syria, in order to give less fuel to the ambitions of future governors, was henceforward divided into two provinces. Soon afterwards Severus felt himself strong enough to break with Albinus, and specifically designated his own son Caracalla as his heir.[22] Albinus, however, was hailed emperor by his own troops,[23] and crossed over to Gaul. There he and Severus confronted one another, but in a savage battle at Lugdunum (Lyon) Albinus was defeated and lost his life (AD 197).

The civil wars of 193–7 lasted longer than those of 68–9, and proved far more damaging to the empire. As deserters and robbers proliferated, the activities of imperial spies and military police intensified,[24] centurions being particularly employed in this role; and the provinces fell under harassing oppression. At Rome, too, twenty-nine senators died because they had supported the losing side. It was true that Severus proclaimed himself the heir of the enlightened Antoninus Pius and Marcus Aurelius, and even adopted himself retrospectively into their family, bestowing their names upon his elder son Caracalla. Yet even if his ideal, or at least his proclaimed ideal, was the bygone Antonine golden age, the recent civil wars had meant that its true revival was out of the question. Indeed Severus's brilliant lawyers were now putting forward the theory that the senate had not delegated its powers to the emperor but had surrendered them, an interpretation that stripped the polite veil from his military autocracy.

The Parthians had collaborated with his enemy Niger, and Severus, determined to strike back, proceeded east, and raised three new legions to fight against them – placing them under the command of knights, rather than under the senators whom by now he distrusted. The ensuing campaign culminated in the fall of the Parthian capital Ctesiphon (winter AD 197–8), and the annexation of northern Mesopotamia, first undertaken over thirty years earlier, was confirmed – a prefect of knightly rank, on the analogy of Egypt, being appointed as its governor. But Severus twice failed to capture the desert fortress of Hatra (Al-Hadr, fifty miles south of Mosul), the possession of which would have enabled him to extend the frontier southwards. Dio Cassius, who had read the reports of these operations as they reached the senate, commented very critically on Severus's eastern wars. He also recorded an anecdote which reveals the increasing reliance of emperors upon legionaries from the west – and illustrates the urgent necessity to keep the troops, of whatever origin, in good temper.

When Severus commanded the soldiers to assault the wall once more, the Europeans, who alone of his army had the ability to do anything, were so angry that not one of them would any longer obey him; and the others, Syrians, who were compelled to make the assault in their place, were miserably destroyed. When one of his associates promised, if he would give him only five hundred and fifty of the European soldiers, to destroy the city without any risk to the other troops, he said within the hearing of all: 'And where am I to get so many soldiers?' – referring to their disobedience.[25]

After the emperor had returned to Rome he created a precedent by stationing one of his new legions within the borders of Italy, indeed just outside Rome itself, at the town of Albanum (Albano). This move has been interpreted as a deliberate indication to the Italians that their supremacy over the provinces was at an end. But it is doubtful whether that was his purpose. For what Severus's measure perhaps revealed, instead, was his recognition that the empire needed a central reserve capable of being sent wherever it was needed – a reserve that had been lacking in the army of Augustus. The new legion was stationed near Rome because this was the central point of the empire, and the point where the emperor himself would normally be. Herodian stated that Severus brought about a fourfold increase in the garrison of Italy.[26] When the posting of the new legion and the enlargement of the city troops are both taken into account, it appears that the historian exaggerated, but not too much. For Severus multiplied the troops in Italy at least threefold, so that they now reached a total of at least thirty thousand.

Augustus had fixed the number of Roman legions at twenty-eight, later reduced by losses to twenty-five. Trajan had thirty legions (of somewhat larger size), and Severus thirty-three. He also increased what had formerly been the 'irregular' soldiery (*numeri*), relying especially on mounted archers from Osrhoene (Mesopotamia) and Palmyra (Syria), who were dispatched around the empire to all fronts, however far from their own countries.[27] Thus his army considerably exceeded the establishment of Augustus and even of Trajan, and its size, guaranteed by recruiting that was now almost wholly compulsory, was better adapted to the defence of the empire and the protection of the emperor's life.

Severus was entirely realistic in this matter. He understood that everything depended on the army, and drew the deduction that if the soldiers were to be loyal and efficient then they had to be given more pay. So legionaries now received five hundred *denarii* instead of the three hundred they had been getting ever since the time of Domitian, more than a hundred years earlier. Conservatives lamented this 'bribery' of the army, which they regarded as conducive to bad discipline. There were, of course, instances of indiscipline, notably at Hatra, but they can hardly be attributed to Severus's over-indulgence, and condemnations of him on this score failed to take account of the inflation which had continued to lower the purchasing value of the *denarius*. As a result of these trends the soldiers could only be satisfied if certain special measures were taken on their behalf. For one thing, some of their bonuses were paid in gold. Most important of all, they increasingly received payments in kind as well as in cash. Moreover, it seems to have been at this time that the deductions from their pay for rations, clothing and arms were lessened or partially offset by allowances. All this meant a great increase in the demands on civilians, who were called upon to supply such goods free, and to provide free personal services of various kinds as well.

In a further attempt to make the army a more attractive career, Severus granted legal recognition to the soldiers' unions with native women. These concubines, who were so often, nowadays, their compatriots, gained official status, and so did their sons, who duly followed their fathers into the army. To encourage this hereditary self-sufficiency, it gradually became more and more customary to assign the garrisons land, in allotments large enough to contribute materially to their subsistence. This policy was designed not only to remedy the dearth of agricultural labour but to reduce the soaring maintenance costs of the armed forces. Once in possession of these allotments, which they often owned themselves, the men took to farming as an additional lucrative, peace-time activity over and above the numerous civilian tasks which were reckoned among their normal duties.[28] And the soldiers also became traders, and speculators in the sale of workshop products and army stores.

The conditions in which the army lived at this time are displayed by the Saalburg fort in the Taunus mountains beyond the upper Rhine.

Today the fort's appearance in the early third century, after it had been rebuilt in stone, has been partially reconstructed.

The stone wall surmounted by battlements [writes Fergus Millar] enclosed barracks, store-rooms, a bathhouse and a headquarters building with a colonnaded courtyard. Outside were large baths with central heating, a number of temples, and a village along the road leading to the main gate. The frontier-line (*limes*) itself ran some two hundred metres to the north. Nothing shows more clearly the strength and settled conditions of the Roman frontiers immediately before the catastrophe of the third century.[29]*

But the most important area for these various developments was not the Rhine border but the Danube, which had been the storm-centre of the crisis under Marcus Aurelius and the starting-point of Severus's successful march on Rome. Here the local racial stock, to which the legions and auxiliaries in the region so largely belonged, was particularly notable for its warlike and patriotic qualities. And this now became, increasingly, the predominant element among the 'European' troops which, as Dio had said, were the best in the army.

Severus tied the soldiery very closely to his own person. He habitually wore a uniform that was a glorified variation upon the formal roles of a triumphant general. At legionary headquarters worship of the ruler himself increasingly overshadowed reverence to the standards. Moreover Severus was the first emperor to follow the example of Mark Antony and issue a large series of coins commemorating his individual legions.[30]

Centurions now received between 8,333 and 33,333 *denarii*, instead of the 5,000–20,000 of Domitian. This, once again, was partly in order to keep step with inflation, though when their new allowances are taken into account it also represented an authentic increase. Indeed, officers of all ranks were now on the crest of the wave. Severus gave them a variety of privileges. For example we begin to hear of clubs (*scholae*) for junior officers, combining social amenities with the sort of protection a modern insurance society provides. Moreover military jobs provided openings to many careers. This was a new military aristocracy, a special caste which supplied the empire with most of its senior administrators – and indeed with most of its emperors as well. And it was an élite that was by no means static but always changing, since the frontiersmen who provided the new sort of army officer had mostly risen from the ranks.

It is surprising to find that even an emperor as strong-minded and

* For Roman camps and forts, see also Appendix 3.

purposeful as Severus became as thoroughly dependent on a praetorian prefect as any ruler before him. Moreover, unlike Tiberius at the time when his reliance on Sejanus had been greatest, Severus was still at the height of his powers when this development occurred. No doubt, however, the personal burden of empire was so enormous that some such confidant seemed indispensable. The man chosen to share the burden was Severus's fellow-African and fellow-townsman Gaius Fulvius Plautianus. After assuming the praetorian command in AD 197, he gradually assumed an extraordinary and almost autocratic authority,[31] extending over almost every branch of government, including the grain supply and taxation. What is more, his daughter Plautilla was married to the emperor's heir, Caracalla. But after Plautianus had held office in this conspicuous fashion for over seven years, the emperor's brother (Lucius Septimius Geta), on his death-bed, disclosed certain unrecorded information that damned him. Plautianus had become estranged from Severus's empress, Julia Domna, a powerful personality herself. He had also incurred the hatred of Caracalla, whose marriage with his daughter was unhappy. And now, in AD 205, Caracalla, who had his own praetorian guard – or a part of his father's guard at his permanent disposal – arranged for three centurions to testify that they and seven others had been ordered by Plautianus to put both Severus and Caracalla to death. And so Plautianus, in their presence, was murdered on Caracalla's orders.

He was succeeded by joint prefects, one of whom was the outstanding jurist Papinian (Aemilius Papinianus).[32] During the immediately following period emperors tended to restrict the military power of the prefects, but they retained and even extended their civilian functions. In particular they served as the ruler's personal deputies on this council. Moreover Severus's initial choice of an eminent lawyer was no accident, since his own keen interest in law caused him to amplify their judicial powers, so that they became the supreme criminal judges in Italy beyond the hundredth milestone from Rome. On the inner side of that circumference the city prefect began to fulfil a similar role.

Severus now decided that the principal crisis area which needed his attention was Britain. The Antonine Wall, from Forth to Clyde, had never been very satisfactory, and by the end of the second century it was abandoned. Part of the responsibility for this evacuation may rest with Clodius Albinus, whose removal of the garrison to Gaul to fight Severus in AD 195–6 invited tribal incursions. In 208 Severus set out for Britain with his wife and two sons, and he was accompanied also by the joint praetorian prefect Papinian, leading a substantial portion of the guard. Large-scale invasions of Caledonia (Scotland) then followed.[33] These yielded, as always, no permanent result. Instead, Hadrian's Wall (Tyne–Solway) was rebuilt and restored as an effective frontier.

Then in AD 211, in his sixty-seventh year, Severus fell gravely ill at Eburacum (York), and called his sons Caracalla and Geta to his bedside. His last words of advice to them were said to have been these: 'Be on good terms with one another, be generous to the soldiers, and don't care about anyone else!'[34] Soon afterwards, he died.

Caracalla and Geta succeeded as imperial colleagues on the model of Aurelius and Verus fifty years earlier. Terminating the British campaigns (on a sound basis, contrary to the aspersions of expansionist historians), they both returned to Rome. But Severus must be blamed for leaving them the empire jointly, since they were manifestly on such bad terms that to advise them to make it up was of no avail. As they took up their residences in different parts of the imperial palace, there was talk of a geographical partition of the empire, such as was to occur later in the century. Their mother Julia Domna exerted herself to prevent this divisive step. Nevertheless, her efforts at reconciling her sons failed, and in about December AD 211 Caracalla had Geta assassinated.

This action, however, did not endear him to the majority of the much expanded praetorian and city troops, who inconveniently remembered that they had sworn an oath of allegiance to both emperors. At first the praetorians would not even admit Caracalla to the camp. When they finally let him in, according to Dio, he succeeded in winning back their dubious allegiance by extravagantly emotional assurances:

On entering the camp he exclaimed: 'Rejoice, fellow-soldiers, for now I am in a position to do you favours!' And before they heard the whole story he had stopped their mouths with so many and so great promises that they could neither think of nor say anything to show proper respect for the dead. 'I am one of you,' he said, 'and it is because of you alone that I care to live, in order that I may confer upon you many favours; for all the treasuries are yours.' And he further said: 'I pray to live with you, if possible, but if not, at any rate to die with you. For I do not fear death in any form, and it is my desire to end my days in warfare. There should a man die, or nowhere!'[35]

But Caracalla was well aware that the praetorians needed financial inducements as well as affectionate words. Next, therefore, he hastened to present them with bonuses of 2,500 *denarii* each, at the same time increasing their ration allowance by half. (Three years later, he gave praetorians accompanying him on a campaign 6,250 *denarii*, and legionaries 5,000.)[36] He also raised legionary pay from Severus's 500 *denarii* to 675 or 750, with proportionate increases for other categories of troops. But by now inflation was reaching such heights that pay was little more than incidental pocket-money, so that Caracalla also had to ensure that the soldiers' payments in kind likewise mounted at a high rate; and this he did.

The death of Geta meant the downfall of a large number of men who had supported him or had remained neutral: and these casualties, as the *Historia Augusta* describes, included the praetorian prefect Papinian.

Men of both senatorial and knightly rank were slain while in the bath, or at table, or in the street, and Papinian himself was struck down with an axe – whereupon Caracalla found fault that the business had not been done with a sword.

At last matters came to the point of a mutiny among the metropolitan soldiery. Caracalla, however, brought them to order with no light hand, and one of their military tribunes was put to death, as some relate, or as others, sent into exile. Yet Caracalla himself was in such fear that he entered the senate-house wearing a cuirass under his broad-striped tunic. Thus clad, he rendered an account of his actions and of the death of Geta.[37]

After these crises Caracalla employed two men named Ulpius Julianus and Julianus Nestor to direct his intelligence service, through the couriers who were placed at their disposal.[38] They were probably *principes peregrinorum* – commandants of the Castra Peregrina at Rome, where the secret police (*frumentarii*) had their headquarters (Chapter 8). The emperor also took steps to ensure that no imperial governor should ever have at his disposal a force that might be large enough to effect a successful revolt. For henceforward no single province was to contain a garrison of more than two legions. Twenty-four legions were assigned in pairs to twelve provinces,[39] the remaining nine (including the one in Italy) being distributed singly elsewhere.[40]*

In 213 Caracalla moved off for Germany, where a people named the Alamanni are named for the first time as enemies of Rome, threatening the upper Danube–upper Rhine re-entrant. The emperor defeated them, but developed earlier precedents, on a larger scale, by buying off another of the south German tribes with financial aid. This was

---

* For the distribution of the legions in AD 215, see Appendix 1.

much criticized, especially by conservative Romans. But it was cheaper than fighting, and in such a delicate area, which was not very far from Italy, it staved off danger for two decades. Moreover this was a policy which corresponded with Caracalla's own tastes, because he was a new sort of emperor with a personal liking for the Germans. He also revived a barbarian bodyguard, composed of handsome and power-fully built Germans and Scythians, who were encouraged to expect eventual promotion to the rank of centurion.[41] Moreover, although his official names were Marcus Aurelius Antoninus, the nickname of Caracalla (or Caracallus), by which he is generally known, was attached to him because of a long Gallic cloak of that name, reaching down to the heels, which he liked to wear and made fashionable at Rome.[42] He even wore a wig consisting of golden locks arranged in the German fashion.

Caracalla's liking for this Germanic style was symbolical of a larger phenomenon. For Caracalla, giving legal reality to a long-growing tendency, bestowed the Roman franchise upon almost the whole free population of the empire, whatever their racial origins.[43] This meant that the principal, traditional difference between citizen legionaries and non-citizen auxiliary troops – a difference which had long been more or less nominal – had now lost whatever small meaning it still retained. The elimination of this distinction, like the measure as a whole, provided a useful, egalitarian uniformity. But it also made it harder to attract ambitious men into the legions. So the need for conscription, far from diminishing, tended to increase.

Caracalla was obsessed with the desire to become an oriental con-queror like Alexander the Great – the ambition which even Caesar and Trajan had failed to fulfil. In AD 214, on the Danube, he mobilized an expeditionary force for the east, including a phalanx of sixteen thousand men equipped like ancient Macedonians. In the following year he moved to the Parthian frontier, and the borders of the pro-vince of Mesopotamia were successfully extended; but an attack on Armenia proved a failure. Wintering in Alexandria, Caracalla allowed his soldiers to run riot and massacre. In 216 he invaded Media, and then returned to Mesopotamia, where, in the following April, he was assassinated.

The deed was planned by one of his joint praetorian prefects, Marcus Opellius Macrinus, whose control of the emperor's correspondence had given him reason to suppose that his own life was in danger.[44] And now Macrinus at once had himself hailed emperor by the troops. It seemed to some that his fellow-prefect, Marcus Oclatinius Adventus, would have been a stronger candidate for the throne, though his record as a former secret military policeman (both *speculator* and *frumentarius*) may not have commended itself to everyone. However Macrinus arranged for Oclatinius to be promoted to senatorial rank, making him his own colleague in the consulate, and he did not attempt any counter-coup of his own. Nevertheless the attitude of the soldiery caused grave anxiety, since they had been so fond of their protector Caracalla. In consequence Macrinus took the precaution of assuring them that his murdered predecessor had died a natural death; and he also assumed Caracalla's name, Antoninus, as part of his own nomenclature.

Macrinus's reign introduces a new epoch, because, being only of knightly rank, he was the very first Roman emperor who did not belong to the senate. Nor did he approach that body with any conspicuous tact, since when he wrote to them he did not ask for the imperial power, but merely told them he had assumed it. Nevertheless, it was not from this quarter that trouble came; for the senate duly confirmed the legions' choice. The only reluctance that it displayed was in agreeing to the deification of Caracalla, when the soldiers demanded this. Nevertheless it was quickly compelled to abandon its objections.

All the same the army was still not satisfied with Macrinus, and although they had proclaimed him emperor they soon showed extreme unwillingness to obey him. Nor did his rapid and somewhat inglorious termination of the Parthian war, ill-concealed by coins inscribed VICTORIA PARTHICA,[45] in any way help to reassure them. The story is told by Dio, whose account of these contemporary events, if one discounts a certain personal bias against the army, carries a good deal of authority.

The soldiers were becoming turbulent. They were angered, for one thing, by their reverses at the hands of the Parthian enemy. But, more important still, they would no longer submit to any hardship if they could help it, but were thoroughly out of training in every respect and wanted to have no emperor who ruled them with a firm hand, but demanded that they should receive everything without limit while deigning to perform no task that was worthy of them ... The long sojourn that they made in practically one and the same spot while wintering in Syria on account of the war strengthened them in their purpose.

Macrinus, indeed, seemed to have shown good generalship and discretion in that he took away no privilege from the men already under arms but preserved to them intact all the privileges established by his predecessor, while at the same time he gave notice to those who intended to enlist in future that they would be enrolled on the old pre-Caracallan terms fixed by Severus. For he hoped that these new recruits, entering the army a few at a time, would refrain from rebellion, at first through peaceful inclination and fear, and later through the influence of time and habit, and that the others, in as much as they were losing nothing themselves, would remain quiet. Now if this had only been done after the troops had retired to their several fortresses and were thus scattered, it would have been a wise measure. For perhaps some of them would not have felt any indignation at all, believing that they were really not going to suffer the loss of any privilege themselves, in as much as they had experienced nothing of the sort immediately; and even if they had been vexed, yet, each body being few in number and under the command of the governors sent out by the senate, they could have done no great harm. But united as they now were in Syria, they suspected, on the one hand, that innovations would be made affecting them, too, if they should once be scattered – for they thought they were only being pampered for the time being on account of the demands of the war.

And thus they caused greater harm to the state than the Parthians themselves. For while the Parthians killed a few soldiers and ravaged portions of Mesopotamia, these men cut down many of their own number and also overthrew Macrinus their emperor. And what is still worse than that, they set up a successor just like him, one by whom nothing was done that was not evil and base.[46]

This successful plot against Macrinus was launched by Julia Maesa, the exceedingly able sister of Septimius Severus's wife Julia Domna. With the assistance of Publius Valerius Comazon Eutychianus, the knight who was in command of the legion from Albanum in Italy, Maesa let it be understood by the Roman soldiers in the east that her fifteen-year-old grandson, whom we know as Elagabalus because he was the priest of the Emesan sun-god El Gabal, had been the bastard offspring of his second cousin Caracalla. Moreover, being extremely wealthy, Maesa was able to back up her grandson's claims by timely gifts on a substantial scale. Macrinus's troops soon began to desert, and Ulpius Julianus, one of his praetorian prefects, died at their hands. Then, near Antioch, a battle was fought between the two factions, in which Maesa's henchman, the eunuch Gannys, though wholly lacking in military experience, proved victorious. Macrinus decided to flee to Rome, adopting the disguise of a military police spy (*frumentarius*). But at Chalcedon (Kadiköy) he was captured by a centurion, and subsequently put to death by another.[47]

Elagabalus, returning to Rome, displayed an almost complete preoccupation with his religious duties, combined, if only one-tenth of the stories about him are true, with exceptional gusto for passive homosexual practices. However he also sought to win the favour of the army by issuing coins in honour of his putative father, Caracalla, inscribed DIVO ANTONINO MAGNO.[48] The government of the empire, except in so far as it was in the hands of Maesa, was left to Comazon, the principal agent of Elagabalus's uprising, who now became joint praetorian prefect.

However he did not remain in that office, passing instead to senatorial rank and the city prefecture.[49] When he had vacated the praetorian command, Elagabalus was perceptive enough to see that all was not well among the guard. For when the senate loaded him with praises, he replied: 'Yes, you are fond of me. And so, by Jupiter, are the people, and the legions abroad, too. But I do not please the praetorians – although I give them so much!'[50]

The crisis came when Maesa began to realize that her imperial grandson's total lack of interest in public affairs meant she had backed a loser. She then prompted the eighteen-year-old Elagabalus to adopt as his heir his thirteen-year-old cousin, who assumed the name of Alexander. When Elagabalus, too late, began to realize that he was being superseded, a judicious distribution of money by Maesa and her daughter Julia Mamaea (Alexander's mother) induced the praetorians to murder Elagabalus. The joint praetorian prefects and city prefect who had now succeeded Comazon in those offices also succumbed.[51]

Maesa died about a year after Severus Alexander's accession (*c.* AD 223), and for most of his reign of thirteen years (222–35) the affairs of the empire were conducted by his mother Mamaea, who was more powerful than any imperial woman had ever been before. Since the life of Severus Alexander in the *Historia Augusta* is almost unrelieved fiction (perhaps contrived to glorify a much later emperor), its suggestion that his reign was a revived 'golden age' of senatorial authority appears to be without any foundation. On the contrary, his mother, and then he himself, had to devote a great deal of care to retaining the goodwill of the army. The *Historia Augusta*'s continual insistence upon Alexander's strict military discipline, though repeated in other sources,[52] merely echoes a conventional eulogistic tradition. In fact the regime, though it lasted longer than most, seems to have been rather weak. Unfortunately, however, it also began to gain a reputation for meanness. Yet the army's initial enthusiasm for the emperor took some time to die down completely, and there is plausibility in at least one passage in the *Historia Augusta*, where Alexander asserts that he is more concerned for the soldiers' welfare than for his own, since it was on them that the safety of the entire community depended.[53]

Nevertheless, these were perilous times, ill-suited for an experiment in feminine rule. An early and ominous development was a three-day-long outbreak of street-fighting, in which the praetorians first clashed with their own commander, the great lawyer Ulpian (Domitius Ulpianus) who was Mamaea's Syrian compatriot and principal adviser. Not unlike Cleander during the reign of Commodus, Ulpian at first apparently held a post of super-praetorian-prefect, presiding over the two joint prefects as their superior. But then the two prefects died, and the guardsmen turned against him – whether because he had killed the pair, or because they hated his old-fashioned disciplinary ideas, is not clear.[54] At all events he was now attacked by them and murdered (AD 223). Mamaea and Alexander, with whom he took refuge, had proved unable to save him, and were even forced to award his murderer, Marcus Aurelius Epagathus, the prefecture of Egypt.

Ulpian's death marked the end of the great juristic praetorian prefects who had been characteristic of the immediately preceding years. From now on their civil duties dwindled, owing to a succession of military crises. The first trouble occurred in AD 227–8, when Alexander's father-in-law, Seius Sallustius Macrianus, fled for refuge to the praetorian camp, perhaps after attempting an insurrection.[55] The historian Dio, too, was unpopular with the praetorians, because (according to his own version), 'I ruled the soldiers in Pannonia with a strong hand'.[56] Earlier on the guardsmen had complained about him to Ulpian, and when Dio became consul for the second time in 229, the emperor advised him to spend his two months of office in unobtrusive safety outside Rome.[57]

The external military situation had now changed gravely and permanently for the worse. This was because, in AD 223–6, the Parthian regime of the past four centuries and more, which had been somewhat easy-going and lacking in full control of its empire, was overcome and superseded by the far more formidable administration of the Sassanian Persians. With grave unrest returning on the Danube and Rhine fronts also, the Romans were at last confronted with a simultaneous double threat such as the armies of Augustus, or Marcus Aurelius, or Septimius Severus, had never been required to encounter.

In AD 231 Alexander and Mamaea, now described as 'Mother of the Emperor and of the Camp',[58] left for the east to repel a Persian invasion of Mesopotamia. After initial setbacks they were able to recover the lost province. Then, however, news reached them of serious trouble on the northern frontier. At this stage the Danubian legions which the emperor had taken on his eastern campaign, already jealous of his preference for the troops of his native east, clamoured to go back home to defend their own countries if these came under attack. In due course Alexander and Mamaea returned to Europe, and proceeded to the Rhine. But when, at Moguntiacum (Mainz), they reverted to Caracalla's prudent but inglorious policy of buying the Germans off, they did not succeed, like Caracalla, in retaining the favour of their troops. Instead they were abandoned by them, and murdered in favour of a tougher and more militant leader (AD 235).

10

Anarchy, Reconstruction, Collapse
AD 235–476

With the final accession of a ruler who was only interested in military affairs, the main part of this story, describing the interplay of military and political interests, is over. The army of the later Roman empire, though its many changes are fascinating, can only be briefly described here.

The new emperor was Maximinus I, an officer of powerful physique from the Danubian area who had risen from the ranks to the centurionate under Septimius Severus and had subsequently held the military commands open to knights.[1] His reign (AD 235–8) is hard to reconstruct, like his predecessor's, but for the opposite reason. For Maximinus, in contrast to Alexander, was profoundly hated by the senators who handed down the historical record.[2] He never troubled, at any time in his reign, to visit Rome. And he removed senators from officers' posts, after mutinous plots against his life, replacing them by his own soldiers.

For Maximinus, being an uneducated man himself, had little sympathy for the bourgeoisie who had been the traditional backbone of the Greco–Roman civilization. Under his rule this upper and middle class, beset by a host of tax-collectors, agents and military spies,[3] had to pay even more heavily than ever before for the defence of the empire: and they had to pay, not in the steadily deteriorating currency, but in bullion and kind. However, Maximinus's harshness was based on a realistic assessment. The empire was desperately hard-pressed. New and

269

grim ways of thinking and acting were needed to keep it above water –
and only a new type of emperor, prepared to subordinate everything
to military needs, could provide them. Maximinus was also a fine commander. He deserves to be regarded as the first of the Danubian
emperors – products of the best fighting peoples in the empire – who
during the next half-century were to strive manfully and in the end
successfully to turn the clock of history back, and enforce military
stability.[4]

Dealing successfully with attempted army revolts, Maximinus crossed
the Rhine near Moguntiacum and moved far into Germany, making
use of his Syrian archers and Mauretanian javelin-men. Then he
heavily defeated the Alamanni in a pitched battle which re-established
peace, for a time, along the Rhine and upper Danube. Next, transferring
his headquarters to Sirmium (Mitrovica in Yugoslavia), he moved
forward once again and won victories against the Sarmatians and
Dacians on the middle and lower Danube.

But meanwhile, in his continued absence from Rome, senatorial
hostility towards him was rising rapidly. It was in Africa, in AD 238,
that the first serious outbreak occurred. Some young nobles of the
province, outraged by his financial exactions, persuaded or forced the
aged senatorial governor of the province, Marcus Antonius Gordianus,
to set himself up as emperor, in association with his son of the same
name.[5] At Rome the senate, probably forewarned, pronounced the
two Gordians joint emperors. They also appointed a commission of
twenty former consuls to conduct military operations against the distant
Maximinus, who was declared a public enemy.

Gordianus senior and junior wrote to Rome promising the praetorians more money than anyone had ever offered them before.[6] They
were obliged to make extravagant offers of such a kind, because theirs
was an insurrection without the serious military backing which alone
would have given it a reasonable chance of success. In the event the
local militia recruited by the Gordians was easily overwhelmed by
Maximinus's imperial governor of Numidia. And so, after a reign of
only three weeks, both father and son met their deaths.

However, the senate, conscious that they could expect little mercy
from Maximinus, immediately appointed another pair of joint
emperors in their place. This time they selected two somewhat elderly
members of their own Board of Twenty, Balbinus and Pupienus. Here,
at last, was the senate in constitutional action, performing their legal
and rightful function of selecting the men who should rule them,

without reference to the army which had made so many emperors before.

Herodian, in the last of his eight books, gives details of this unique and historic procedure.

Since they had already cast the die, the senate voted to issue a declaration of war and choose two men from their own ranks to be joint emperors, dividing the imperial authority so that the power might not be in one man's hands and thus plunge them again into autocracy. They did not meet as usual in the senate-house but in the temple of Jupiter Capitolinus, the god whom the Romans worship on the Capitoline Hill. They shut themselves up alone in this temple, as if to have Jupiter as their witness, their fellow council member, and the overseer of their actions.

Choosing the men most distinguished for their age and merit, they approved them by ballot. Other senators received votes but on the final count Pupienus and Balbinus were elected joint emperors by majority opinion. Pupienus had held many army commands; appointed city prefect, he administered the office with diligence and enjoyed among the people a good reputation for his understanding nature, his intelligence and his moderate way of life. Balbinus, an aristocrat who had twice served as consul and had governed provinces without complaint, had a more open and frank nature. After their election the two men were each proclaimed Augustus, and the senate awarded them by decree all the imperial honours.[7]

The new emperors at first had a stroke of almost unimaginable good luck. For when Maximinus, without delay, abandoned the northern frontier and launched an invasion on Italy, his progress was arrested by the staunch resistance of the city of Aquileia. As the siege of the place proceeded without success, his severity towards senior officers caused the army, already suffering hardship from a failure of the supply services, to become gravely disaffected. Moreover the legionaries from Albanum near Rome were worried that his plan to ravage Italy would endanger their wives and children. So they turned against Maximinus, and, in association with a group of praetorians, succeeded in murdering him.

Pupienus hastened northwards from Rome to Aquileia, and then returned to the capital triumphantly. However his triumph was short-lived, because the praetorians were feeling very resentful because of their exceptional exclusion from the emperor-making process by the senate. In an endeavour to secure continuity, the joint rulers appointed as Caesar and heir the thirteen-year-old Gordian III, who, although the grandson and nephew of the two recent senatorial nominees of the same name,[8] appears to have been popular with the troops. However, the guardsmen remained unpropitiated, and before long they stormed into the palace. As they must have known very well, the relationship between the two emperors was an unhappy one. The principle of collegiality, however dear to the senate, could clearly prove fatal in such circumstances: and very soon it did.

Herodian describes the scene.

Both men were led to covet the sole rule because of their distinguished birth, aristocratic lineage and the size of their families. This rivalry was the basis of their downfall. When Pupienus learned that the praetorian guard was coming to kill them, he wished to summon a sufficient number of the German bodyguard to resist the conspirators. But Balbinus, thinking that this was a ruse intended to deceive him (he knew that the Germans were devoted to Pupienus), refused to allow him to issue the order, believing that the Germans were coming not to put down a praetorian uprising but to secure the empire for Pupienus alone.

While the two men were arguing, the praetorians rushed in with a single purpose. When the guards at the palace gates deserted the emperors, the praetorians seized the old men and ripped off the plain robes they were wearing because they were at home. Dragging them both naked from the palace, they inflicted every insult and indignity upon them. Jeering at these emperors elected by the senate, they beat and tortured them, pulling their beards and eyebrows and doing them every kind of physical outrage. They then brought the emperors through the middle of the city to the praetorian camp, unwilling to kill them in the palace. They preferred to torture them first, so that they might suffer longer. When the Germans learned what was happening, they snatched up their arms and hastened to the rescue. As soon as the praetorians were informed of their approach, they killed the mutilated emperors.[9]

The last time the senate had tried to make an emperor by themselves was in AD 96, when their nominee Nerva had very rapidly been obliged to yield to a military man (Chapter 8). This year AD 238, when they appointed two pairs of emperors in rapid succession, had even more speedily taken a catastrophic turn, not once but twice, on each occasion in turn. Moreover the action of the praetorians taken to thwart them was purely negative and destructive. For when they slew Balbinus and Pupienus they had no candidate of their own. Indeed they now proceeded to salute the young Gordian III as emperor, although he was only a boy.

The new emperor, or rather those who took control on his behalf, inherited an unhappy empire. We happen to have an inscription from the year of his accession, in which the villagers of Scaptopare in Thrace complain to the emperor about their oppression by soldiers and others, who have been insisting on the provision of hospitality free of charge.

We live and own land in the aforesaid village, which is very pleasant owing to its possessing hot springs and lying between two military camps in your Thrace; and as long as the inhabitants in the old days remained free from disturbance and extortion, they used to pay the tribute and the other requirements without fail. But since in our time some people have begun to take to injury and violence, the village, too, has begun to decline. Two miles from our village a celebrated fair is held and those who go there for the fair and stay for fifteen days do not stop at the site of the fair, but leave it and come to our village and force us to give them lodging and provide much else for their entertainment without payment. And, in addition to this, soldiers sent to various places leave their own routes and come to us, and similarly force us to furnish them with lodgings and provisions without paying any price.[10]

The villagers of Scaptopare presented their petition through one of their number who was a member of the praetorian guard, hoping that he might receive special attention from the emperor. But Gordian III, like other rulers, replied that they must ventilate their grievance through the usual and proper channels. And such must have been the outcome of innumerable complaints during this period of oppression and over-taxation, in which the needs and wishes of the army came first and foremost, and no one else got very much attention at all.

From AD 241 to 243 the supreme authority in Gordian's empire was exercised by a very able adviser, Timesitheus, who had risen from the ranks to become a centurion, or knight, and then praetorian prefect.[11] Accompanying the youthful emperor to the east, Timesitheus won important victories against the Persians.[12] But then he died, and his successor Philip, the son of an Arabian chieftain, exploited a food-shortage, which he himself had artificially created, to induce the soldiers to assassinate Gordian and salute himself instead (244). After concluding the usual indeterminate peace with the Persians, Philip returned to Rome and established satisfactory relations with the senate. Next he proceeded to the northern frontiers, where he conducted successful campaigns. The Millenary of Rome was then celebrated with great pomp (247–8).

But in spite of these apparently hopeful manifestations, it was in Philip's reign that two parallel, catastrophic, military situations intensi-fied and converged. First, the tendency for individual army garrisons to set up their own generals as emperors began to reach alarming and, it might seem, almost incredible proportions. Between AD 247 and 270 no less than thirty such emperors were proclaimed.[13] Second, the pressure from martial tribes on the northern frontiers became almost uncontrollably great.

In 248 the Goths, tempted by Roman disunity, surged across the Danube and Philip's city prefect Decius, who came from Pannonia and had served his fellow-Danubian Maximinus as imperial governor of nearer Spain, was given the supreme command in his own homeland and in Moesia. There he quelled invasions and mutinies with such success that his troops declared him emperor, whereupon Philip, moving northwards to confront him, was killed in a battle near Verona (249). Assuming the glorious name of Trajan, Decius, on an unprecedented series of coins, explicitly celebrated the glories of the Danubian and Illyrian peoples and their armies.[14] However, he, in his turn, fell in battle, two years later, fighting against the Goths at Abrittus (near Cobadin in the Dobrogea). His end was probably hastened by treachery from his subordinate general in lower Moesia, Trebonianus Gallus, who became his successor. Gallus was compelled to face what emperors had always dreaded, attacks by external enemies on the northern and eastern frontiers at the same time. But then he, too, was murdered, by the governor of lower Moesia, an African named Aemilian (253).

However, after further civil strife, the emperor who emerged was Valerian (Publius Licinius Valerianus), a senator of distinguished origin who was the imperial governor of Raetia. Valerian immediately appointed his son Gallienus as his colleague. In this same year the Goths plunged southwards through the Balkans and Asia Minor; and then another German people, the Franks, overran Gaul and Spain. Under these repeated, continuous, external attacks, accompanied by an epidemic of internal usurpations, the empire almost fell to pieces. The culminating horror and humiliation was the capture of Valerian himself by the Persian king (260).[15]

Gallienus did not even try to rescue his father, but struggled on as best as he could with the problems that assailed him on all sides. He was faced by a massive breakaway of all the western provinces under Postumus (259), who established his capital at Colonia Agrippinensis (Cologne), and created his own praetorian guard. Then followed a similar secession involving most of the eastern provinces, under Queen Zenobia of Palmyra in Syria.

Nevertheless, even in these unprecedented and apparently desperate circumstances, Gallienus found time to give a new shape to his army. The Romans had long since made use of mounted javelin-men and archers, and for over a century past they had also employed certain heavily armoured units of horse. But now the formidable heavy cavalry with which the Persians and Sarmatians were confronting them demonstrated that this branch of the army needed extension on a very large scale. And so Gallienus took the significant step of creating a major cavalry corps (264-8). This corps, a very expensive institution since a horse's feed cost as much as a soldier's rations, was intended to serve not only as a striking force but as a central military reserve, which had so long been lacking until Severus made a start by his expansion of the military establishment in Italy at the end of the previous century (Chapter 9). The principal base of the new army was Mediolanum (Milan). Located at a convenient equidistance both from the frontiers and from Rome, this centre rapidly assumed even greater practical importance than the venerable capital itself. Moreover it was joined to other north Italian towns in a new system of defence and potential offence. This new strategic arrangement was rendered all the more necessary because the Agri Decumates, the area in the re-entrant between the upper Rhine and upper Danube, had now been overrun and permanently lost, so that the barbarians were that much nearer to the borders of Italy.

The coins of Gallienus appeal to various virtues of the new élite force,[16] and in particular to its loyalty (FIDEI EQVITVM).[17] And one of the large gold medallions, which it had become customary to hand out to high-ranking officers as personal rewards,* was now bluntly inscribed 'Because you have remained loyal' (OB FIDEM RESERVATAM).[18] In order to keep the officers of the new cavalry corps in this blessed condition, they were enrolled by Gallienus, together with a number of other officers, in a select staff group of household troops (*protectores domestici*), who encamped in the proximity of the emperor himself, and were attached to his own person. Nevertheless, it was precisely over this matter of loyalty that the new army reform proved most vulnerable. The commanders of the new cavalry corps were as unable to resist rebellion as the praetorian prefects before them. For the very first man to hold the post, Aureolus, revolted and had himself proclaimed emperor at Mediolanum. Gallienus defeated and killed him, but then succumbed to assassination at the hands of other officers (AD 268).

* See below, Appendix 5.

These were still years of disastrous internal separatist movements and equally catastrophic enemy irruptions. Yet three successive Danubian emperors reigning during the next fourteen years, Claudius II, Aurelian and Probus were able, in spite of the shortness of their reigns, to perform the astonishing double feat of stamping out the separatist regimes and at the same time rolling back the tide of hostile tribesmen. When the Alamanni surged into Italy itself, Claudius II overwhelmed them, and then defeated the Goths in additional battles which earned him the designation of Gothicus. After his death from plague (270), Aurelian, who had been his cavalry commander, began his reign by fighting two further north Italian engagements, in which he crushed further hordes of invading Germans. Then he defeated and obliterated both the principal secessionists, Postumus's successor Tetricus in the west and Zenobia in the east; and their provinces were brought back into the central empire.

Distrusting the future, Aurelian surrounded Rome by a massive fortified wall extended to enclose the praetorian camp. He also felt it necessary to evacuate Dacia – Rome's last major conquest under Trajan, and now the first to be abandoned. Nevertheless, the coin inscriptions hailing him as 'Restorer of the Army' (RESTITVTOR EXERCITI) and 'Pacifier of the World' (PACATOR ORBIS) were thoroughly deserved. And so was a dedication to the Courage of the Danubians (VIRTVS ILLVRICI).[19]

When Aurelian fell at the hands of an assassin (275),[20] Probus rapidly resumed his compatriot's victorious progress. Utterly shattering a great threefold invasion of Gaul by the Germans,[21] he moved east to confront another of their peoples, the Vandals, on the middle Danube frontier. He also revived, on a massive scale, the policy of settling northern barbarians in Roman territory.

Probus remarked that, at this rate, armies would soon become superfluous.[22] But he proved over-optimistic.

With the accession of Diocletian, a Dalmatian of humble birth who had become commander of the household troops (*protectores domestici*),[23] a new epoch was about to begin (AD 284). For before long the empire was formally divided between two Augusti, each with a Caesar as his deputy,[24] and each of the four members of this tetrarchy had his own geographical area and his own praetorian prefect; Diocletian himself resided at Nicomedia (Izmit in north-western Asia Minor). As part of a large-scale reorganization in many fields, he and his fellow tetrarchs extensively overhauled the entire structure of the army. Pursuing his predecessors' interest in mobile formations, he created a new barbarian mounted bodyguard, named *scholae palatinae* after a portico in the palace where they awaited imperial orders. These *scholae* were incorporated into one of the two major branches into which the entire army was now divided, the field force (*comitatenses*, 'soldiers of the retinue'). This mobile force, of which each of the four rulers controlled his own sections, included infantry units, but it was in cavalry that its particular strength appeared.

The second major division of Diocletian's armed forces was the frontier force (subsequently known as *limitanei* or *riparienses*), stationed along the strengthened fortifications of the borders. The total strength of the Roman army was now half a million, perhaps about 20 per cent larger than the army of Severus a century earlier. It was recruited by systematic annual conscription among Roman citizens. But extensive use was also made of the warlike tastes and various specialist skills of barbarian tribesmen. These included numerous Germans, as well as men from the highlands of Asia Minor. Successful operations in the east extended the frontier on the upper Tigris, and a breakaway government established by Carausius in Britain was suppressed.[25] Diocletian also reorganized the navy, adding a number of small provincial fleets.

In AD 305 he voluntarily and deliberately abdicated – a unique phenomenon in Roman history. However on his abdication the whole tetrarchic system collapsed. After prolonged civil wars, one of the numerous contenders, Constantine, conducted a final series of operations against his last surviving rival Licinius, in which both sides made extensive use of their fleets for naval and amphibious operations. Constantine won decisive victories on land and sea alike,[26] and emerged as sole ruler (324). He then established his capital at Byzantium (Constantinople, now Istanbul), which he chose for its unique strategic advantages, including equal proximity to the Danube and Euphrates fronts.

Constantine continued reorganizing the army, which received unceasing commemoration on his coins and medallions. Like Diocletian he greatly expanded the German element, since he keenly appreciated the particular qualifications of the Germans for fighting against their hostile compatriots on the other side of the frontier. High status, therefore, was conferred on German units, and favour was lavished upon

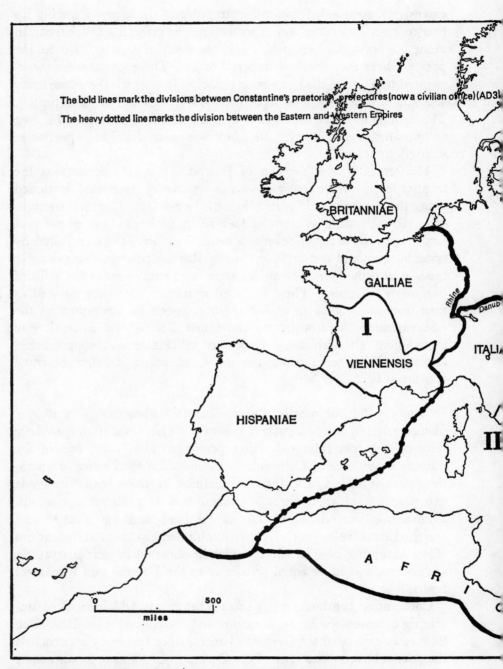

The bold lines mark the divisions between Constantine's praetorian prefectures (now a civilian office) (AD3

The heavy dotted line marks the division between the Eastern and Western Empires

BRITANNIAE

GALLIAE

Rhine

Danub

I

VIENNENSIS

ITALI

HISPANIAE

II

A F R I

O 500
miles

A F R I C

14 Administrative Divisions of the Roman Empire AD 305

German generals. The praetorian cohorts had fought on the side of a hostile ruler Maxentius, from whom Constantine, at an earlier stage of his rise to power, had captured Rome (312)[27] – a pagan, unlike Constantine, who was now about to make Christianity the state religion. So now the praetorian guard (together with the city cohorts and the Watch) was finally abolished, thus ending its stormy and chequered career of three and a half centuries. It was replaced by the largely German mounted guard, the *scholae*, which had been founded by Diocletian.

Furthermore, many other Germans as well as Sarmatians, admitted inside the empire as settlers, were incorporated into new cavalry and infantry units which Constantine now established. These, supplemented by detachments drawn from the frontiers, were drafted into the mobile field force, whose units of one thousand infantrymen (for which the name of legion was now employed) and five hundred cavalrymen now constituted a central striking force and strategic reserve substantially larger than any that had existed before.

In Diocletian's time, before the praetorian cohorts were abolished, their prefects had often commanded in the field. But although the posts of prefect still remained in existence, and these were usually four in number, their functions, like those of the city prefect, were now civilian (mainly financial and judicial). Constantine therefore placed his field army under two different officers whose posts were newly created: a Master of the Horse and Master of the Foot. The second main branch of the army, the frontier troops, consisting of static cavalry and infantry formations, did not receive as much pay as the field force. Nevertheless their role remained essential, since Constantine, in the course of repulsing the Goths on the Danube and restoring the eroded lower Rhine frontier,[28] carried out a large-scale rearrangement and supplementation of the frontier garrisons. The privileges of frontier-army veterans were extended to their sons. However recruitment was also enforced by severe penalties, which caused widespread terror, especially in the less militarized provinces.

When Constantine the Great died (AD 337), the empire was once again divided, between his three sons and the two sons of his half-brother. The most durable of these princes proved to be his second son Constantius II (d. 361). In this period a further subdivision of the army took place, the field force being split into two sections, the *comitatenses* themselves and a new central élite corps the *palatini*, 'soldiers of the palace', who included not only cavalry but infantry formations, some of them of novel types. However, intensified imperial espionage did not succeed in preventing continued uprisings by military usurpers, and the Franks and Alamanni did their best to profit from these dissensions; so Constantius II was compelled to send his cousin Julian to deal with them in as conclusive a manner as possible.

With Julian's campaign we have entered a period of particular military interest, because it is covered by the surviving portion of the *History* of Ammianus Marcellinus, who based his account of contemporary wars upon an unusually full and expert personal experience. After serving with the household troops in the east, Ammianus took part in Julian's fighting on the Rhine frontier. There is therefore a special value in his account of the great battle of Argentorate (Strasbourg), in which Julian, encountering thirty thousand Alamanni with a far smaller force, defeated them utterly.[29]

It was a victory worthy of the greatest days of Rome, displaying amply that there was nothing degenerate or disloyal about the massive Germanized Roman armies of these later imperial times. Nevertheless such successes, unlike those of a century earlier, could not set the tide of history into reverse; and the Germans from across the Rhine now won permanent footholds on the Roman bank.

Two years after the battle of Argentorate, Constantius II, engaged in a war against King Sapor (Shapur) II of Persia, lost a fortress on the Tigris, Amida (Diyarbakir), after a formidable siege. And Ammianus was there once again. The Persians brought up stone-throwers (*ballistae*) on iron-clad towers, which the Romans countered by other siege engines known as scorpions.* But the enemy prevailed, and the city was overrun.[30]

Then, after the brief reign of Julian (AD 361–3), who earned the title of Apostate because of his reversion to paganism, the empire was more or less permanently divided into a western and an eastern half. It was felt that this definitive step was necessitated by the requirements of defence, since no single emperor would be strong enough to deal with the external threats and internal usurpations in every part of the empire at the same time. But the division also inevitably meant that the weaker of the two empires, namely the west with its more vulnerable frontiers and feebler economy, would before long cease to be able to maintain itself. The two emperors who took over in AD 364 were Christians from

* For Roman siege-machinery, see Appendix 4.

Pannonia, Valentinian 1 and his brother Valens. Valentinian 1, who
ruled the west, was a great military emperor, who spent most of his
reign on the northern frontiers, where his skill and energy put off the
evil day. But he died in 375, and in the following year the armies of
Valens clashed with large immigrant masses of Visigoths. These were
members of the western branch of the Gothic peoples who, in panic, had
fled over the Roman frontiers into the empire to escape the Huns, a
nomadic, non-German people whose extraordinary skill as horsemen
was enabling them to advance into huge areas of central Europe. In 378
these Visigoths, under their king Fritigern, subjected Valens to a shattering defeat at Hadrianopolis (Edirne) in Thrace, resulting in the
emperor's death. This battle, too, is described by Ammianus.

At dawn on 9 August the Roman army began its march with extreme
haste, leaving all its baggage and packs near the walls of Hadrianopolis with
a suitable guard of legions. For the treasury, and the insignia of imperial
dignity besides, with the praetorian prefect and the emperor's council, were
kept within the circuit of the walls. So after hastening a long distance over
rough ground, while the hot day was advancing towards noon, finally at
about two in the afternoon they saw the wagons of the enemy, which, as the
report of the scouts had declared, were arranged in the form of a perfect
circle. And while the barbarian soldiers, according to their custom, uttered
savage and dismal howls, the Roman leaders so drew up their line of battle
that the cavalry on the right wing were first pushed forward, while the greater
part of the infantry waited in reserve. But the left wing of the horsemen
(which was formed with the greatest difficulty, since very many of them were
still scattered along the roads) was hastening to the spot at swift pace. And
while that same wing was being extended, still without interruption, the
barbarians were terrified by the awful din, the hiss of whirring arrows and
the menacing clash of shields; and since a part of their forces under Alatheus
and Saphrax, was far away and, though sent for had not yet returned, they
sent envoys to beg for peace.

The emperor scorned these men because of their low origin, demanding,
for the execution of a lasting treaty, that suitable chieftains be sent. Meanwhile the enemy purposely delayed, in order that during the pretended
truce their cavalry might return, who, they hoped, would soon make their
appearance; also that our soldiers might be exposed to the fiery summer heat
and exhausted by their dry throats while the broad plains gleamed with fire,
which the enemy were feeding with wood and dry fuel for this same purpose.
To that evil was added another deadly one, namely, that men and beasts
were tormented by severe hunger . . .

When battle was joined, the Roman left wing, which had made its way
as far as the very wagons, and would have gone farther if it had had any

support, found itself deserted by the rest of the cavalry, and was so hard pressed by the enemy's numbers that it was crushed and overwhelmed, as if by the downfall of a mighty rampart. The foot-soldiers thus stood unprotected, and their companies were so crowded together that hardly anyone could pull out his sword or draw back his arm. Because of clouds of dust the heavens could no longer be seen, and echoed with frightful cries. Hence the arrows whirling death from every side always found their mark with fatal effect, since they could not be seen beforehand nor guarded against. But when the barbarians, pouring forth in huge hordes, trampled down horse and man, and in the press of ranks no room for retreat could be gained anywhere, and the increased crowding left no opportunity for escape, our soldiers also, showing extreme contempt of falling in the fight, received their death-blows, yet struck down their assailants; and on both sides the strokes of axes split helmet and breastplate.

Here one might see a barbarian filled with lofty courage, his cheeks contracted in a hiss, hamstrung or with right hand severed, or pierced through the side, on the very verge of death, threateningly casting about his fierce glance; and by the fall of the combatants on both sides the plains were covered with the bodies of the slain strewn over the ground, while the groans of the dying and of those who had suffered deep wounds caused immense fear when they were heard. In this great tumult and confusion the infantry, exhausted by their efforts and the danger, when in turn strength and mind for planning anything were lacking, their lances for the most part broken by constant clashing, content to fight with drawn swords, plunged into the dense masses of the foe, regardless of their lives, seeing all around that every loophole of escape was lost ... And so the barbarians, their eyes blazing with frenzy, were pursuing our men, in whose veins the blood was chilled with numb horror. Some fell without knowing who struck them down, others were buried beneath the mere weight of their assailants. Some were slain by the sword of a comrade. For, though they often rallied, there was no ground given, nor did anyone spare those who retreated. Besides all this, the roads were blocked by many who lay mortally wounded, lamenting the torment of their wounds, and with them also mounds of fallen horses filled the plains with corpses. To these ever irreparable losses, so costly to the Roman state, a night without the bright light of the moon put an end.

At the first coming of darkness the emperor Valens, amid the common soldiers as was supposed (for no one asserted that he had seen him or been with him), fell mortally wounded by an arrow, and presently breathed his last breath. And he was never afterwards found anywhere.[31]

It was an overwhelming catastrophe. Yet Ammianus, in the true Roman military tradition, is unabashed. 'For if you look at earlier times or those which have recently passed, these will show that such dire disturbances have often happened.'[32] However a study even of his own narrative of events shows that this was a greatly over-optimistic conclusion, and makes it clear that the situation was, in fact, unprecedentedly and indeed fatally grave. The historian himself shows successive emperors constantly engaged in trying to dam breakthroughs at one point and another along the frontiers, while usurpers in the provinces still continued to proliferate. But Ammianus refuses to see that the situation is desperate, and only concludes that the empire must be defended with redoubled determination.

The greatest problem of the day was the influx of these vast quantities of 'barbarians' into the provinces. The historian, good military writer though he is, fails to recognize that these men fulfilled a real need; since the Roman army, unless it could be enabled to enrol them as recruits, would no longer continue to exist at all. Ammianus is also steadfastly opposed to 'buying off' or subsidizing underdeveloped neighbours, although this was longstanding practice and made military as well as political sense. But in any case, Ammianus had a prejudice against Germans and other outsiders, whom he described so frequently as mere savages – though at the same time he was fair enough to recognize that their bad treatment by Rome was one of the causes why the defeat at Hadrianopolis had taken place.

At all events the disastrous battle irremediably threw the empire wide open to uncontrollable German immigration. It had been the eastern empire which was defeated at Hadrianopolis. But henceforward it was upon the west, with its longer European frontier, inferior economic resources, and more glaring class differences, that the successive, catastrophic hammer-blows descended. Theodosius I (379–95) made a treaty conceding the existence of a Gothic state on Roman territory. From now on further German states, in similar treaty relations with the western empire, continued to establish themselves within the frontiers, which gradually became fainter, and were finally obliterated altogether. Leading an army of Visigoths from lower Moesia in AD 395, Alaric penetrated the borders of Italy six years later. A German (Vandal) general, in Roman employment, Flavius Stilicho, for a time the effective ruler of the western empire, twice defeated him and then collaborated with him and annihilated a further horde of invading Ostrogoths, the eastern branch of the Gothic nation.[33] Then, however, on the orders of his emperor Honorius, the younger son of Theodosius I, he was put to death (AD 408). Two years later Alaric captured Rome, and plundered the city for three days. But by this time it had not been the effective capital of the western empire for many years past; first Mediolanum and then in 404 Ravenna had become the successive capitals of the western empire in its place.

In the 440s Attila and his Huns erupted into the Balkans and subsequently transferred their attentions to the west,[34] where a brilliant Danubian general, Flavius Aetius,[35] united with the Visigoths to repel the Hun invaders at the battle of the Catalaunian plains in Gaul (451). Yet the western provinces were all falling away from Roman rule, and becoming independent barbarian kingdoms. In the year after his defeat in Gaul Attila invaded Italy itself, but in 453 he died. In the next year, however, the great Aetius, like Stilicho before him, was struck down by his emperor (Valentinian III). Soon afterwards Gaiseric and his Vandals captured Rome (455), and occupied the city for two weeks, carrying off many works of art and precious objects. The last western Roman emperors, who, even at this last critical phase, still included numerous usurpers thrown up by the army, were mostly puppets under the control of German or other barbarian generals, of whom one of the most important was Ricimer, partly Visigothic and partly Suebian (d. 472). In 476 the western empire ceased to exist. For a time the eastern emperors, whose Byzantine empire had nearly another thousand years to rule, remained the titular controllers of Italy. But its real rulers were the German kings Odoacer (476–93) and Theodoric (493–526). The western Roman state and army were no more.

Epilogue

The foregoing pages have demonstrated the extent to which the Roman army influenced and dominated the internal development and administration of the empire for nearly half a millennium. The power of this army had set the emperors a singularly intractable problem. On the one hand an army must exist, and a formidable one at that, in order to guard the empire against its external and internal foes. But at the same time each ruler had only too good cause to feel anxious about the loyalty of his soldiers, since there was always a grave danger that they would overthrow him. This is, up to a point, a familiar enough theme in discussions of Roman history. But sufficient emphasis has not always been laid upon the incessant preoccupation of every successive emperor with this worry, and upon its influence very often on all their actions for every waking moment of the day.

It was one of the many great strengths of Edward Gibbon, the bicentenary of whose first quarto volume of the *Decline and Fall of the Roman Empire* is almost with us, that he fully appreciated this factor. The army, as he rightly saw it, was a constant peril to its imperial master. 'How precarious', he says of Augustus, 'was his own authority over men whom he had taught to violate every social duty! He had heard their seditious clamours; he dreaded their calmer moments of reflection.' And the plans, arrangements and policies of the emperors were continually affected by this ever-present fear. The army was indeed a double-edged weapon; or, as the emperor Tiberius feelingly remarked, to try to control it was like holding a wolf by the ears.

To return to Gibbon's more rotund phrases, 'The army is the only order of men sufficiently united to concur in the same sentiments, and powerful enough to impose them on the rest of their fellow-citizens. But the temper of soldiers, habituated at once to violence and to slavery, renders them very unfit guardians of a legal or even a civil constitution.' To this statement only one qualification needs to be added. Fortunately for the emperors on some occasions, unfortunately at other more numerous times, the different branches of the army did not always 'concur in the same sentiments'. The great legionary garrisons were sometimes discordant with one another, and more frequently still all or some of them were at odds with the praetorian guard. Although this guard, under its praetorian prefects, has been the subject of excellent specialist studies, too few historians of the army in recent years have followed Gibbon's lead in treating it as the truly integral part of the Roman armed forces that it was, fulfilling a military and political role quite out of proportion to its small size.

The difficulty presented by the existence of an army which had to be strong enough to keep the empire in existence, and was therefore also strong enough to threaten each successive emperor, was never surmounted. Or rather it was surmounted to a certain extent, but only by the continual exertions of every emperor in turn. Had it not been for these exertions, the empire would not have continued for so many hundreds of years. Yet, in the course of their attempts, a great many of those same emperors prematurely and violently lost their lives – and lost their lives at the hands of the soldiers, or more frequently of their officers. It was due to the army that the empire went on and on. But it was also due to the army that internal stability never was and never could be achieved. And because of this fatal weakness at the top – which was directly caused by the preponderance of the army – the empire sustained enormous, continuing losses, amounting sometimes to total paralysis.

This is a phenomenon of timeless, and modern, significance. Throughout the centuries military rule has continued in many lands. The French Marshal Louis Lyautey, who died in 1934, declared: 'I love the soldiers, I detest *les militaires*.' He was primarily offering a contrast between the rank and file, who do the fighting, and the bureaucratic, uniformed, army administrators, who do not. But the same remark could also have served, in France as in imperial Rome, to point a contrast between the ordinary soldiers who regard it as their job to fight for their country, and *les militaires* who make it their concern to project the army into its internal politics. Today, in the 1990s, the world still contains many states, dozens and scores of them, in which the army either controls the administration or is in a position to bring down and set up another one at any time it wishes. The study of the Roman imperial army reveals that the price of such an arrangement is permanent instability. The Roman empire, for all its governmental sophistication, failed to overcome this obstacle — or only overcame it, precariously, at the cost of extremely frequent and damaging upheavals.

The upheavals continue in numerous lands today – on the very day that these words are being written the newspapers announce two attempted military coups – and as long as such disturbances continue, world peace is endangered. The lessons of more than two thousand years of political science have not been learnt; in many countries scarcely a beginning has been made in learning them. The army of the Caesars, which displayed the same phenomenon on such a massive and spectacular scale, is therefore not only highly significant on its own account, but markedly relevant to a problem which bedevils huge tracts of the world today.

Appendices

I

The Location of the Legions[1]

Province	AD 20 (Tiberius)	December AD 68 (Galba)	AD 112 (Trajan)	AD 215 (Caracalla)
Nearer Spain (Hispania Tarraconensis)	IV Macedonica (until 39–43) VI Victrix X Gemina (to Pannonia in 63)	VI Victrix X Gemina (returned 68–71, then to lower Germany)	VII Gemina (since 71)	VII Gemina
Upper Germany	II Augusta XIII Gemina (until 45) XIV Gemina (until 43) XVI	IV Macedonica (cashiered in 70) XXI Rapax (destroyed on Danube in 92) XXII Primigenia (raised by Caligula)	VIII Augusta (since 70) XXII Primigenia	VIII Augusta XXII Primigenia
Lower Germany	I V Alaudae XX XXI Rapax	I (cashiered in 70) V Alaudae (destroyed in Dacian War in 86) XV Primigenia (raised by Caligula,	I Minervia (raised in 83[?]) VI Victrix (since 70)	I Minervia XXX Ulpia Victrix

Province	AD 20 (Tiberius)	December AD 68 (Galba)	AD 112 (Trajan)	AD 215 (Caracalla)
Lower Germany— *cont.*		cashiered in 70) XVI cashiered in 70		
Britain	—	II Augusta IX Hispana XX Valeria Victrix	II Augusta IX Hispana (destroyed in 119–20[?]) XX Valeria Victrix	*Upper Britain* II Augusta XX Valeria Victrix *Lower Britain* VI Victrix (since 122)
Italy	—	—	—	II Parthica (raised in 197)
Raetia	(see upper Germany)			III Italica (raised in 168)
Noricum	—	—	—	II Italica (since 176, raised in 168)
Dalmatia	VII XI	XI (Claudia Pia Fidelis) XIV in transit	—	—
Pannonia	VIII Augusta IX Hispana XV Apollinaris	VII Gemina (Galbiana) (raised in Spain in 68) XIII Gemina (since 45)	*Upper Pannonia* X Gemina (from lower Germany, 105) XIV Gemina Martia Victrix XV Apollinaris (returned from east in 71) XXX Ulpia Victrix (raised in 101[?]) *Lower Pannonia* II Adiutrix (raised from marines at Ravenna in 69; from Britain in 85[?])	*Upper Pannonia* X Gemina XIV Gemina Martia Victrix *Lower Pannonia* I Adiutrix II Adiutrix

Province	AD 20 (Tiberius)	December AD 68 (Galba)	AD 112 (Trajan)	AD 215 (Caracalla)
Moesia	IV Scythica V Macedonica	III Gallica (from Syria in 68) VII Claudia Pia Fidelis (from Dalmatia in *c.* 56–7) VIII Augusta (from Pannonia in 45)	*Upper Moesia* IV Flavia (raised by Vespasian) VII Claudia Pia Fidelis *Lower Moesia* I Italica V Macedonica (since 71) XI Claudia Pia Fidelis	*Upper Moesia* IV Flavia VII Claudia Pia Fidelis *Lower Moesia* I Italica XI Claudia Pia Fidelis
Dacia	—	—	I Adiutrix (?) XIII Gemina	*Upper Dacia* V Macedonica XIII Gemina
Galatia–Cappadocia	—	—	XII Fulminata XVI Flavia (raised by Vespasian)	XII Fulminata XV Apollinaris (since 114)
Syria	III Gallica VI Ferrata X Fretensis XII Fulminata	IV Scythica (from Moesia in 56–7) VI Ferrata XII Fulminata	III Gallica (from Moesia in 69) IV Scythica II Trajana (raised in 101[?])	*Syria Coele* IV Scythica XVI Flavia *Syria Phoenice* III Gallica
Judaea	—	V Macedonica (in east from 61) X Fretensis XV Apollinaris (in east from 62)	X Fretensis	*Syria Palaestina* VI Ferrata X Fretensis
Mesopotamia	—	—	—	I Parthica (raised in 197) III Parthica (raised in 197)
Arabia	—	—	VI Ferrata (?)	III Cyrenaica
Egypt	III Cyrenaica XXII Deiotariana	III Cyrenaica XXII Deiotariana	III Cyrenaica XXII Deiotariana (destroyed in Second Jewish Revolt in 132–4)	II Trajana

Province	AD 20 (Tiberius)	December AD 68 (Galba)	AD 112 (Trajan)	AD 215 (Caracalla)
Africa	III Augusta	III Augusta	III Augusta	*Numidia* III Augusta
TOTAL	25	30	30	33

2

Some Different Kinds of
Military Uniform*

A[2] *The centurion* Marcus Caelius from Bononia (Bologna).[3] He fell in
theam bush of Varus and his three legions in the battle of the Saltus
Teutoburgensis, in AD 9 (Chapter 5). The inscription describes his
origin and career.

The dead man, who was fifty-three years of age, is shown in full
uniform, dressed in his woollen tunic, over which he wears a leather
corselet or cuirass (*lorica*). This is bordered round the bottom with
leather strips which were movable and covered the abdomen. The
cloak (*sagum*) is hung over the left shoulder and the left arm, and its
lappet is held in the centurion's hand. Over the front of the shoulders
hang two Celtic neck-rings (*torques*) attached to a scarf worn round the
neck. These neck-rings, which are very thick, are ornamented with
Celtic patterns. At the bottom the neck-rings are open, their ends
being thickened into a trumpet-like shape. The officer's chest is
decorated with orders and medals (*phalerae*). These circular discs are
carried on a holder made of leather straps. On the left and right of the
phalerae a youthful head with a wreath of ivy can be seen, while in the
centre is engraved a head of Medusa, to ward off evil. The fourth medal
shows a lion's head turned to the right, and the fifth is concealed by the
wearer's right arm. There are also two lions' heads looking straight

* Many of the forms of armour and equipment described here are shown in the Plates.

ahead over his shoulders; they are perhaps additional *phalerae*, or may form part of shoulder-belts.

In his hair Marcus Caelius wears a wreath made of oak leaves and acorns – the *corona civica*, adorned in the centre with a round vignette: this very high decoration was awarded for the rescue of a Roman citizen from danger in the face of the enemy. The two broad bangles (*armillae*) on the wrists can also be regarded as decorations for bravery in battle. Finally Caelius holds a staff (*vitis*) in his right hand with a pommel on the top – the command staff of the centurion, cut from a vine – and it is on account of this that we deduce that he held that rank, although the accompanying inscription is not explicit on the point.

B *The Eagle-bearer* (*aquilifer*) Cnaeus Musius,[4] from Veleia (Velleia in Lombardy). The Eagle-bearer, who came next in rank to a centurion, is depicted in full war-dress. Over his tunic he is wearing mail armour, with leather armour over it. Like the centurion Marcus Caelius, he displays a number of decorations on his chest, comprising nine *phalerae* and two *torques*. On his right wrist there are either bangles (*armillae*), or a protective leather covering. From his right hip hangs a dagger, of which only the hilt is visible. On one end of the belt there is a large buckle, and the other end is divided into a number of straps which hang down at the front and terminate in leather tongues. His left hand rests on an oval shield adorned with a winged badge. In his right hand he carries his Eagle-topped standard; the bird's uplifted wings are bound with a wreath of oak leaves. A hook on the shaft of the standard enables it to be held more easily, especially when carried over the shoulder.

C *Standard-bearers ranking below the Eagle-bearer, namely the* signiferi *and* imaginiferi *and the three kinds of trumpeters or* aeneatores (Introduction, note 34).

These did not wear a helmet, but a special head-dress of bear-skin (lion-skin for the *signiferi* of the praetorian guard), the skull of the beast (without his jaw) being used as a hood, while the furry skin fell on to the shoulders and down the back, and was fastened at the neck by tying the forelegs together. Further they lacked the segmented cuirass, and wore instead a coat of chain-mail (see the Trophy of Trajan at Adamklissi), or a leather or cloth corselet. Their shields (*parmae*) were round in shape and probably small.[5]

D *The auxiliary cavalryman* Titus Flavius Bassus of the Noricum regiment from Dansala in Thrace.[6] He is forty-six and died at Colonia Agrippinensis (Cologne, where the gravestone was discovered). His name Flavius indicates that he was not demobilized and enfranchised before the beginning of the Flavian dynasty (Vespasian, Titus and Domitian AD 69–96). He is represented jumping over an enemy, his spear raised for the death blow, while the enemy desperately defends himself with sword and shield uplifted, and apparently begs for mercy. Bassus appears to be wearing leather armour. His head is protected by a helmet (*cassis*) with cheek-shields. With his right hand he raises his spear (*hasta*), and his left hand holds a long, oval-shaped shield (*clipeus*), of which the inside edge is visible behind the neck and head of his horse. A long sword (*ensis*) hangs in a body-strap from his right hip. Behind the rider, his batman (*agaso* or *strator*) carries two spears (or lances) and a shield.

The horse is adorned with decorative bridle and saddle gear, and wears a plaited mane. The harness (*frena*) of leather straps is decorated with bronze and silver discs. From under the saddle protrudes a saddle-cloth (*ephippium*), hemmed with a zig-zag band. From the front saddle-pommel, a wide belt, adorned with a decorative fringe, leads round the horse's chest. The centre of this belt is adorned with a large disc which may be a head of Medusa to ward off evil.

G. L. Cheesman adds the following comments on the 'service uniform' of auxiliary cavalry and the 'irregular' units which became recognized under the designation of *numeri*:

Auxiliary cavalry. In the first century AD 'the cavalry uniform consisted of a tunic, breeches reaching a little below the knee, both probably of leather, and the *caligae* or military boots. Over the tunic was worn a leather breastplate with extra shoulder-pieces to guard against a down-cut. Metal breastplates however, although rare, are not unknown. The shield is usually an oblong with the longer sides slightly curved, but occasionally an angle in these longer sides transforms it into an elongated hexagon. This shield was borrowed from the Celtic or Teutonic tribes. The helmet had a projection behind to cover the neck in the manner of the English cavalry helmet of the seventeenth century. It was also furnished with an extra band of metal or a peak in front, to protect the forehead, and large cheek-pieces which clasped over the chin.

'The auxiliary cavalryman's equipment as he appears on the Column of Trajan (early second century AD) is essentially the same, except that he now wears a shirt of chain-mail over his tunic instead of the leather breastplate, and his shield has changed from an oblong to a narrow oval shape.

'Irregular cavalry (*numeri*). The horse archers, if one may judge by a soldier of a cavalry squadron from Ituraea (south Syria) represented on a Danubian relief, carried no shield, and possibly no body armour, and wore a leather cap in place of a helmet.[7] Arrian also mentions that some regiments carried a specially heavy spear (*contus*) and devoted themselves to shock tactics.[8] The Moors of Trajan's reign are represented on the Column wearing nothing but a short tunic; their weapons consist of a spear and a small round shield (*cetra*), and they ride their horses without saddle or bridle, guiding them simply by a halter round the neck.'[9]

E *An auxiliary infantryman* of the fourth Dalmatian cohort from the Rhine.[10] He is dressed in a short tunic, which is looped up at the sides so as to hang down in front in a series of folds. The cloak (*sagum*) covers his shoulders and hangs down his back. A long broad sword (*spatha*) and a short dagger are suspended from two waistbelts (*cingula*) at his right and left sides respectively. His only body armour is a sporran composed of strips of metal. (Other monuments, however, display a leather breastplate similar to those worn by the auxiliary cavalry at this period.) His legs are bare, and he wears no helmet. In his right hand he holds two long spears and in his left an oblong rectangular shield, which is not curved like the legionary *scutum*, but looks as flat as a board.

'The Trajanic reliefs,' adds G.L.Cheesman,[11] 'show several other varieties of uniforms also. The flying column which the emperor leads down the Danube includes men who wear, instead of the ordinary helmet, an animal's skin arranged over the head and shoulders in the manner usually confined to standard-bearers (*see* C above).

'*A barbarian* who appears in this scene and elsewhere clad only in long, loose breeches and a *sagum*, and whose chief weapon is a knotted club must belong to the irregular regiments (*numeri*). Others of these regiments are probably represented by the archers clad in long tunics and pointed caps, or wearing helmet and shirt of scale armour, who appear in one or two scenes.'

3

The Roman Camp[12]

The legionary camps of the Roman army were normally located on strategic sites and became, early in the empire, permanent defensive establishments. They were always of rectangular shape, covering fifty or sixty acres. In the centre of each camp, displaying a great façade to impress visitors, stood the headquarters (*principia*). Arranged round a courtyard were offices, store-rooms, colonnades and a covered hall (*basilica*) for all formal functions, with its shrine. Near this was the *praetorium*, the commander's house, and the houses of the military tribunes. The greater part of the camp was filled with barrack blocks,[13] each pair of rooms belonging to one *contubernium*, the tent- and mess-unit of eight men. Centurions had quarters here too. Other buildings comprised the granaries, baths, stables, cook-houses, lavatories, workshops and a large hospital.[14]

Gates on each of the four sides of the camp gave access to the central roadways. The gates were inserted in the rampart or palisade surrounding the camps, which were constructed first of turf and timber, later of stone. This rampart, including inward-curving sections to protect the gates, contained timber watchtowers from which signals could be rapidly transmitted along main routes, and torches moved in a simple semaphore system to spell out detailed messages. Outside the rampart was a ditch.* Outside the camp there was usually a stream to provide water for men and horses.

* Cf. also a description of the fortress camp at Saalburg, Chapter 9, note 29.

In contrast to these great permanent conglomerations was the most temporary form of encampment, the marching camp. According to Vegetius there were three ways of constructing a marching camp, depending upon urgency.

1 If danger is not too pressing, turves are dug from the earth all round, and from them a kind of wall is built, three feet high above the ground, in such a way that there is the ditch in front from which the turves have been cut; and then an emergency ditch is dug, nine feet wide and seven deep.
2 If the enemy force is rather more threatening, then it is worthwhile to fortify the circuit of the camp with a full-scale ditch. This should be twelve feet wide and nine feet deep 'below the line', as the technical term has it. Above this, placing supports on both sides, a mound is raised to a height of four feet, by using the earth from the ditch. At this stage the defences are thirteen feet high and twelve feet wide. On top of this mound the soldiers fix the stakes of stout wood which they always carry with them. For this task of entrenchment it is desirable to have entrenching tools, shovels, wicker baskets and other kinds of equipment always at hand.
3 But if the enemy is pressing, then the whole of the cavalry and half of the infantry are drawn up in line to repel an attack, while behind them the remainder of the men fortify the camp by digging ditches.
A herald marks out the task of Number One century, Number Two, Number Three, etc. Afterwards the ditch is inspected by the centurions, and measured. Men whose work is found to have been negligent are punished.
The recruit, therefore, should be trained in this task, so that when the need arises he may be able to fortify the camp without panic, quickly and carefully.[15]

G.R.Watson, to whom most of this translation is owed, comments that in such descriptions Vegetius, or the earlier authorities upon whom he is relying, show an obsession with defence – a Maginot Line mentality. (Another military writer of a slightly earlier date, however, the Anonymous de Rebus Bellicis, is concerned principally with attack.[16]*) Indeed, when Hadrian inspected his troops at Lambaesis (Lambèse) in north Africa, the Second (Spanish) Auxiliary Cohort chose to display its skill by the rapid construction of a stone wall for its camp (Chapter 8, note 87).

* See Bibliography, Section B, Latin Writings.

4

Roman Siege-Machines

At the siege of Amida (Diyarbakir) by the Persians in AD 359, the historian Ammianus Marcellinus, who was there, describes how the besiegers brought up the arrow-shooting catapults known in his time as *ballistae*, which the Romans successfully countered by another type, the *scorpio* (Chapter 10, note 30). About these, Graham Webster writes:

The smaller siege-machines, to which Vitruvius gives the general term of catapult (*catapulta*), were in various sizes. The smaller ones appear to have been called *scorpiones* and the larger *ballistae*, but the names are used by various ancient writers without much precision. They operated in much the same way as the later crossbow. The pair of vertical coil chambers was at the front, the bow being drawn back by windlass to the required limit of tension and held by a rack and pinion. The bow was released by a trigger, and the bolt shot along a trough through an aperture in the front.[17]

From the time of Trajan at least there were also *carroballistae*, mounted on mobile carriages. Vegetius allotted eleven men to each.

However, there was also a machine which was sometimes of much greater size, known in the later empire as the *onager* (wild ass).[18] At Titus's siege of Jerusalem in AD 70, these engines hurled stones weighing about fifty-five pounds for a distance of 440 yards or more,[19] and indeed a range of as much as 700 yards is recorded.[20] The best material for the springs of such machines was probably not horse-hair or women's hair, as have been suggested, but sinew. The stones were thrown by a single wooden arm, and the machines were erected on massive stone platforms packed in stiff clay. They were operated by four soldiers who twisted the rope, while another released the trigger.[21]

Further siege-equipment included a battering ram (*aries*) enclosed in a wheeled shed (*testudo*, tortoise), mobile towers with bridges or draw-bridges, iron-plated mobile screens (*musculi*) to protect attackers, protective galleries (*porticus*, sometimes formed by a line of mobile screens), iron-pointed wall-borers (*terebrae*), and hooks and crowbars (*falces*, *vectes*) for dislodging masonry.[22]

5

The Value of the Soldiers' Pay

Soldiers' pay is generally reckoned in *denarii* or *sestertii,* of which there were four to the *denarius,* each *sestertius* being worth four *asses.* To facilitate comparisons between one period and another, this book quotes all sums in *denarii.*

In the time of Caesar silver *denarii* were coined, but not *sestertii.* Under Augustus, the monetary system, in so far as it concerned these two denominations, was as follows. The *denarius* was the standard silver coin, valued at one-twenty-fifth of the standard gold coin, the *aureus.* The *sestertius* was at this period a large brass token coin. Unfortunately it is quite impossible to give any useful modern equivalents of these denominations, owing to the notorious absence of ancient economic statistics: our fragmentary pieces of evidence do not enable us to draw up a reliable list of prices – and, in any case, these varied from one date, and one region, to another. Besides, the purchasing value of our own currencies diminishes so rapidly that any modern equivalents I guessed at today will, almost certainly, be out of date before these words have reached print.

The Romans did not understand or appreciate token currencies. But Augustus, by transforming an ugly old bronze coinage into shining pieces of yellow brass and red copper, performed yet another of his conjuring tricks, and persuaded the western public to accept this sleight of hand. However the population was never prepared to admit a token principle for the coinage in precious metals, which they invariably expected to contain gold and silver worth one *aureus* and one *denarius* respectively. Yet one emperor after another failed to resist the temptation to erode these values, by issuing coins that were increasingly debased or light-weight, or both, and thus gradually forfeited the public confidence. In the third century AD this and other economic misfortunes caused an acute inflation which brought widespread misery and destitution (H.Mattingly, *Roman Coins*, 2nd edn, 1960, pp. 124ff.; M.Grant, *Roman Imperial Money*, 1972 edn, pp. 239ff.). The inflation also meant that the soldiers, whom the emperors so urgently needed to satisfy, had to be paid a great deal more money, and also had to be given substantial payments in kind, as well as additional allowances (Chapters 9 and 10). In addition the rulers sought to retain the loyalty of their officers by the presentation of large gold and silver medallions.

Abbreviations

BMC. Emp.	*Coins of the Roman Empire in the British Museum* (1923)
CIL.	*Corpus Inscriptionum Latinarum* (1863–)
Crawford	M.H.Crawford, *Roman Republican Coinage* (1973)
Dio	Dio Cassius, *Roman History*, including summaries (Epitomes).
Gnecchi	F.Gnecchi, *I medaglioni romani* (1912)
ILS.	H.Dessau, *Inscriptiones Latinae Selectae* (1892–1916)
M.&S.iv,3	H.Mattingly, E.A.Sydenham and C.H.V.Sutherland, *The Roman Imperial Coinage*, iv, 3 (1949)
M.&S.v,1	P.H.Webb, *ibid.*, v, 1 (1927)
SHA.	*Scriptores Historiae Augustae* (*The Augustan History*)
Toynbee	J.M.C.Toynbee, *Roman Medallions* (Numismatic Studies, v, American Numismatic Society, 1944)

Notes

Introduction: The Roman Soldier

1 Polybius, VI, 23.

2 In the second century BC, and perhaps earlier, a lighter lance was also used.

3 Polybius, *loc. cit.* Bronze bindings, too, were sometimes employed. Oval shields were also used. The emperor's bodyguard in the field sometimes carried round shields (Josephus, *Jewish War*, III, 94).

4 Metal plates, too, were sometimes worn over leather jackets – and such plates, or mail, could be worn under them as well.

5 These belts could be embellished with ornamental buckles, plates and inlay. They were sometimes replaced by shoulder-belt straps.

6 Cicero, *Tusculan Disputations*, II, 16, 37.

7 For camp-building, see Appendix 3. As for roads (largely the creation of the army):

Methods of construction varied with available materials. There is usually a foundation of large stones overlaid by smaller stones and gravel; occasionally the use of cement has been recorded to bind the matrix. Sometimes the surface is cobbled or even paved with large blocks. Always a camber was obtained for drainage and side ditches or gutters were normally provided; main roads were often carried on a high mound. Engineering is careful; roads run with remarkable directness in open country and in broken country keep to high ground shunning narrow valleys. Their alignments sometimes demonstrate the remarkable accuracy of long-distance survey. (G.H. Stevenson and S.S. Frere, *Oxford Classical Dictionary*, 2nd edn [1970], p. 925.)

8 Cf. Josephus, *Jewish War*, III, 95.

9 The highest of all decorations for valour was a wreath of grass, which Augustus was the last man ever to be awarded.

10 Tacitus, *Annals*, XIV, 24.1.

11 G.Webster, *The Roman Imperial Army*, p. 255.

12 Plutarch, *Galba*, 1.

13 This appears to be the correct interpretation of Livy, XXII, 38.

14 Crawford, 28/1. For the sacrificial pig, cf. Virgil, *Aeneid*, VIII, 638f.

15 A.H.M.Jones, *Studies in Roman Government and Law*, p. 51 (*jus gladii*).

16 Gellius, *Attic Nights*, XVI, 4, 2 (trans. J.C.Rolfe).

17 Juvenal, XVI, 1–4, 7–24, 32–4, 58–60 (trans. P.Green). Soldiers also possessed (perhaps from the time of Augustus) the unique right to dispose of all they acquired on service and leave it by will, even if their father was living (*testamentum militare, peculium castrense*).

18 *Revue de philologie*, XVII (1943), pp. 111–19.

19 Luke 3: 14.

20 *Berliner Griechische Urkunden (Ägyptische Urkunden aus den Königlichen Museen zu Berlin)*, XIII, 51, 1 (adapted from H.M.D.Parker).

21 Vegetius, I, 11 (trans. G.R.Watson).

22 Vegetius, I, 26–7; II, 3.

23 Josephus, *Jewish War*, III, 102–8 (trans. H.St.J.Thackeray).

24 Arrian, *Tactics*, 34 (trans. G.Webster). For this special parade-armour see also G.L.Cheesman, *The Auxilia of the Roman Imperial Army*, pp. 127f. For the trappings worn by horses, see Appendix 2(D).

25 G.Webster, *The Roman Imperial Army*, p. 155.

26 Josephus, *Jewish War*, III, 76–8 (trans. H.St.J.Thackeray).

27 Caesar, *Gallic War*, II, 19, 2.

28 Josephus, *Jewish War*, III, 116–26.

29 Summarized by G.Webster, *The Roman Imperial Army*, pp. 221f.

30 Velleius Paterculus, II, 15, 2 quotes the Italian contribution in personnel as double the Roman.

31 Vegetius, II, 25.

32 Cf. Cicero, *On Behalf of Caelius*, V, 11.

33 Livy, XLII, 34.

34 These 'NCO ranks' (known as the *principales* from at least *c.* AD 107) comprised a group within each century and a headquarters group within each legion. The former, when the army was fully developed, included a *signifer* (standard-bearer: cohorts had these too, and possibly maniples); *optiones* (deputy centurions) and *tesserarii* (orderly sergeants). The legionary headquarters group included an *aquilifer*, Eagle-bearer; *imaginiferi*, who carried standards incorporating medallions with the portraits of reigning and deified emperors; *cornicularii*, senior NCOs in charge of clerical duties; *beneficiarii*, including orderly-room staffs; *speculatores* and *frumentarii*, couriers who developed intelligence duties, see Chapters 4 and 8; *quaestionarii*,

torturers; *aeneatores*, trumpeters (of three kinds, *tubicines*, *bucinatores*, *cornicines*: for their uniforms and those of the *signiferi* and *imaginiferi* see Appendix 2). For details of pay grades and ranks below the level of the centurionate see D.J.Breeze, *Journal of Roman Studies* (1971), pp. 130–5.

Part I Two Styles of Leadership

Chapter 1 Army Leadership in the Failing Republic 107–31 BC

1 Plutarch, *Marius*, 13f.
2 Plutarch, *Comparison between Lysander and Sulla*, 1.
3 Cicero, *On the Agrarian Law*, II, 27, 73.
4 Sallust, *Catiline*, 16, 4.
5 Livy, XLIII, 7, 5.
6 Cicero, *For the Manilian Law*, XXII, 66; XIII, 37–8.
7 Cicero, *Letters to Atticus*, V, 21 (50 BC).
8 *Ibid.*, VI, 2.
9 Examples in N.Lewis and M.Reinhold (eds), *Roman Civilization*, I (1951), pp. 376ff.
10 Cicero, *On the State*, III, 23, 35.
11 Diodorus, XXXVIII–XXXIX, 12.
12 Sallust, *Histories, fragment I*, 55, 19.
13 Plutarch, *Sertorius*, 23.
14 Lucretius, II, 10–13 (trans. R.Humphries).
15 Velleius Paterculus, II, 29, 1.
16 His province combined Transalpine Gaul (Gallia Narbonensis), Cisalpine Gaul (north Italy) and Illyricum (Yugoslavia), of which part of the coast had been under Roman control since 167 BC.
17 F.E.Adcock, *Cambridge Ancient History*, IX (1932), p. 705.
18 Caesar, *Gallic War*, VIII, 4, 1.
19 *Ibid.*, I, 24, 1–26, 2 (trans. R.Warner).
20 Suetonius, *Divus Julius*, 67, 1–2 (trans. J.C.Rolfe).
21 Caesar, *Gallic War*, II, 21, 1.
22 *Ibid.*, VII, 17, 4–8 (trans. R.Warner).
23 *Ibid.*, VII, 52, 1–53, 1 (trans. R.Warner).
24 Lucan, *Pharsalia*, I, 148f. (trans. N.Rowe).
25 [Caesar], *African War*, 10.
26 Cf. Caesar, *Gallic War*, VI, 35, 2.
27 *Ibid.*, II, 19, 7–20, 4 (trans. R.Warner).
28 *Ibid.*, V, 44, 1–14 (trans. R.Warner).
29 *Ibid.*, I, 39, 2–7 (trans. R.Warner).
30 Labienus belonged to the region of Picenum which owed dependence (*clientela*) to Pompey. He may also have been dissatisfied by Caesar's advancement of Antony.

31 Caesar, *Gallic War*, VI, I, I–4 (trans. R.Warner).

32 Suetonius, *Divus Julius*, 38, I.

33 [Caesar], *Spanish War*, 17 (Tiberius Tullius); Caesar, *Civil War*, III, 91, 2.

34 Caesar, *Civil War*, III, 28 (trans. R.Warner).

35 Appian, *Civil Wars*, II, 77 (trans. H.White).

36 Caesar, *Civil War*, III, 92–4 (trans. Jane F.Mitchell).

37 Lucan, *Pharsalia*, III, 93ff.; I, 13ff., 428ff.

38 *Ibid.*, II, 52f., 59ff.; VII, 210f., 416f. (trans. J.W.Duff).

39 Cicero, *Letters to Atticus*, VII, 14.

40 [Caesar], *African War*, 46.

41 Caesar, *Civil War*, I, 72.

42 Suetonius, *Divus Julius*, 69–70 (trans. J.C.Rolfe). Earlier he had called them 'comrades' (note 20 above).

43 Lucan, *Pharsalia*, III, 168.

44 Crawford, 466/1.

45 Incorrectly expressed by Dio, XLIII, 44, 2.

46 Suetonius, *Divus Julius*, 45, 2.

47 Lucretius, V, 1145f. (trans. R.Humphries).

48 Cicero, *On Duties*, III, 21, 82.

49 Suetonius, *Divus Julius*, 86, 2.

50 Sallust, *Jugurtha*, III, 2

51 The War of Perusia (Perugia), between Octavian and Antony's brother Lucius Antonius, supported by Antony's wife Fulvia (41 BC), was notorious for its savagery.

52 Appian, *Civil Wars*, V, 405–7 (trans. H.White).

53 Octavian assumed the laurel-wreath first as an occasional, and then as a permanent, distinction (Dio, XLVIII, 16; XLIX, 16; 40 and 36 BC). This was part of what has been described as his 'Theology of Victory'.

54 Crawford, 534/1. In the same year, 38 BC, Agrippa refused a Triumph for himself.

55 Cf. also Octavian's leading commanders Marcus Tarius Rufus and Quintus Salvidienus Rufus, and Publius Ventidius who defeated the Parthians on behalf of Antony.

56 During Antony's retreat from Media (36 BC), there was an outbreak of robbery among his troops (Plutarch, *Antony*, 48).

Chapter 2 The Iron Hand in the Velvet Glove 31–18 BC

I Dio, LI, 3, 2. It is estimated that Octavian's armies included 85,000 soldiers recruited before Philippi (42 BC), 60,000 recruited in 42–40 BC, 65,000 recruited up to 35 BC, and 40,000 recruited from 34 BC onwards.

2 Virgil's First and Ninth *Eclogues* reflect this situation.

3 Dio, LI, 4, 3.

4 Horace, *Odes*, III, 6, 13f., etc.

5 *Ibid.*, III, 14, 14–16.

6 Lucan, *Pharsalia*, I, 40; cf. I, 670.

7 Virgil, *Aeneid*, VIII, 678, 681.

8 Tacitus, *Histories*, I, 11, 1.

9 Some minor provinces, however, were governed by knights, e.g. Judaea after its annexation in AD 6.

10 Tacitus, *Annals*, II, 59, 3; Suetonius, *Tiberius*, 52, 2.

11 *BMC. Emp.* I, p. 112, no. 691.

12 Suetonius, *Augustus*, 28, 1.

13 Between 18 BC and AD 11 only twenty-five out of eighty-one consuls were from new families, and almost all of those were *suffecti* (i.e. replacements for the *consules ordinarii* during the course of the year).

14 *Res Gestae Divi Augusti*, 1.

15 E.g. Gallia Narbonensis was transferred from the emperor to the senate (22 BC), and Illyricum (known as upper Illyricum from *c.* AD 9, and later as Dalmatia) from the senate to the emperor (11 BC). New provinces acquired during the reign, Galatia, Raetia, Noricum, Moesia and lower Illyricum (later known as Pannonia), came under the control of the *Imperator*.

16 13 and 8 BC, and AD 3 and 13.

17 E.Gibbon, *Decline and Fall of the Roman Empire*, Chapter III.

18 Horace, *Odes*, III, 3, 2f.

19 Tacitus, *Dialogue on Orators*, 41, 5.

20 Cf. also Orosius, *Historiae adversum Paganos*, VI, 22.

21 A.H.M.Jones, *The Decline of the Ancient World* (1966), p. 15. The senate's property qualification was fixed at the figure indicated in 13 BC, if not earlier.

22 A fourth revision of the senate was also undertaken by a special commission (AD 4). Sulla's senate had been six hundred strong.

23 Macrobius, *Saturnalia*, II, 4, 18.

24 Dio, LII, 26, 6.

25 Suetonius, *Augustus*, 19, 1.

26 Suetonius, *Domitian*, 10 (cf. Chapter 8, note 43).

27 Dio, LIV, 15, 2.

28 Dio, LII, 31, 10.

29 Dio, LII, 31, 10; cf. LV, 16, 5.

30 Lucan, *Pharsalia*, VIII, 491ff. (trans. J.W.Duff).

31 Dio, LIV, 3, 2f.

32 Either Aulus Terentius Varro Murena, a successful general who was consul with Augustus in 23 BC and was the brother-in-law of Maecenas, or Lucius Licinius Murena who had been imperial governor of Syria.

33 Velleius Paterculus, II, 91, 2 ('a good man').

34 Livy, I, praef., 4f., 12f.; Horace, *Odes*, I, 2; III, 6.

35 *Res Gestae Divi Augusti*, 6.

36 Strabo, xvii, 839f.

37 E.g. Lex Manilia (67 BC), Lex Trebonia (55 BC).

38 Dio, LIV, 10, 5 ('consular power for life').

39 Augustus was directing military movements in the east (with his stepson Tiberius in command), which led to a reconciliation with Parthia.

40 *Digest*, XLVIII, 4, 3.

41 Dio, LIV, 15, 1ff.

42 E.g. tribunician power (23 BC) – a power divorced from office but reminiscent of the ancient rights of the tribunes of the people to protect the populace from oppression, and now treated as symbolic of the principate; also *pontifex maximus* (12 BC), *pater patriae* (2 BC).

Part II The Army of Augustus

Chapter 3 The Imperial Army in the Provinces 31 BC–AD 6

1 Sixteen of Augustus's twenty-eight legions outlived him by two hundred years. One (v Macedonica) still survived in the sixth century AD, under Justinian.

2 The worst disturbances were in AD 68–70 and 193–7.

3 The cavalry regiments of five hundred were eventually divided into sixteen squadrons or troops (*turmae*), each commanded by a *decurio*. The regiments of a thousand were organized in twenty-four squadrons. Later there is also evidence for part-mounted cohorts (*cohortes equitatae*), e.g. three cited by F.Millar, *The Roman Empire and its Neighbours* (1967), p. 124; cf. Chapters 8 (Lambaesis, note 86) and 9 (Dura-Europus, note 27).

4 With the exception of certain auxiliary units of Roman citizens named *cohortes civium Romanorum*. These enjoyed the same treatment as legionaries in Augustus's will (Tacitus, *Annals*, I, 8, 3), but seem to have disappeared gradually during the decades that followed.

5 Dio, LII, 27, 3 (alleged speech of Maecenas).

6 Herodian, II, 11, 5.

7 Possibly Augustus's right of conscription was only recognized in 23 BC.

8 Suetonius, *Augustus*, 24, 2 (trans. J.C.Rolfe). For Caesar's practice when addressing the troops, cf. above, Chapter 1, notes 20, 42.

9 *BMC. Emp.*, I, pp. 108–9, nos 671ff. According to a tactful suggestion by Propertius, IV, 6, 79ff., the subjugation of the east was only postponed for subsequent members of Augustus's house.

10 The advance into Moesia, at an uncertain date, consolidated the earlier operations of Marcus Licinius Crassus in 29 and 28 BC.

11 The Altar of Peace (Ara Pacis) at Rome was consecrated in 13 and dedicated in 9 BC.

12 Julian, *Caesars*, 317 B, ranked Augustus as a conqueror with Julius Caesar nd Trajan.

13 Perhaps the process had been started by Agrippa, who in 38 BC had brought the tribe of the Ubii, at their own request, across the lower Rhine, where they were settled in Oppidum Ubiorum, later the Roman settlement of Colonia Agrippinensis (Cologne). The colony of Raurica on the upper Rhine, later Augusta Raurica (Augst near Basel), had been founded in 44 BC.

14 These legions were temporarily removed by Drusus senior for his campaigns.

15 Siscia had been captured in 35 BC, and garrisoned.

16 Their first legionary camp was probably at Naissus (Niş) in Dardania (upper Moesia). Occupation did not at first extend eastwards as far as the Black Sea.

17 A legion (perhaps preceded by detachments from three legions) was subsequently moved from Cantabria to Caesaraugusta (Zaragoza).

18 The legion in the Thebaid was stationed either at Thebes (Karnak, Luxor) or at Coptos (Kuft).

19 Near Cyrrhus (Khoros), Raphaneae (Rafniyeh) and Laodicea ad Mare (Latakia).

20 Dio, LII, 20, 4 (alleged speech of Maecenas).

21 Tacitus, *Annals*, II, 36, 1.

22 Army doctors (*medici*) were mainly Greeks. A very few of the most senior among them possibly held a rank equivalent to that of centurion. There were also *medici ordinarii* (orderlies) and *capsarii* (dressers). The equipment of military surgeons has been found, e.g. at a doctor's quarters at Aquae Helveticae (Baden in Switzerland). Cornelius Celsus (*De Medicina*, VII, 5) offers advice on the extraction of weapons from the body, and describes an implement devised for the purpose. 'Although', remarks Graham Webster (*The Roman Imperial Army*, p. 250, n. 1), 'anaesthetics were unknown – except for the liberal use of alcohol – Celsus lists a number of antiseptics which include pitch, turpentine, salt, disulphide of arsenic, silphium and a variety of oils. Most of these, judiciously used, would have been helpful, but mixed with them are other remedies which are purely magical.' For military hospitals, see Appendices, note 14.

23 Appian, *Civil Wars*, III, 44 (under Antony).

24 Suetonius, *Augustus*, 38.

25 Or, more rarely, these military tribunes had been centurions.

26 Lawyers were sometimes exempted from these officer posts.

27 E.g. *ILS.* 2648: Marcus Vettius Valens, who held a series of commands, was no doubt related to Claudius's doctor Vettius Valens.

28 Suetonius, *Augustus*, 46.

29 Philo, *Embassy to Gaius*, V, 30.

30 *BMC. Emp.*, I, p. 7, no. 36; p. 10, no. 51.

31 Suetonius, *Augustus*, 24.

32 Horace, *Odes*, III, 2, 1–4 and 13 (trans. J.Michie).

33 Propertius, II, 7, 14; cf. I, 6, 29f.

34 Ovid, *Amores*, I, 9; cf. II, 19–24.

35 Cf. Juvenal, *Satires*, XIV, 193.

36 Tacitus, *Histories*, III, 49 (Antonius Primus).

37 *CIL.*, VIII, 217 (under Antoninus Pius).

38 Pliny the elder, *Natural History*, III, 31.

39 Southern Spain (Baetica) probably became a senatorial province in 27 BC, and southern France (Narbonensis) in 22. The Spanish recruits came from ordinary provincial cities as well as from the communities of Roman citizens. The only city in the imperial provinces of Gaul (Lugdunensis, Belgica and Aquitania) to furnish legionaries was the colony of Lugdunum (Lyon).

40 The latest assessment estimates the population of Italy at this time at 7 million, including 4 million Roman citizens.

41 The legionaries recruited in Cisalpine Gaul came especially from towns which had native tribes attached to them.

42 This legion (named after the former Galatian King Deiotarus) was sent to Egypt, probably at once. No legions were permanently stationed in Galatia until the time of Vespasian.

43 *ILS.*, 1987, etc.

44 Perhaps this tendency did not become strongly marked until after Augustus.

45 Geneva Papyri, 1 (Domitian).

46 Tacitus, *Annals*, I, 2, 1.

47 Dio, LI, 21, 3. It is uncertain whether the auxiliaries received bonuses: cf. also note 57 below.

48 *Res Gestae Divi Augusti*, 15.

49 Dio, LV, 6, 4.

50 Vegetius, II, 20.

51 Suetonius, *Augustus*, 25, 3.

52 S.Riccobono (*et al.*), *Fontes Iuris Romani Antejustiniani*, 2nd edn, III, 19.

53 Suetonius, *Augustus*, 24, 1.

54 Philostratus, *Life of Apollonius*, V, 35.

55 *BMC. Emp.*, II, p. 364, no. 301 (Domitian). The type was repeated by Trajan.

56 Berlin Papyri, 628; S.Riccobono, *Fontes Iuris Romani Antejustiniani*, I, 56 (trans. N.Lewis and M.Reinhold). Octavian is still speaking in his capacity as triumvir (though this office had ended), and he is acting under the Lex Munatia Aemilia of 42 BC which authorized the triumvirs to grant exemption from taxes (and confer citizenship). Earlier, Octavian had granted similar privileges to a retired officer Seleucus of Rhosus (Arsuz) in Syria (P.Roussel, *Syria*, 1934, pp. 33f.).

57 It is not known if any auxiliaries received land grants (or cash gratuities later): cf. also note 47 above.

58 *Res Gestae Divi Augusti*, 16.

59 Strabo, III, 5, 1, 167. For another reference to the procurators, see passage quoted above (note 56).

60 Dio, LII, 6, 4.

61 Dio, LIV, 25, 5.

62 Dio, LV, 24, 8.

63 In AD 5 according to Dio, LV, 23, 1.

64 Suetonius, *Augustus*, 49, 2.

65 Dio, LIV, 25, 6.

66 Dio, LV, 23, 1.

67 *Res Gestae Divi Augusti*, 17.

Chapter 4 The Protection of Rome and the Regime 31 BC–AD 14

1 Misenum was equidistant from Sicily, Sardinia and Corsica. A detachment of the Misenum fleet was on duty in Rome to organize naval spectacles, to arrange for the awnings which protect the audiences at places of public entertainment from the sun, and to assist the Watch when necessary.

2 The Danube flotilla was subsequently divided into Pannonian and Moesian fleets, based on Taurunum (Zemun) and Tomis (Constanta) respectively.

3 *ILS.*, 2688, etc.

4 At Forum Julii, after Gallia Narbonensis had been transferred to the senate in 22 BC, the naval personnel may have been thought of as belonging to Augustus's private household.

5 Dio, LII, 10, 4; LV, 14, 8.

6 Suetonius, *Augustus*, 35, 1f.

7 E.g. Caesar, *Civil War*, I, 75, 2 (Petreius in Spain).

8 E.g. Appian, *Iberian Wars*, 84: Scipio Africanus the younger (Aemilianus).

9 Festus, 249L.

10 Sallust, *Jugurtha*, 98, 1.

11 Cicero, *Letters to Atticus*, XIII, 52.

12 Plutarch, *Antony*, 53.

13 Crawford, 544/1.

14 Suetonius, *Augustus*, 49, 1.

15 Tacitus, *Histories*, I, 38; cf. *Annals*, XVI, 27, 1, and reliefs from the Palazzo della Cancelleria in the Vatican Museums.

16 Tacitus, *Annals*, IV, 5, 5.

17 Evidence from Gallia Narbonensis, Spain, Noricum and Macedonia.

18 Virgil, *Aeneid*, VIII, 678.

19 Tacitus, *Histories*, I, 84.

20 [Caesar], *Spanish War*, 13.

21 Crawford, 544/12. These coins show three standards ornamented with two wreaths and a prow, possibly indicating that the cohort was partly composed of former marines (cf. Chapter 8, note 51) – or that it possessed certain naval duties.

22 *ILS.*, 2014.

23 *ILS.*, 1993 (Vespasian).

24 Suetonius, *Augustus*, 74.

25 Tacitus, *Histories*, II, 11.

26 Suetonius, *Galba*, 18.

27 Suetonius, *Augustus*, 49, 3.

28 Dio, LII, 37, 2.

29 Augusta Praetoria (Aosta) was founded for praetorian veterans in 24 BC. It formed a linked communications system with Augusta Raurica (Augst) and Augusta Vindelicorum (Augsburg). Coins show that praetorians were also settled at Philippi in Macedonia.

30 *ILS.*, 1993 (Vespasian).

31 One from Macedonia and one from Epirus are known.

32 The first man appointed to this vital post was Gaius Turranius, after AD 6.

33 Dio, LII, 24, 2.

34 *ILS.*, 8996.

35 A city cohort was also stationed (probably by Vespasian) at Carthage, where it could be called upon throughout the province of Africa.

36 They could also, on occasion, be used to deal with disturbances even in distant Italian towns, e.g. at Pollentia (Pollenzo) under Tiberius (Suetonius, *Tiberius*, 37, 3).

37 Possibly Agrippa and Maecenas, when on earlier occasions they had been left in charge of the city, had been thought of informally as its prefects.

38 Tacitus, *Annals*, VI, 11, 4; cf. Jerome in Eusebius, *Chronicle*, VIII, p. 551 (Migne).

39 Dio, LIV, 19, 6, states that he was placed in charge of the whole of Italy.

40 It is conceivable, however, that the post continued to exist, but was largely in abeyance when the *princeps* was at Rome.

41 The pay of the praetorian guardsmen did not come from the state treasury until the reign of Tiberius (Dio, LVIII, 18, 3).

42 Tacitus, *Annals*, VI, 10, 3–11, 6, analyses the city prefect's position.

43 *Ibid.*, XIV, 41, 2, records a potential clash with a praetor's jurisdiction under Nero. In about the time of Domitian the city prefect was beginning to attract cases from the rest of Italy.

44 This was also the arrangement for the grain supply during the years immediately preceding the appointment of Gaius Turranius (see note 32 above).

45 In the Republic the aediles and *tresviri capitales* or *nocturni* had possessed responsibilities in this field.

46 According to Dio, LV, 26, 4, Augustus at first expected that this would be a temporary arrangement.

Part III The Breakdown of the Augustan System

Chapter 5 The Transmission of Military Power AD 4–21

1 Suetonius, *Tiberius*, 16, 1.

2 *Ibid.*, 21, 5; cf. Dio, LVI, 12, 2.

3 Pliny the elder, *Natural History*, VII, 149.

4 Dio, LV, 31, 1. For the 'eighth cohort of volunteers in Dalmatia', cf. A.E. Gordon, *Album of Dated Latin Inscriptions*, 1 (1958), no. 112.

5 Tacitus, *Annals*, I, 31, 4.

6 Suetonius, *Tiberius*, 21, 4f.

7 Site unidentifiable; the Teutoburger Wald was not given that name until the seventeenth century.

8 Dio, LVI, 23, 4.

9 Suetonius, *Augustus*, 23, 2.

10 Dio, LVI, 23, 2.

11 Tacitus, *Annals*, I, 11, 7.

12 In AD 19 Maroboduus, his position undermined by the Romans, fled into Roman territory, and was interned at Ravenna.

13 Earlier Marcellus (d. 23 BC) had been married to Augustus's daughter Julia. Her next husband was Agrippa (the father of Gaius and Lucius), and then Tiberius (their son died in infancy).

14 Dio, LV, 10, 15.

15 In 6 BC Tiberius had been granted tribunician power (Chapter 2, note 42) for five years, but he had retired from public life and gone to Rhodes in the same year.

16 Tacitus, *Annals*, IV, 57, 5; Suetonius, *Gaius*, 4.

17 As Dio, LV, 14–22 (in 16–13 BC according to Seneca, *On Clemency*, I, 9).

18 Velleius Paterculus, II, 104. The Vindelici lived in the eastern part of the province of Raetia.

19 Dio, LV, 27, 1f.

20 Dio, LV, 20, 5f.

21 Suetonius, *Augustus*, 19, 2. According to another account Julia had been allowed to move to Rhegium (Reggio Calabria) on the mainland in *c.* AD 4.

22 Possibly this had occurred in *c.* AD 1.

23 *BMC. Emp.*, I, p. 87, no. 506. Tiberius's head had already appeared on official token coinage at Rome and Lugdunum (Lyon).

24 According to alternative theories, (1) Tiberius's provincial command had lapsed on Augustus's death, and (2) his grant of AD 13 did not include Italy.

25 Tacitus, *Annals*, i, 7, 7.
26 *Ibid.*, i, 7, 3.
27 *Ibid.*, i, 7, 8 – 'as though he were already emperor'.
28 Livia was Augustus's joint personal heir, and was adopted into the Julian family as Julia Augusta.
29 Also to the Roman citizens in auxiliary units (the *cohortes civium Romanorum*), cf. Chapter 3, note 4.
30 That the peril was not wholly unreal was shown by the daring attempt of a slave of Agrippa Postumus to impersonate his late master in AD 17.
31 Velleius Paterculus, ii, 124, 1, somewhat over-dramatizes this, under-estimating the arrangements already made in AD 4.
32 The names of Lucius Arruntius, Marcus Aemilius Lepidus (consul AD 6), Gaius Asinius Gallus and Cnaeus Calpurnius Piso were mentioned.
33 Tacitus, *Annals*, i, 8–15.
34 Suetonius, *Tiberius*, 25, 1 (Greek proverb).
35 The theory that this was a restrictive gesture by the senate is unlikely.
36 Tacitus, *Annals*, i, 16f.
37 *Ibid.*, i, 23, 4.
38 *Ibid.*, i, 24, 3.
39 The camp at Carnuntum (Petronell) may have received its first stone wall at this time (or a little later, cf. Chapter 6). Carnuntum was at the north-western extremity of the province. At the south-eastern end an important base was growing up at Sirmium (Mitrovica). In between (for the time being), tribal buffer states were relied upon to defend the frontier. In south-western Pannonia, Emona (Ljubljana), which now ceased to be a legionary base, instead received a veteran colony of about fifteen hundred settlers, who would afford Italy safer protection, it was estimated, than any legion could.
40 Tacitus, *Annals*, i, 31, 1–5. Gaius Silius's full name was Gaius Silius Aulus Caecina Largus, cf. R.Syme, *Ten Studies in Tacitus* (1970), p. 142n.
41 Though one of Silius's legions had hesitated at first. Among the Chauci, on the coast beyond the Rhine, an outbreak was prevented by the camp prefect, Manius Ennius.
42 Tacitus, *Annals*, i, 48, 3–49, 4.
43 The soldiers also complained of deductions of pay for rations, clothing, arms and rents – but not food, presumably because this was accepted as a reasonable demand.
44 Dio, LVII, 3, 2.
45 Tacitus, *Annals*, i, 47, 1–4.
46 *Ibid.*, ii, 22, 1.
47 Vegetius, iii, 4.
48 Tacitus, *Annals*, ii, 16–18.
49 Timber buildings had been used for food storage under Augustus. According to one view, the establishment of legionary fortresses at

Argentorate (Strasbourg) and Vindonissa (Windisch), attributed in the text of this chapter to *c.* AD 12, should be ascribed instead to *c.* AD 17.

50 Tacitus, *Annals*, IV, 4, 4, records a plan by Tiberius in AD 23 (subsequently abandoned) to proceed on a provincial tour to organize conscription.

51 *Ibid.*, II, 26, 3.

52 Suetonius, *Gaius*, 4.

53 Tacitus, *Annals*, II, 44, 1 ('Illyricum').

54 There was also a war in the client kingdom of Thrace (AD 19), and an incipient slave revolt near Brundusium led by a former praetorian guardsman and suppressed by a local quaestor (with naval personnel) and a praetorian tribune (AD 24 [Tacitus, *Annals*, IV, 27, 1–3]).

Chapter 6 Emperors Made by the Guard AD 21–62

1 It was said afterwards that Sejanus was abetted by Livilla or Livia Julia, the wife of Drusus junior and sister of Germanicus.

2 The elder of the twins was Tiberius 'Gemellus'. For their heads in cornucopiae, see *BMC. Emp.*, I, p. 133, no. 95 (before the death of Drusus junior).

3 Tacitus, *Annals*, I, 21, 2; III, 22, 5.

.4 *Ibid.*, IV, 2.

5 Dio, LVII, 19, 6.

6 He was the last private person to be hailed *Imperator* (AD 23).

7 Sejanus obliged the highly influential Lucius Arruntius to govern nearer Spain (Hispania Tarraconensis) *in absentia*, through deputies, for ten years or more.

8 This youth Drusus, a son of Claudius, had thrown a pear in the air, caught it in his mouth, and choked to death.

9 Tacitus, *Annals*, IV, 2, 4.

10 Suetonius, *Tiberius*, 48, 2.

11 Dio, LVIII, 4, 3.

12 Tacitus, *Annals*, IV, 2, 4; cf. Dio, LVIII, 4, 3.

13 Bruttedius Niger: Juvenal, *Satires*, x, 82 (cf. Tacitus, *Annals*, III, 66, 5).

14 Velleius Paterculus, II, 127, 3.

15 For the ambiguous function of the guardsmen, cf. Tacitus, *Annals*, II, 31, 1, Suetonius, Tiberius, 25, 1 (Marcus Scribonius Libo Drusus, charged with magic but perhaps secretly plotting rebellion).

16 Dio, LVII, 19, Ib.

17 Dio, LVII, 24, 2; Tacitus, *Annals*, IV, 34, 2.

18 Dio, LVII, 24, 5.

19 Josephus, *Jewish Antiquities*, XVIII, 181.

20 Tacitus, *Annals*, IV, 41, 3.

21 *Ibid.*, IV, 60, 1; cf. 67, 6.

22 *Ibid.*, IV, 59, 5.

23 *Ibid.*, IV, 67, 6.

24 *Ibid.*, V, 4, 5.

25 E.g. their joint consulship was honoured on a coin of Bilbilis (Calatayud) in Spain (M.Grant, *Aspects of the Principate of Tiberius* [1950], p. 141 and n. 32).

26 Josephus, *Jewish Antiquities*, XVIII, 182; Dio, LXV, 14, 1: the details differ.

27 Perhaps a group of senators, led by Lucius Arruntius, had been working on Tiberius against Sejanus. Tacitus's account of this period is missing.

28 Seneca, *Letters*, 83, 14.

29 Dio, LVIII, 11, 4.

30 Suetonius, *Tiberius*, 65, 2 (trans. J.C.Rolfe).

31 Tacitus, *Annals*, VI, 24, 3.

32 Suetonius, *Tiberius*, 61, 1.

33 Juvenal, *Satires*, X, 66–77 (trans. P.Green). But Sejanus, being a knight by origin, could not have aspired at this period, with even the slightest chance of success, to become emperor himself (the first knight to become an emperor was Macrinus, AD 217).

34 Tacitus, *Annals*, VI, 2, 6.

35 Dio, LVIII, 18, 2.

36 Tacitus, *Annals*, VI, 3, 1f.

37 *Ibid.*, 30, 5.

38 *Ibid.*, 50, 6.

39 Philo, *Embassy to Gaius*, 2, 8.

40 *BMC. Emp.*, I, p. 155, no. 55.

41 Caligula wanted to pay the legacies not only of Tiberius but of Livia (d. 29), which Tiberius had not paid.

42 Thus the Watch replaced the auxiliary *cohortes civium Romanorum* which had appeared in Augustus's will but had subsequently faded, or were fading, away (Chapter 3, note 4).

43 *BMC. Emp.*, I, p. 151, no. 33. Augustus had employed a similar design, but without the inscription.

44 Philo, *Embassy to Gaius*, VIII, 52ff.

45 Tacitus, *Histories*, IV, 68.

46 In AD 39 Aulus Avillius Flaccus was first banished and then executed, perhaps on a charge of plotting with Macro and Gemellus.

47 Philo, *op. cit.*, 30.

48 Dio, LIX, 18, 4.

49 Tacitus, *Histories*, I, 48.

50 Suetonius, *Gaius*, 43.

51 It was perhaps now that legions were moved to Bonna (Bonn) from Argentorate (Strasbourg) and Oppidum Ubiorum, the later Colonia Agrippinensis (Cologne).

52 Suetonius, *Gaius*, 55, 2.

53 Josephus, *Jewish Antiquities*, XIX, 18. He attributes the leadership to Gaius Cassius Chaerea, who later murdered Caligula.

54 Dio, LIX, 25, 8; a slightly different version in Suetonius, *Gaius*, 56, 1.

55 Seneca, *On Clemency*, 1, 4, 3.

56 Britannicus, the son of Claudius and Messalina, was born about three weeks later.

57 Other suggested, or possible, candidates were Marcus Vinicius, brother (?) of Vinicianus and husband of Caligula's sister Julia Livilla; Decimus Valerius Asiaticus, who had recently calmed the praetorians; and Servius Sulpicius Galba, who had succeeded Gaetulicus as army commander in upper Germany and became emperor twenty-seven years later (Chapter 7).

58 Josephus, *Jewish Antiquities*, XIX, 252.

59 Suetonius, *Claudius*, 10, 1–4 (trans. J.C.Rolfe). The guardsman who discovered him in hiding was named Gratus (Josephus, *Jewish Antiquities*, XIX, 217).

60 Josephus, *Jewish Antiquities*, XIX, 274.

61 *Ibid.*, 247.

62 *BMC. Emp.*, I, pp. 165f., nos 5, 8: the former type continued to be issued until AD 46–7, the latter until AD 44–5.

63 Suetonius, *Claudius*, 21, 4 (but they were not very costly).

64 Dio, LX, 12, 4. It is possible that previous emperors had done this also.

65 Dio, LX, 15, 2; cf. 27, 5 (Gaius Asinius Gallus, AD 46).

66 *ILS.*, 976 (of his son).

67 Scribonia, and Gaius and Lucius Caesars.

68 Suetonius, *Claudius*, 36, 2.

69 *Ibid.*, 13.

70 Tacitus, *Histories*, II, 75.

71 E.g. rumours that Decimus Valerius Asiaticus, a Gaul by birth, was about to visit the legions in Germany caused him to be suppressed by the praetorian prefect Rufrius Crispinus (AD 47).

72 Suetonius, *Claudius*, 25, 1.

73 Claudius left Lucius Vitellius, formerly imperial governor of Syria and father of the later emperor Aulus Vitellius, in charge at Rome.

74 Probably Raetia also became a province under Claudius with its own imperial governor.

75 E.g. Argentorate, Vindonissa. Stone work at Carnuntum had also been attributed to a date prior to Claudius (Chapter 5, note 39). The only camps where a complete plan has so far been uncovered are Novaesium (Neuss) and Inchtuthil (in Scotland), both of later date. Cf. Appendix 3. The plan of a general's headquarters (*praetorium*) can best be seen at Castra Vetera (Birten). Veteran colonies were established at Oppidum Ubiorum (Colonia Agrippinensis, Cologne) and probably Augusta Trevirorum (Trier), as well as on the lower and middle Danube, where Viminacium (Kostolac) in upper

Moesia probably became a legionary camp under Nero (*c.* AD 56–7). Two colonies of Nero at Tarentum (Taranto) and Antium (Anzio) failed, perhaps because the settlers were too heterogeneous.

76 *ILS.*, 1985, cf. 1986.

77 Tacitus feels his own account of this may seem incredible (*Annals*, XI, 27, 1), but he ignores the serious military significance of the plot.

78 Sosia Galla, the wife of Silius's father Gaius Silius Aulus Caecina Largus, had been a friend of Agrippina senior.

79 Rufrius Crispinus (whom Claudius had separated from his wife Poppaea Sabina) was told to stay in Rome, and Lusius Geta was not trusted.

80 Tacitus, *Annals*, XII, 41, 3.

81 *Ibid.*, XII, 41, 5.

82 *ILS.*, 1321.

83 At some stage in his reign Claudius had executed a joint prefect, Rufrius Pollio, who was serving as the colleague of Catonius Justus.

84 Seneca, *On Clemency*, II, 1, 2.

85 Tacitus, *Annals*, XII, 56, 3.

86 The only historian who avoids committing himself on this point is Josephus, *Jewish Antiquities*, XX, 151.

87 Tacitus, *Annals*, XII, 69, 1–3.

88 *Ibid.*, XIII, 4, 1.

89 The historians are not agreed whether this was because the will favoured Britannicus, or did not favour him.

90 Tacitus, *Annals*, XII, 41, 5.

91 E.g. at Amisus (Samsun), *L'Année épigraphique* (1959), 224.

92 *BMC. Emp.*, I, p. 202, no. 11.

93 Tacitus, *Annals*, XI, 19, 1.

94 *Ibid.*, XIII, 35, 1–10.

95 Across the lower Danube, a hundred thousand tribesmen were transported to Roman Moesia, and Wallachia was brought into the province.

96 Tacitus, *Annals*, XIII, 21, 7 (*cohortes in urbe temptatas*).

97 Dio, LXI, 9, 1.

98 Tacitus, *Annals*, XIII, 18, 3–19, 1.

99 *Ibid.*, XIV, 10, 2.

100 *Ibid.*, XIV, 10, 5–11, 2.

101 *BMC. Emp.*, I, p. 226, no. 142.

102 Seneca, *Natural Investigations*, VI, 8, 3; Pliny the elder, *Natural History*, VI, 181.

Part IV Revolution and Recovery

Chapter 7 The Guard and the Armies Stake their Claims AD 62–70

1 These victims were Faustus Cornelius Sulla Felix and Rubellius Plautus.

Sulla was a descendant of the dictator Sulla and Pompey, and had married Claudius's daughter Claudia Antonia: it was reported that he was intriguing with the German armies and Gaulish tribesmen. Plautus, a great-grandson of Tiberius, was reported, wrongly, to have escaped to Corbulo and the eastern armies.

2 Tacitus, *Annals*, xiv, 59–62.

3 Lusitania had been split off from Hispania Tarraconensis (nearer Spain) and made a separate imperial province by Augustus.

4 Nero lost popularity during the Great Fire (AD 64), in which metropolitan troops and personnel of the Watch were accused of arson (Dio, LXII, 17, 1).

5 Caligula had obliged Piso to hand over the woman he was engaged to, Livia Orestilla, who then became the emperor's second wife (Caesonia, who died at the same time as he did, was his fourth).

6 I.e. especially Lucius Junius Silanus Torquatus (Tacitus, *Annals*, xv, 52, 3).

7 Tacitus, *Annals*, xv, 50, 4, admits this in passing, but does not make it sufficiently clear in his narrative.

8 Tacitus, *Annals*, xv, 50, 6f.

9 However, Piso himself was happily married: though this might not have deterred him from replacing his wife by an imperial princess in order to obtain the throne.

10 According to Dio, LXII, 24, 1, Faenius and Seneca (not Piso) were the leaders of the plot.

11 *BMC. Emp.*, I, p. 241, no. 212. However the inscription could also possess the secondary meaning of 'the Security *given* by the emperor', cf. Vitellius's LIBERTAS AVGVSTI.

12 Tacitus, *Annals*, xvi, 7, 3.

13 *Ibid.*, xvi, 9, 3f.

14 *Ibid.*, xvi, 27, 1f.

15 *Ibid.*, xvi, 30, 1.

16 Dio, LXII, 3, 2f. (Loeb edn, p. 142) (trans. E. Cary).

17 *BMC. Emp.*, I, p. 215, no. 113.

18 Dio, LXII, 23, 6 (Loeb edn, p. 126).

19 The Arval Brethren gave thanks on 19 June for the suppression of the plot. Cf. Suetonius, *Nero*, 36, 1.

20 Corbulo was also the half-brother of Quintus Pomponius Secundus, who had joined the revolt of Scribonianus in AD 42.

21 Dio, LXII, 17, 6 (Loeb edn, p. 164).

22 They had earlier been entrusted with the joint command of praetorian cohorts sent to restore order at Puteoli (Pozzuoli) (Tacitus, *Annals*, xiii, 48, 3).

23 *BMC. Emp.*, I, p. 214, no. 107.

24 Suetonius, *Nero*, 19, 2.

25 Caesar, *Gallic War*, iii, 10, 3.

26 *BMC. Emp.*, I, pp. 294f., 298ff.

27 Zonaras, II, p. 41, 12–19 (ed. Dindorf).

28 *BMC. Emp.*, I, p. 293. The type MONETA (*ibid.*, p. 291n.) assures his troops of his capacity to pay them.

29 Pliny the younger, *Letters*, IX, 19, 1.

30 Tacitus, *Histories*, I, 6.

31 *BMC. Emp.*, pp. 285f. For the emblem of Sicily, *ibid.*, p. 287, no. 5.

32 Plutarch, *Galba*, 8.

33 Suetonius, *Nero*, 47, 1 (Rubrius Gallus). Or Nero may have learnt of the move to make Verginius Rufus emperor.

34 Suetonius, *Nero*, 47–9.

35 Tacitus, *Histories*, I, 6 and 24.

36 *Ibid.*, I, 5. Partial checks on this work can be obtained from Suetonius, Plutarch, Dio, Josephus and the coins. Translations from Tacitus, *Histories*, are by K. Wellesley.

37 *BMC. Emp.*, I, p. 357, no. 255.

38 Tacitus, *Histories*, I, 54.

39 Suetonius, *Vitellius*, 7, 3.

40 Tacitus, *Histories*, I, 18.

41 Suetonius, *Otho*, 5, 2; *ibid.*, 10, 1, his father a *tribunus angusticlavius* of Otho.

42 It is uncertain, however, on which day the news of the events on the Rhine of 1 and 2 January reached Rome.

43 Suetonius, *Otho*, 6, 3.

44 Tacitus, *Histories*, I, 40–1.

45 *BMC. Emp.*, I, p. 367, no. 21.

46 Dio, LXIII, 13, 1 (Loeb edn, p. 214).

47 Rome was full of army spies in disguise belonging to both sides (Tacitus, *Histories*, I, 85).

48 *BMC. Emp.*, I, pp. 305f., 384ff.

49 Tacitus, *Histories*, II, 29. He hid in the quarters of a cavalry non-commissioned officer (*decurio*), disguised as a slave.

50 Tacitus, *Histories*, I, 80.

51 Suetonius, *Otho*, 8, 2. Suetonius refers to the removal of arms from the praetorian camp by marines, who were ordered to load them on shipboard (presumably for an abortive naval expedition which Otho was sending to Gallia Narbonensis). The incident is described differently by every surviving historian.

52 Tacitus, *Histories*, I, 46.

53 Dio, LXIII, 10, 1 (Loeb edn, p. 210).

54 Tacitus, *Histories*, II, 37–8.

55 *BMC. Emp.*, I, p. 392, no. 119.

56 Tacitus, *Histories*, II, 70.

57 *Ibid.*, 87–9.

58 Suetonius, *Vitellius*, 10, 1.

59 Tacitus, *Histories*, II, 94.

60 One of the eastern legions, at the Second Battle of Bedriacum, saluted the rising sun in the Syrian fashion (Tacitus, *Histories*, III, 24).

61 Suetonius, *Vespasian*, 6, 1–3 (trans. J.C.Rolfe).

62 *BMC. Emp.*, II, pp. 88ff.

63 Josephus, *Jewish War*, IV, 605.

64 Dio, LXIV, 9, 4 (Loeb edn, p. 234).

65 Mucianus's withdrawal of most of the Black Sea fleet to Byzantium (Istanbul) caused serious disorders and plundering there (Tacitus, *Histories*, III, 47).

66 The Misenum fleet, too, later changed its allegiance (Tacitus, *Histories*, III, 57).

67 Tacitus's introduction of common soldiers at such meetings (cf. also at Berytus [Beirut] and Poetovio [Ptuj]) is of dubious authenticity.

68 Tacitus, *Histories*, III, 23.

69 Though Tiberius, Claudius and Nero were also rumoured to have considered abdication at one time or another.

70 Tacitus, *Histories*, III, 71f. Lars Porsenna of Clusium in Etruria was believed to have attacked and perhaps captured Rome in *c.* 509 BC. Its capture by the Gauls was ascribed to 390 or 387 BC.

71 Vitellius had sent praetorian cohorts and other troops (two thousand strong) to hold the snow-bound Apennines, but they deserted.

72 Tacitus, *Histories*, III, 83. Lucius Cornelius Cinna was the Marian leader in control of Rome in 87–4 BC.

73 Suetonius, *Vitellius*, 16, 1–17, 2 (trans. J.C.Rolfe). The Stairs of Wailing (Scalae Gemoniae), on which the bodies of executed criminals were exposed, were a flight of steps from the Capitol down to the forum.

74 *ILS.*, 244 (*Lex de imperio Vespasiani*).

75 In Britain, where serious discontent occurred, there had been sharp friction between legionaries and auxiliaries (Tacitus, *Histories*, I, 60).

76 Tacitus, *Histories*, IV, 54.

77 Also Julius Sabinus of the tribe of the Lingones, who claimed descent from Julius Caesar.

78 Tacitus, *Histories*, IV, 57.

79 *BMC. Emp.*, I, p. 308 (LEGION. XV. PRIMIG.).

Chapter 8 Emperor and Army United AD 69-180

1 E.g. also Otho, Caecina, Valens.

2 Vespasian's paternal grandfather was a private soldier and his father a tax-collector and moneylender. He had an uncle in the senate and a maternal grandfather who was a knight.

3 Primus's soldiers had demanded an extra bonus in vain, though they were

said to have obtained the equivalent by plundering (Tacitus, *Histories*, III, 50).

4 Suetonius, *Vespasian*, 8, 3. For the period that follows Tacitus is lost, and Suetonius and Dio are our main literary sources.

5 *Ibid.*

6 *BMC. Emp.*, II, p. 129, no. 597, etc.

7 Tacitus, *Histories*, II, 80.

8 A Roman colony was established at Caesarea Maritima (Sdot Yam), and eight hundred veterans were settled at Emmaus (Qalonia).

9 In the extreme north a legionary fortress was established near Noviomagus (Nijmegen), a Batavian town which had been destroyed in the revolt of Civilis.

10 Pliny the younger, *Letters*, VII, 1. In the new peaceful province of Hispania Tarraconensis (nearer Spain), it was probably from *c.* AD 74 that the single legion was stationed at Legio (Leon).

11 But Titus's use of the name *Imperator* as prefix on the earliest eastern coins issued under Vespasian was deemed irregular and was dropped.

12 *BMC. Emp.*, II, p. 183, no. 752.

13 Suetonius, *Vespasian*, 25, 1.

14 Tacitus, *Histories*, II, 77; IV, 52. Doubts about the political reliability of Titus (Philostratus, *Life of Apollonius*, 6, 30) can probably be ignored.

15 For provincial recruitment areas, cf. Chapter 4, note 17, and passage quoted in Chapter 9 (reference in note 21).

16 According to one interpretation of *CIL.*, IV, 1009.

17 Suetonius, *Titus*, 6, 1 (trans. J.C.Rolfe).

18 Helvidius's mother-in-law Arria had been the wife of Thrasea Paetus (forced to commit suicide in AD 66) and was the daughter of Aulus Caecina Paetus (an associate of Lucius Arruntius Camillus Scribonianus who rebelled in AD 42).

19 Epictetus, *Discourses*, I, 2, 5.

20 Dio, LXV, 16, 3 (Loeb edn, p. 292).

21 Suetonius, *Titus*, 6, 2.

22 The head of Flavia Julia (Julia Titi) was placed on coins, under both Titus and Domitian. She was said to be the mistress of Domitian.

23 From Hönningen on the Rhine as far as Lorch in Württemberg, where the frontier-line joined on to the Raetian lines.

24 *BMC. Emp.*, II, p. 384, no. 389 (AVGVST. two years earlier, in AD 84, *ibid.*, p. 361, no. 288).

25 Domitian exempted veterans from customs duties (*portoria*) and probably from the requirement to provide for official travellers (*vehiculatio*).

26 Pliny the younger, *Panegyricus*, 18, 1–3; *Letters*, VIII, 14, 7.

27 *BMC. Emp.*, II, p. 364, no. 301: an officer is seen with an Eagle-bearer (*aquilifer*) and standard-bearer (*signifer*).

28 The location of the battle of 'Mons Graupius' is uncertain.

29 The frontier of lower Moesia was protected by a wall of earth across the Dobrogea.

30 Cf. *CIL.*, xvi, 81 (AD 88–100).

31 Dio, LXVIII, 9, 3 (Loeb edn, p. 374); Jordanes, *Getica*, XIII, 76.

32 Juvenal, *Satires*, IV, 111f. (trans. P.Green).

33 The first battle of Tapae (near the Iron Gates of Transylvania), won by Tettius Julianus.

34 The Sarmatians were a racially mixed group of tribes, including Iranian elements akin to the Scythians. The original home of the Jazyges had been the region of the Sea of Azov.

35 Cf. Suetonius, *Domitian*, 10, 3 (execution of Sallustius Lucullus).

36 For the Pseudo-Neros of AD 69, 79 and 88, cf. M.Grant, *Nero* (1970), pp. 250f., and note 4.

37 Dio, LXVII, 11; Suetonius, *Domitian*, 6f.

38 Two legions were, exceptionally, still located together in Egypt in AD 119.

39 According to another view, this change had already taken place in *c.* AD 85.

40 *CIL.*, vi, 2066.

41 *ILS.*, 1448.

42 Pliny the younger, *Letters*, VIII, 12.

43 Suetonius, *Domitian*, 21; cf. also Chapter 2 (note 26).

44 Dio, LXVII, 14, 4.

45 *Ibid.*, 15, 2; cf. Eutropius, VIII, 1.

46 *BMC. Emp.*, III, p. 21*. Trajan repeated the type.

47 Aurelius Victor, XI, 9.

48 Suetonius, *Domitian*, 23, 1.

49 *BMC. Emp.*, III, p. 14*.

50 *Ibid.*, p. 1, no. 4.

51 The standard rests on a ship's prow, cf. coins of Galba and Vespasian, and a relief from San Marcello, Rome (G.Webster, *The Roman Imperial Army*, pl. X). This may indicate that the legion honoured was composed of former marines. But the same feature is found on a standard of the *speculatores* (Chapter 4, note 21).

52 Pliny the younger, *Panegyricus*, 8, 5.

53 Philostratus, *Lives of the Sophists*, I, 7, 2.

54 Pliny the younger, *Letters*, IX, 13, 11.

55 Pliny the younger, *Panegyricus*, 5, 7.

56 Later he plotted against Trajan and was removed to an island, where he was killed during Hadrian's reign.

57 According to one theory Nerva himself had possessed pro-Domitianic tendencies, and was still prepared to assert them at least tentatively.

58 John of Antioch, fragment 110 M, cf. Dio, LXVIII, 3, 3.

59 Pliny the younger, *Panegyricus*, 6, 1f. (trans. B.Radice).

60 *Ibid.*, 7, 4.

61 Though a victory in Pannonia was announced at this very moment: *ibid.*, 8, 2; cf. *ILS.*, 2720.

62 Pliny the younger, *Panegyricus*, 35, 4.

63 *Ibid.*, 7, 3; cf. 8, 4.

64 *Ibid.*, 7, 6.

65 Dio, LXVIII, 4, 1 (Loeb edn, p. 366).

66 Pliny the younger, *Panegyricus*, 94, 5.

67 *SHA. Hadrian*, 11, 6.

68 *SHA. Maximus* (i.e. Pupienus) and *Balbinus*, 3. In the later empire the large corps of the *agentes in rebus* sometimes performed similar duties, though they were principally inspectors of the post.

69 P.K.Baillie Reynolds, *Journal of Roman Studies* (1923), p. 168.

70 Scholiast on Juvenal, *Satires*, VI, 480, *Codex Theodosianus*, 16, 12, 3.

71 Epictetus, *Discourses*, IV, 13, 5 (trans. W.A.Oldfather).

72 The innovation is variously attributed to Trajan while in Germany (AD 98–9), or to the dynasty of Vespasian.

73 Dacia was divided into upper and lower provinces in AD 118–19, and part of upper Dacia was detached to form a third province (Dacia Porolissensis) in c. AD 124. Pannonia, too, had been divided into upper and lower provinces in c. AD 103, with capitals at Carnuntum (Petronell) and Aquincum (Budapest) respectively. The upper province was the more important of the two. Apulum (Alba Julia) in upper Dacia, and Durostorum (Silistra) and Troesmis (Iglitza) in lower Moesia, became legionary camps.

74 When the Danubian legions were decreased from twelve to ten, this did not represent an overall numerical reduction of troops in the area, since its auxiliary and irregular units were increased. In lower Germany, Trajan established two new colonies, at Noviomagus (Nijmegen) and Ulpia Trajana (Xanten, near the camp of Castra Vetera).

75 L.Rossi, *Trajan's Column and the Dacian Wars* (1971). The Trophy at Adamklissi in Rumania, with crude vigorous sculptures, was also dedicated in AD 109 (?) to commemorate Trajan's Dacian victories.

76 D.E.Strong, *Roman Imperial Sculpture* (1961), pp. 37f.

77 *SHA. Marcus Antoninus* (i.e. Marcus Aurelius), 11, 7; cf. *Hadrian*, 12, 4: Italian settlers in Spain were exempted.

78 Pliny the younger, *Letters*, X, 30, 2.

79 *BMC. Emp.*, III, p. 223, no. 1045 (REX PARTHIS DATVS).

80 *BMC. Emp.*, III, p. 237, no. 5, celebrates Hadrian's ADOPTIO. *Ibid.*, p. 124*, allegedly depicts Hadrian as 'Caesar' before his accession. The only known specimen is now lost, but was apparently genuine. However, it may have been issued, disingenuously, after his accession.

81 Septicius and Suetonius were supposedly both dismissed in AD 121–3 for discourtesy to Hadrian's empress Sabina, *SHA. Hadrian*, 11, 3.

82 But the serious Second Jewish Revolt raged in Judaea from AD 132–5, and Flavius Arrianus, imperial governor of Cappadocia and author of a *Tactical Manual* (see Bibliography, section [A]), beat off an attack by the tribe of the Alani in 136.

83 In upper Moesia, for example, the old principle that camp and town must not be united was abandoned.

84 *BMC. Emp.*, 111, p. 318, no. 602.

85 The Exercitus Britannicus, Cappadocicus, Dacicus, Germanicus, Hispanicus, Mauretanicus, Moesiacus, Noricus, Raeticus and Syriacus. Presumably it was not considered fitting to celebrate the Judaean army while the Jewish rebellion was still raging (note 82 above).

86 The single legion in the province of Africa, to which Numidia still belonged, had been at Lambaesis (Lambèse) since the end of the first century AD.

87 *ILS.*, 2487 (trans. A.H.M. Jones). Catullinus, as commander of the legion (which had now been removed from the control of the senatorial governor) was also responsible for the operations of the auxiliaries attached to him.

88 British Museum Papyri, 2851 (*cohors I Hispanorum veterana*).

89 Michigan Papyri, VII 1951), no. 465. For the *principales*, see Introduction, note 34.

90 *Digest*, L. 6, 7 (trans. G.R. Watson).

91 Cnaeus Pedianus Fuscus Salinator. Servianus had succeeded Trajan as imperial governor of upper Germany.

92 Antoninus's sole salutation as *Imperator* was for these successes of Quintus Lollius Urbicus in Britain (AD 139-after 142). Urbicus's career culminated with the city prefecture.

93 Cf. earlier long tenures: R. Syme, *Journal of Roman Studies* (1980), p. 77.

Part V The Army of the Later Empire

Chapter 9 Growing Crisis and Army Domination AD 180-235

1 *SHA. Verus*, 4, 3; *SHA. Marcus Antoninus* (Marcus Aurelius), 7, 9.

2 Lucian, *Alexander*, 48.

3 Dio, LXII, 17 and 22-8 (Loeb edn, pp. 36ff.).

4 *BMC. Emp.*, IV, p. 488, no. 704 (MATRI CASTRORVM).

5 Avidius Cassius claimed he had already been appointed emperor by troops that were then in Pannonia (Dio, LXII, 23, 1).

6 M. Grant, *The Climax of Rome* (1968), p. 87.

7 E.g. Dio, LXXIII, 2, 2 (Loeb edn, p. 73).

8 Herodian, 1, 9, 1.

9 Dio, LXXIII, 9, 1f. (Loeb edn, p. 88, trans. E. Cary).

10 Herodian, I, 9, 10.

11 Moretti, *Rivista di filologia*, XXXVIII (1960), p. 68.

12 Dio, LXXIII, 13, 6.

13 H.Keil and A. von Premerstein, *Dritte Reise* (*Denkschriften der Wiener Akademie*, LVII, 1914–15), no. 9, lines 16ff. The term used here for military police is *colletiones*.

14 S.Riccobono, *Fontes Iuris Romani Antejustiniani*, 2nd edn, I, 103.

15 Dio, LXXIV, 8, 4.

16 Cf. *SHA. Divus Claudius* (i.e. Claudius II Gothicus), 12, 5.

17 Dio, LXXIV, 11, 3–6 (trans. E.Cary).

18 Dio added that Didius Julianus eventually paid even more than he had agreed to pay, but Herodian said he paid less.

19 Herodian, II, 6, 12–14 (trans. E.C.Echols).

20 *Ibid.*, 13, 1–5 (trans. E.C.Echols).

21 Dio, LXXV, 2, 2–6 (trans. E.Cary).

22 *BMC. Imp.*, V, p. 52, no. 193 (DESTINATO IMPERAT[*ori*]). Caracalla became joint Augustus in AD 198, and Geta in 209.

23 *Ibid.*, pp. 63ff.

24 Dio, LXXVIII, 17, 1.

25 *Ibid.*, LXXVI, 12, 3 (trans. E.Cary).

26 Herodian, III, 13, 4.

27 For the duties of a part-mounted Palmyrene cohort in *c.* AD 208–51, see C.B.Welles, R.O.Fink and J.F.Gilliam, *The Excavations at Dura-Europus, Final Report*, V, 1 (1959). Cf. above, Chapter 3, note 3.

28 Cf. Chapter 8, notes 88–90.

29 F.Millar, *The Roman Empire and its Neighbours* (1967), p. 125.

30 *BMC. Emp.*, V, pp. 21ff. (AD 193).

31 Plautianus had his co-prefect Quintus Aemilius Saturninus murdered (AD 199).

32 Papinian's first co-prefect was Quintus Maecius Laetus.

33 Coins of Caracalla of AD 208 celebrate a crossing (TRAIECTVS), possibly of the Firth of Forth, *BMC. Emp.*, V, pp. 353, clxxiv; Gnecchi, III, p. 40, no. 9.

34 Dio, LXXVII, 15, 2 (Loeb edn, pp. 271f.).

35 *Ibid.*, LXXVIII, 3, 1f. (Loeb edn, pp. 282f., trans. E.Cary).

36 Herodian, IV, 4, 7; Dio, LXXVIII, 24, 1 (Loeb edn, p. 336).

37 *SHA. Geta*, 6, 3ff. (trans. D.Magie). Papinian's latest co-prefect Valerius Patruinus was killed with him. But it is not certain that Papinian was still prefect at the time of his death.

38 Dio, LXXIX, 15, 1 (Loeb edn, p. 372).

39 Upper Britain (the province had been divided, probably by Caracalla and Geta: the legions were at Isca Silurum [Caerleon] and Deva [Chester]), upper Germany, lower Germany, upper Pannonia, lower Pannonia, upper Moesia, lower Moesia, Dacia (reunited under a single governor since

AD 168: the legions were at Apulum [Alba Julia] and Potaissa [Turda]),
Galatia–Cappadocia, northern Syria (Syria Coele), Syria Palaestina (the
former Judaea), Mesopotamia.

40 Nearer Spain (Hispania Tarraconensis), lower Britain (the legion was
at Eburacum [York]), Raetia, Noricum, southern Syria (Syria Phoenice),
Arabia, Egypt, Numidia (detached from Africa as a separate province by
Septimius Severus after AD 198–9).

41 Dio, LXXIX, 6, 1 (Loeb edn, p. 350).

42 *SHA. Antoninus Caracalla*, IX, 7f.; cf. (rather differently) Herodian, IV, 7, 3.

43 The *Constitutio Antoniniana*: Dio, LXXVIII, 9, 5 (Loeb edn, p. 296); Giessen
Papyrus, i, 40.

44 Herodian, IV, 12, 7.

45 *BMC. Emp.*, V, p. 525, no. 143.

46 Dio, LXXIX, 28, 1–29, 2 (trans. E. Cary).

47 *Ibid.*, 39, 3–40, 2.

48 *BMC. Emp.*, V, p. 531, no. 7.

49 Dio, LXXX, 4, 1f., is particularly scandalized by these appointments of
Comazon.

50 *Ibid.*, 18, 4 (Loeb edn, p. 474).

51 Comazon survived to become city prefect for the third time.
Elagabalus's mother Julia Soaemias was murdered with her son.

52 Aurelius Victor, XXIV, 3; Eutropius, VIII, 23.

53 *SHA. Severus Alexander*, 47, 1.

54 Cf. R. Syme, *Emperors and Biography* (1971), pp. 150f., 154ff. The two
prefects were Julius Flavianus, who had held the post in AD 218 as colleague of
Comazon, and Geminius Chrestus, who had been prefect of Egypt (219–21).
However Ulpian's responsibility for their murder is uncertain. Zosimus, I,
11, 3, suggests that it was Mamaea who destroyed them.

55 Herodian, VI, 1, 9f., cf. *SHA. Severus Alexander*, 49, 3f.

56 Dio, LXXX, 4, 2 (Loeb edn, p. 484). Dio was imperial governor first of
Dalmatia and then of upper Pannonia, probably in AD 224–6 and 226–8
respectively.

57 *Ibid.*, 5, 3.

58 Gnecchi, II, p. 83, no. 3; Toynbee, p. 164.

Chapter 10 Anarchy, Reconstruction, Collapse AD 235–476

1 He was called 'Thracian' but probably came from the region of Oescus
(near Nikopol) on the Danube; cf. R. Syme, *Emperors and Biography*, pp. 185f.

2 However about 56 per cent of the senators, too, were provincials at this
period.

3 Cf. Anonymous, *To the King*, XXI, 62 (in the time of Philip).

4 It is customary to reckon the 'Danubian emperors' from Claudius II
Gothicus (AD 268–70).

5 Herodian, VII, 5, 6.

6 *Ibid.*, 6, 4.

7 *Ibid.*, 10, 2–5 (trans. E.C.Echols).

8 *ILS.*, 498, 500.

9 Herodian, VIII, 8, 4–7 (trans. E.C.Echols).

10 W.Dittenberger, *Sylloge Inscriptionum Graecarum*, 3rd edn, 888 (trans. A.H.M.Jones).

11 Gordian III's wife Tranquillina was the daughter of Timesitheus.

12 The whole of the province of Mesopotamia, overrun by the great Persian king Sapor (Shapur) I, was recovered.

13 For details, cf. M.Grant, *The Climax of Rome* (1968), pp. 13ff. and notes.

14 PANNONIAE, GEN[*ius*] EXERCITVS ILLVRICIANI, EXERCITVS ILLVRICVS, GEN[*ius*] ILLVRICI, DACIA, DACIA FELIX: M.&S.IV,3, pp. 120, 122, 124, 134.

15 For the differing accounts see Wickert, Pauly-Wissowa-Kroll, *Realencyclopädie für die classische Altertumswissenschaft*, s.v. Licinius (Valerianus), col. 492.

16 E.g. the Courage of the cavalry (VIRTVS EQVIT[*um*]), and its Speed (ALACRITATI with Pegasus): M.&S.V,I, p. 276, no. 100; p. 179, no. 545; cf. Toynbee, p. 165, n. 196.

17 M.&S.V,I, p. 133, no. 33. There are also coins celebrating the loyalty of the legionaries and praetorians.

18 Toynbee, p. 113, n. 8. The characteristic religion of the officers of this period was the stern faith of Mithras, related to the prevailing cult of the Sun (M.Grant, *The Climax of Rome*, pp. 172–86).

19 M.&S.V,I, p. 306, no. 366; p. 265, no. 4; and p. 307, no. 378.

20 The tradition in the *SHA.* of a 'senatorial restoration' under the emperor Tacitus (AD 275–6) is likely to be wholly fictitious.

21 However, since AD 276 at latest, the lower German frontier was evacuated, for half a century. Franks were settled on the left bank of the Rhine (cf. the Ubii in 38 BC).

22 Aurelius Victor, XXXVII, 3; Eutropius, IX, 17, 3.

23 On his accession, Diocletian executed Lucius Flavius (?) Aper, the praetorian prefect who had probably murdered his own son-in-law Numerian (joint emperor with his brother Carinus [283–4]: they were the sons of Carus [282–3], who was much admired by *SHA.* because he marched to Ctesiphon (and for his German victories cf. Gnecchi, II, p. 83, no. 3; Toynbee, p. 88).

24 The first Augusti were Diocletian and Maximian (286), and the first Caesars Galerius and Constantius I (the father of Constantine the Great).

25 Carausius (287–93) was murdered and succeeded by Allectus, who was defeated by Asclepiodotus, the praetorian prefect of Constantius I (296).

26 Constantine was victorious at Hadrianopolis (Edirne), Chrysopolis (Üsküdar, Scutari) and in the Hellespont (Sea of Marmara).

27 Maxentius, the son of Maximian, had been elevated to the throne by a section of the praetorian guard in 306, and succumbed to Constantine's invasion at the battle of the Milvian Bridge in 312.

28 Cf. Gnecchi, I, p. 15, no. 6 (DEBELLATORI GENTIVM BARBARARVM).

29 Ammianus, XVI, 27ff.; for the army as known to him, see G.A.Crump, *Historia* [1973], pp. 91–103). He uses the old word *turmae* for cavalry squadrons, but the squadrons of the frontier force were also now known as *cunei* and those of the field force as *vexillationes*.

30 *Ibid.*, XIX, 2ff.

31 *Ibid.*, XXXI, 12, 10–13; 13, 1–5 and 10–12 (trans. J.C.Rolfe).

32 *Ibid.*, 5, 10.

33 The Ostrogoths had built up a large empire in the Ukraine, but it was overrun by the Huns.

34 Already, earlier, the Huns had driven other tribes before them into Italy and Gaul, e.g. the Vandals who, with the Suebi and Alani, severely devastated Gaul and Spain (AD 406–9).

35 Aetius had destroyed the Burgundian kingdom centred since AD 413 upon Civitas Vangionum (the former Borbetomagus and the present Worms), an event commemorated in the *Nibelungenlied*.

Appendices

1 The substance of this table is owed to J.P.V.D.Balsdon, *Rome: The Story of an Empire* (1970), pp. 88–91. He comments:

It illustrates the build-up of the Danube army (12 legions in AD 112 as against 7 in AD 20) at the expense of the Rhine army (8 legions in AD 20; 4 in AD 112); also of the army in the east (Egypt excluded), which from 4 legions in AD 20 rose to 7 in 112 and 10 in 215. It also shows that, apart from sending detachments to wars elsewhere, a number of legions were virtually stationary throughout the period: III Augusta in Africa; XXII Primigenia in Germany from the time of its creation by Caligula; II Augusta and XX Valeria Victrix in Britain from the time of the invasion; and VII Gemina, recruited by Galba, in Spain. Two legions, VII and XI (both *Claudia Pia Fidelis* since they had second thoughts about mutinying in AD 42) stayed in the Balkans. The eastern legions, too, remained continuously in the east. Legion XX won its title Valeria Victrix for suppressing Boudicca's revolt in Britain in AD 61.

2 Sections A, B and C are based on descriptions by P.La Baume, *The Romans on the Rhine*, 2nd edn (1972), pp. 25f., 33f., 28.

3 *ILS.*, 2244; from Castra Vetera (Birten). Rheinisches Landesmuseum, Bonn.

4 *ILS.*, 2341; Romisch-Germanisches Zentralmuseum, Mainz.

5 L.Rossi, *Trajan's Column and the Dacian Wars* (1971), p. 88. For the *signa*, *ibid.*, p. 106.

6 *ILS.*, 2512; *Bonner Jahrbücher*, Supplement 81, p. 104.

7 Hofman, *Sonderschrift des Oesterreichischen Archäologischen Institutes in Wien*, vol. v (1905), fig. 23.

8 Arrian, *Tactics*, 4, 2. In Josephus's time spears of two sizes had been carried, one for thrusting and one for throwing.

9 G.L.Cheesman, *The Auxilia of the Roman Imperial Army* (1914), pp. 125–9.

10 Rheinisches Landesmuseum, Bonn (Lehner, *Catalogue*, plate v, no. 3).

11 G.L.Cheesman, *The Auxilia of the Roman Imperial Army*, p. 131. These descriptions are owed to him.

12 This account is based on *The Roman Army* (*Sunday Times* Wall Chart [1969]). In addition to the legionary camps there were also permanent or semi-permanent encampments for auxiliary troops, e.g. Birovicium (Housesteads) on Hadrian's Wall.

13 At Isca Silurum (Caerleon), the mess-unit has a room fifteen feet square. In marching camps, the legionaries' leather tents (220 men to an acre) were behind the headquarters and the auxiliaries' tents were in front of the area, facing the enemy. The eight-man tents measured ten square feet, and were rolled up for the march, like a chrysalis (hence their name *papilio*, butterfly). Officers' tents, which were larger, were erected on box frames and had floors of newly cut turf.

14 Each legionary fortress was provided with a hospital (*valetudinarium*), and remains survive, e.g. at Novaesium (Neuss), Castra Vetera (Birten), Carnuntum (Petronell) and Inchtuthil. For plans, see Webster, *The Roman Imperial Army*, pp. 196f.: some of these hospitals were large buildings with an internal courtyard and a continuous circulating corridor containing sixty wards, arranged in pairs. For the military medical service see above, Chapter 3, note 22. 'Every permanent fort,' adds Webster (p. 251), 'had its bath-house which with its pattern of rooms of different temperatures and humidities was far better for the promotion of health and cleanliness than our modern practice of wallowing in dirty water . . . Drains and latrines were constantly flushed with the overflow from the water supply.'

15 Vegetius, I, 24 (trans. G.R.Watson, *The Roman Soldier* [1969], p. 67).

16 E.A.Thompson, *A Roman Reformer and Inventor* (1952), p. 79.

17 G.Webster, *The Roman Imperial Army* (1969), pp. 234f.

18 Confusingly, the *onager* (Ammianus Marcellinus, XXII, 4) was known in earlier times as *scorpio*, and the *ballista* as *catapulta*.

19 Josephus, *Jewish War*, v, 63. Vitruvius gives rules covering ranges between 2 and 360 pounds, but many of his calculations are apparently theoretical. *Onagri* were also employed for defensive purposes.

20 Athenaeus Mechanicus, *On Engines* (late Hellenistic or early imperial epoch). This was with the three-span catapult furnished with sinew springs.

21 It appears likely that artillery was normally provided for the first cohort of the legion only, which constructed machines and trained men for the rest of the legion as required. It has been suggested, though without general

agreement, that the administrative staff of the legion was concentrated in its first cohort, which was doubled in size from the early second century AD.

22 *Anonymous De Rebus Bellicis* (*c.* AD 366–75) propounded a series of inventions of new or improved siege-artillery, as well as a new warship, scythed chariot, and portable bridge. But none of these proposals were put into effect, cf. E.A.Thompson, *A Roman Reformer and Inventor*, pp. 78f. On the history of ancient siege-machinery in general, see E.W.Marsden, *Greek and Roman Artillery* (1971).

Bibliography

A Greek Writings

ARRIAN (of Nicomedia [Izmit in Turkey], *c.* AD 95–175), *Tactical Manual* (*Techne Tactice*), AD 136.

DIO CASSIUS (of Nicaea [Iznik in Turkey], consul in *c.* AD 205 and 229), *Roman History* from beginnings until AD 229, of which portions from 68 BC survive, partly in abbreviated form.

JOSEPHUS (of Jerusalem, AD 37/8–after 94), *Jewish War* (*Bellum Judaicum*), about the First Jewish Revolt (First Roman War) of AD 66–73 (with introductory section), published in AD 75–9; *Jewish Antiquities* (*Antiquitates Judaicae*), a history of the Jews to AD 66, published in AD 93–4.

PLUTARCH (of Chaeronea, before AD 50–after AD 120), twenty-three surviving pairs of *Parallel Lives*, mostly published between AD 105 and 115.

POLYBIUS (of Megalopolis, *c.* 200–after 118 BC), *Histories* of period 220–146 BC in forty books, of which large portions survive.

B Roman Writings

AMMIANUS MARCELLINUS (of Antioch [Antakya in Turkey], *c.* AD 330–95), *History* covering the years AD 96–378; the parts relating to AD 353–78 are still extant.

ANONYMOUS, *Alexandrian War* (*Bellum Alexandrinum* 48–7 BC), wrongly attributed to Julius Caesar; possibly written by his officer Aulus Hirtius.

ANONYMOUS, *African War* (*Bellum Africum*, 47–6 BC), wrongly attributed to Julius Caesar.

ANONYMOUS, *Spanish War* (*Bellum Hispaniense*, 45 BC), wrongly attributed to Julius Caesar.

337

Bibliography

ANONYMOUS, *On the Fortification of Camps* (*De Munitionibus Castrorum*), probably of third century AD, wrongly attributed to Hyginus.

ANONYMOUS, *On Matters relating to Warfare* (*De Rebus Bellicis*), probably AD 366–75.

CAESAR, JULIUS (100–44 BC), *Commentaries*: *Gallic War* (*De Bello Gallico*), covering the years 58–2 BC (completed to 50 BC by Aulus Hirtius); *Civil War* (*De Bello Civili*), on 49–8 BC.

FRONTINUS (*c.* AD 30–104); his treatise on Greek and Roman military science (*De Re Militari*) is not extant, but a work on *Strategies* (*Strategemata*) has survived.

HISTORIA AUGUSTA; title given in the seventeenth century to collection of biographies of Roman emperors from AD 117 to 284; the names of the authors attached to them are fictitious, and so is a substantial proportion of the contents (especially in the middle and later Lives); date of publication much disputed; perhaps near the end of the fourth century AD.

JUVENAL (AD 50/65–after 127); his sixteenth *Satire* outlines the privileges of a soldier's life.

LUCAN (AD 39–65), epic poem the *Civil War* (*Bellum Civile*), generally known as the *Pharsalia*, on the war between Julius Caesar and Pompey (49–8 BC).

SALLUST (*c.* 86–35 BC), *Jugurthine War* (*Bellum Jugurthinum*), on the operations against King Jugurtha of Numidia (112–5 BC).

SUETONIUS (perhaps of Hippo Regius [Bône] in Numidia, *c.* AD 69–after 130), *Lives of the Caesars*, from Julius Caesar to Domitian.

TACITUS (*c.* AD 56–after 115 or 117 [?]), *Agricola* (AD 98), eulogy of his father-in-law Cnaeus Julius Agricola of Forum Julii (Fréjus); *Germania* (*De Origine et Situ Germanorum*, AD 98), a description of the tribes north of the Rhine and the Danube; *Histories*, on period AD 68–96, of which AD 68–70 survives: published *c.* 109; *Annals*, on period AD 14–68, of which the major part survives (with part of AD 37 to part of AD 47, and part of AD 66–8 missing).

VEGETIUS (writing AD 388–91), *Epitome of Military Science* (*Epitome Rei Militaris*), the only ancient manual of Roman military institutions to have survived intact; includes much information from sources of earlier periods, notably of the second century AD (e.g. Tarrutenius Paternus, the praetorian prefect of Commodus) and third century AD.

VELLEIUS PATERCULUS (*c.* 19 BC–after AD 30), *Roman Histories*, from beginnings until AD 30; the surviving sections begin in the second century BC.

VITRUVIUS (Roman architect and military engineer, of Augustus's reign and shortly before); the last (tenth) book of his work *On Architecture* (*De Architectura*) deals with military artillery.

C *Other Ancient Sources*

Selections from the huge amount of evidence provided by inscriptions, papyri and coins are supplied in source-books such as V.Ehrenberg and A.H.M. Jones, *Documents illustrating the Reigns of Augustus and Tiberius,* 2nd edn (1955); E.M.Smallwood, *Documents illustrating the Principates of Gaius, Claudius and Nero* 1967); M.McCrum and A.G.Woodhead, *Select Documents of the Principates of the Flavian Emperors (including the year of Revolution)* (1961); E.M.Smallwood, *Documents illustrating the Principates of Nerva, Trajan and Hadrian* (1966). For later reigns, the search is harder. Among very numerous and valuable papyri, the military calendar of Dura-Europus (*Feriale Duranum,* of the third century AD) is outstanding: see book by R.O.Fink, A.S.Hoey and W.F.Snyder in section D of this bibliography, and R.Cavenaile, *Corpus Papyrorum Latinorum* (1958), no. 324.

For the coins and medallions of the Roman state, which are extremely informative about the aspects of the Roman army with which this book is concerned, see Abbreviations (above, p. 305). The evidence of the local coinages of the cities of the Roman empire, for this as for other aspects of Roman history, has never been completely collated: but many such issues – notably of Tomis (Constanţa), Perga (Aksu), Caesaraugusta (Zaragoza), Viminacium (Kostolac), Philippi, Berytus (Beirut) – possess military significance (and could usefully be published together in a single volume).

Archaeological and artistic material is of immense value. For the archaeological evidence, see the standard textbooks on the Roman army indicated below, section D. Among the very numerous works of art that are relevant and informative, the Columns of Trajan and Marcus Aurelius at Rome and the Trophy of Trajan at Adamklissi (near the ancient town of Tropaeum Trajani) may be singled out: see, in section D, books by L.Rossi, C.Caprino *et al.,* and F.B.Florescu respectively.

D *Modern Books*

ADCOCK, F.E., *The Roman Art of War under the Republic* (Cambridge, Massachusetts, 1940).

AIGNER, H., *Die Soldaten als Machtfaktor in der ausgehenden Fümischen Republik* (Graz, 1974).

ANDERSON, A.S., TOMLIN, R.S.O., and WATSON, G.R., *The Army,* in WACHER, J. (ed.), *The Roman World,* Vol. I (London, 1987).

ANDERSON, J.K., and WEBSTER, G., *Wars and Military Science* (Greece, Rome) in GRANT, M., and KITZINGER, R. (eds.), *Civilization of the Ancient Mediterranean,* Vol. I (New York, 1988).

BIRLEY, E., *Roman Britain and the Roman Army* (Kendal, 1953).

BRUNT, P.A., *Italian Manpower 225 B.C.–A.D. 14* (Oxford, 1971).

CAMPBELL, J.B., *The Emperor and the Roman Army: 31 B.C.–A.D. 235* (Oxford, 1984).

Bibliography

CAPRINO, C. (et al.), *La colonna di Marco Aurelio* (Rome, 1955).

CHEESMAN, G.L., *The Auxilia of the Imperial Roman Army* (Oxford, 1914, reprint 1971).

CHEVALLIER, R., *Les voies romaines* (Paris, 1972).

CONNOLLY, P., *Greece and Rome at War* (London, 1981).

CONNOLLY, P., *The Roman Army* (London, 1975).

COUISSIN, P., *Les armes romaines* (Paris, 1926).

DAVIES, R., *Service in the Roman Army* (Edinburgh, 1989).

VON DOMASZEWSKI, A., *Die Rangordnung des römischen Heeres,* 2nd edn (revised by B. Dobson) (Cologne—Graz, 1967).

VON DOMASZEWSKI, A., *Die Religion des römischen Heeres* (Trier, 1895, New York, 1978).

DURRY, M., *Les cohortes prétoriennes* (Paris, 1938).

ERDMANN, E.H., *Die Rolle des Heeres in der Zeit von Marius bis Caesar* (Neustadt, 1972).

FINK, R.O., *Military Records on Papyri* (Cleveland, Ohio [American Philological Association], 1970).

FINK, R.O., HOEY, A.S. and SNYDER, W.F., *The Feriale Duranum* (Yale Classical Studies, VII, New Haven, 1940).

FLORESCU, F.B., *Tropaeum Traiani* (Bucharest—Bonn, 1965).

FORNI, G., *Il reclutamento delle legioni da Augusto a Diocleziano* (Milan, 1963).

FRANK, R.I., *Scholae Palatinae* (Rome [American Academy], 1969).

FREIS, H., *Die Cohortes Urbanae* (Bonner Jahrbücher, Supplement no. 21, Cologne, 1967).

FULLER, Major-General J.F.C., *Julius Caesar: Man, Soldier and Tyrant* (London, 1965).

GABBA, E., *Esercito e società nella tarda repubblica romana* (Florence, 1973).

GABBA, E., *Per la storia dell'esercito romano in età imperiale* (Bologna, 1974).

GABBA, E., *Republican Rome: The Army and the Allies* (Oxford, 1977).

GARLAN, Y., *War in the Ancient World: A Social History* (London, 1975).

GROSSE, R., *Römische Militärgeschichte von Gallienus bis zum Beginn der byzantinischen Themenfassung* (Berlin, 1930).

HARMAND, J., *L'armée et le soldat à Rome de 107 à 50 avant notre ère* (Paris, 1967).

HARMAND, J., *La querre antique de Sumer à Rome* (Paris, 1973).

HODGE, P., *The Roman Army* (London, 1977).

HOLDER, P.A., *The Auxilia from Augustus to Trajan* (Oxford, 1980).

HOWE, L.L., *The Praetorian Prefect from Commodus to Diocletian* (Cambridge, 1942).

HUMBLE, R., *Warfare in the Ancient World* (London, 1980).

JAL, P., *La guerre civile à Rome: étude littéraire et morale* (Paris, 1963).

JONES, A.H.M., *The Later Roman Empire* (Oxford, 1964).

KEPPIE, L., *The Making of the Roman Army: From Republic to Empire* (London, 1984).

KIENAST, D., *Untersuchungen zu den Kriegsflotten der römischen Kaiserzeit* (Bonn, 1966).

KNEISSL, P., *Die Siegestitulatur der römischen Kaiser* (Hypomnemata, 23, Göttingen, 1969).

KOCH, W. and BAUMHAUER, H., *Cäsaren, Herren am Limes* (Stuttgart, 1969).

KROMAYER, J. and VEITH, G., *Heerwesen und Kriegführung der Griechen und Römer* (Munich, 1928).

LA BAUME, P., *The Romans on the Rhine*, 2nd edn (Bonn, 1972).

LUTTWAK, E.N., *The Grand Strategy of the Roman Empire from the First Century A.D. to the Third* (Baltimore, 1976).

MACMULLEN, R., *Enemies of the Roman Order* (Cambridge, Massachusetts, 1967).

MACMULLEN, R., *Soldier and Civilian in the Later Roman Empire* (Cambridge, Massachusetts, 1963).

MARIN Y PEÑA, M., *Instituciones militares romanas* (Madrid, 1956).

MARSDEN, E.W., *Greek and Roman Artillery* (Oxford, 1971).

MILLAR, C.M.H., *The Roman Army* (London, 1955).

MILLAR, F., *Cassius Dio* (Oxford, 1964).

PARKER, H.M.D., *The Roman Legions* (Cambridge, revised edn 1958).

PASSERINI, A., *Le coorti pretorie* (Rome, 1939; reprint 1972).

PFLAUM, H.-G., *Les carrières procuratoriennes équestres sous le haut-empire romain* (Paris, 1960–1).

PRITCHETT, W.K., *Ancient Greek Military Practices*, vol. I (Berkeley, 1971).

PRITCHETT, W.K., *The Greek State at War* (Berkeley, 1974).

PUSCH, M., *Die Römer: Politik mit Legionen* (Munich, 1977).

RADKE, G., *Viae Publicae Romanae* (Pauly-Wissowa offprint, Munich, 1971).

REYNOLDS, P.K. BAILLIE, *The Vigiles of Imperial Rome* (London, 1926).

ROBINSON, H.R., *The Armour of Imperial Rome* (London, 1975).

ROSSI, L., *Trajan's Column and the Dacian Wars* (London, 1971).

ROSTOVTZEFF, M.I., *The Social and Economic History of the Roman Empire*, 2nd edn (revised by P.M. Fraser) (Oxford, 1967).

ROUGE, J., *La marine dans l'antiquité* (Paris, 1975).

SADDINGTON, D.B., *The Development of the Roman Auxiliary Forces from Caesar to Vespasian* (Harare, 1982).

SAXER, R., Untersuchungen zu den Vexillationen (Cologne—Graz, 1967).

SCHLEIERMACHER, W., *Der römische Limes in Deutschland* (Berlin, 1961).

SIMKINS, M., *The Roman Army from Caesar to Trajan* (London, 1982).

SIMKINS, M., *Warriors of Rome* (London, 1988).

SIMPSON, GRACE, *Britons and the Roman Army* (Farnborough, 1964).

SMITH, R.E., *Service in the Post-Marian Roman Army* (Manchester, 1958).

SPEIDEL, M.P., *Die Equites Singulares Augusti* (Bonn, 1965).

SPEIDEL, M.P., *Guards of the Roman Armies* (Bonn, 1978).

SPEIDEL, M.P., *Roman Army Studies* (Amsterdam, 1984, 1988).

STARR, C.G., *The Roman Imperial Navy*, 2nd edn (Cambridge, 1960).

SYME, R., *Emperors and Biography: Studies in the Historia Augusta* (Oxford, 1971).

SYME, R., *The Roman Revolution* (Oxford, 1939; reprint 1971).

SYME, R., *Tacitus* (Oxford, 1958).

TIMPE, D., *Untersuchungen zur Kontinuität des frühen Prinzipats* (Historia Einzelschriften, 5, Wiesbaden, 1962).

VERSNEL, H.S., *Triumphus* (Leiden, 1970).

VITUCCI, G., *Richerche sulla praefectura urbi in età imperiale* (Rome, 1956).

WATSON, G.R., *The Roman Soldier* (London and New York, 1969).

WEBSTER, G., *The Roman Army,* (Chester, 1956; 1968, 1985).

WEBSTER, G., *The Roman Imperial Army* (London, 1969, 1979). *

*Webster is largely concerned with what the British army calls the 'Q side' of military life—above all, with weapons, camps and barracks—whereas Watson, in the book listed above, has concentrated on the 'A side', the conditions of service of the individual soldier.

E *Some Books on the Ancient Historians*

GREEK AND ROMAN HISTORIANS: GENERAL
H.E. Barnes, *A History of Historical Writings* (2nd ed., 1963); A.B. Breebaart, *Clio and Antiquity: History and Historiography of the Greek and Roman World* (1987); A. Cameron, *History as Text: The Writings of Ancient History* (1989); J.W. Eadie and J. Ober (eds.), *The Craft of the Ancient Historian* (C.G. Starr, 1985); M.I. Finley, *Ancient History; Evidence and Models* (1985), and *The Use and Abuse of History* (1975); C.W. Fornara, *The Nature of History in Ancient Greece and Rome* (1983, 1988); B. Gentili and G. Cerri, *History and Biography in Ancient Thought* (1988); A. Momigliano, *Essays in Ancient and Modern Historiography* (1977); I.S. Moxan, J.D. Stuart and A.J. Woodman (eds.), *Past Perspectives: Studies in Greek and Roman Historical Writing* (1986); G.A. Press, *The Development of the Idea of History in Antiquity* (1982); C.G. Starr, *Essays on Ancient History* (1979); D.R. Stuart, *Epochs in Greek and Roman Biography* (1928); S. Usher, *The Historians of Greece and Rome* (1969, 1985); F.W. Walbank, *Selected Papers: Studies in Greek and Roman History and Historiography* (1985); A.J. Woodman, *Rhetoric in Classical Historiography: Four Studies* (1988).

GREEK HISTORIANS: GENERAL
N. Austin, *The Greek Historians*, (1968); J.B. Bury, *The Ancient Greek Historians* (1909, 1958); M.I. Finley, *The Greek Historians* (1959); K. von Fritz, *Die griechische Geschichtsschreibung*, I (1967); W.P. Henry, *Greek Historical Writings* (1966); D. Kagan, *Studies in the Greek Historians* (1975); K.H. Kinzl (ed.), *Problems and Methods in Greek History* (1988); A. Momigliano, *The Development of Greek Biography* (1971); C.G. Starr, *The Awakening of the Greek Historical Spirit* (1968); R. Thomas, *Oral Tradition and Written Record in Classical Athens* (1989); F.W. Walbank, *Speeches in Greek Historians* (1965).

HERODOTUS
H.F. Burnitz, *Herodotstudien*, (1968); J.A.S. Evans, *Herodotus* (1982); D. Fehling, *Herodotus and his 'Sources'* (1989); S. Flory, *The Archaic Smile of Herodotus* (1987); C.W. Fornara, *Herodotus: An Interpretative Essay* (1971); J. Gould, *Herodotus* (1989);

D. Grene, *Herodotus* (1987); J. Hart, *Herodotus and Greek History* (1982); V.J. Hunter, *Past and Process in Herodotus and Thucydides* (1982); H.R. Immerwahr, *Form and Thought in Herodotus* (1967); M.L. Lang, *Herodotean Narrative and Discourse* (1984); J.L. Myres, *Herodotus: the Father of History* (1953); J.E. Powell, *The History of Herodotus* (1939, 1967); A. de Selincourt, *The World of Herodotus* (1962); K.H. Waters, *Herodotus the Historian* (1984).

THUCYDIDES

F.E. Adcock, *Thucydides and his History* (1963); L. Cantora, *Tucidide: l'oligarèa imperfetto* (1988); C.N. Cochrane, *Thucydides and the Science of History* (1929, 1965); W.R. Connor, *Thucydides* (1984, 1987); F.M. Cornford, *Thucydides Mythistoricus* (1907, 1965); K.J. Dover, *Thucydides* (1973); L. Edmunds, *Chance and Intelligence in Thucydides* (1975); H. Erbse, *Thukydides Interpretationen* (1989); J.H. Finley, *Three Essays on Thucydides* (1967); A.W. Gomme (etc.), *A Historical Commentary on Thucydides*, 4 vols. (1945-1970); G.B. Grundy, *Thucydides and the History of his Age* (1948); V.J. Hunter, *Thucydides the Artful Reporter* (1973); N. Marinatos, *Thucydides and Religion* (1981); P.R. Pouncey, *The Necessities of War: A Study of Thucydides' Pessimism* (1980); D. Proctor, *The Experience of Thucydides* (1980); H.E. Rawlings, *The Structure of Thucydides' History* (1981); J. de Romiley, *Thucydides and Athenian Imperialism* (1963); P.A. Stadter, *The Speeches in Thucydides* (1973); H.-P. Stahl, *Thucydides: Die Stellung des Menschen im geschichtlichen Prozess* (1966); R. Syme, *Thucydides* (1963); F.L. Tasolambros, *In Defence of Thucydides* (1979); H.D. Westlake, *Studies in Thucydides and Greek History* (1989); A.G. Woodhead, *Thucydides on the Nature of Power* (1970); J.E. Ziolkowski, *Thucydides and the Tradition of Funeral Speeches at Athens* (1981).

XENOPHON

J.K. Anderson, *Xenophon* (1974); F. Delebecque, *Essai sur la vie de Xénophon* (1957); P. Gauthier, *Un commentaire historique des Poroi de Xenophon* (1976); V. Gray, *The Character of Xenophon's Hellenica* (1989); W.E. Higgins, *Xenophon the Athenian* (1977); S.W. Hirsch, *The Friendship of the Barbarians: Xenophon and the Persian Empire* (1985); J. Luccioni, *Les idées politiques et sociales de Xénophon* (1957); R. Nickel, *Xenophon* (1979); G.R. Nussbaum, *The Ten Thousand* (1967); G. Proietti, *Xenophon's Sparta: An Introduction* (1987); L. Strauss, *Xenophon's Socrates* (1972); J. Tatum, *Xenophon's Imperial Fiction On the Education of Cyrus* (1989).

POLYBIUS

K.F. Eisen, *Polybiosinterpretationen* (1966); G.A. Lehmann, *Untersuchungen zur historischen Glaubwürdigkeit des Polybios* (1967); P. Pédech, *La méthode historique de Polybe* (1962); *Polybe* (Entretiens Sur l'Antiquité Classique, xx, 1974); K. Sacks, *Polybius on the Writing of History* (1981); F.W. Walbank, *A Historical Commentary on Polybius*, 3 vols. (1957-1959), and *Polybius* (1972).

Bibliography

ROMAN HISTORIANS: GENERAL

T.A. Dorey, *Latin Biography* (ed. 1967), and *Latin Historians* (1966); M.L.W. Laistner, *The Greater Roman Historians* (1963).

JULIUS CAESAR

F.E. Adcock, *Caesar as Man of Letters* (1956); J.P.V.D. Balsdon, *Julius Caesar and Rome* (1967); M. Borda (etc.), *Gaio Giulio Cesare* (1957); M. Gelzer, *Caesar: Politician and Statesman* (1968); M. Grant, *Caesar* (1974, 1975), and *Julius Caesar* (1969, 1972); M. Rambaud, *L'art de la déformation historique dans les Commentaires de César* (1953), and *Autour de César* (1987); D. Rasmussen (ed.), *Caesar* (1967); O. Seel, *Caesarstudien* (1967); Z. Yavetz, *Julius Caesar and his Public Image* (1983).

SALLUST

E. Bolaffi, *Sallustio e la sua fortuna nei secoli* (1949); K. Büchner, *Sallust* (1960); G. Cipriani, *Sallustio e l'immaginario: per una bigorafia eroica di Giugurta* (1988); D.C. Earl, *The Political Thought of Sallust* (1961); A. La Penna, *Sallustio e la rivoluzione romana* (1968); P. McGushin, *Sallust: The Conspiracy of Catiline* (1987); G.M. Paul, *A Historical Commentary on Sallust* (1984); L.O. Sangiacomo, *Sallustio* (1954); T.F. Scanlon, *Spes Frustrata: A Reading of Sallust* (1987); W. Steidle, *Sallusts Historische Monographien* (1958); R. Syme, *Sallust* (1964).

LIVY

R. Bloch, *Tite-Live et les premiers siècles de Rome* (1965); E. Burck (ed.), *Wege zu Livius* (1967); T.A. Dorey (ed.), *Livy* (1971); I. Kajanto, *God and Fate in Livy* (1957); E. Lefère and E. Olshausen, *Livius: Werk und Rezeption* (1983); T.J. Luce, *Livy: The Composition of his History* (1977); M. Mazza, *Storia e ideologie in Tito Livio* (1966); R.M. Ogilvie, *A Commentary on Livy I–V* (1965); P.G. Walsh, *Livy: His Historical Aims and Methods* (1961) and *Livy* (1974).

JOSEPHUS

S.J.D. Cohen, *Josephus in Galilee* (1979); L. Feldman, *Josephus and Modern Scholarship 1937–1980* (1984); F.J. Foakes Jackson, *Josephus and the Jews* (1930); P. Fornaro, *Flavio Giuseppe, Tacito e l'impero* (1980); T. Rajak, *Josephus: The Historian and his Society* (1983); R.J.H. Shutt, *Studies in Josephus* (1961); H.St.J. Thackeray, *Josephus: The Man and the Historian* (1929); P. Vidal-Nacquet, *Il buon uso di tradimento: Flavio Giuseppe e la Guerra Giudaica* (1980); P. Villalba i Varneba, *The Historical Method of Flavius Josephus* (1986); G.A. Williamson, *The World of Josephus* (1964).

TACITUS

H.W. Benario, *An Introduction to Tacitus* (1975); T.A. Dorey (ed.), *Tacitus* (1969); D.R. Dudley, *The World of Tacitus* (1968); J. Ginsburg, *Tradition and Theme in the Annals of Tacitus* (1981); F.R.D. Goodyear, *Tacitus* (1970); R. Häussler, *Tacitus und das historische Bewusstsein* (1965); H.Y. McCulloch, *Narrative Cause in the Annals of Tacitus* (1984); R. Martin, *Tacitus* (1981); C.W. Mendell, *Tacitus: The Man and his*

Work (1958); R. Paratore, *Tacito* (1951, 1962); R. Syme, *Tacitus* (1958), and *Ten Studies in Tacitus* (1970); B. Walker, *The Annals of Tacitus* (1952, 1961); G. Wille, *Der Aufbau der Werke des Tacitus* (1983).

PLUTARCH

G.J.D. Aalders, *Plutarch's Political Thought* (1982); R.H. Barrow, *Plutarch and his Times* (1967); C.P. Jones, *Plutarch and Rome* (1971); D.A. Russell, *Plutarch* (1973); B. Scardigli, *Die Römerbiographien Plutarchs* (1979); C. Theander, *Plutarch und die Geschichte* (1951); A.E. Wardman, *Plutarch's Lives* (1974).

SUETONIUS

B. Baldwin, *Suetonius* (1983); F. della Corte, *Svetano: eques Romanus* (1958, 1967), and *Svetonio: grammatici e retori* (1968); J. Gascou, *Suétone historien* (1984); H. Gugel, *Studien zur biographischen Technik Suetons* (1977); U. Lambrecht, *Herrscherbilo und Prinzipatsidee in Suetons Kaiserbiographien* (1984); R.C. Lounsbury, *The Arts of Suetonius* (1987); W. Steidle, *Sueton und die antike Biographie* (1951); A. Wallace-Hadrill, *Suetonius: The Scholar and the Caesars* (1983).

EUSEBIUS

T.D. Barnes, *Constantine and Eusebius* (1982); R.M. Grant, *Eusebius as Church Historian* (1980); A.A. Mosshammer, *The Chronicle of Eusebius and Greek Chronographic Tradition* (1979); J. Stevenson, *A New Eusebius* (1957, 1987); D.S. Wallace-Hadrill, *Eusebius of Caesarea* (1960).

AMMIANUS MARCELLINUS

N.J.E. Austin, *Ammianus on Warfare* (1979); R.C. Blockley, *Ammianus Marcellinus: A Study of his Historiography and Political Thought* (1975); P.M. Camus, *Ammien Marcellin* (1967); G.A. Crump, *Ammianus Marcellinus as a Military Historian* (1975); A. Denandt, *Zeitkritik und Geschichtsbild im Werk Ammianus* (1965); D. Drexler, *Ammianstudien* (1974); G. Elliott, *Ammianus Marcellinus and Fourth Century History* (1983); J. Matthews, *The Roman Empire of Ammianus* (1989); K. Rosen, *Ammianus Marcellinus* (1982); H.T. Rowell, *Ammianus Marcellinus; Soldier-Historian of the Late Roman Empire* (1964); R. Seager, *Ammianus Marcellinus: Seven Studies in his Language and Thought* (1986); R. Syme, *Ammianus and the Historia Augusta* (1968); E.A. Thompson, *The Historical Work of Ammianus Marcellinus* (1947, 1969); J. Vogt, *Ammianus Marcellinus als erzählender Geschichtsschreiber der Spätzeit* (1963).

List of Roman Emperors

	Julio–Claudian Dynasty
BC 31–AD 14	Augustus
AD 14–37	Tiberius
37–41	Caligula (Gaius)
41–54	Claudius
54–68	Nero

	Civil Wars
68–69	Galba
69	Otho
69	Vitellius

	Flavian Dynasty
69–79	Vespasian
79–81	Titus
81–96	Domitian

	Adoptive and Antonine Emperors
96–98	Nerva
98–117	Trajan
117–138	Hadrian

138–161	Antoninus Pius
161–180	{ Marcus Aurelius
161–169	{ Lucius Verus
180–192	Commodus

Civil Wars

193	Pertinax
193	Didius Julianus

Severan Dynasty

193–211	Septimius Severus
211–217	{ Caracalla
211	{ Geta
217–218	Macrinus (not a member of the dynasty)
218–222	Elagabalus
222–235	Severus Alexander

Danubian and other Emperors

235–238	Maximinus I (*Danubian*)
238	{ Gordian I Africanus
	{ Gordian II Africanus
238	{ Balbinus
	{ Pupienus
238–244	Gordian III
244–249	Philip the Arab
249–251	Trajanus Decius (*Danubian*)
251–253	Trebonianus Gallus
253	Aemilian
253–260	{ Valerian
253–268	{ Gallienus
268–270	Claudius II Gothicus (*Danubian*)
270	Quintillus (*Danubian*)
270–275	Aurelian (*Danubian*)
275–276	Tacitus (*Danubian ?*)
276	Florian (*Danubian ?*)
276–282	Probus (*Danubian*)
282–283	Carus

283–284	{ Carinus { Numerianus

The Tetrarchy

284–305	⌠ Diocletian
286–305	{
306–308	⌡ Maximian
305–306	⌠ Constantius I Chlorus
305–311	⌡ Galerius
306–312	Maxentius
306–307	Severus II
308–313	Maximinus II Daia
306–337	Constantine I the Great
308–324	Licinius

The Dynasty of Constantine

306–337	Constantine I the Great (see above)
337–340	⌠ Constantine II
337–350	{ Constans
337–361	⌡ Constantius II
361–363	Julian 'the Apostate'
363–364	Jovian (not a member of the dynasty)

The Dynasty of Valentinian

364–375	⌠ Valentinian I
364–378	{ Valens (*in east*)
367–383	{ Gratian
375–392	⌡ Valentinian II

The Dynasty of Theodosius

378–395	Theodosius I
392–408	⌠ Arcadius (*in east*)
393–423	⌡ Honorius
408–450	Theodosius II (*in east*)
425–455	Valentinian III
450–491	five emperors in east
455–475	seven emperors in west
475–476	Romulus Augustulus

Genealogical Tables

1 The Family of Augustus

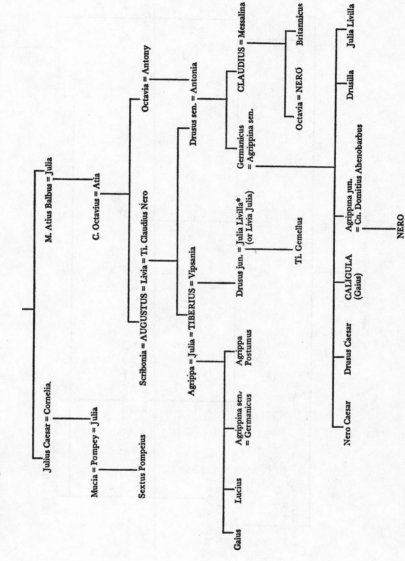

* After the death of Drusus jun., it is believed that Julia Livilla was betrothed to Ti. Aelius Sejanus, the praetorian prefect.

2 The family of Vespasian

Flavius Sabinus, city prefect

Flavia Domitilla = VESPASIAN

Flavius Sabinus = Vespasia Polla

Flavius Sabinus (? consul AD 69)

Cn. Domitius Corbulo

Domitia = DOMITIAN Longina

Flavia Domitilla

Flavius Clemens = Flavia Domitilla

TITUS (praetorian prefect under Vespasian)

Titus Flavius Sabinus = Flavia Julia (d. AD 82)

Vespasian jun.

Domitian jun.

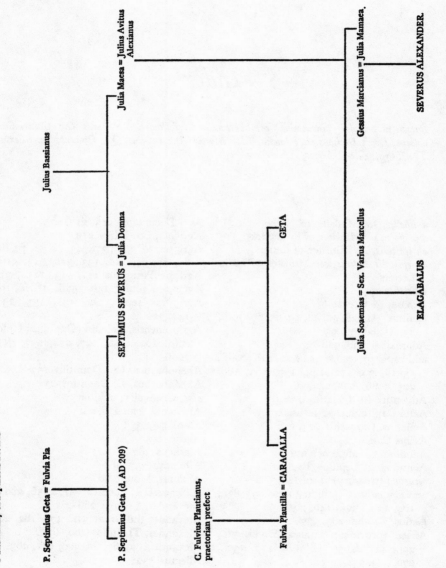

9 The Family of Septimius Severus

P. Septimius Geta = Fulvia Pia

Julius Bassianus

P. Septimius Geta (d. AD 209)

SEPTIMIUS SEVERUS = Julia Domna

Julia Maesa = Julius Avitus Alexianus

C. Fulvius Plautianus, praetorian prefect

Fulvia Plautilla = CARACALLA

GETA

Julia Soaemias = Sex. Varius Marcellus

Gessius Marcianus = Julia Mamaea.

ELAGABALUS

SEVERUS ALEXANDER.

Index

Roman first names (praenomina) are abbreviated as follows: A.: Aulus, C.: Gaius, Cn.: Cnaeus, Dec.: Decimus, L.: Lucius, M.: Marcus, P.: Publius, Q.: Quintus, Sex.: Sextus, T.: Titus, Ti.: Tiberius.

Clemens, M. Arrecinus (praetorian prefect under Caligula) 144, 147f.
Clemens, M. Arrecinus (praetorian prefect under Vespasian) 214f.
Clemens, Flavius 217, 224f.
Cleopatra VII 29, 34f., 37ff., 85
client kingdoms, armies of 77, 147, 155, 176
cloaks xx, xxii, 263, 295, 298
clubs, junior officers', *see scholae*
Clusium 325
Clyde, R. 219, 242, 260
Coele Syria, *see* Syria
cohors speculatorum, see speculatores.
cohortes civium Romanorum 312, 318, 320
cohortes equitatae, see part-mounted cohorts
cohortes legionariae xxxiff., 27, 56, 59, 73, 239
cohortes praetoriae, see praetorian guard
cohortes urbanae, see city cohorts
cohortes voluntariorum 104, 317
collegia juvenum, see Juventus
collegium custodum corporis, see German bodyguard
colletiones 330
Colonia Agrippinensis, *see* Agrippinensis
'colonies' (*coloniae civium Romanorum*) 30, 78, 80, 237
Column of Aurelius (Aurelian Column), *see* Aurelius, M.
Column of Trajan, *see* Trajan
Comazon Eutychianus, P. Valerius 265f. 331
comitatenses, see field force
Commagene 240
commander of legion, *see legatus legionis*
Commodus (emperor) 248–51, 267
Commodus, L. Ceionius, *see* Aelius Caesar
concubines, *see* marriage laws, military conscription, *see* recruitment
Constantine I the Great 277, 280, 332f.
Constantinople 277; *see also* Byzantium
Constantius I Chlorus 332
Constantius II 280f.
contubernium, see mess unit
Coptos 313
Corbulo, Cn. Domitius 146, 160ff., 173ff., 198, 200, 213, 217, 219, 225, 323
Cordus, Cremutius 134
Corinth 165
corn supply, *see* grain supply, rations

Cornelia 145
Cornelius, *see* Balbus, Celsus, Cinna, Gallus, Laco, Lentulus, Sulla
corona civica, see decorations
corselet, breastplate xix-xxii, xxix, 161, 193, 239, 262, 283, 295–8, 307
Crassus Frugi Licinianus, C. Calpurnius 226
Crassus, M. Licinius (consul 30 B.C.) 40, 312
Crassus, M. Licinius (triumvir) 11ff., 226
Crassus, Otacilius 25f.
Crastinus 25
Cremona 190, 194f., 201f.
Crispinus, Rufrius 154, 321
Crispinus, Tullius 253
Crispinus, Varius 191
Crispus, C. Sallustius 115
crowns, *see* decorations
Ctesiphon 233, 256, 332
cuirass, *see* corselet
Cumae 88
curator custodum corporis, see German bodyguard
curator veteranorum 81
Cyprus 10
Cyrrhus 313

Dacia 206, 219ff., 231f., 270, 276, 328ff.
daggers xviii, 250, 296, 298
Dalmatia 34, 76, 86, 104ff., 123, 128, 149, 152f., 176, 192, 200, 276, 298, 311, 317, 331
Dansala 297
Danube, R. xxviii, 25, 40, 60, 64–7, 76, 86, 105, 120, 127, 176, 182, 187, 193f., 199f., 206, 211, 213, 217, 219f., 223, 228, 232, 245ff., 253f., 259, 263, 267–270, 274–7, 285, 298, 315, 321f., 328, 331ff.
Dardania 25, 313; *see also* Moesia
De Rebus Bellicis 300, 335
Dead Sea 208
Decebalus 219, 221, 231
Decius, Trajanus 274
decorations, military xx, xxii, xxv, xxxiii, 78, 113, 197, 295f., 308
Decumates, Agri, *see* Agri Decumates
decuriones (cavalry) 312, 324
decursio, see ceremonial
deductions from pay, *see* pay